ISTE® National Educational Technology Standards for Teachers

http://cnets.iste.org/teachers/t_stands.html

NETS for Teachers

EDUCATIONAL TECHNOLOGY STANDARDS AND PERFORMANCE INDICATORS FOR ALL TEACHERS

Building on the NETS for Students, the ISTE NETS for Teachers (NETS*T), which focus on preservice teacher education, define the fundamental concepts, knowledge, skills, and attitudes for applying technology in educational settings. All candidates seeking certification or endorsements in teacher preparation should meet these educational technology standards. It is the responsibility of faculty across the university and at cooperating schools to provide opportunities for teacher candidates to meet these standards.

The six standards areas with performance indicators listed below are designed to be general enough to be customized to fit state, university, or district guidelines and yet specific enough to define the scope of the topic. Performance indicators for each standard provide specific outcomes to be measured when developing a set of assessment tools. The standards and the performance indicators also provide guidelines for teachers currently in the classroom.

1. TECHNOLOGY OPERATIONS AND CONCEPTS

   Teachers demonstrate a sound understanding of technology operations and concepts. Teachers:
   - demonstrate introductory knowledge, skills, and understanding of concepts related to technology (as described in the ISTE National Education Technology Standards for Students).
   - demonstrate continual growth in technology knowledge and skills to stay abreast of current and emerging technologies.

2. PLANNING AND DESIGNING LEARNING ENVIRONMENTS AND EXPERIENCES

   Teachers plan and design effective learning environments and experiences supported by technology. Teachers:
   - design developmentally appropriate learning opportunities that apply technology-enhanced instructional strategies to support the diverse needs of learners.
   - apply current research on teaching and learning with technology when planning learning environments and experiences.
   - identify and locate technology resources and evaluate them for accuracy and suitability.
   - plan for the management of technology resources within the context of learning activities.
   - plan strategies to manage student learning in a technology-enhanced environment.

3. TEACHING, LEARNING, AND THE CURRICULUM

   Teachers implement curriculum plans that include methods and strategies for applying technology to maximize student learning. Teachers:
   - facilitate technology-enhanced experiences that address content standards and student technology standards.
   - use technology to support learner-centered strategies that address the diverse needs of students.
   - apply technology to develop students' higher order skills and creativity.
   - manage student learning activities in a technology-enhanced environment.

4. ASSESSMENT AND EVALUATION

   Teachers apply technology to facilitate a variety of effective assessment and evaluation strategies. Teachers:
   - apply technology in assessing student learning of subject matter using a variety of assessment techniques.
   - use technology resources to collect and analyze data, interpret results, and communicate findings to improve instructional practice and maximize student learning.
   - apply multiple methods of evaluation to determine students' appropriate use of technology resources for learning, communication, and productivity.

5. PRODUCTIVITY AND PROFESSIONAL PRACTICE

   Teachers use technology to enhance their productivity and professional practice. Teachers:
   - use technology resources to engage in ongoing professional development and lifelong learning.
   - continually evaluate and reflect on professional practice to make informed decisions regarding the use of technology in support of student learning.
   - apply technology to increase productivity.
   - use technology to communicate and collaborate with peers, parents, and the larger community in order to nurture student learning.

6. SOCIAL, ETHICAL, LEGAL, AND HUMAN ISSUES

   Teachers understand the social, ethical, legal, and human issues surrounding the use of technology in PK–12 schools and apply those principles in practice. Teachers:
   - model and teach legal and ethical practice related to technology use.
   - apply technology resources to enable and empower learners with diverse backgrounds, characteristics, and abilities.
   - identify and use technology resources that affirm diversity.
   - promote safe and healthy use of technology resources.
   - facilitate equitable access to technology resources for all students.

Reprinted with permission from *National Educational Technology Standards for Teachers: Preparing Teachers to Use Technology,* © 2002, ISTE® (International Society for Technology in Education), iste@iste.org, www.iste.org. All rights reserved.

A Teacher's Quick Reference Guide to Technology Tutorials

Type	Package	Publisher	Distribution	Tutorials
Web Browser	Firefox	Mozilla http://www.mozilla.com/en-US/firefox/	Free	Firefox FAQ: http://www.mozilla.org/support/firefox/faq.html Atomic Learning: http://www.atomiclearning.com/tutorials (subscription)
	Netscape	Netscape http://browser.netscape.com/ns8/	Free	Gateway Web designs: http://www.getawaydesigns.com/email/emailsmain.htm Internet4Classrooms: http://www.internet4classrooms.com/on-line_netscape.htm
	Internet Explorer	Microsoft Corporation http://www.microsoft.com/	Free	Internet4Teachers: http://www.internet4classrooms.com/on-line_ie.htm Atomic Learning: http://www.internet4classrooms.com/on-line_ie.htm
	Google	Google http://www.google.com/	Free	Google Guide: http://www.googleguide.com/ LearnWebSkills: http://www.learnwebskills.com/search/google.html
	NetTrekker	Thinkronize http://www.nettrekker.com/di/	Commercial	Atomic Learning: http://www.atomiclearning.com/nettrekker_di
	Safari	Apple Computer http://www.apple.com/	Free—Mac only	Atomic Learning: http://www.atomiclearning.com/safari Lakeland College: http://www.lakeland.cc.il.us/online/tutorials/Browsers/safari/index.htm
Operating Systems	Mac OS (Tiger, Panther)	Apple Computer http://www.apple.com/	Bundled with Apple computers	J. Overton—Mac Options: http://www.macoptions.com/os85/ Internet4Classrooms: http://www.internet4classrooms.com/on-line_macintosh.htm
	Windows (Vista, XP)	Microsoft http://www.microsoft.com/	Bundled with PCs	Atomic Learning: http://www.atomiclearning.com/freetrial CNET Windows Vista Tutorials: http://vista-tutorials.classes.cnet.com/ Internet4Classrooms: http://www.internet4classrooms.com/on-line_ibm.htm Microsoft Help and How-To: http://windowshelp.microsoft.com/Windows/en-GB/winbasics.mspx
	Linux	Varies—see Wikipedia http://en.wikipedia.org/wiki/Linux	Free	The Linux Tutorial: http://www.linux-tutorial.info/
	Unix	The Open Group http://www.unix.org/	Free	Unix Tutorial for Beginners: http://www.ee.surrey.ac.uk/Teaching/Unix/
Office Software	Excel	Microsoft http://www.microsoft.com/	Commercial	Atomic Learning: http://www.atomiclearning.com/freetrial Internet4Classrooms: http://www.internet4classrooms.com/
	PowerPoint	Microsoft http://www.microsoft.com/	Commercial	Atomic Learning: http://www.atomiclearning.com/freetrial Internet4Classrooms: http://www.internet4classrooms.com/
	Word	Microsoft http://www.microsoft.com/	Commercial	Atomic Learning: http://www.atomiclearning.com/freetrial Internet4Classrooms: http://www.internet4classrooms.com/
	ThinkFree Show (presentation)	ThinkFree http://www.thinkfree.com/common/main.tfo	Free	http://www.seniormanagementservices.com/SHOW-TUTORIAL/0_welcome_to_show_tutor.html
	Open Office http://www.open	Sun Microsystems/OpenOffice.org	Free	Tutorials for OpenOffice: http://www.tutorialsforopenoffice.org/

Category	Software/Tool	Vendor / URL	Cost	Tutorials / Resources
		office.org / http://www.openoffice.org/		LearnOpenOffice.com: http://www.learnopenoffice.org/tutorials.htm
Web Development Tools	Front Page	Microsoft http://www.microsoft.com/	Commercial	West Loogootee Schools: http://www.siec.k12.in.us/west/online/website/ FrontPage: http://www.kent.k12.wa.us/KSD/IT/TSC/prof_dev/tutorials.html#web
	Dreamweaver	Adobe http://www.adobe.com	Commercial	Dreamweaver Support Center: http://www.adobe.com/support/dreamweaver/tutorial_index.html Internet4Classrooms: http://www.internet4classrooms.com/
Graphics/ Drawing/ Mapping	KidPix	Broderbund http://www.broderbund.com	Commercial	KidPix http://www.kent.k12.wa.us/KSD/IT/TSC/prof_dev/tutorials.html#kidpix LearningElectric.com: http://www.learningelectric.com/kidpix.htm
	Inspiration	Inspiration http://www.inspiration.com	Commercial	Internet4Classrooms: http://www.internet4classrooms.com/ Inspiration: http://www.kent.k12.wa.us/KSD/IT/TSC/prof_dev/tutorials.html#inspiration LearningElectric.com: http://www.learningelectric.com/inspiration7.htm
	Kidspiration	Inspiration http://www.inspiration.com	Commercial	Kidspiration Quick Start: http://www.inspiration.com/popups/kidstutorial/index.cfm
	Photoshop	Adobe http://www.adobe.com	Commercial	Atomic Learning; http://www.atomiclearning.com/freetrial Photoshop Elements: http://www.kent.k12.wa.us/KSD/IT/wwwdev/photoshop/index.html
Social software	Blogging	Various, e.g., http://www.blogger.com, http://www.wordpress.com, http://blog.com	Free	Atomic Learning: http://www.atomiclearning.com/freetrial How to Start a Blog: http://www.wikihow.com/Start-a-Blog
	Internet Classroom Assistant (ICA)	Nicenet http://www.nicenet.org/	Free	ICA FAQ: http://www.nicenet.org/ica/ica_faq.cfm
	Podcasts	Various, e.g., www.podcast.net, www.podcastalley.net, www.cnn.com, www.epn.org	Free	Atomic Learning: http://www.atomiclearning.com/freetrial How to Create Your Own Podcast—A Step-by-Step Tutorial: http://radio.about.com/od/podcastin1/a/aa030805a.htm How to Podcast: http://www.how-to-podcast-tutorial.com/17-audacity-tutorial.htm
Learning Activities	Web Inquiry Projects	P. Molebash/SDSU http://edweb.sdsu.edu/wip/	Free	Templates for Creating WIPs: http://edweb.sdsu.edu/wip/templates.htm
	WebQuests	B. Dodge/SDSU http://webquest.sdsu.edu/	Free	Internet4Classrooms: http://www.internet4classrooms.com/ Readings and Training Materials: http://webquest.sdsu.edu/materials.htm
Authorable Software	Quandary	Half-Baked Software http://www.halfbakedsoftware.com/ quandary.php	Free	Tutorials and Examples: http://www.halfbakedsoftware.com/quandary_tutorials_examples.php
	Hyperstudio	Sunburst Technology http://www.hyperstudio.com/	Commercial	Internet4Classrooms: http://www.internet4classrooms.com/ Building Learning with Technology: http://www.education.umd.edu/blt/hyperstudio/
	MovieMaker	Microsoft http://www.microsoft.com/	Bundled with the Windows OS	Atomic Learning; http://www.atomiclearning.com/freetrial Get Started with Windows Movie Maker: http://www.microsoft.com/windowsxp/using/moviemaker/getstarted/default.mspx
	iMovie	Apple www.apple.com	Bundled with the Mac OS	Atomic Learning: http://www.atomiclearning.com/freetrial iMovie Tutorial: http://www.apple.com/support/imovie/tutorial/

Supporting Learning with Technology
Essentials of Classroom Practice

Joy Egbert
Washington State University

PEARSON

Merrill
Prentice Hall

Upper Saddle River, New Jersey
Columbus, OH

Library of Congress Cataloging-in-Publication Data
Egbert, Joy.
    Supporting learning with technology: essentials of classroom practice / Joy
Egbert.
        p. cm.
Includes bibliographical references and index
ISBN-13: 978-0-13-172118-0 (pbk.)
ISBN-10: 0-13-172118-6 (pbk.)
1. Educational technology.   I. Title.
LB 1028.3.E424 2009
371.33—dc22

                                                    2007034966

Vice President and Executive Publisher: Jeffery W. Johnston
Executive Editor: Darcy Betts Prybella
Editorial Assistant: Nancy Holstein
Development Editor: Amy J. Nelson
Production Editor: Sarah Kenoyer
Photo Coordinator: Lori Whitley
Production Coordination: Thistle Hill Publishing Services, LLC
Design Coordinator: Diane C. Lorenzo
Text Designer: Candace Rowley
Cover Designer: Ali Mohrman
Cover Image: Jupiter Images
Production Manager: Susan Hannahs
Director of Marketing: Quinn Perkson
Marketing Coordinator: Brian Mounts

This book was set in Berling Roman by S4 Carlisle Publishing Services. It was printed and bound by
R.R. Donnelley & Sons Company. The cover was printed by R.R. Donnelley & Sons Company.

Pearson Education Ltd.   Pearson Education Australia Pty. Limited
Pearson Education Singapore Pte. Ltd.   Pearson Education North Asia Ltd.
Pearson Education Canada, Ltd.   Pearson Educación de Mexico, S.A. de C.V.
Pearson Education–Japan   Pearson Education Malaysia Pte. Ltd.

10 9 8 7 6 5 4 3 2 1
ISBN-13: 978-0-13-172118-0
ISBN-10:   0-13-172118-6

Dedication

For Jamie and David, love to infinity and beyond, and to the memory of the incomparable Sylvia Bodolay.

Preface

FOCUS ON LEARNING

During my years working in the fields of educational technology and computer-assisted language learning, I have reviewed and used many books in these areas. Somehow they were never really appropriate for what I thought my students needed to know and be able to do in classrooms with technology. Many of those texts took a very technocentric view of technology use, and others seemed to have unrealistic expectations for what teachers could and were willing to do in their classrooms. Some of the texts take a simplistic approach (e.g., "only use technology as a tool," "technology should be used only for constructivist purposes"). This text is my answer to what I see as problematic in other texts and in the ways that technology is talked about and taught in teacher education. Following my own good advice in earlier works, my focus is on pedagogical goals and student learning first, and then on presenting technology as something that may or may not help teachers and learners to reach these goals. In developing the content and applications in this book, I assume that good teachers teach well because they adhere to certain understandings about what learners need to learn and how learners can best be helped to do so. Having these understandings at the core of each chapter makes it much easier for teachers to concentrate on the question of what constitutes effective technology-enhanced learning and why.

The points in this book derive from the ideas I discovered during teaching, discussions with colleagues, and reading while I put this book together. All told, it illustrates what technology-enhanced learning can be like today and prepares teachers and administrators for what may come tomorrow.

HOW-TO VERSUS WHY-TO

The emphasis in this text is what I consider *essential* for effective technology-enhanced teaching and learning. Research shows clearly that teacher education students will focus on the essentials and disregard much of what else they are exposed to during their programs. Therefore I have tried to avoid software or hardware how-to's that may be outdated or impossible within specific school contexts. For the most part, the examples throughout the chapters present ideas for tasks that can be completed with a variety of tools rather than one specific tool that teachers may not have access to. In addition, each chapter and example presents reasons "why-to" use technology—thereby broadening the possibilities of specific technologies that teacher education students can learn to those that they see as necessary.

TRANSFER TO THE CLASSROOM

Each chapter includes a brief summary of research from educational technology, learning theory, and other areas to build a foundation for chapter examples and activities. The research is explained and explored in a manner appropriate to a teacher education audience. I then present tips, examples, and activities for teachers to consider in developing technology-enhanced activities. Because I do not speak to one specific theory of teaching, those following philosophies as different as behaviorism and constructivism can find use in these basic ideas about what's essential for effective learning. Chapters provide examples for learning in a variety of contexts and content areas and have been developed to be applied easily to teaching other ideas and subjects.

Skills learning is integrated, as is a focus on meeting the needs of all learners. Activities and ideas overlap throughout the book, demonstrating that it is not just the technology or the content that is important, but a whole learning environment system that teachers can create with their students. I suggest that if teachers come away from this text with a good general understanding of what learning is and how to support it with technology, there is a greater chance that they will transfer this knowledge to their classrooms than if they learned soon-to-be-outdated technologies or generic, context-free problem-solving.

RESPONSIVE TEACHING

Many of the educational technology texts on the market treat language, social status, culture, physical and cognitive ability, and other learner differences in a separate chapter, then neglect to mention them again. This text integrates, both explicitly and implicitly, the learning of all students in every chapter. This not only supports culturally responsive teaching as advocated by Geneva Gay and others but also emphasizes teacher responsiveness to all learners. This is a crucial aspect of learning and reflection for all teacher education students.

CONCLUSION

The purpose of this text is to address what teachers should know and be able to do, but the focus is on learners and learning rather than on the technology itself. In this way, I hope to help prepare teachers who can address problems with learning as they arise, integrate new technologies with ease in pedagogically sound ways, and share their knowledge and understandings with their colleagues and students.

ACKNOWLEDGMENTS

There are many people to thank for their help and support in creating this work. Len Jessup made the suggestion, and Debbie Stollenwerk at Pearson saw its potential. Thanks go to them and to: my Merrill/Prentice Hall development editor, Amy Nelson, for patience and support throughout the process (in spite of being a new mom); Darcy Betts, acquisitions editor, who had to step in at the last minute; the fabulous reviewers whose suggestions made this a much stronger and more effective text. They are Sherry L. Allen, University of Southern Indiana; Donna Baumbach, University of Central Florida, Orlando; David Bolton, West Chester University; Valerie Bryan, Florida Atlantic University; David Bullock, Portland State University; Kathleen Conway, Hofstra University; Carrie Dale, Eastern Illinois University; Lorana A. Jinkerson, Northern Michigan University; Lisa Kunkleman, Baker College–Flint; Valerie Larsen, University of Notre Dame & Indiana University; S. Kim MacGregor, Louisiana State University; Lisa Owen, Rhode Island College; Robert Perkins, College of Charleston; Thomas Smyth, University of South Carolina–Aiken; Jean Swenk, National University; and Patricia Weaver, Fayetteville Technical Community College.

Thanks to the public school students and teachers who contributed their ideas, art, and interest; colleagues and students at Washington State University for listening; and my family for believing that it would happen. Of particular help were Jennifer and Russell Robinson, Jamie Jessup, Daisy Ward, Lucy Ward, and Henry Ward, LeAnne Spragg, Judy Tseng, and Leslie Huff. Thanks to the Web site managers and copyright holders who permitted the reproduction of their materials in this text.

Finally, deep appreciation to those who helped keep me sane during the process—Cary Anderson, Mary Roe, Dawn Shinew, Kelly Ward, Levi McNeil, Joanne Sellen, Pam Bettis, and my Rebel 250. Those whom I have not mentioned by name know who they are, and for their understanding and encouragement I am eternally grateful.

Welcome to the "Essentials"

Created for teachers new to educational technology, this text provides the basics on how to integrate technology into classrooms while providing classroom examples that can be used with a variety of technology tools. *Supporting Learning with Technology: Essentials of Classroom Practice* provides opportunities for readers to learn about technology-enhanced learning today and prepares them for what may come tomorrow. Major headings, as well as tabbed color sections along the edges of the pages, highlight "Essential" sections. This provides a convenient way for students to easily locate specific sections.

Supporting Learning with Technology provides a new, unique approach tailored for future educators. This text offers:

- An organization supported by learning goals
- An opportunity to learn how to meet the needs of today's learners
- Application opportunities for today's classroom

Organized by Student Learning Goals

Unique in its presentation of student learning goals first rather than the technology tool, it focuses you on the *learner* and *learning* rather than the technology.

Explore a clear and predictable chapter framework that provides you with:

- A learning goal with supporting research and theory that builds a foundation for each chapter's examples and activities
- Guidelines, examples, and activities to consider when creating technology-enhanced lessons
- A variety of technology tools for that learning goal, with lesson activities across grade levels and content areas

Learn how technology can be used to help you meet the following learning goals:

- Content learning
- Communication
- Critical thinking
- Creativity
- Problem solving
- Production

Meet the Needs of Today's Learners

Diverse Students—The author recognizes that not every classroom is the same—all students are diverse and all instruction must meet the learning needs of *ALL* students. Therefore, each chapter integrates the learning of *ALL* students with marginal icons highlighting discussion of English language learners (ELL) and other students with diverse needs.

Most teachers probably think of telecommunication tools as those mentioned in Table 3.2, but software packages can both directly and indirectly support communication. Even common software packages such as word processors can be used for collaboration; as noted in chapter 2 and above, the "comment" function in Microsoft Word allows learners to comment on one another's work in writing inside the document. Voice (oral) annotations are also possible and are a good alternative for students who do not type well, who have physical barriers, or whose written skills are not understandable.

In addition, much of the software from educational software companies such as Tom Snyder Productions (www.tomsnyder.com) is based on student collaboration. Packages such as the Inspirer (geography/social studies), Decisions, Decisions (government/social studies), and Fizz and Martina (math) series are aligned with content-area standards and have built-in mechanisms for collaboration. The teachers' guides that accompany these software packages also include ideas about how to make the collaboration work for all learners, including ELLs. Perhaps essential for some contexts, much of the Tom Snyder software is intended for students to work with as a class in the one-computer classroom. However, more important than *how* the software connects learners is *why* and *with whom* learners connect. Much content-based software guides students into predetermined conclusions, and teachers must take care to make sure that those conclusions are equitable and socially responsible. See the Tool CloseUp: Asia Inspirer on the previous page for more information about students interacting around the computer.

Choose a communication tool to investigate further. What features might be useful for the way you plan to teach? Why? Be creative in your thinking and response.

_____

_____

_____

Inclusion / ELL

Inclusion / ELL

FIGURE 3.13 Cooperative Learning Project Rubric

Cooperative Learning Project Rubric A: Process

Name: _____

Date: _____

Class: _____

	Exceptional 4 points	Admirable 3 points	Acceptable 2 points	Amateur 1 point
Group Participation	All students enthusiastically participate	At least 3/4 of students actively participate	At least half the students confer or present ideas	Only one or two persons actively participate
Shared Responsibility	Responsibility for task is shared evenly	Responsibility is shared by most group members	Responsibility is shared by 1/2 the group members	Exclusive reliance on one person
Quality of Interaction	Excellent listening and leadership skills exhibited; students reflect awareness of others' views and opinions in their discussions	Students show adeptness in interacting; lively discussion centers on the task	Some ability to interact; attentive listening; some evidence of discussion or alternatives	Little interaction; very brief conversations; some students were disinterested or distracted
Roles Within Group	Each student assigned a clearly defined role; group members perform roles effectively	Each student assigned a role but roles not clearly defined or consistently adhered to	Students assigned roles but roles were not consistently adhered to	No effort made to assign roles to group members

Integrated Assessment—Providing practical support for assessment, assessment tools such as rubrics, checklists, and other assessment forms are found throughout the text.

Application for Today's Classroom

The following features are located in every chapter.

Cases—Immerse yourself in the classroom through school or class-related cases that illustrate the use of technology to support learning. Providing a framework for the chapter discussion that follows, these compelling classroom snapshots help you understand educational concepts by connecting them to the real world of classrooms and schools.

3
Supporting Student Communication

Case: Geography Mystery

As you read the following case, pay attention to how and with whom the teacher plans for the students to communicate during their telecommunications project.

Mr. Finley, a junior high school social studies teacher, is planning a telecommunications project for his seventh-grade students while they study the geography of the United States. His project will employ technology to support interaction among students at a distance from each other. Participating in this project will help students understand the use and importance of latitude and longitude and the role of geographical features in people's lives. It will also help the students to meet other content, language, and technology goals and standards.

During this project, Mr. Finley's class will work on geography mysteries via email with Ms. Stewart's sixth-grade class in a different state. Mr. Finley's students will work in teams of three students. Each team will choose a place somewhere in the United States. Team members will pretend that they were dropped unexpectedly in that particular place and need help figuring out the name of the place where they are located. They may choose a city, a landmark, the top of a mountain, or some other specific point for which they will figure out such details as the latitude, longitude, nearby geographic features, how the people in the area use the land, and mileage to nearby landmarks. They will send clues about their location in email messages to a team in Ms. Stewart's class, who will respond through email to try to discover where Mr. Finley's students are. A message from a team in Mr. Finley's class might look like this:

A pen logo follows integrated questions throughout the chapter, providing you with an opportunity to write down your thoughts as you read the chapter.

Answer these questions about the case. There are no right or wrong answers to this chapter preview—the goal is for you to respond before you read the chapter. Then, as you interact with the chapter contents, think about how your answers might change.

1. *What learning benefits might the sixth- and seventh-grade students derive from participating in this telecommunications project?*

_____

_____

_____

Revisit the case at the end of the chapter and reconsider the questions based on your chapter reading.

CASE QUESTIONS REVIEW

Reread the case at the beginning of the chapter and review your answers. In light of what you learned during this chapter, how do your answers change? Note any changes below.

1. *What learning benefits might the sixth- and seventh-grade students derive from participating in this telecommunications project?*

_____

_____

_____

Meeting the Standards—
Providing guidance, this feature shows you how the National Educational Technology Standards connect to the learning goal of each chapter. Additional specific state standards connections are included on the text's Companion Website (http://www.prenhall. com/egbert).

• • • • **Meeting the Standards:** Communication • • • •

Guidelines for every content area include communication as an essential component for meeting national standards. For example, the education technology standards (NETS*S) address student mastery of technology communication tools, including being able to "interact, collaborate, and publish with peers, experts, and others," and "communicate information and ideas effectively to multiple audiences using a variety of media and formats." The national math standards have a complete section on math communication that emphasizes students "organizing and consolidating their mathematical thinking through communication" and being able to "communicate their mathematical thinking coherently"

(NM–COMM PK–12). Fine arts standards ask students to work together to develop improvisations; English focuses on communication skills, strategies, and applying language skills (4, 5, and 12); the first goal of the foreign language and ESL standards is communication; and even PE standards support the goal of communicating about health (NPH-H.5). In every area, communication is understood to be a foundation of learning, and technology can help students to communicate with a variety of audiences for a variety of purposes by connecting them both online and off. Some of the communication standards are mentioned in this chapter in the activities section.

Review the national or state standards for a content area that you will teach. How many of the standards address communication in some way? What kinds of connections do your students need to make to meet those standards? How do you think technology can help?

_____

_____

_____

 As you read the rest of the chapter, look for ways to use technology to help your students communicate and make connections in the ways you outlined above. See national standards and your state standards for communication in the **Standards module** on this text's Companion Website.

• • • •

Guidelines—Highlighting a focus on instruction, this section in each chapter provides quick, quality teaching guidelines at your fingertips.

FIGURE 3.7 Guidelines for Designing Opportunities for Communication	
Guidelines	**Explanation**
Consider the context.	• Use technologies that work with the students, audience, and task.
Make safety a primary focus.	• Review the classroom and school safety policies. • Choose safe technologies and a safe audience. • Work with parents.
Teach group dynamics and team-building skills.	• Help students understand how to work effectively in groups with people of all kinds.
Provide students with a reason to listen.	• Provide opportunities for students to listen actively for important information. • Make the information crucial to their success.

Technology Tools—Utilize this section in each chapter to quickly identify what technology tools will help you reach your intended learning goals.

TABLE 3.2 Examples of Communication Tools

Tool and Examples	Description	Sample Classroom Uses
MOO • Schmooze schmooze.hunter.cuny.edu (cross-cultural communication) • Digital Space Traveler www.digitalspace.com/traveler (any) • Mundo Hispano www.umsl.edu/moosproj/mundo.html	• Text- or graphics-based virtual worlds • Accessible by a large number of users simultaneously • Users type in words to "talk" to other users • Synchronous • Some have voice capabilities and include 3D and color graphics	*MOO visitors can:* • Converse with people from many different places • Collaborate on building new parts of the MOO • Play interactive games • Find resources and ideas A collaborative MOO treasure hunt can be fun!

Tool CloseUp—Explore the features of technology tools in more detail through the *Tool CloseUp* features in the text and online tutorials located on the text's Companion Website (www.prenhall.com/egbert).

Tool CloseUp: Assistive Support in Windows and Apple Operating Systems

T O O L S

As technology improves, it becomes more accessible to everyone who needs to access it. Communication becomes possible even for severely challenged students. Formerly most assistive tools were add-ons or special purchases, but now a host of tools can be found on every new computer.

Mr. Finley's project can take advantage of many of these tools. For example, because Gaggle.net is Web based, students with visual impairments and those who learn best orally can use *screen readers* that turn text into speech to read the emails to them. Screen readers are built into most new operating systems. Windows XP includes Narrator, and Apple OS X includes the screen reader VoiceOver. For a list of other screen readers see the "list of screen readers" at wikipedia.org.

In addition, during the computer-supported project students with visual impairments can use the magnifier function built into the computer's accessibility features to make the text large enough for them to read comfortably. The user can choose the level of magnification and how the magnified items will appear. In Windows, the user can choose start>control panels and find the magnifier easily.

Students who have trouble typing can use the sticky keys function, which allows the user to press a keyboard command such as Shift or Control only once and have it stay active until pressing another command key. In addition, an onscreen keyboard can make it easier for some students to type. Other accessibility features contained in the computer's operating system are available as needed. Some of the options in Windows XP are shown here.

Find the accessibility options offered by the operating system on your computer and list them here. Which ones might help you use the computer more effectively?

_____

_____

_____

_____

For more information on Assistive Support in Windows and Apple Operating Systems, see the Assistive Support in Windows and Apple Operating Systems in the Tutorials module on the Companion Website (http://www.prenhall.com/egbert).

Most teachers probably think of telecommunication tools as those mentioned in Table 3.2, but software packages can both directly and indirectly support communication. Even common software packages such as word processors can be used for collaboration; as noted in chapter 2 and above, the "comment" function in Microsoft Word allows learners to comment on one another's work in writing inside the document. Voice (oral) annotations are also possible and are a good alternative for students who do not type well, who have physical barriers, or whose written skills are not understandable.

In addition, much of the software from educational software companies such as Tom Snyder Productions (www.tomsnyder.com) is based on student collaboration. Packages such as the Inspirer (geography/social studies), Decisions, Decisions (government/social studies), and Fizz and Martina (math) series are aligned with content-area standards and have built-in mechanisms for collaboration. The teachers' guides that accompany these software packages also include ideas about how to make the collaboration work for all learners, including ELLs. Perhaps essential for some contexts, much of the Tom Snyder software is intended for students to work with as a class in the one-computer classroom. However, more important than *how* the software connects learners is *why* and *with whom* learners connect. Much content-based software guides students into predetermined conclusions, and teachers must take care to make sure that those conclusions are equitable and socially responsible. See the Tool CloseUp: Asia Inspirer on the previous page for more information about students interacting around the computer.

Choose a communication tool to investigate further. What features might be useful for the way you plan to teach? Why? Be creative in your thinking and response.

_____

_____

_____

LEARNING ACTIVITIES: COMMUNICATION TASKS

Communication opportunities are mentioned throughout this book because learning results from the interaction that takes place during these opportunities, regardless of the task goal. Many of the activities in this book have a communication component. Although examples of telecommunications projects like Mr. Finley's abound, there are fewer examples of communication projects in which students work around and with the support of technologies, as in the Asia Inspirer example in the Tool CloseUp. However, in addition to the tools listed previously, Web sites and other Internet tools, such as the free tools on the Intel Education Thinking Tools Web site (http://www.intel.com), provide an amazing number and variety of opportunities for ... communicate around, with, *and* through technology.

This section presents examples of communication activities. Each of the example ... begins with a content-area standard as its goal. All examples also address the techno... dard that students learn to communicate effectively with and to a variety of audien... ences for the examples are included; an internal peer refers to a classmate or schoolma... external peer is someone in another school, district, region, or country. Teachers are n... as participants in these examples because it is a given that much classroom communi... be aimed at or filtered through them.

In the activities, students work around, with the support of, and through the co... you read the activities, reflect on how the guidelines from this chapter might be appl... case and which technologies from Table 3.2 starting on page 79 might be used to s...

Inclusion ELL

Inclusion ELL

LEARNING ACTIVITIES

Learning Activities—Refer to the chapter's Guidelines and Technology Tools sections as you explore a variety of learning activities related to various grade levels and content areas.

SAMPLE LESSON

Sample Lesson—Using a lesson plan based on the opening case, walk through the steps a teacher took to adapt it to meet learners' needs by utilizing the text's *Lesson Analysis and Adaptation Worksheet* provided in chapter 1.

Lesson Analysis and Adaptation Worksheet

Content Area/Topic: *Current events/News*
Location and Title of Lesson: *http://www.sites4teachers.com/, Current Events Awareness*
Intended Audience for the Adaptation: *3rd grade*

The lesson . . .	Indicators	Comments
Works toward appropriate goals.	• Content and technology standards are mentioned. • Standards are for the correct grade level and content area. • Objectives are aligned with standards. • Tasks focus clearly on obtaining the objectives.	The goal of increasing student awareness is stated, but the standards are not. These need to be listed for grade 3 and tied to the objectives and tasks.
Requires the use of higher order thinking skills and "new" literacies.	• Students are asked to do more than memorize or understand (e.g., summarize, synthesize, predict, etc.). • Media, visual, communicative, technological, mathematical, and/or other nontraditional literacies are addressed.	The lesson includes summarizing, some synthesizing. It could easily include predicting and other literacy skills. For third graders, visual literacy is important and there should be a segment about WHERE they got the story and why they believe it. It doesn't have to be in depth, but should raise awareness.
Integrates the learning goals.	• Communication • Production • Critical thinking • Creativity • Content • Problem solving • Inquiry/research	It includes one-way communication and simple production but needs to integrate research, critical thinking, and content learning more.
Includes a variety of resources.	• Students have choices of materials at different levels. • Materials are available in a variety of modes (e.g., graphics, sound, text, video) and media (e.g., books, films, photos, computer).	The resources need to be made explicit—is it *USA Today* and the local paper or something else? Reading levels differ, and using online papers and magazines made specifically for students would help more students have choices and include other types of news like video reports.
Engages all students actively in authentic tasks.	• Students have roles/tasks to perform throughout the lesson. • Connections are made between the task and real life. • Students must actively search for answers to essential questions.	There are groups but no specific tasks. Students need to be given some recommendations here. It's too easy for one or two students to control this task. A general connection is made at the start to students' lives but not carried through. More specifics could help form an essential question.
Uses technology effectively, efficiently, and as a learning tool.	• The technology makes the task more authentic. • The technology makes the task easier to accomplish. • The technology helps students learn faster than without it. • The technology is secondary to the content and goals.	Technology is not used. Students could print news from many different sources from the Internet and thereby get a much broader picture of each event. Saves the teacher time from trying to get enough newspapers and gives students more options, especially for the follow-up stories.
Addresses the needs of a variety of students, including ELLs and students with physical and other challenges.	• All students can access task instructions. • All students can access task materials and resources. • Students have different ways to accomplish the same objectives.	Not all students can read a newspaper. Using the Internet to find a variety of levels of news would help these students access the lesson content. Also, instead of an oral report at the end of the week, students should be allowed to draw, graph, or whatever else they need to do to show their understanding. A class journal might work, too.
Includes appropriate assessments.	• Assessment is aligned to the standards and objectives. • Assessments are fair for all students and not based on one ability (e.g., writing). • Assessments allow students to show what they know/can do rather than what they cannot.	No real assessment is mentioned. It needs to be made explicit and tied to the standards/objectives. Adding choices for presentation would also make the assessment fairer.

Extension Activities—Separated into three major groups—*Adapt, Practice,* and *Explore*—these activities encourage you to go beyond the text to learn about endless technology applications, tools, and resources.

CHAPTER EXTENSIONS • • • • • • • • • •

To answer any of the following questions online, go to the Chapter 3 Extensions module for this text's Companion Website (http://www.prenhall.com/egbert).

Adapt • • • •

Choose a lesson for your potential subject area and grade level from the lesson plan archives at Educators Desk Reference (http://www.eduref.org/). Use the Lesson Analysis and Adaptation Worksheet from chapter 1 on page 33 (also available in the Lesson Planning module of the Companion Website) to consider the lesson in the context of *communication*. Use your responses to the worksheet to suggest general changes to the lesson based on your current or future students and context.

Practice • • • • •

1. *Integrate the standards.* Choose one or more of the activities in the chapter and note which technology standard(s) the tasks can help to meet.
2. *Improve an activity.* Choose a technology-supported activity example from the chapter and add details that would help to make it successful. For example, you may need to outline specific roles, choose a specific technology, or note an important safety tip.
3. *Think about learning.* Choose an activity from the chapter and explain how the communication might lead to learning. Say *what* students will learn, both what is obvious and less obvious.

Explore • • • •

1. *Revise an activity.* Choose one of the learning activities in the chapter and adapt it for your content area and/or grade level. Add or change technology and change the existing audience as necessary. Briefly explain your changes.
2. *Assess.* Review the sample rubric in the assessment section of the chapter. Keeping the general structure and intent, change the question to evaluate a different activity.
3. *Create a project.* Choose a grade level and content area and create a telecommunications project following the guidelines from this chapter. Note what other ideas not mentioned in this chapter should be included, e.g., a different form of assessment or another type of technology.

Support and Trends for Today's Teachers and Students

Teacher Productivity—This unique chapter helps support future educators in their everyday tasks. Teachers need to prepare their students not only for what they have to do today, but also for what they're going to need tomorrow. Therefore, they have to know what's coming for their students, and that means keeping up with trends in areas such as technology.

9

Supporting Teacher Development

My oldest cousin is Ryan, who is in college. He has a little sister Emily who is my third oldest cousin. These are the names of my cousins on my mom's side in order of how old they are: Ryan, Jarrod, Emily, Anthony, Marissa, Camille, Liam and Donald, Brier and Ellie. I like it when me and my family go to New Jersey because it is hot and is very fun too. I think the most fun part is the beach and miniature golf because those are the tings we do together most of the time. Even though my uncle owns a big golf course in Florida, where he lives, this is the first time we have all gone to the miniature golf course together with all of my relatives.
Me and my family and relatives have lots of fun in New Jersey!

Case: Lifelong Learning

As you read the following scenario, think about how you will continue to develop professionally in technology-supported learning.

• •

The teachers at Pierce Junior High School had just participated in an in-service provided by the state education department. The focus of the meeting was the new state technology standards for students. The teachers learned that, in addition to content area standards and grade level indicators, the state was requiring all teachers to address the technology standards throughout the curriculum. During the workshop the presenter provided a resource list that included many print and electronic resources that teachers could use to help them learn about the technology standards and integrate them into instruction.

Patricia Morello, an eighth-grade English teacher, used technology regularly in her classes, particularly word processing. Her students typed their essays, looked for resources on the Web, and sometimes made graphic organizers to lay out the structure of a text. Patricia felt that she

From the Classroom—Read excerpts from teachers that provide advice and activities regarding the use of educational technologies in real classrooms.

Resources

FOR EVERY STUDENT'S SUCCESS

The features and materials listed below offer you resources that allow you to be successful in your coursework as well as in your first classroom.

Companion Website—This text's Companion Website (CW) is located at http://www.prenhall.com/egbert. The CW provides you with resources and immediate feedback on exercises and other activities. These activities, projects, and resources also enhance and extend chapter content. Each topic on the CW contains the following modules (or sections), unless specified otherwise.

- Extensions—This module extends chapter content and offers additional reflection questions, exercises, and current issues/trends regarding technology.
- Lesson Planning—Explore additional lesson plans and access a downloadable version of chapter 1's *Lesson Analysis and Adaptation* worksheet.
- Chapter Web Links—Annotated Web links are provided in one easy location for you to access.
- Resources—Explore a variety of resources including, but not limited to, Accessibility and Special Education, Assessment, Copyright and Plagiarism, Grants and Funding, Learning Theories, Standards, and Videos.
- References—Visit this module to explore additional articles, journals, and books.
- Technology Tools—This module includes annotated resources such as virtual libraries and virtual field trips.
- Tutorials—Go to this link to visit Web sites with quality, step-by-step tutorials. Tools highlighted in the *Tool CloseUp* features are included in this module.
- Self-Review—Test your knowledge by answering true/false, short answer, and essay questions and receive immediate feedback.
- PowerPoints—PowerPoint presentations for each chapter highlight key concepts and summarize content from the text.

FOR EVERY PROFESSOR'S SUCCESS

The text has the following ancillary materials to assist instructors in their attempts to maximize learning for all students.

- *Online Instructor's Manual/Media Guide and Test Bank* provides concrete, chapter-by-chapter instructional and media resources.
- *Online PowerPoint Slides* are available on the Companion Website and the Instructor Resource Center.
- *Online TestGen* questions give professors access to multiple choice, short-answer, and essay questions for each chapter. These questions are also available online on the Instructor Resource Center.
- **Instructor Resource Center**

  Instructor supplements can also be accessed at our Instructor Resource Center located at http://www.prenhall.com. The Instructor Resource Center provides a variety of print and media resources in downloadable, digital format. Resources available for instructors include:

  - Instructor's Manual/Media Guide and Test Bank
  - Computerized Test Bank
  - PowerPoint slides

Your one-time registration opens the door to Prentice Hall's premium digital resources. You will not have to fill out additional forms or use multiple usernames and passwords to access new titles and/or editions. Register today, and maximize your time at every stage of course preparation.

For instructors who have adopted this text and would like to receive book-specific supplements, please contact your Prentice Hall sales representative, call Faculty Services at 1-800-526-0485, or e-mail us at merrillmarketing@prenhall.com. We look forward to hearing from you.

Brief Contents

Contents

Note: Every effort has been made to provide accurate and current Internet information in this book. However, the Internet and information posted on it are constantly changing, so it is inevitable that some of the Internet addresses listed in this textbook will change.

Special Features

Learning Activities

Sample Lessons

PART I

What Teachers Need to Know About Supporting Learning with Technology

CHAPTER 1   Understanding Classroom Learning and Technology Use

1 Understanding Classroom Learning and Technology Use

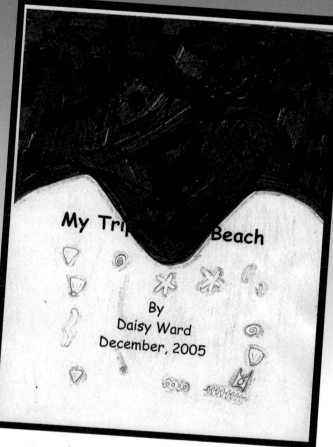

My Trip ... Beach

By
Daisy Ward
December, 2005

INTRODUCTION

Fun, interesting, engaging, effective, meaningful, crucial, powerful, empowering, real. These are words that teachers want to hear about their instruction. Their goal is to provide instruction that makes a difference in learners' lives. Technology is a powerful resource that is helping many teachers meet this goal. The purpose of this text is to help *you* meet this goal by addressing what you should know and be able to do with technology. Unlike most technology education texts, the focus of this text is on *learners* and *learning* rather than only on the technology itself. This focus will help you to address problems with learning as they arise, integrate new technologies with ease in pedagogically sound ways, and share your knowledge and understandings with your colleagues and students.

Technology should be seen as support for what teachers know and do. Instead of providing a prescription for how to teach, viewing technology as a support for teaching and learning allows teachers to discover ways to do what they already do more efficiently, more effectively, more interestingly, or in new and innovative ways. From this point of view, this text focuses on foundational, or essential, ideas for effective technology-enhanced learning and teaching.

This first chapter provides a firm foundation for the rest of this text by demonstrating and explaining why you should employ a learning focus to plan technology use and how such a focus might help you effectively meet content and technology standards to address the needs of all learners.

PREVIEW

Each chapter in this text begins with a case. Many are taken from actual experience; others have been created to provide a clear example. The purpose of the case is to stimulate your thinking and background knowledge and to focus your attention on essential chapter information.

Case: Balancing Act

As you read the following scenario, think about what teachers need to know in order to support learning with technology effectively.

• •

"Let's discuss why you're taking this class," said Dr. Ritter on the first day of her education technology class for pre-service teachers. "What do you think teachers need to know about supporting learning with technology, and why do they need to know it?"

She wrote "What" and "Why" at the top of the whiteboard at the front of the room.

"I don't know why we need to take an ed tech class," lamented Barbara, a first semester pre-service teacher. "I've been using computers since I was 4. We don't have a class that just talks about using books, do we?"

"Interesting point. Can you put that in a form that I can list here, please?" Dr. Ritter replied.

"Oh, okay," said Barbara. "Under 'Why' you can write: so they know why they need to know."

As the class laughed, Dr. Ritter smiled and asked, "What do others of you think?"

"Well, I can say that I use computers every day," said Josh. "But I don't really know how to use them in a classroom except for writing and maybe sending email to someone. So I need to know how to use them with students."

Dr. Ritter wrote "How to use computers in classroom" under "What" on the board.

Brittany added, "There's a lot of software and other technologies out there that I have never used. So I need to know more about technical stuff. But how can we learn everything in one course?"

Dr. Ritter said, "Good question—we'll need to answer that one" and wrote "Technical stuff" under "What."

The conversation continued for several more minutes. When the students ran out of ideas, the short lists on the board looked like this:

What	Why
• How to use computers in classroom	• To meet state requirements
• Technical stuff (all of it)	• Because we have to
• What's available	• To meet student standards
• What's required/expected	• To keep up with students
• The best software and activities	• To have an edge in job searches
• Exactly what to do	

"Those don't seem like very strong reasons for you to spend 5 hours per week in class for a whole semester, do they?" said Dr. Ritter. "There must be additional whats and whys that we haven't considered yet. Let's think about the questions in another way."

She displayed a PowerPoint slide on the screen in the front of the classroom. On it was written:

Teaching is not a science; it is an art. If teaching were a science there would be a best way of teaching and everyone would have to teach like that. Since teaching is not a science, there is great latitude and much possibility for personal differences. (George Polya, cited in O'Connor & Robertson, 2002)

"What do you think this quote has to do with the reasons you're here?" she asked.

• •

Answer these questions about the case with your current level of knowledge. There are no right or wrong answers to this chapter preview—the goal is for you to respond before you read the chapter. Then, as you interact with this chapter's content, think about how your answers might change.

1. *What would you add to the lists the class made? Why?*

   _____

   _____

   _____

2. *What does the quote from Polya have to do with learning about educational technology?*

   _____

   _____

   _____

3. *What role(s) do you believe technology should play in education? Why?*

   _____

   _____

   _____

4. *What are your goals in taking this course? What do you hope to accomplish?*

   _____

   _____

   _____

The questions from Dr. Ritter help to set the tone for the rest of her course and stimulate her students' previous knowledge so that they can make connections between *what they know* and *what is to come* in the course, as this chapter does for the rest of this text. As mentioned above, this text focuses on foundational, or essential, ideas for effective technology-enhanced learning and teaching. More specifically, this chapter will help you to understand how technology has been defined and why it has become such an important educational topic. The chapter also discusses some initial fears that you may have as you begin to integrate technology into your teaching, as well as benefits and barriers to using technology. Additionally, examples of tools and activities provide an overview of what is happening in today's classrooms. Refer to this chapter and to resources on this text's Companion Website at http://www.prenhall.com/egbert for support while you read the rest of the text.

This text cannot, and does not try to, include everything about supporting learning with technology—there are millions of educational Web sites, hundreds of useful software programs, and an enormous amount of pedagogical and technical information to explore. Wonderful texts such as Mills and Roblyer (2006) help teachers learn technical aspects of software programs. However, because research clearly shows that teacher education students choose to learn only what they believe they will use in their future teaching (Egbert, Paulus, & Nakamichi, 2002), this text focuses on what is essential in supporting learning with technology.

Following each chapter's case is a list of objectives that you should be able to meet after completing the chapter. For example, when you finish this chapter, you will be able to meet the following objectives:

- Explain why a learning focus is important to supporting learning with technology.
- Describe the relevant standards and the 21st-century skills that ground the learning in this text.
- Define "educational technology" and related terms.

- Discuss the use of technology tools to provide access to learning for physically challenged students, English language learners, and others who might face barriers to learning.
- Present an overview of computer-based and computer-assisted assessment practices.
- Understand how and why to adapt lesson plans for more effective learning.

The format, content, and objectives for each chapter have been developed to help you to meet the National Educational Technology Standards for Teachers (NETS*T). These include:

1. Teachers demonstrate a sound understanding of technology operations and concepts.
2. Teachers plan and design effective learning environments and experiences supported by technology.
3. Teachers implement curriculum plans that include methods and strategies for applying technology to maximize student learning.
4. Teachers apply technology to facilitate a variety of effective assessment and evaluation strategies.
5. Teachers use technology to enhance their productivity and professional practice.
6. Teachers understand the social, ethical, legal, and human issues surrounding the use of technology in PK–12 schools and apply that understanding in practice. (iste.org, 2000)

Look at the objectives for this chapter listed above. Which NETS*T do they address, at least in part?

_____

_____

_____

Foundational Standards for Students

Each chapter in the text contains a feature called "Meeting the Standards" that discusses the content and technology standards for students relevant to the topic of each chapter. In this chapter, Meeting the Standards describes an overview of standards and presents how they underscore the **learning goals,** or the expected outcomes, that frame the uses of technology presented in this text. These goals, often termed "21st-century skills" because of their perceived need in the near future, include:

- Content learning
- Critical thinking
- Communication
- Problem-solving
- Production
- Creativity

The standards cited throughout this text are taken from two main resources. The first is the International Society for Technology in Education (ISTE) Web site (http://www.iste.org). ISTE is the central organization for technology standards for teachers, administrators, and students. The student technology standards from ISTE are listed in Figure 1.1. Notice that the student standards have much in common with the standards for teachers.

1. **Creativity and Innovation**

   Students demonstrate creative thinking, construct knowledge, and develop innovative products and processes using technology. Students:

   a. apply existing knowledge to generate new ideas, products, or processes.
   b. create original works as a means of personal or group expression.
   c. use models and simulations to explore complex systems and issues.
   d. identify trends and forecast possibilities.

2. **Communication and Collaboration**

   Students use digital media and environments to communicate and work collaboratively, including at a distance, to support individual learning and contribute to the learning of others. Students:

   a. interact, collaborate, and publish with peers, experts, or others employing a variety of digital environments and media.
   b. communicate information and ideas effectively to multiple audiences using a variety of media and formats.
   c. develop cultural understanding and global awareness by engaging with learners of other cultures.
   d. contribute to project teams to produce original works or solve problems.

3. **Research and Information Fluency**

   Students apply digital tools to gather, evaluate, and use information. Students:

   a. plan strategies to guide inquiry.
   b. locate, organize, analyze, evaluate, synthesize, and ethically use information from a variety of sources and media.
   c. evaluate and select information sources and digital tools based on the appropriateness to specific tasks.
   d. process data and report results.

4. **Critical Thinking, Problem-Solving, and Decision-Making**

   Students use critical thinking skills to plan and conduct research, manage projects, solve problems and make informed decisions using appropriate digital tools and resources. Students:

   a. identify and define authentic problems and significant questions for investigation.
   b. plan and manage activities to develop a solution or complete a project.
   c. collect and analyze data to identify solutions, and/or make informed decisions.
   d. use multiple processes and diverse perspectives to explore alternative solutions.

5. **Digital Citizenship**

   Students understand human, cultural, and societal issues related to technology and practice legal and ethical behavior. Students:

   a. advocate and practice safe, legal, and responsible use of information and technology.
   b. exhibit a positive attitude toward using technology that supports collaboration, learning, and productivity.
   c. demonstrate personal responsibility for lifelong learning.
   d. exhibit leadership for digital citizenship.

6. **Technology Operations and Concepts**

   Students demonstrate a sound understanding of technology concepts, systems, and operations. Students:

   a. understand and use technology systems.
   b. select and use applications effectively and productively.
   c. troubleshoot systems and applications.
   d. transfer current knowledge to learning of new technologies.

The technology standards are also available with national content standards in the aggregated list posted at the Education World Web site (http://www.educationworld.com). Each standard from Education World used in this text is designated with a content area identifier, as illustrated in Table 1.1. The grade level and standard number typically follow the identifier. All of the standards can also be found at the sites of the organizations that created them. Find a list of additional standards Web sites in the Resources module for this chapter on the text's Companion Website (http://www.prenhall.com/egbert).

TABLE 1.1 Standards Identifiers			
NA	National	Arts	
NA-D	National	Arts	Dance
NA-M	National	Arts	Music
NA-T	National	Arts	Theatre
NA-VA	National	Arts	Visual Arts
NL	National	Language Arts	
NL-ENG	National	Language Arts	**ENG**lish
NL-FL	National	Language Arts	Foreign Language
NM	National	Math	
NM-NUM	National	Math	**NUM**ber and Operations
NM-ALG	National	Math	**ALG**ebra
NM-GEO	National	Math	**GEO**metry
NM-MEA	National	Math	**MEA**surement
NM-DATA	National	Math	**DATA** Analysis and Probability
NM-PROB	National	Math	**PROB**lem Solving
NM-REA	National	Math	**REA**soning and Proof
NM-COMM	National	Math	**COMM**unication
NM-CONN	National	Math	**CONN**ections
NM-REP	National	Math	**REP**resentation
NPH	National	Physical Education & Health	
NPH-H	National	Physical Education & Health	Health
NS	National	Science	
NSS	National	Social Sciences	
NSS-C	National	Social Sciences	Civics
NSS-EC	National	Social Sciences	**EC**onomics
NSS-G	National	Social Sciences	Geography
NSS-USH	National	Social Sciences	US History
NSS-WH	National	Social Sciences	World History
NT	National	Technology	

Source: Reprinted with permission of Education World, Inc.

• • • •   Meeting the Standards: 21st Century Skills **• • • •**

Standards, instructional goals, curricula, legislation, teacher beliefs, student experience, resources, and many other variables guide technology use in classrooms. Ultimately educational stakeholders agree that the use of technology is to prepare students, but there is often little agreement on what they are being prepared for (jobs? citizenry? life in general?) and how that preparation should be conducted (drill? experiential learning? discovery?). Nonetheless, for teachers looking to understand what is essential to support learning with technology, the common components integrated into national technology and content area standards and state requirements provide a good start. For example, following are categories from the math (representation subsection) and English standards.

Math

- NM-REP.PK-12.1 Create and Use Representations to Organize, Record, and Communicate Mathematical Ideas
- NM-REP.PK-12.2 Select, Apply, and Translate Among Mathematical Representations to Solve Problems
- NM-REP.PK-12.3 Use Representations to Model and Interpret Physical, Social, and Mathematical Phenomena

English

- NL-ENG.K-12.1 Reading for Perspective
- NL-ENG.K-12.2 Reading for Understanding
- NL-ENG.K-12.3 Evaluation Strategies
- NL-ENG.K-12.4 Communication Skills
- NL-ENG.K-12.7 Evaluating Data
- NL-ENG.K-12.8 Developing Research Skills
- NL-ENG.K-12.9 Multicultural Understanding

Source: Reprinted with permission of Education World, Inc.

Across these standards, the terms used to describe them combine readily into the six "21st-century" learning goals mentioned previously in this chapter. In fact, NETS have recently been revised with a focus on these goals. Using these learning goals as a framework for supporting learning with technology considers virtually all of the standards and addresses many curricular and legislative goals. Other chapters in this text discuss how to meet these learning goals and how technology can support the process.

Which of the six learning goals are you confident that you know how to support? Which do you need more work with? Why do you think so?

_____

_____

_____

 See your state standards for 21st Century Skills in the **Standards module** on this text's Companion Website (http://www.prenhall.com/egbert).

• • • •

OVERVIEW OF LEARNING AND TECHNOLOGY

In each chapter of this text, the overview section presents definitions, explanations, and examples of the chapter focus. The discussion gives readers a consistent understanding of the ideas to be presented and grounds the information in the rest of the chapter. In the current chapter, the overview focuses on a basic understanding of learning and technology.

What Is Learning?

This text discusses learning before it addresses technology because the central focus of technology use should be *what students learn*. The concept of *learning* is discussed in more detail in chapter 2, but clearly there are many ways to understand what it is and how it happens. For example, the learning theories seen in Figure 1.2 are only a few of those that exist.

FIGURE 1.2 Learning Theories from the Theory into Practice Database
(http://tip.psychology.org/theories.html)

The Theories

- <u>ACT* (J. Anderson)</u>
- <u>Adult Learning Theory (P. Cross)</u>
- <u>Algo-Heuristic Theory (L. Landa)</u>
- <u>Andragogy (M. Knowles)</u>
- <u>Anchored Instruction (J. Bransford & the CTGV)</u>
- <u>Aptitude-Treatment Interaction (L. Cronbach & R. Snow)</u>
- <u>Attribution Theory (B. Weiner)</u>
- <u>Cognitive Dissonance Theory (L. Festinger)</u>
- <u>Cognitive Flexibility Theory (R. Spiro)</u>
- <u>Cognitive Load Theory (J. Sweller)</u>
- <u>Component Display Theory (M.D. Merrill)</u>
- <u>Conditions of Learning (R. Gagne)</u>
- <u>Connectionism (E. Thorndike)</u>
- <u>Constructivist Theory (J. Bruner)</u>
- <u>Contiguity Theory (E. Guthrie)</u>
- <u>Conversation Theory (G. Pask)</u>
- <u>Criterion Referenced Instruction (R. Mager)</u>
- <u>Double Loop Learning (C. Argyris)</u>
- <u>Drive Reduction Theory (C. Hull)</u>
- <u>Dual Coding Theory (A. Paivio)</u>
- <u>Elaboration Theory (C. Reigeluth)</u>
- <u>Experiential Learning (C. Rogers)</u>
- <u>Functional Context Theory (T. Sticht)</u>
- <u>Genetic Epistemology (J. Piaget)</u>
- <u>Gestalt Theory (M. Wertheimer)</u>
- <u>GOMS (Card, Moran & Newell)</u>
- <u>GPS (A. Newell & H. Simon)</u>

Constructivist Theory (J. Bruner)

A major theme in Bruner's theoretical framework is that learning is an active process in which learners construct new ideas or concepts based on their current/past knowledge.

Experiential Learning (C. Rogers)

Rogers distinguished two types of learning: cognitive (meaningless) and experiential (significant). The former corresponds to academic knowledge such as learning vocabulary or multiplication tables, and the latter refers to applied knowledge such as learning about engines in order to repair a car.

Many technology texts focus on *one* learning theory or philosophy as a guide for technology use. However, good teachers follow all kinds of philosophies, and good teaching is not necessarily a matter of behaviorism vs. constructivism or any other "-ism" (Ketterer, 2007). Good teachers keep students engaged and challenged and work with both language and content to develop student skills, abilities, knowledge, and experience (Aaronsohn, 2003). Obviously this can happen in any number of ways, depending on students, context, goals, and tools. Sometimes it calls for a more behavioristic approach and sometimes for a more cognitive or social approach to teaching and learning. This text points out that whether teachers believe that knowledge is to be memorized or constructed through social interaction, there are ways that technology can help, from providing resources for content learning to supporting independent thought.

To illustrate this and other points throughout the text, each chapter includes a feature titled From the Classroom. This feature integrates ideas, suggestions, and opinions from classroom teachers about the topics in the chapter. Read how one teacher works through her understanding of how technology theories fit together for her in From the Classroom: Theory and Practice.

For more resources about learning theories, see this chapter's Resources module on the Companion Website (http://www.prenhall.com/egbert). Also, note Figure 1.3, which defines terms that are used often throughout this text in the discussions of learning goals.

What is your theory of how people learn? How does your personal theory affect how you plan to teach?

_____

_____

_____

> ### FROM THE CLASSROOM
> #### Theory and Practice
> Our questions and frustrations reminded me of the three main theories which exist. . . . The first is the behaviorist: [learning] is acquired through imitation, direct instruction, practicing through drills, memorization, etc. The second is innatist: [learning] is acquired naturally, just by listening to it and being immersed in an authentic environment. No direct instruction or correction is needed. The last is interactionist, which says that [learning] is acquired naturally, but it really stresses the interaction portion, and also says that sometimes it is necessary to teach specific rules or correct student output. These are coming from the experts and it seems to me that perhaps pieces from each are true. I doubt any one theory could ever explain how every unique individual will learn. I think there is a time and a place for flashcards and memorization, but I think it is also crucial to have meaningful interaction. (Jennie, first-grade teacher)

What Is Technology?

As with the word *learning*, the term *technology* has many definitions. According to a variety of sources, **technology** is:

- Mechanisms for distributing messages, including postal systems, radio and television broadcasting companies, telephone, satellite and computer networks. www1.worldbank.org/disted/glossary.html
- Electronic media (such as video, computers, or lasers) used as tools to create, learn, explain, document, analyze, or present dance. www.openc.k12.or.us/start/dance/glosd.html
- The application of knowledge to meet the goals, goods, and services desired by people.
- The set of tools, both hardware (physical) and software, that help us act and think better. Technology includes all the objects from pencil and paper to the latest electronic gadget. Electronic and computer technology help us share information and knowledge quickly and efficiently.
- The application of scientific or other organized knowledge—including any tool, technique, product, process, method, organization or system—to practical tasks. www.nlm.nih.gov/ nichsr/hta101/ta101014. html

In general, a broad definition of technology ranges from mechanical assembly lines to Nintendo, from drugs to knowledge. In an even more global sense, technology is seen as a "driver of change" and "the fundamental cause for social shifts toward globalization and the new economy" (NCREL, 2004, p. 1). Technologies of all kinds hold an important place in society, and it is natural that education has been and will continue to be affected by technology.

What Is Educational Technology?

Educational technology is a subset of all existing technologies. To many educators, the term **educational technology** is synonymous with computers. Although the major focus of this text and of the field of educational technology is on computers, teachers use many other technologies in the course of a day, including the pencil, the telephone, and the stapler. Most teachers, however, do not need lessons on how to use a pencil well, so this text follows the trend to define educational technology as electronic technologies with an emphasis on computing. Basic components of technology include hardware, software, and connection, discussed later in this chapter.

FIGURE 1.3 Learning Terms

Assessment: Assessment means gathering evidence about student needs, skills, abilities, experience, and performance. Assessment happens in technology-enhanced classrooms in many ways, as described in each of the upcoming chapters.

Context: Context is the environment or circumstances that surround something. For example, if a student poses a problem to be solved, it must be put into context by describing the events that led to it, what features it has, who is involved, and so on. The case at the start of each chapter in this book helps to provide a context for the discussions and examples.

Effective: In essence, effective means the capability to achieve a goal. In other words, if a technology-enhanced task is effective, it has the potential and means to help students reach the learning goal. In this text, a crucial element for tasks is that they are effective.

Engagement: When students are engaged, they are motivated and find the task meaningful. Engagement can be evidenced by willingness to stay on task, progress toward task goals, and ability to apply task content to life. According to McKenzie (1998), we can judge our classrooms "engaged" when we witness the following indicators:

- Children are engaged in authentic and multidisciplinary tasks.
- Students participate in interactive learning.
- Students work collaboratively.
- Students learn through exploration.
- Students are responsible for their learning.
- Students are strategic.

Evaluation: Although many educators equate assessment with evaluation, there are qualitative differences in the terms. While assessment covers a range of processes and focuses, evaluation means making a judgment about something. Typically this means assigning a grade or other value to whatever is being evaluated. Because schools and teachers have different requirements for evaluation, assessment is given more emphasis in this text.

Feedback: Responses to student work, questions, and processes are feedback. Feedback can be positive, negative, clarifying, or interactive, and it can be provided in many forms such as spoken, written, or graphical. Feedback is discussed in every chapter as an essential component of the learning process.

Goal: A goal is a general statement about what should happen or what the expected outcomes are. For example, a goal for technology use in science might be for students to understand scientific inquiry. The learning goals presented at the beginning of this chapter serve as the foci for this text.

Objective: An objective is a specific statement about what students will be able to do when they complete the task or lesson. For example, for the science goal noted above, objectives could be that students will be able to define "inquiry," to describe each part of the process, and to demonstrate the process. Objectives are usually stated with measurable action verbs—find a thorough list of them at http://www.schoolofed.nova.edu/sso/acad-writing/verbs.htm. Because student outcomes are vital in understanding how to support learning with technology, objectives are mentioned in many chapters.

Process: A process is a sequence of events or procedure for accomplishing something. Each chapter in this text describes the process for achieving a learning goal. These processes overlap but each goal also has its own particularities.

Scaffold: A scaffold is information, feedback, a tool, or some other form of support that helps students grow from their present level of knowledge, skill, or ability to the next level.

Each type of technology affords opportunities for different actions and can help fulfill learning goals in different ways. For example, students can learn to communicate and write with word processing and email tools; they can learn to organize and analyze with database, spreadsheet, and graphical organizer programs; they can learn about the importance of visuals using drawing software. Educational technology has been categorized in different ways based on these different goals. It has been looked at as:

- A tutor that presents information to be memorized (e.g., drill-and-practice software, instructional video)
- Support for student exploration (e.g., through electronic encyclopedias, simulations, and hypermedia-based data presentations that students can control)
- A creativity and production tool (e.g., word processing, videotape recording)
- A communications tool (e.g., email, electronic discussion forums)

Levin and Bruce (2001) define technology as *media* for (a) inquiry, (b) communication, (c) construction, and (d) expression. There are many more ways to describe educational technology, but across all of these descriptions, two main ideas emerge. First, as technology changes, so does the uses to which it is put and the ways in which it is characterized. The Internet, for example, has revolutionized the way that many students obtain and use resources. The second, and seemingly apparent, idea is that a computer by itself is nothing but a plastic box with wires and silicon. In other words, a computer cannot do anything by itself. Therefore, what people do with it is central to what it does for people (Ascione, 2006).

Read this accompanying feature that describes how one teacher supports this text's suggestion about how to define technology in From the Classroom: Definition of Technology.

> **FROM THE CLASSROOM**
>
> ### Definition of Technology
>
> I think we need to be careful not to get too specific (i.e., technology = computers), while at the same time not getting so broad that our definition of technology includes everything from pencil and paper to lasers and computers. I'd like to see us define technology in a manner that looks at electronic tools we use to enhance teaching and learning. This eliminates some simple learning tools such as chalkboards, pencil and paper, but leaves a broad definition of "electronic" devices that might include calculators, PDAs, computers, overhead projectors, VCRs, etc. (Sally, fifth/sixth-grade teacher)

Technology Effectiveness in Classrooms

In fact, although widely believed to cause better achievement, technology has not been shown overall to be effective at increasing student achievement. In part, this is because the research on effectiveness is "contradictory and/or seriously flawed" (Burns & Ungerleider, 2002–2003, p. 45). However, that does not mean that technology *cannot* be used to support student achievement in specific contexts. For example, Burns and Ungerleider (2002–2003) note that when age, task, and autonomy are considered in the use of computers, there are benefits to group work, high-level concept understanding for older students, and improvement in student attitudes toward computer technologies. Schacter (1999) cites studies showing that

- Students can learn faster in computer-based instructional contexts.
- Student attitudes toward their classes are more positive when they include computer-based instruction.
- Children with special needs can achieve more in technology-rich environments.
- Students of all ages and levels can achieve more across the curriculum in technology-rich environments.

However, Schacter also notes that for technology to have a positive effect, learning objectives must be clear and the technology must be used for specific, targeted goals. Research also clearly shows that the effectiveness of technology use is based not on learning theory but on context—in other words, it depends on the learner, the learning environment, the knowledge, experience, and attitude of the teacher, the technology used, and the task (Burns & Ungerleider, 2002–2003; Schacter, 1999). Most important is that effective teaching and learning drive technology use. McKenzie (1998) supports this view, noting that "there is no credible evidence that [technologies] improve student reading, math, or thinking skills unless they are in service of carefully crafted learning programs" (p. 2).

What Drives the Use of Educational Technology?

In spite of mixed reports on its effectiveness for learning, technology is used in classrooms across the nation. For some teachers their interest in doing something innovative drives technology use. For other teachers, obligations imposed by their schools or districts, for example, required lab use, does. Other impetuses include community/parental pressure, student demands, and economic rewards. State and federal laws push technology use by requiring that teachers and students be proficient and demonstrate learning. For example, the current federal No Child Left Behind legislation requires that every student be technology literate by the end of the eighth grade, and teachers must be knowledgeable enough to help students reach this goal. The increase in student excitement, motivation, and achievement that teachers see as a result of technology use is another teacher motivator to use educational technology.

What are your reasons for learning about educational technology?

_____

_____

_____

STUDENTS AND TECHNOLOGY

In addition to the possible benefits listed above, why else do students need to be taught with and about technology? According to Gordon (2001), "Students may perform a Web search faster and better than their teachers, but they still need to be taught to filter and critically engage with what they read, see, and hear from the multimedia devices they so deftly operate. And school is still the place where they will need to develop the skills they need to function effectively in the world—to read and write, to add and subtract, to understand how nature and societies are organized and where they fit in" (pp. vii–viii). There are many other reasons why students should study about and with technology. Each chapter in this text presents benefits to students related to the topic of the chapter; some general benefits are presented here.

Student Benefits from Learning With and About Technology

One of the benefits of students learning with technology is that they will be engaged in new **literacies,** or new ways of being knowledgeable. Within the learning goals, a number of literacies are becoming more focal because technology calls attention to them. Three main literacies include:

- *Information literacy,* which is the ability to "recognize when information is needed and have the ability to locate, evaluate, and use effectively the needed information" (American Library Association [ALA], 1998). Students cannot recognize when information is needed if they do not have a grasp of the information that has already been presented to them. For example, conducting an accurate Web search and finding information that is appropriate and factual is part of being information literate. Information literacy implies that learners also have visual, numerical, computer, and basic (text) literacy. Information literacy standards are included in the NETS. More detail on these standards is available from www.ala.org.

- *Technological literacy.* A second important but often overlooked literacy, this is the ability for students to be able to make "informed, balanced and comprehensive analysis of the technological influences on their lives and then be able to act on the basis of their analysis" (Saskatchewan Education, n.d., p. 1). In other words, students must understand not only how to use technology, but understand the many ways in which technology affects their lives. Computers are only one of the many technologies that this literacy addresses.

- *Media literacy* addresses technology and more as it involves critically thinking about the influences of media (including books, TV, radio, movies, and the Internet). It means choosing, reflecting on, appreciating, responding appropriately to, and producing media of all kinds. For example, media-literate students understand the motivations behind television commercials and can judge the merits of the product despite the persuasive techniques employed by advertisers. A great source for media literacy information is Media Awareness Network at http://www.media-awareness.ca/english/.

Clearly, these literacies are tightly linked to the learning goals, and student achievement in these areas provides lifelong benefits. These literacies are integrated, even where not specifically mentioned, throughout the activities and ideas in this text.

Another benefit of student technology use is a change in how learning occurs in classrooms. If we think about how children learn at home and in the world, we can see that there is a disconnect between natural learning and classroom learning. Outside of school, children are encouraged to explore, to inquire, to experiment, and to come to their own conclusions with the help of adults and peers. In classrooms, children are often asked to listen, memorize, and not to question. Technology can make it more possible for students to learn in ways that resemble natural learning by providing resources, support, and feedback that teachers alone may not be able to provide. Of course, technology will not have these benefits if it is not used in ways that support this vision of learning. As a number of scholars have noted, just because you can do something with technology doesn't mean that you should. The goal is to make the technology use itself transparent, while examining the interactions, content, and process of the learning that occurs with technology.

Now read how two teachers support a learning focus in using educational technology in From the Classroom: Learning Focus.

What do you remember about using technology when you were a K–12 student? What ideas do you already have about using technology in your instruction?

_____

_____

_____

FROM THE CLASSROOM

Learning Focus

We can't just throw the kids on a computer and expect learning to take place any more than we would show them the text and tell them to learn it by the end of the year. No matter what tools we use, we need to use good teaching practices, or our teaching will be ineffective. (Susan, fifth-grade teacher)

[A reading] says that computers are not capable of teaching, that teachers are the ones who actually perform this. I completely agree with this because it is important to keep in mind as technology continues advancing. This is why I feel that we need to rely on the content of our lessons in incorporating technology rather than using technology just because it will be fun when the activity itself might be better without it. Learning occurs best when it is driven by the human processes, not the technology. When this occurs, students are involved in their learning through negotiation of meaning with one another and are focused on the content of the project. (Cammie, student teacher)

TEACHERS AND TECHNOLOGY

As a technology-using teacher, you are central to meeting the goals of technology-supported learning. However, two-thirds of teachers describe themselves as unready to use technology for instruction (Loschert, 2003). To support learning with technology effectively, teachers must learn how to integrate technology into effective learning tasks and understand what their roles are during the technology-supported learning process. Each text chapter provides characteristics of effective learning tasks based specifically on the chapter's learning goal. It also provides insights into teacher roles that effectively support learning with technology.

Characteristics of Effective Learning Tasks

In general, effective student tasks are those that result in authentic, meaningful, engaged learning. For a technology-supported task to be effective in this sense, it should have these general characteristics:

1. *Focuses on goals.* Goals are developed based on standards, curricular requirements, and student needs, wants, and interests. Each chapter presents examples of goals.
2. *Includes technology that is working and available.* However, it must be more than just *some* technology, it has to be the *right* technology. Guidelines to assist in making appropriate technology choices are presented throughout this text.
3. *Includes teacher training and support.* Each chapter describes ways that teachers might find, discover, request, or use training and support.
4. *Allows time to learn relevant technologies.* Guidelines in all the chapters discuss ways to do this efficiently.

FIGURE 1.4 Effective Task Characteristics

An effective technology-enhanced task:
- Focuses on goals
- Includes relevant technology
- Includes teacher support
- Integrates time to learn
- Provides a variety of relevant resources
- Uses technology only if it is necessary

FIGURE 1.5 Technology Can't. . .

What can't technology do?
- Design a seating chart, taking into consideration understandings about children and their attitudes toward one another.
- Make friends or show respect.
- Create lessons that address the needs of diverse students.
- Decorate a classroom.
- Choose a textbook.
- Manage 20 third graders.
- Make a decision based on a gut feeling.
- Give creative feedback.
- Understand.
- Search for or create knowledge.
- Teach.

FIGURE 1.6 Technology Can . . .

What can technology do?
- Manipulate streams of meaningless data.
- Repeat itself endlessly.
- Help make learning more efficient by controlling large amounts of data quickly.
- Help make learning more effective by providing a great wealth of resources and allowing students choices.
- Operate in environments where humans cannot.
- Connect people who could not connect cheaply or easily otherwise.
- Provide means to improve students' acquisition of basic skills and content knowledge (Kleiman, 2001).
- Motivate students (Kleiman, 2001).
- Work quickly and objectively.
- Strengthen teachers' preferred instructional approaches—for example, those who lecture can use computer-enhanced visual support, those who prefer inquiry-based approaches can use raw data on the Web and databases or spreadsheets for analysis.
- Help to change the vision of a classroom as a room with four walls that depends solely on the teacher for information.

---

5. *Provides needed resources.* Resources include lab time, online and offline information sources, and skills lessons. Suggestions for how and when to provide such resources are presented throughout this text.

6. *Uses technology only if appropriate.* Effective tasks do not use technology if goals can be reached and content can be better learned, presented, and/or assessed through other means and tools. Each chapter includes a section on learning activities that demonstrate appropriate uses of technology.

Figure 1.4 summarizes these characteristics. For more information about effectiveness and educational technology, see National School Boards Foundation (n.d.).

Teachers' Roles

Teachers' roles in classrooms have changed. Although some teachers continue to work within a curriculum in which *teaching* is central, the trend is toward goal-centered and student-centered curricula in which *student learning* is focal. This new focus has changed the teacher's role in the classroom. A student-centered focus that includes understanding and addressing students' interests, for example, means that teachers need to vary their teaching so that student interests are connected to classroom content and tasks.

Challenges for Teachers

Teachers using technology may face environmental, physical, attitudinal and philosophical, access, equity, cultural, financial, legal, and other obstacles. These challenges are presented in every chapter and discussed in depth in chapter 9. One challenge that teachers often voice is the idea that computers will put them out of a job. But there are many things that teachers can do that technology cannot. Figure 1.5 presents a very incomplete list that shows why teachers cannot be replaced by technology.

As important as understanding what technology cannot do is understanding what it can. Plotnik (1999) notes that "technology, in all of its various forms, offers users the tools to access, manipulate, transform, evaluate, use, and present information" (p. 3). How do teachers help it do this? Teachers can treat it as the tool that it is and integrate its use into every content area. In addition, instead of learning technology itself as the goal, teachers can employ technology to meet curricular goals in all areas. Figure 1.6 presents some of the things that technology is typically more efficient or effective at than teachers are.

Some teachers fear, often rightly, that technology learning may take the place of content learning and that the curriculum will not be covered. Teachers often do not understand at first how to balance technology and content and worry that there is not enough time to learn the technology they need. In these cases, teachers often stop using technology to focus on content, use only one technology repeatedly, or just jump in and hope for an eventual best. But it does not need to be this way. Support from students and parents, willingness to set aside an hour a week for additional learning, and/or a district that is willing to support grant writing are some of the ways discussed in this text to help teachers find the time they need to learn. Chapters 8 and 10 address these issues. In addition, the Guidelines section in each chapter supports teachers in understanding the roles of technology in classroom learning and how they might plan their learning about technology. Read one teacher's concerns about integrating technology in From the Classroom: Teacher Concerns.

What else would you add to this list?

_____

_____

_____

Whatever choices they make, teachers need choice, just as learners do, to reach their potential and become independent technology learners and users. Read From the Classroom: Teachers' Role to understand one teacher's perspective on her role and the role of technology.

GUIDELINES FOR USING EDUCATIONAL TECHNOLOGY

In each chapter, the Guidelines provide practical suggestions for teachers to help meet learning goals and overcome potential barriers. In this chapter, the guidelines present general issues to help you meet goals for technology use. These guidelines are summarized in Figure 1.7 on page 18.

Guideline #1: Understand the realities of technology use. In addition to understanding what technology can and cannot do, there are other significant realities that teachers need to understand. For example, learning to use technology *well* takes time—for everyone to learn, for effective uses to be discovered, and for implementation to be complete. Learning technology will not always be smooth, but help is available from members of the school community, including parents, technology specialists, knowledgeable students, and other teachers. In addition, teachers can join online teacher-based groups such as the Global SchoolNet Foundation (http://www.globalschoolnet.org/index.html) for help, ideas, and resources.

The special effects of technology (often called **bells and whistles**) may take precedence for students over task content at first, but well-designed tasks following the guidelines in this text can help avoid this problem. In addition, there are resources to help with just about every technology need, from using the icons in Microsoft Word (see http://www.med.miami.edu/psychiatry/wordvocab.html) to finding appropriate content for diverse learners (see the WestEd site at http://www.wested.org/cs/tdl/view/tdl_tip/45). This text will help you to explore and find additional technology resources by presenting a variety of Web sites, software packages, and support information and by suggesting places to look for further ideas and information. This text will also encourage you to share your findings with other educators.

Guideline #2: Examine equity and access for your students. Loschert (2003) reports that although the average school has over 100 computers, each student typically has only 20 minutes per week on the computer. In addition, girls, minorities, and students with special needs

FROM THE CLASSROOM
Teacher Concerns
I [keep] thinking about "how do I keep up?" I would love to see my students with digital notebooks, me videoconferencing with parents and students, using voice-generated technology. First, district and state will need to support technology growth and use in the classrooms with monies for technical support: training, maintenance, wiring. Second, respect for equipment needs to be taught to students and families (now, if a student misplaces a book, parents may or may not pay). Thirdly, as professionals we (educators) will need to embrace the new technology. I am ready! (Jean, sixth-grade teacher)

FROM THE CLASSROOM
Teachers' Role
I also wonder how much the role of teachers will change as technology advances. I even applied for a tutoring job with [a company where] you tutor online with a digital pencil and headset! Pretty crazy. Also, if we can listen and learn from history . . . there were so many predictions that new technology would revolutionize teaching and they really never did. For example, when the radio, TV, and mainframe computer came out, they were all expected to change the entire educational scene, but in reality, the changes were minute. From my reading, educational technology researchers always warn not to get overly excited about the future of technology based on history. (Jennie, first-grade teacher)

FIGURE 1.7 Guidelines for Using Educational Technology

Guideline	Summary
#1: Understand the realities of technology use.	Learning to use technology effectively takes time. Give yourself and your students that time.
#2: Examine equity and access for your students.	Not all students have equal access to technology. Teachers must make sure that everyone who needs it is given fair opportunities.
#3: Consider student differences.	Students who are physically and/or socially challenged or have other barriers to learning must be considered while technology-enhanced instruction is being designed.

often have less access than other students (Kleiner & Farris, 2002; Male, 2003). If everyone is to learn with these tools, everyone must be able to access them. Other chapters in this text provide ways to arrange and use technology to make access more equitable; these include making the best use of classroom computers and creating arrangements to share technology equitably and effectively within schools.

Guideline #3: Consider student differences. Students bring skills and backgrounds that can add to or detract from technology-enhanced learning experiences. Teachers should assess student needs by first investigating their learning preferences, cultural and language differences, and background experience and knowledge. Teachers must then address these needs by applying the techniques and strategies presented throughout the text. These techniques include, for example, using content resources at multiple levels, giving students choice in the products they develop, and providing extra support for students who need it.

In addition to specific instructional strategies, computer technologies can also help address the needs of diverse students and help to include students with a variety of abilities in classroom tasks. For example, special technologies called **assistive devices** can help teachers to provide larger text for sight-impaired students, voice recognition for students with physical disabilities, and extra wait time, feedback, or practice for those who need it. Assistive devices are presented later in this chapter and throughout the text.

Technology can also provide support for English language learners (ELLs) and other students by providing resources in a variety of languages and many different ways to work (Egbert, 2005), from supportive team-based software to individual remediation Web sites. Suggestions for supporting the learning of ELLs with technology are noted throughout the text.

What might be some of the barriers to learning for the students you plan to teach? Ideally, how could technology help overcome these barriers?

_____

_____

_____

TECHNOLOGY-ENHANCED LEARNING ACTIVITIES

The Learning Activities section in each chapter presents suggestions and examples to use as models to effectively use technology. In this chapter, you will read real-life educational technology uses taken directly from school reports. These examples provide an initial idea of effective ways that technology is being applied in classrooms today.

• •

Elaine Insinnia, an eighth-grade language arts teacher from Berkeley Heights, New Jersey, uses Internet research to help her students understand the novels she assigns. Using questions to help focus the students, Insinnia directs them as they research a book's author, the story's time period, and key historical events related to the plot. In the past, Insinnia and her students conducted similar research in the school's library, which often took several class periods. With the Internet, "you can get the same amount of information in 25 to 30 minutes," she says. "It saves you lots of time and the kids pay attention." The project lets students take control of their learning as they explore Web sites and information that interests them, Insinnia says. The project also teaches students how to evaluate the validity of information they find on the Web. After they complete their research, students share their findings in an online chat room [a Web site that allows communication in real time]. "When you are in a classroom discussion, the same kids dominate the discussion," Insinnia says. "In the chat room everyone gets a chance to answer and they are engaged." The chat room discussion also provides a record of each student's contribution, which Insinnia can review later, she adds. (Loschert, 2003, n.p.)

● ●

Tony Vincent, a fifth-grade classroom teacher in Omaha, Nebraska, reports: "Using a computer program called Sketchy, which functions like a digital flip book, students create short cartoons that show each step they take to solve a math problem. They move the numbers around the screen as they solve a problem and add 'thought bubbles' to explain their work. Students find the programs so engaging they watch their cartoons, and ones created by their classmates, re-peatedly. The process of creating the product and reviewing it reinforces the thought process students should use to solve the problems. . . . As a result, a lesson that used to take two weeks now takes just three days for students to comprehend." (Loschert, 2003, n.p.)

For more about Sketchy and handhelds, see http:/ /www. goknow.com/Products/ Sketchy/ (GoKnow, 2003). Figure 1.8 shows the Sketchy interface and the step-by-step animation process.

● ●

When Jane McLane first mentioned her upcoming sabbatical to bicycle around the world to Kristi Rennebohm Franz, a fellow teacher at Sunnyside Elementary in Pullman, Washington, she never dreamed she'd end up with 25 virtual companions. But somehow she did—Kristi's first and second graders! By carrying a digital camera and a small computer, Jane was able to communicate on a daily basis with Kristi and her students. Along the way, Kristi's students learned to write, read, and communicate as they interacted with Jane about world languages, cultures, geography, art, time zones, and architecture. (Learning Point Associates, 2004)

● ●

In a challenge described by FermiLab LInC (2000), seventh-grade students will be chal-lenged to develop a schoolwide recycling program. The challenge will be for everyone, stu-dents, teachers, administrators and especially the cafeteria and lunch program to recycle waste products. Students will form teams to investigate waste and waste management. They will also contact other schools throughout the country (via email) and collect data on school recycling programs. Do they exist? How are they managed? What percentage of waste has to be hauled away? What are the costs for running such a program? The teams will be encouraged to develop a Total School Recycle Program to either internally handle waste, or to find resources that will productively utilize waste products. This will involve investigating the means of disposing or recycling all the waste generated from their school building. Can it be done? (FermiLab LInC, 2000)

● ●

FIGURE 1.8 Sketchy Example

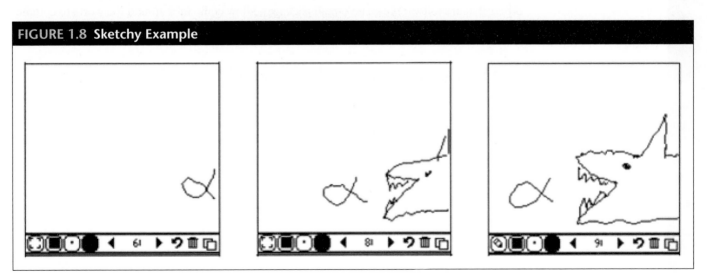

Source: Reprinted with permission of GoKnow.

All of these examples are adaptable for a variety of grade levels and students. More important, they demonstrate the effective task characteristics presented in Figure 1.4 and focus on 21st-century learning goals such as critical thinking and problem solving. The technology is employed as support for effective student learning. This learning focus is important because technology changes so rapidly. In fact, even by the time you finish reading this text, much of the technology mentioned in it may be in a new version, may have a new format, or may be obsolete entirely. However, having a firm grounding in the learning goals that will continue to be essential—for example, critical thinking, problem solving, content, and communication—means that teachers and students will be able to continue to integrate technology, deal with change, and work toward success.

TECHNOLOGIES FOR SUPPORTING LEARNING

Each chapter in this text presents a variety of technologies that can be used to support learning. This chapter presents a general overview of technology for reference at any time during your reading of the text. It focuses on a basic understanding of educational technology that includes awareness of the components of any tool.

Components of Electronic Tools

Electronic tools generally consist of **hardware, software,** and **connection** components. Table 1.2 presents a basic overview and broad definitions of hardware components listed in alphabetical order. For hardware, the three main types are input, processing, and output. **Input devices** are used to enter information into the computer. **Output devices** display or deliver the information in a format that users can understand. **Processing devices** change the input into output. There are also **communication devices** that connect computers to each other. The components listed in the table will also be mentioned in other chapters in this text.

Software is composed of a set of instructions that controls the operation of a computer. The most important software is the **operating system,** or OS. The OS manages the rest of the software on the computer. Typically software is developed for one OS or **platform,** either Macintosh OS or Windows, but some software can run on these and other less common operating systems such as Unix and Linux. Find tutorials for these common operating systems in the Tutorials module on the Companion Website (http://www.prenhall.com/egbert).

Information about types of software, software functions, and parts of a software package is presented in Table 1.3 on page 22. These terms are used throughout this text.

Connection components, some of which are technically hardware (e.g., a modem) and others that are software (e.g., an e-mail package), allow computers around the world to communicate. A short list of important components is presented in Table 1.4 on page 22.

The World Wide Web as Educational Technology

Probably the most-used tool in classrooms today, the World Wide Web has an astounding number of resources to offer educators. See this chapter's Tool CloseUp on page 24 for more details on how to understand and use the Web.

Assistive Technologies

This text addresses supporting learning with technology for students with a wide range of abilities, skills, and needs. In some instances, the choice of resource or student role in an activity will be enough to help students access academic content. In other cases special technologies, called **assistive devices,** will be needed for students to access the information they need. In general, assistive devices are hardware and software designed for specific needs. Table 1.5 on page 23 presents examples of some of these devices, and others are presented throughout this text.

TABLE 1.2 Hardware Components

Hardware	Function	Uses
CD-ROM (compact disc, read-only memory) DVD (digital video disc)	Storage device	Portable optical recording devices that store massive amounts of data
Central processing unit (CPU)	Processing	The "brains" of the computer, the central processing unit contains the motherboard, disk drives, and chips. Loads the operating system to enable the computer to turn on and work; performs operations.
Digital camera	Input device	Entering video and images
Flash drive	Storage device	Portable, very small storage devices are also known as thumb drives and USB drives. Flash drives fit in a computer's USB port—very convenient for storage.
Floppy disk	Storage device	Portable magnetic recording devices that keep user files—these are not used in new computers because they have been replaced by more stable CDs and DVDs with a larger capacity.
Handheld	Combination device	These small computers have almost the same range of uses as their desktop-size counterparts, but they are more portable, cheaper, and wireless.
Hard drive	Storage device	Storing information long-term on a computer. The hard drive contains any software installed on the computer and files that the user has created and saved.
Keyboard	Input device	Enter text and numbers
Microphone	Audio input device	Enter audio information, particularly for speech recognition
Modem	Communication device	A device that allows one computer to talk to another over a phone or cable line
Monitor	Output device	Display information on the computer
Mouse/touch screen/touch pad	Input device	Pointing to and selecting information
Printer	Output device	Print a hard copy of graphics and text on paper or paper products.
Projector	Visual/audio output device	Provides a bigger picture than a monitor that can be broadcast for a group
RAM (Random-access memory) /ROM (Read-only memory)	Storage device	RAM is the computer's primary memory and stores what is currently in use. ROM stores the computer's instruction set and cannot be changed by the user.
Scanner	Input device	Enter drawings, documents, and designs
Speakers	Output device	Listening to audio output
VCR	Input and output device	Entering or printing video
Web cam	Input device	Take pictures to be displayed on the Internet and communicate in real-time with other users who can see you.

In addition, the Microsoft (www.microsoft.com) and Apple (www.apple.com) Web sites list all of the assistive devices included in their operating systems.

The benefits of access to technology for students with disabilities include:

- Being able to bridge ideas
- Sequential practice to master concepts step by step
- Control over their environment

TOOLS

TABLE 1.3 Software

Software	Category	Examples	Explanation
Commercial	Software type	Microsoft Office Suite	Software from publishers that is sold for profit
Communications	Software function	Email, courseware (addressed in chapter 3)	Any software that allows users to communicate
Freeware	Software type	Programs from sites such as download.com and tucows.com	Software that is free
Operating system	Software component	Mac OS X, Microsoft XP, Windows Vista, Linux	Software that coordinates the working of the computer
Personal productivity	Software function	Word processor, database, spreadsheet, presentation software (addressed in chapter 7)	Also called "office software," allows users to produce, analyze, present, and describe data
Programming software, formatting languages	Software function	C++, Java/ FrontPage, Netscape Composer	Used by programmers to write applications and by users to format Web pages. Web page editors avoid the need to learn the Web formatting codes (called hypertext markup language, or html) by providing clickable visual formatting.
Shareware	Software type	Found at sites such as http://www.macintoshos.com/shareware.library/educational/educational.shtml	Software that users can test and, if they decide to keep it, they pay a small fee to the developer
Teacher tools	Software function	Grade books, letter generators, rubric makers	Administrative software that teachers use to support instruction
User interface	Software component	All software programs	Allows the user to communicate with the computer; it's what the user sees on the screen

- Timely feedback
- Access to multimodal (visual, auditory, tactile, and kinesthetic) and multiintelligence materials (Barry & Wise, n.d.)

Teachers need to understand why and how to use assistive technologies to help students effectively. For example, teachers may not think about how students with different abilities will access information from the Web. For students who are visually impaired or physically challenged, access is an important issue. Simple solutions to access problems range from making the text in the Web browser bigger so that sight-impaired students can see it to providing a special, large mouse that needs only a light touch to work. For ways to make the Web more accessible to all students, see www.phschool.com/about_ph/web_access.html and the Accessibility section of the Resources module on this chapter's Companion Website (http://www.prenhall.com/egbert).

TABLE 1.4 Connection Components

Connection	Function
Internet	Connects computer networks around the world so that they can "talk" to each other. Computers must typically have a modem (see hardware).
ISP	Internet Service Providers (ISPs) provide connection to the Internet, typically for profit.
LAN	Local area networks (LANs) connect computers on the same network through wireless or cable connections to share printers and applications.
WAN	Wide area networks connect local computers to a broader network (such as the Internet) or connect LANs together.
World Wide Web	Part of the Internet that enables electronic communication of text, graphics, audio, and video.

TABLE 1.5 Assistive Technologies

Device	Function	Uses	Examples
Accessibility testers	Test whether a Web site is as accessible as possible	For all teacher- and student-made Web pages	Bobby software (Watchfire)
Closed-captioned TV	Shows the TV audio in text	For students who are hearing-impaired	Every TV sold in the U.S. since 1993 must have closed-captioning capability
Touch screen	Students touch the monitor screen to give instructions to the computer, e.g., to click on links.	Can be used instead of a mouse for students who cannot control a mouse well. Touch screens are often used with young children.	Other "mouse emulators" include special keyboards, laser or infrared pointers, keyboard overlays, trackballs, and a variety of devices that can be tailored to students' needs. Figure 1.9 shows a trackball.
Screen magnifiers and screen readers	To make screen text bigger and/or to have the text read aloud	Helps sight-impaired users	Usually part of the operating system on computers; there are also free magnifiers like the one shown in Figure 1.10.
Signing avatars	Animated characters who use sign language	For students who use sign language	See the Signing Science Dictionary at http://signsci.terc.edu/ and find out more at the University of Toronto's Adaptive Technology Resource Centre, http://atrc.utoronto.ca/
Voice recognition software	Turns oral language into text on a computer screen	For students who cannot physically enter data other ways	Dragon Naturally Speaking and IBM's ViaVoice.
Universally designed software	Features include spoken voice, visual highlighting, and document or page navigation.	Makes software accessible to struggling readers and students with disabilities and enables struggling readers to read the same books as their peers.	eReader software (CAST) and Thinking Reader software (Tom Snyder Productions) For more information on universal design, see this chapter's Resources module on the Companion Website.

FIGURE 1.9 Trackball

Source: Used with permission of Kensington Computer Products Group.

FIGURE 1.10 Screen Magnifier

Source: Used with permission of Site Point Pty Ltd.

TOOLS

Tool CloseUp: The World Wide Web

Each chapter provides a detailed view of two software applications in Tool CloseUps. In this chapter, the Tool CloseUp features the World Wide Web (WWW). Because the Web is one of the most popular applications of educational technology, teachers need at least a basic understanding of what it is and how it works. More about the Web is presented in each chapter of this text.

What Is the Web?

Many teachers believe that the Internet and World Wide Web are one and the same. However, whereas the **Internet** is a massive global network of linked computers, the **Web** is a "way of accessing information over the medium of the Internet. It is an information-sharing model that is built on top of the Internet" (from www.webopedia.com, "The Difference between the Internet and the World Wide Web"). In other words, the Web is a part of the Internet.

How Does the Web Work?

Documents on the Web are formatted in special languages, most commonly **hypertext markup language,** or HTML. Users access documents and resources on the Web by using a **Web browser,** which is software that can translate HTML into a readable display. Popular browsers include Internet Explorer (Microsoft), Firefox (Mozilla), Safari

(Apple, for Macs only), and Netscape Navigator (Netscape). Sometimes, in order to display audio or video, special components called **plug-ins** are necessary.

Documents are located on the Web through a **Uniform Resource Locator (URL),** also known as a Web address. The URL indicates the **domain** where the document can be found and what kind of organization the domain belongs to. For example, the domain www.wsu.edu indicates that the document will be found on the site of Washington State University (WSU), which the suffix, or final set of letters at the end of the domain name (.edu), specifies as an educational institution. There are only a few suffixes in use, but they may signify quite different information and views. The main suffixes are:

- .gov—government agencies
- .edu—educational institutions
- .org—nonprofit organizations
- .mil—military
- .com—commercial business
- .net—network organizations

Countries also have suffixes that designate the name of the country in which the domain is located.

Uses of the Web to support learning are presented in each chapter of this text.

Being media literate requires that students understand the source of their information. How can understanding the parts of a URL aid in this understanding?

_____

_____

_____

_____

Tutorial

CW

For support in searching the Web efficiently, see the Web browser tutorials in the Tutorials module on the Companion Website (http://www.prenhall.com/egbert).

The University of Washington's DO-IT program provides teachers with outstanding resources such as videos and articles for understanding and working with assistive technologies. See Figure 1.11 for an example of some of the resources, and read more about this program on the Web at http://www.washington.edu/doit/. Additionally, find information in this chapter's Resources module on the Companion Website (http://www.prenhall.com/egbert).

Appropriate Tool Use

Most important to understand in the discussion of technological tools is that if the tool does not make the task more effective or more efficient, a different tool should be employed. In addition, if there is no appropriate electronic technology that fits the task, electronic technology should not be used. For example, asking first graders to type sentences on the computer might be fun for them, but teachers need to evaluate whether the time students spend hunting for the correct keys and making editing mistakes might be better spent with a pencil or crayons. Or, setting ninth graders free on the Internet to research famous Americans might result in chaos that could better be organized by employing a

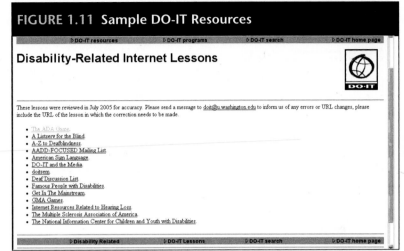

FIGURE 1.11 Sample DO-IT Resources

Source: Used with permission from DO-IT (Disabilities, Opportunities, Internetworking, and Technology), University of Washington.

more manageable information set in an electronic encyclopedia such as Encarta. This theme of principled technology use is repeated throughout the text. The thoughtless use of technology and the problems it causes is well documented and discussed (Bowers, 2000; Ferneding, 2003; Postman, 1993) and can be avoided.

Have you ever witnessed or participated in a thoughtless use of technology? What did you learn from the experience?

_____

_____

_____

ASSESSMENT

After you have reviewed the goals for your lesson, decided on an effective task, integrated technology in appropriate and effective ways, and supported students through the task process, it's time to assess. Each chapter in this text presents ways to appropriately assess student progress toward learning goals. Most important in the discussions of assessment is that both the *product* of student learning and the *process* of student learning are the foci of assessment. In the examples given throughout this text, technology is the focus of assessment (for example, did students use it well? was it appropriate for the task?) and used to assess (for example, an observation checklist on the teacher's handheld computer). However, it is important that assessments fit the specific context and students for whom they are developed. Therefore, note that the assessments in this text only serve as models. They probably cannot be used without at least some adaptations to fit specific classroom, task, and student conditions. For example, a **rubric,** or detailed scoring outline, that is made to evaluate a technology-supported presentation for fifth graders is most likely inappropriate to evaluate a presentation by 10th-grade students.

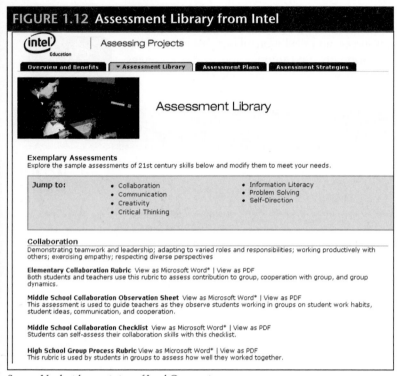

FIGURE 1.12 Assessment Library from Intel

Source: Used with permission of Intel Corporation.

FROM THE CLASSROOM

Assessment

I see [the] point about finding the purpose of assessment before deciding what type is more appropriate. However, I feel it's even more important to find out what type of student we are dealing with before deciding which assessment works better. For example, when we test our students in our building, we know certain students with extra barriers (language, attention span, etc.) will benefit more or will show their abilities better in a computer assessment versus paper/pencil. So, teachers decide to give them the computer assessment! It's not really a matter of what but WHO is taking the test! (Andrea, third-grade teacher)

The text addresses a number of assessments, including:

- Scoring guides (chapter 2)
- Rubrics (chapter 3)
- Multiple-choice tests (chapter 4)
- Checklists and peer team reports (chapter 5)
- Performance assessments (chapter 6)
- Problem-solving notebooks (chapter 7)
- Electronic portfolios (chapter 8)

These assessments can be used in a variety of contexts other than those described in the chapters. The text's brief theoretical discussions that accompany assessment examples will help you to understand *how* and *when* to employ them effectively.

One of the best places to start learning about assessments for technology-supported learning is the Assessing Projects Web site by Intel (http://www97.intel.com/en/Assessing Projects/). The three main sections of this site—Assessment Library (Figure 1.12), Assessment Plans, and Assessment Strategies—focus on 21st-century skills for elementary through high school. The site provides resources, examples, and practice that can be used for a variety of assessment purposes. Many of these resources are presented in this text.

Read as one teacher discusses the importance of looking at who students are when developing classroom assessments in From the Classroom: Assessment.

TECHNOLOGY-SUPPORTED LESSON EXAMPLE

Chapters 2–8 include a lesson section that has three parts: (1) a sample technology-enhanced lesson, (2) a lesson analysis, and (3) suggestions for adaptation to better fit the classroom or situation addressed in the case. Each sample lesson is written by a classroom teacher and is tied to the chapter's opening case. Each chapter's lesson is chosen because it demonstrates ideas from that particular chapter. This section not only shows how the chapter concepts fit together but also demonstrates how technology-enhanced lessons created for one context might be adapted to work effectively in another context. Note that any adaptation must be based on who the students are, the teacher's experience and knowledge, and the context (available technology, support structure, curriculum, and so on).

This chapter explores an example of a lesson developed for grades 5–7 that is being adapted for grade 3.

The Lesson

Following is a plan on current events from http:// www.sites4teachers. com/. Note that the lessons in other chapters might follow different formats because there is not one right way to create a lesson plan, and teachers usually personalize their lessons in some way. However, certain elements such as objectives, goals, materials, and procedures will almost always be present and can be analyzed for appropriateness.

Current Events Awareness
An Educator's Reference Desk Lesson Plan

Author: NIE Curriculum Guide—The Montana Standard—Butte, MT.

Grade Level(s): 5, 6, 7

Subject(s):
• Social Studies/Current Events/Issues

Objective: To increase student awareness of current events at local, national and international levels

Materials Needed: Newspapers, scissors

To Start:
Ask students to recall some of the biggest local news events of the year. Can they do the same for national news? World news? Which stories affect them directly (teachers' strikes, park closings, etc.)? Which stories affect them indirectly (world hunger, rising oil prices, etc.)? Which stories do not affect them at all?

Group Activity:
Section off the class bulletin board into three categories: local, national, and world news. Break the class into three groups, one for each category. Every day for a week or so, have each group clip from the newspaper two or three articles and photos they feel are most important or interesting. Each group should arrange its examples on the bulletin board.
At the end of the week, have students report on one of the events pictured on the board. The oral reports should include the 5Ws and H—the who, what, when, where, why, and how of the story—as well as why the group felt the event was important.

Follow-Up:
When a major local, national, or world news story breaks, bring it to the class' attention; challenge students to find follow-up stories in the days that follow. Have them summarize events that have occurred. Story examples might include natural disasters, political crises, major crime investigations, disease outbreaks, organ transplant operations, etc. (Note that as the days go on and the story becomes less timely, it may be harder to find follow-ups. You might make the assignment a challenge: Who will be the first to uncover the news?)

Source: Reprinted with permission if *The Montana Standard.*

Analysis

The lesson in each chapter is analyzed according to the categories from the following Lesson Analysis and Adaptation Worksheet (also found in the Lessons module of this text's Companion Website at http://www.prenhall.com/egbert). The first column contains criteria for an effective lesson. Indicators (explanations) of the criteria are in the middle column. The third column in the worksheet is for teacher comments about whether and how the lesson meets each criterion and, if it does not, how the lesson might be adapted. Following on page 28 is a sample analysis of the current events lesson.

From the analysis, it is clear that the lesson has some good aspects. However, a number of areas can be improved or changed to work better in general and for third graders specifically. Following are some adaptations that could be made to this lesson based on the analysis.

Adaptations

A synthesis of the comments on the worksheet indicates that, to work better for the range of third graders in any class, these adaptations could be made:

1. *Make the standards explicit and tie them to the objectives and tasks.* Standards could include those addressing media and technological literacy, thinking skills, current events, and reading and writing.

2. *Include handouts for reading strategies.* Content reading strategies such as predicting and inferencing could be addressed by having students complete a handout for each article. The handout would provide scaffolding and help students focus their reading. The handout could include simple questions such as:
   • "What do you already know about this topic?"
   • "What does the title mean?"

Lesson Analysis and Adaptation Worksheet

Content Area/Topic: *Current events/News*

Location and Title of Lesson: *http://www.sites4teachers.com/, Current Events Awareness*

Intended Audience for the Adaptation: *3rd grade*

The lesson . . .	Indicators	Comments
Works toward appropriate goals.	• Content and technology standards are mentioned. • Standards are for the correct grade level and content area. • Objectives are aligned with standards. • Tasks focus clearly on obtaining the objectives.	The goal of increasing student awareness is stated, but the standards are not. These need to be listed for grade 3 and tied to the objectives and tasks.
Requires the use of higher order thinking skills and "new" literacies.	• Students are asked to do more than memorize or understand (e.g., summarize, synthesize, predict, etc.). • Media, visual, communicative, technological, mathematical, and/or other nontraditional literacies are addressed.	The lesson includes summarizing, some synthesizing. It could easily include predicting and other literacy skills. For third graders, visual literacy is important and there should be a segment about WHERE they got the story and why they believe it. It doesn't have to be in depth, but should raise awareness.
Integrates the learning goals.	• Communication • Production • Critical thinking • Creativity • Content • Problem solving • Inquiry/research	It includes one-way communication and simple production but needs to integrate research, critical thinking, and content learning more.
Includes a variety of resources.	• Students have choices of materials at different levels. • Materials are available in a variety of modes (e.g., graphics, sound, text, video) and media (e.g., books, films, photos, computer).	The resources need to be made explicit—is it *USA Today* and the local paper or something else? Reading levels differ, and using online papers and magazines made specifically for students would help more students have choices and include other types of news like video reports.
Engages all students actively in authentic tasks.	• Students have roles/tasks to perform throughout the lesson. • Connections are made between the task and real life. • Students must actively search for answers to essential questions.	There are groups but no specific tasks. Students need to be given some recommendations here. It's too easy for one or two students to control this task. A general connection is made at the start to students' lives but not carried through. More specifics could help form an essential question.
Uses technology effectively, efficiently, and as a learning tool.	• The technology makes the task more authentic. • The technology makes the task easier to accomplish. • The technology helps students learn faster than without it. • The technology is secondary to the content and goals.	Technology is not used. Students could print news from many different sources from the Internet and thereby get a much broader picture of each event. Saves the teacher time from trying to get enough newspapers and gives students more options, especially for the follow-up stories.
Addresses the needs of a variety of students, including ELLs and students with physical and other challenges.	• All students can access task instructions. • All students can access task materials and resources. • Students have different ways to accomplish the same objectives.	Not all students can read a newspaper. Using the Internet to find a variety of levels of news would help these students access the lesson content. Also, instead of an oral report at the end of the week, students should be allowed to draw, graph, or whatever else they need to do to show their understanding. A class journal might work, too.
Includes appropriate assessments.	• Assessment is aligned to the standards and objectives. • Assessments are fair for all students and not based on one ability (e.g., writing). • Assessments allow students to show what they know/can do rather than what they cannot.	No real assessment is mentioned. It needs to be made explicit and tied to the standards/objectives. Adding choices for presentation would also make the assessment fairer.

- "What do you think will happen next?"
- "Is the source trustworthy?"
- "What did you learn about this topic?"

This could lead to great discussions around media literacy, content learning, and personal experience. In addition, this could give each student a task that the teacher could assess.

3. *Include a greater variety of resources.* Third graders, like all students, vary greatly in reading and thinking skills and preferred learning strategies, so materials at a number of levels should be available. The Internet can help by allowing students to access Time for Kids, CNN Online, local news in repeatable video clips, and so on. This allows students with a variety of challenges to participate and work toward the same goals.

4. *Include specific, differentiated assessment.* Third graders cannot always explain in text what they want to say. They should have the option of using other modes (e.g., speaking or drawing) to present their stories, but a rubric should be included that evaluates all of the presentations on the same criteria tied to whichever standards the lesson is based on. Depending on these standards and the related outcome goals, sample categories could be completeness, expression, explanation, ability to answer questions, and use of technology or other aids.

These four important changes make the lesson content more relevant, more consistent, and focused on language and content standards that are easily integrated into the third-grade lesson topic. Just as important, incorporating the use of technology makes all of these goals possible.

Based on your reading of this chapter, what else would you change about this lesson? Why?

_____

_____

_____

Chapter 2, "Supporting Student Content Learning," points out how content learning can be addressed using higher order thinking skills. It discusses how content is best learned and how technology can effectively support content learning. As you move on to the rest of this text, keep in mind the underlying premise of this chapter, that learning comes before technology. Be sure to review ideas in the chapter as needed and to use the glossary of terms and table data to support your learning throughout the text.

CHAPTER REVIEW

Key Points

Each chapter in this text includes a Key Points Review that summarizes chapter ideas and reminds readers how the chapter objectives were met.

- **Explain why a learning focus is important in supporting learning with technology.**

  Technology is a tool that teachers can use to support learning, but learning must be foremost. If teachers do not understand how to support learning, technology use will be ineffective and inefficient. Kleiman (2001) summarizes the focus of this text, noting that "while modern technology has great potential to enhance teaching and learning, turning that potential into reality on a large scale is a complex, multifaceted task. The key determinant of our success will not be the number of computers purchased or cables installed, but rather how we define educational visions, prepare and support teachers, design curriculum, address issues of equity, and respond to the rapidly changing world" (p. 14).

- **Describe the relevant standards and the 21st-century skills that ground the learning in this text.**

    The integration of content area and technology standards, along with standards for English language learners, results in six 21st-century skills that can serve as learning goals in the creation of technology-supported learning tasks:

    - Content learning
    - Critical thinking
    - Communication
    - Problem solving
    - Production
    - Creativity

- **Define "educational technology" and related terms.**

    Pencils, chalkboards, and overhead projectors are all educational technologies. However, in today's classrooms, educational technology is usually understood to be electronic technologies, particularly computers, that are used to support the learning process.

- **Discuss the use of technology tools for providing access to learning for all students, including physically challenged students, English language learners, and others who might face barriers to learning.**

    Hardware, software, and connection are the main components of electronic technologies. Specific applications of these components can determine whether students can access the content and demonstrate their skills.

- **Present an overview of computer-based and computer-assisted assessment practices.**

    There are many ways to assess student learning in every classroom. This idea does not change when technology is integrated, but technology use can make assessment easier and more effective.

- **Understand how and why to adapt lesson plans for more effective learning.**

    Evaluating lessons according to criteria for effective technology-supported learning can help you provide instruction that is accessible, engaging, and useful for all students in your classroom.

Which information in this chapter is most valuable to you? Why? How will you use it in your teaching?

_____

_____

_____

CASE QUESTIONS REVIEW

Reread the case at the beginning of the chapter and review your answers. In light of what you learned during this chapter, how do your answers change? Note any changes below.

1. *What would you add to the lists the class made? Why?*

_____

_____

_____

2. What does the quote from Polya have to do with learning about educational technology?

_____

_____

_____

3. What role(s) do you believe technology should play in education? Why?

_____

_____

_____

4. What are your goals in taking this course? What do you hope to accomplish?

_____

_____

_____

CHAPTER EXTENSIONS • • • • • • • • • • •

In addition to the following extensions, the Companion Website offers additional cases, reflection questions, and other exercises to support your learning from this chapter. To answer any of the following questions online, go to the Chapter 1 Extensions module for this text's Companion Website (http://www.prenhall.com/egbert).

Adapt • • •

Choose a lesson for your potential subject area and grade level from the Lesson Plans Library at Discovery Schools (http://school.discovery.com/lessonplans/). Use the Lesson Analysis and Adaptation Worksheet presented in this chapter on page 33 (also available in the Lesson Planning module on the Companion Website at http://www.prenhall.com/egbert) to analyze the lesson. Use your responses to the worksheet to suggest general changes to the lesson based on your future students and context.

Practice • • •

These activities will allow you to apply the ideas from the chapter and use your understandings of the foundations of technology use.

1. *Map the standards*. List the 6 learning goals for this text in a table. Use the Education World Web site (http://www.educationworld.com/) to find standards for your specific grade and content area. Put each standard under one or more of the learning goals. What did you find?
2. *Think about technology*. List the ways in which you interact with technology in a typical day. What does this technology interaction imply about what students need to do in real life with technology?
3. *Outline your personal teaching philosophy*. What do you believe education is and can do? How do you believe learning happens? Why?

4. *Explore literacy needs.* Explore a piece of software or a Web site from a multiliteracy viewpoint. Which literacies listed in this chapter do students need to employ to use the software you chose? How will you teach them?

5. *Find an example.* Using one of the Web sites mentioned in the chapter or one you find yourself, find a real-life example of classroom technology use. State whether the use might be effective or not and explain why you think so.

6. *Examine task characteristics.* Using the characteristics of effective tasks outlined in this chapter, examine one of the classroom examples provided in the Learning Activities section. Explain how it has or does not have these characteristics.

Explore • • • • •

These activities will help you to explore possibilities outside the chapter.

1. *Interview a K–12 student.* Think about what students in a specific grade and/or content area need to know about technology and technology use. Prepare questions ahead of time to discover what your student knows about technology. Prepare a summary of the interview to share.

2. *Interview a K–12 teacher.* Find out what technologies are most useful for the teacher and what else he or she would like to know about technology and learning.

3. *Make a list.* Research information on students with special needs from the DO-IT Web site (http://www.washington.edu/doit/) or conduct a Web search. List some of the needs that students in your future classes may have. List any other kinds of differences that you may find in children in your future classes that could affect both learning and technology use.

Lesson Analysis and Adaptation Worksheet

Content Area/Topic:

Location and Title of Lesson:

Intended Audience for the Adaptation:

The lesson . . .	Indicators	Comments
Works toward appropriate goals.	• Content and technology standards are mentioned. • Standards are for the correct grade level and content area. • Objectives are aligned with standards. • Tasks focus clearly on obtaining the objectives.	
Requires the use of higher order thinking skills and "new" literacies.	• Students are asked to do more than memorize or understand (e.g., summarize, synthesize, predict, etc.). • Media, visual, communicative, technological, mathematical, and/or other nontraditional literacies are addressed.	
Integrates the learning goals.	• Communication • Production • Critical thinking • Creativity • Content • Problem solving • Inquiry/research	
Includes a variety of resources.	• Students have choices of materials at different levels. • Materials are available in a variety of modes (e.g., graphics, sound, text, video) and media (e.g., books, films, photos, computer).	
Engages all students actively in authentic tasks.	• Students have roles/tasks to perform throughout the lesson. • Connections are made between the task and real life. • Students must actively search for answers to essential questions.	
Uses technology effectively, efficiently, and as a learning tool.	• The technology makes the task more authentic. • The technology makes the task easier to accomplish. • The technology helps students learn faster than without it. • The technology is secondary to the content and goals.	
Addresses the needs of a variety of students, including ELLs and students with physical and other challenges.	• All students can access task instructions. • All students can access task materials and resources. • Students have different ways to accomplish the same objectives.	
Includes appropriate assessments.	• Assessment is aligned to the standards and objectives. • Assessments are fair for all students and not based on one ability (e.g., writing). • Assessments allow students to show what they know/can do rather than what they cannot.	

REFERENCES

Aaronsohn, E. (2003). *The exceptional teacher.* San Francisco, CA: Jossey-Bass.

American Library Association and Association for Educational Communications and Technology. (1998). Information power: Building partnerships for learning. Chicago: Author.

Ascione, L. (2006). Study: Ed tech has proven effective. eSchool News Online. www.eschoolnews.com.

Barry, J., & Wise, B. (n.d.). http://www.netc.org/cdrom/fueling/html/fueling.htm.

Bowers, C. (2000). Let them eat data: How computers affect education, cultural diversity, and the prospects of ecological sustainability. Athens, GA: The University of Georgia Press.

Burns, T., & Ungerleider, C. (2002–2003). Information and communication technologies in elementary and secondary education: State of the art review. *International Journal of Educational Policy, Research, and Practice, 3*(4), 27–54.

Egbert, J. (2005). *Call Essentials.* Alexandria, VA: TESOL.

Egbert, J., Paulus, T., & Nakamichi, Y. (2002). The impact of CALL instruction on classroom computer use: A foundation for rethinking technology in teacher education. *Language Learning and Technology, 6*(3), 108–126.

FermiLab LInC. (2000). Project examples. http://www-ed.fnal.gov/lincon/el_proj_examples.shtml.

Ferneding, K. (2003). *Questioning technology: Electronic technologies and educational reform.* New York: Peter Lang.

GoKnow. (2003). Sketchy Pro Quick Start Guide Version 1.9. Author. Available: www.goknow.com.

Gordon, D. (2001). *The digital classroom: How technology is changing the way we teach and learn.* Cambridge, MA: Harvard Education Letter.

Ketterer, K. (2007). Online learning in harmony. *Learning and Leading with Technology, 34*(6), 19.

Kleiman, G. (2001). Myths and realities about technology in K-12 schools. In D. Gordon (Ed.), *The digital classroom.* Cambridge, MA: Harvard Education Letter.

Kliener, A., & Farris, E. (2002). Internet access in U.S. public schools and classrooms: 1994–2001. National Center for Education Statistics (NCES 2002018). Web version available: http://nces.ed.gov/pubsearch/pubsinfo.asp?pubid=2002018.

Learning Point Associates (2004). 21st century skills: Kristi Rennenbohm Franz's primary classroom. http://www.ncrel.org/engauge/skills/glimpse1.htm.

Levin, J., & Bruce, B. (2001, March). Technology as media: The learner centered perspective. Paper presented at the 2001 AERA Meeting, Seattle, WA. Available: http://tepserver.ucsd.edu/~jlevin/jim-levin/levin-bruce-aera.html.

Loschert, K. (2003, April). Are you ready? *NEA Today.* Available: http://www.nea.org/neatoday/0304/cover.html.

Male, M. (2003). *Technology for inclusion: Meeting the special needs of all students* (4th ed.). Boston, MA: Allyn & Bacon.

McKenzie, J. (1998, September). Grazing the Net: Raising a generation of free range students. *Phi Delta Kappan.* Online version available: http://fno.org/text/grazing.html.

Mills, S., & Roblyer, M. (2006). *Technology tools for teachers: A Microsoft Office tutorial* (2nd ed.). Upper Saddle River, NJ: Pearson.

NCREL (2004). enGAUGE resources what works—Enhancing the process of writing through technology: Integrating research and best practice. http://www.ncrel.org/engauge/resource/techno/whatworks. Learning Point Associates.

National School Boards Foundation (n.d.). *Technology's effectiveness in education.* Available: http://www.nsba.org/sbot/toolkit/teie.html.

O'Connor, J., & Robertson, E. (2002). *George Polya.* MacTutor History of Mathematics Archive, http://www-groups.dcs.st-and.ac.uk/~history/Mathematicians/Polya.html.

Plotnik, E. (1999). Information literacy. ERIC Digest. ED427777, http://searcheric.org/digests/ed427777.html.

Postman, N. (1993). *Technopoly: The surrender of culture to technology.* New York: Vintage Books.

Saskatchewan chapter V: Technological literacy. Education. Understanding the common essential learnings. Regina, SK, Canada: Author. http://www.sasked.gov.sk.ca/docs/policy/cels/el5.html.

Schacter, J. (1999). The impact of education technology on student achievement: What the most current research has to say. Santa Monica, CA: The Milken Family Foundation. Available online through http://www.milkenexchange.org.

PART II

Supporting Student Learning with Technology

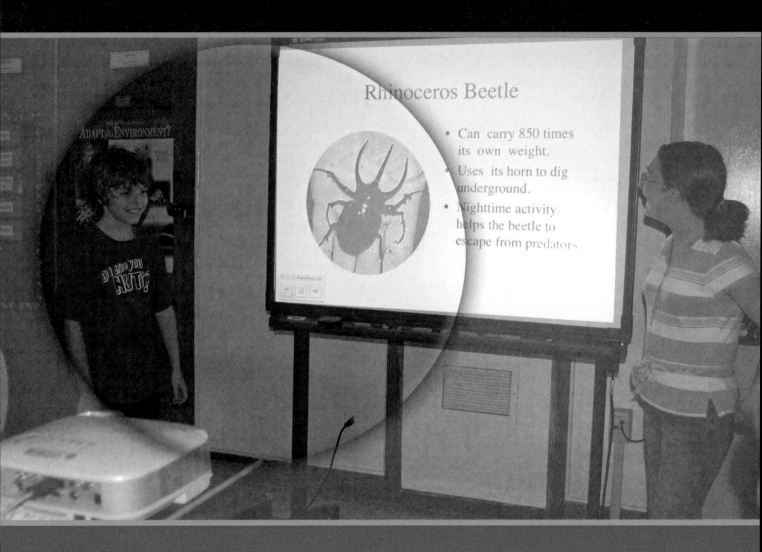

2
Supporting Student Content Learning

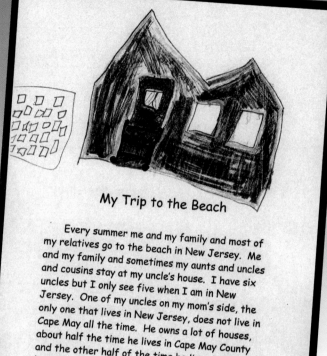

My Trip to the Beach

Every summer me and my family and most of my relatives go to the beach in New Jersey. Me and my family and sometimes my aunts and uncles and cousins stay at my uncle's house. I have six uncles but I only see five when I am in New Jersey. One of my uncles on my mom's side, the only one that lives in New Jersey, does not live in Cape May all the time. He owns a lot of houses, about half the time he lives in Cape May County and the other half of the time he lives in New York because he works there.

Case: What Do You Know?

As you read the following scenario, note the different concerns that policymakers, administrators, and other educational stakeholders have about how technology is implemented in schools.

● ●

Because of its status as a high-poverty school with students who do not make adequate yearly progress (AYP) on the state's high-stakes test, East Park High School recently received a large federally funded technology grant. The grant requires the school to create a technology plan before receiving funding. The plan must be tied to district goals and national and state standards and must provide a specific action plan that addresses how technology will help meet the content learning achievement of the school's high-needs population. In addition to other information, the plan must include a rationale for the school's proposed computer/student ratio, specific objectives with standards and timelines, and projected yearly improvement in test scores over the next five years. The technology funded by the grant is to be aimed primarily at students who are not performing at grade level or who have not passed the state-mandated exit test after at least one attempt; this includes a large population of English language learners. However, all students at the school are expected to use the technology at some time for content learning.

Mr. Yates, the technology teacher, is the chair of the Technology Committee (TC) at East Park. In addition to Mr. Yates, the TC consists of the vice principal, one teacher from each department at the school, and several staff members. The committee's job is to draft the technology plan. To address the criteria required by the grant, they decide to suggest first how the technology will be assigned, to whom, and in what configurations, what types of hardware and software will be purchased, and how the technology will be accessed equitably and effectively by teachers and students. The TC will also be responsible for creating professional development opportunities for the teachers. The overall focus of its work is to figure out which needs are the most crucial and how technology can help meet those needs.

● ●

Answer these questions about the case with your current level of knowledge. Change or add to your answers as needed as you read and understand the issues in this chapter.

1. *What kinds of hardware components should the committee choose? Why?*

   _____

   _____

   _____

2. *What kind of software and/or Internet access should the computers have? Why?*

   _____

   _____

   _____

3. *How can the needs of ELLs and other students with special needs be addressed in the technology plan?*

   _____

   _____

   _____

4. *How should the computers be assigned and laid out?*

   _____

   _____

   _____

5. *Do you see any problems in the way the grant was awarded or how it will be implemented? If so, what are the problems?*

   _____

   _____

   _____

Mr. Yates and the Technology Committee have quite a job ahead of them, but others also have knowledge and experience that can help. Teacher input in particular will be very important to the effective development and implementation of the school's technology plan. All teachers need to understand the implications of the issues that the committee is addressing to help make effective choices for their districts, schools, classrooms, and individual students. To this end, when you finish this chapter, you will be able to:

- Explain how content learning takes place.
- Explain the role of content learning in meeting other instructional goals.
- Discuss guidelines and techniques for using technology in content learning and teaching.
- Analyze technologies that can be used to create opportunities for content learning for all students, including simulations, raw data sites, and even word processing.
- Describe and develop effective technology-enhanced content learning activities.
- Create appropriate assessments for technology-enhanced content learning activities.

Review the NETS for teachers in chapter 1. After mastering the content of this chapter, which of these standards will you be able to meet?

_____

_____

_____

There are many theories about how the learning of "facts" takes place, from behaviorism that emphasizes the importance of practice to constructivism that focuses on the social construction of knowledge. Regardless of which theory seems most believable to individual teachers, all teachers must consider certain principles of learning, particularly when teaching with technology. This chapter will consider many of these principles. To start, see the Meeting the Standards feature for standards that address content learning.

• • • • **Meeting the Standards:** Content Learning and Technology • • • •

Because content knowledge is seen as fundamental to what schools do, the standards in every subject area list, sometimes explicitly, what content students should grasp to be considered knowledgeable. Words like "understand," "identify," "memorize," and "recognize" are used to describe the content that students should be able to work with. For example, in math, students in grades 6–8 are supposed to "Understand both metric and customary systems of measurement" (NM-MEA.6–8.1) and in health K–4 students should be able to "describe the basic structure and functions of the human body system" (NPH-H.K–4.1). In science,

secondary students need to develop an understanding of the structure of atoms, the cell, energy, and other concepts (NS.9–12.2,3,4) and in social studies to explain how the national government is organized (NSS-C.9–12.3). The national K–12 educational technology standards for students (NETS*S) also address content learning—content in this case includes how to use tools, what responsible use implies, and the "nature and operation of technology systems" (NT.K–12.1). The key to content learning is to understand how content is learned, including what skills are needed and how technology can help.

Find the content-learning standards for your state, grade level, and content area in the Standards section of the Resources Module on the Companion Website. List some of the content that your students will be expected to know.

_____

_____

_____

CW

• • • •

OVERVIEW OF CONTENT LEARNING AND TECHNOLOGY IN K–12 CLASSROOMS

Content knowledge is essential for students in order to meet student learning goals such as problem solving and effective communication. Teachers should first understand the importance of content learning and then how it can be learned and supported by technology while students work toward learning goals.

What Is Content Learning?

There are two parts to the question "What is content knowledge?" The first, what content is, seems rather basic, but the second, what learning is, can be fairly complicated. A look at how content knowledge is acquired can help to answer both parts of the question.

FIGURE 2.1 Creating Connections with Kidspiration

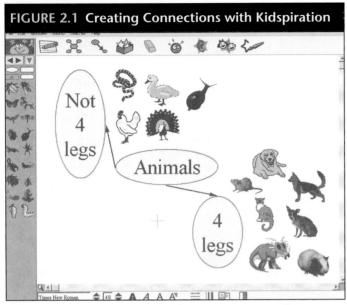

Source: Diagram created in Kidspiration® by Inspiration Software®, Inc.

Researchers and educators typically divide knowledge into three categories: declarative, structural, and procedural. **Declarative knowledge** consists of discrete pieces of information that help us identify things and events (Wignall, 2005). For example, declarative knowledge includes the definition of "democracy" or the names of all the U.S. presidents. Declarative knowledge forms the basis for all other types of knowledge and is essential for students to achieve more complex goals such as creative and critical thinking, communication, production, and inquiry. It is often learned through memorization, drill, and practice, although a variety of scaffolding strategies such as mnemonics, concept mapping, and metaphoric techniques support the acquisition of simple facts. Software packages such as Where in the World Is Carmen SanDiego (Broderbund) and Reader Rabbit (The Learning Company), in which specific facts are the focus, can help students to acquire and practice declarative knowledge. However, students must also have structural and procedural knowledge to carry out the functions in these software packages.

Structural knowledge is an understanding of how pieces of declarative knowledge fit together. When students have pieces of information among which relationships are created in their minds, this information has been *contextualized* and/or *schematized.* Another way to describe structural knowledge is as information that has been developed into a mental model. For example, structural knowledge includes the understanding that a toothbrush is necessary to brush teeth, or that evaporation is related to liquids. Structural knowledge can be represented through, for example, concept maps, categorizations, and classifications, and it is supported by concept-mapping software such as Inspiration or Kidspiration. An example of animal classification using Kidspiration is shown in Figure 2.1. Jonasson and Wang (1992) note that when learners focus on structural relationships among pieces of information, they acquire structural knowledge. This leads to the ability to use higher order thinking skills.

Procedural knowledge is the knowledge of action, or the knowledge of how to do something (Williams, 2000). Examples include how to speak Spanish, how to teach with technology, how to drive a car or use a cell phone. It is based on declarative knowledge but learned through the relationships in structural knowledge. Teachers often access procedural knowledge through student performance, having students construct a technology-enhanced product such as an essay, a presentation, or a graphical representation of a concept.

Figure 2.2 presents a simple model of the relationships among these knowledge types.

Make a short list of ways that students might acquire declarative knowledge. What techniques or strategies can they use? How might this process affect the technology plan under development? Why?

_____

_____

_____

_____

FIGURE 2.2 Simple Model of Knowledge Acquisition

Declarative knowledge
"This is the computer's 'on' switch"

fits into

Structural knowledge

This is the computer's "on" switch

Switches can be pressed

The computer works if you turn it on

This is a computer

Switches often require electricity to work

can lead to

Procedural knowledge
To make this computer work, turn on the computer by pressing the "on" switch.

Traditionally, many educators have thought of declarative knowledge as "content," and some of the standards reinforce this view by listing discrete pieces of information that students should know. However, many standards also list procedures that students should be able to carry out, so simple declarative knowledge is not enough to say that students "know" something. Students must also be able to do something with the knowledge/content to show that they have mastered it.

Educators have mixed views of when students can be deemed knowledgeable about a subject—and legislators and tests often determine the current understanding. For example, some claim it to be when students have memorized the names of the scientific elements and others when they can use the periodic chart to make statements about living things. In other words, while *information-knowing* is the goal set for some students, *knowledge creation* is the goal for others. Teachers who do not go beyond declarative knowledge teaching and testing, however, are doing their students a disservice by ignoring students' needs to be able to make connections and to use knowledge to act.

It seems a rather simple matter for students to learn content, but it is far more complex than most people think. Some content, and the relevant skills needed to learn it, is disciplined-based; for example, science uses a different form of exploration and expression than English literature, and the way that math is presented, used, and produced is different still. This implies that different ways to learn and teach content might be necessary across disciplines.

In addition, although brain science is making great strides in providing information about how and why people learn, the factors that make students learn in different ways are still not entirely clear. It is clear, however, that individual sets of factors such as culture, economic status, first language, educational background, and age can affect learning on a person-by-person and day-by-day basis (Norman, 2004). In addition, brain research has also shown that stress hinders learning and that "emotionally important content learned in school is very likely to be permanently remembered" (Erlauer, 2003, p. 13). That means that content that is tied in some important way to learners' lives will have more impact on their learning. Clearly, both internal (i.e., learner characteristics) and external (i.e., environmental) factors contribute to knowledge acquisition. Teachers can consider all of these ideas as they plan content lessons supported by technology.

Among the external factors that affect learning, the classroom environment, focusing on the arrangement of technology, is important to discuss. Although some external factors are not under the teacher's control, the teacher often has choices in setting up technology in the classroom and school.

Physical Contexts for Technology-Supported Learning

The physical arrangement of the classroom, including placement of desks, whiteboard, and other resources, can affect how students learn because the roles that these resources, including technology, can play vary by how the classroom is designed. Most teacher education programs address the physical environment in their classroom management course, but the importance of the location of technology, particularly computers, is often overlooked. As McKenzie (1998) notes, classroom design can actually work against good teaching by restricting the use of the equipment or creating barriers to good use.

Technology can be configured in many ways. Typical designs are a one-computer classroom, multiple-computer classroom, and lab, and all of these configurations can be used for different activities at different grade levels.

One-computer classroom

Although not typically the optimal situation for all students to receive maximum benefit from the power of computing, a lot can be done with one computer. For example, the teacher can use the computer to provide prereading exercises, focus whole-class discussion, or lead teams through a game or simulation (other examples are provided throughout this book). However, the computer must be accessible to all students; in other words, it should have a high-quality projector or large monitor attached, and there must be room for all students to sit, view, and participate. In addition, students with special needs must have access to tools that help them to participate. These include special keyboards, screen readers, and other tools described later in this chapter.

Inclusion

Excellent content software and resources for K–12 that make effective use of the one-computer classroom are available from Tom Snyder Productions (www.tomsnyder.com) and Sunburst (www.sunburst.com). For example, in Tom Snyder's Decisions, Decisions series, the

FIGURE 2.3 Learning in a One-Computer Classroom

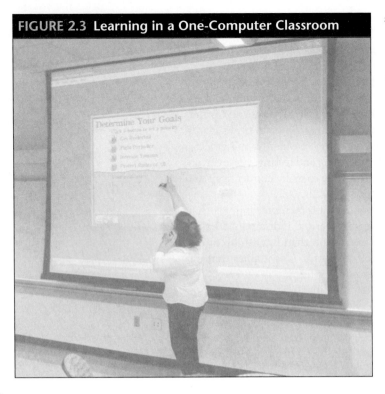

software presents a scenario and then offers students choices of how to proceed. With the teacher facilitating, the students discuss the issues and come to a decision as to which choice is best based on the information they have. The software shows the consequences of that action and presents students with another choice, and the task concludes after several additional decisions. The photo in Figure 2.3 shows teacher Jennifer Robinson leading her students through Tom Snyder's Decisions, Decisions: Prejudice software.

Multiple computers

In a classroom of 25 students, three to five computers do not seem like much help, and they are not if they are relegated to a corner of the room and only used for free time or remediation. However, separated into "activity zones" or "interest centers" (McKenzie, 1998), they can blend into the daily workings of the class and be integrated into classroom goals. For example, in a classroom where students are producing books, one center could be used for research, one for development, and one for printing. Or, where students are studying ancient Egypt, each team of students could work with their topic in a different area of the classroom.

Lab

There are all kinds of designs for computer labs. Unfortunately, the most common is still computers in separate carrels or in rigid rows that create physical barriers between the students and teacher or the students and their peers. This makes it difficult for students to collaborate, use other spaces for learning, and observe modeling by and receive feedback from the teacher. In fact, Theroux (2004) notes that the "most difficult and least effective way to integrate technology is to consistently take all students into the computer lab to work on the same activities at the same time" (p. 1). In part this is because the individual nature of the lab setting is a barrier to working with the teacher or other students, and the activity does not consider differences among students in technology skill or content knowledge.

A variety of effective alternative arrangements can make a lab setting a more flexible and useful space. These arrangements include furniture such as hideaway desks into which the monitor can be completely recessed (shown in Figure 2.4), groupings such as pods of four to six computers, and tables where students can work offline. These arrangements can all contribute to making the computer classroom a place where instructional goals can be met.

FIGURE 2.4 Hideaway Desk

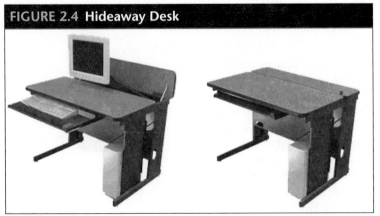

Source: Used with permission of Computer Comforts, Inc.

Flotillas

According to McKenzie, another useful layout for schools that do not have a critical mass of computers is a **flotilla,** or a set of computers that rotate among classrooms. Students use the computers for several weeks to participate in technology-intensive projects, and then the technology moves on to another classroom. Many schools use mobile labs (moveable carts that store 20–30 laptops) to provide computers to classrooms when needed.

Equal access

Whichever layout is chosen, the Americans with Disabilities Act (ADA) and state and local regulations require that all students have equal access to the technology. To make sure that there are as few physical barriers as possible, teachers, students, and school staff can make it a point to make sure that:

- Pathways in classrooms and labs are wheelchair accessible.
- One or more desks allows for wheelchair access.
- The printer and other peripherals are located in easily accessed locations.
- Any tables or other work spaces are at a variety of heights.
- Assistive devices such as screen glare reducers, alternative keyboards, and screen readers that might be used fairly often are immediately available.
- Any important documents are available in a variety of formats and prints so that diverse users can access them.
- Web sites and other technologies are accessible.

The Tool CloseUp: AlphaSmart provides a description of a tool that supports equal access. For more information about equal access, see the Accessibility section of the Resources module for this chapter on the Companion Website (http://www.prenhall.com/egbert).

To determine the technology's layout and design, we must consider what students need to do with the technology and what design allows them to do it. McKenzie (1998) recommends that teachers view other classrooms and expert designs before making decisions about the layout of technology. Some ideas are available in photo shots at www.fno.org.

Other technologies

The availability and accessibility of cameras, handhelds, microphones, tape recorders, overhead projectors, printers, and other hardware tools also need to be considered for effective student learning. How will they be accessed? Where will students need to and be able to use them? Yatvin (2004) points out that printers should be in the workspace with computers so that students do not get frustrated by having to travel or wait to get their printed products. Similarly, tools that are locked in a closet on the other side of the school or can only be checked out on Thursday morning provide little support for content learning.

Other considerations in the physical space

McKenzie and other educators suggest that a computer is needed for every 3–4 students for all students to have the access they need to participate in effective technology-enhanced tasks. Not all the computers need to be the newest; rather, students can draft assignments on lower-end computers and use better ones for more advanced tasks. An important consideration is that students have storage space on the network so that they can move from computer to computer on the network and not be tied to one computer or to an (easily lost) CD or floppy disk.

There is no one right way to design the layout of technology to support student learning. Whichever layout teachers and technology coordinators decide on, they need to understand the implications for learning. This goes for other tools as well; sometimes electronic technologies do not provide authentic information and sometimes the information is not exactly what students need. Therefore the physical space assigned to desktop computers should also provide access to other basic resources such as books, films, and a variety of other tools that might be more reliable, easier to access, and easier to carry.

Which of these designs should Mr. Yates and the TC choose for the high school? Why?

_____

_____

_____

Characteristics of Effective Technology-Supported Content Learning Tasks

Teachers teach from different philosophical standpoints, and students learn based on many different variables—such as the arrangement of the classroom, as noted above—many of which are discussed throughout this text. However, there are basic principles of teaching and learning that

TOOLS

Tool CloseUp: AlphaSmart

A teacher recently introduced the AlphaSmart to her peers in this way:

> An AlphaSmart is a portable word processor. Usually it allows the student to see 2–3 lines of their typing. It is used with a lot of my students on IEPs [individualized education programs, typically written for students in special education] whose handwriting and the motor act of writing keeps them from demonstrating their thinking and writing skills so keyboarding is a better option. It is also used to teach typing. They can then be connected to a computer and the piece can be transferred on the computer for editing or to be saved to the student's folder on the server. The down side to the AlphaSmart is the inability to see the whole essay or story so sometimes it makes for tricky editing and I find it really impacts paragraphing. Some of my students have the newer super version that also has Inspiration loaded on it. With the newer ones there are cords that allow the student to transfer from AlphaSmart to Mac back to AlphaSmart then to home onto PC and then back to AlphaSmart to be used at school and repeat the cycle as needed.

There is even more that the AlphaSmart can do. These portable keyboards can be set up for right-hand only or left-hand only use. In addition, the amount of time that a key must be pressed to make it work can be adjusted so that students who cannot move quickly can type accurately. These relatively inexpensive machines can also be adapted to specific students in other ways; for example, less nimble students can use one-finger (rather than the usual two-finger) capitalization; the font size can be changed easily for those with visual impairments; and the Alpha-Smart DANA model can translate text into speech. Most important for schools that allow students to take Alpha-Smarts home, the AlphaSmart is extremely durable—unlike most PCs, the AlphaSmart can be dropped and even smashed and come out unscathed.

In inclusive classrooms, all students can be equipped with AlphaSmarts for the price of about three new high-end PCs. Giving each student this tool means not singling out certain students and ensuring that students can help each other make use of the technology. For more information and lessons that use AlphaSmarts, see http://www1.alphasmart.com.

The AlphaSmart 3000

Source: Used with permission of AlphaSmart, LLC.

How could an AlphaSmart help to meet the guidelines in this chapter? Should Mr. Yates include it in the technology plan? Why or why not?

_____

_____

_____

_____

Tutorial

CW

To learn more about AlphaSmarts, see the AlphaSmart tutorial in the Tutorial module on the Companion Website (http://www.prehall.com/egbert).

support all of the learning goals. Following these principles in task development can help teachers to support all students, including those who are often underserved, such as ELL, gifted, and students with special needs.

In general, effective content learning tasks

1. *Engage students.* Students are motivated and find the tasks meaningful. Work does not always have to be "fun," but it should be interesting and meaningful and take place in an environment that is emotionally safe (Erlauer, 2003).

2. *Help students become responsible for their own learning, in whole or in part.* If students are engaged, teachers can use a gradual release of responsibility to move students toward independent learning (Pearson & Gallagher, 1983). To do so, tasks must allow students to investigate some of their own questions rather than having them supplied.

3. *Encourage students to be strategic.* During effective tasks, students make systematic, thoughtful choices of how to meet learning challenges. They decide which strategies, resources, and tools will help them complete the task (see New Horizons for Learning, 2002, for strategy descriptions and research support).

4. *Require collaboration.* Effective learning takes place through interaction with others, so tasks must require that students work together, share information, and contribute to the understanding of others (Vygotsky, 1978).

5. *Focus on essential questions.* Rather than just gathering information, students need tasks during which they frame and investigate important questions. Such tasks are more likely to use technology well, engage students, and lead to gains in learner achievement. According to McKenzie (2004a), these questions include:

   - Why do things happen the way they do?
   - How could things be made better?
   - Which do I select?

These questions integrate the need for declarative knowledge, or data, with a requirement to consider, transform, and make decisions that result in insight. Instead of content knowledge being only the forebear of other types of thinking such as problem solving or creativity, gains in content knowledge are also a *result* of those types of thinking. Examples of student research with essential questions can be found at http:// questioning.org/. A more thorough explanation of the research process can be found in Falk & Blumenreich (2005).

In other words, content can be learned before, throughout, and as a result of working toward learning goals such as critical and creative thinking, communication, production, and inquiry. Students who learn content as procedural knowledge can also perform well on tests of declarative knowledge and on performance assessments. On the other hand, learning content solely through information gathering can result in students handing in hundreds of pages of data printed directly from the Internet and not understanding a single page. Figure 2.5 sums up the characteristics of effective content learning tasks.

How do the characteristics of effective content learning tasks affect decisions that Mr. Yates and the TC will make? Remember to consider the structure of high schools and the fact that this high school is in a high-poverty area.

FIGURE 2.5 Characteristics of Effective Technology-Supported Content Learning Tasks	
Characteristic	**Example**
Students are engaged.	Students work on tasks that are important and meaningful to them.
Students are encouraged to become responsible for their own learning.	Students ask and answer their own questions.
Students are strategic.	Students can plan their learning.
The task requires collaboration.	Students must work with each other throughout the task, not just compile individual results at the end.
The task focuses on essential questions.	Why? How? Which?

Student Benefits from Technology-Supported Content Learning

Content learning, if we define it only as the acquisition of declarative knowledge, is important because it forms the basis for gaining other kinds of knowledge. Some educators believe that students only need to know *where* to find and *how* to obtain declarative knowledge rather than controlling or mastering the information itself, and that computer technologies are best suited to this purpose. However, this focus leaves students with researching skills but without content to which to apply these skills. For students to benefit from content study they must build schema and learn how to act in various situations. This will result in both the acquisition of information and the knowledge that can result from interacting with it.

THE TECHNOLOGY-SUPPORTED CONTENT LEARNING PROCESS

Figure 2.2 showed relationships among declarative, structural, and procedural knowledge. Although the exact biological and psychological mechanisms that lead to the acquisition of declarative knowledge, and in turn to the other types of knowledge, are not known, it is fairly clear that new content is attached to old content in the brain in some way (Erlauer, 2003; Johnson, 2004); therefore, for tasks to be meaningful they must activate students' prior knowledge.

Although we do not yet know the specifics of how the brain processes content, teachers can still teach and observe student outcomes to help understand how these links are made in classrooms. Content learning in classrooms occurs through general stages of planning, engaging, and evaluating. During an effective content learning process, students:

1. *Understand where they are supposed to go.* Goals and objectives are clear and accessible to all students, including those who speak different first languages and others who access information in diverse ways.

2. *Assess their current knowledge and skills and the level of each.* Students should reflect on how they can reach the goals and what knowledge and skills they need to get there. Planning is facilitated by the teacher, peers, and others.

3. *Engage in activities that help them to acquire the knowledge and skills they need.* Students must find and be given resources that directly apply.

4. *Evaluate how they did.* Feedback from the teacher and others, self-reflection, standardized tests, comprehension questions, and interviews contribute to an understanding of the extent to which goals were met.

This outline does not really speak to how each step in the process is carried out specifically—teachers have to make that choice knowing their students. For example, in a diverse class of first graders, the teacher may decide that both a teacher-fronted discussion and a cooperative group work will help the students understand their task. After she has worked with her learners for a while, she may skip the teacher-fronted discussion and go right to the cooperative group format for task instruction. In eighth grade, one English teacher may use a spontaneous writing task to evaluate the level of written proficiency for her class; another English teacher may decide to give both a standardized test and interviews because she knows that her students perform differently on different tasks. Figure 2.6 presents an overview of the content learning process.

FIGURE 2.6 Overview of the Technology-Supported Content Learning Process

Student Stage	Ideas for Technology-Supported Implementation
Understand	Make overall learning goals and objectives clear. Present them in many ways—text, audio, graphics— and refer back to them during the process.
Assess	Help with personal goal-setting and current understanding of content knowledge. Use Inspiration and other graphical organizers to describe declarative, structural, and procedural knowledge.
Engage	Provide appropriate resources and make sure that tasks work toward learning objectives. Give students access to Web sites, book lists, content software, and experts.
Evaluate	Provide feedback through test scores, interviews, and other assessments and allow opportunities for self-reflection. Students can use a word processor to create knowledge summaries and digital sound recorders to record observations and ideas.

What does this process imply for the development of the technology plan at East Park High School?

_____

_____

_____

Teachers and Technology-Enhanced Content Learning

In any classroom, the teacher's role in the content learning process may change from task to task, and task-specific challenges may arise for both teachers and students. Understanding both possible roles and potential challenges is crucial for teachers.

The teacher's role in content learning

To help students move from declarative knowledge to structural and procedural knowledge, teachers can guide students to make connections, test hypotheses about how things work, and explore how ideas go together. Realistically, for expediency and to meet some student needs, the teacher's role must sometimes be to model, demonstrate, or lecture to the whole class. At other times, the teacher can facilitate and support as students explore.

Challenges for teachers

Because content teaching often occurs while students work toward the learning goals of critical thinking, problem solving, communicating, and so on, many of the same challenges are present whether electronic technologies are used or not. However, computer use presents some particular challenges. For example, plagiarism (discussed in chapter 6) can be particularly rampant with Web-based research or content-gathering projects. However, by asking students to answer essential questions rather than just having them gather information, plagiarism can be controlled to some extent.

A real challenge for teachers using technology is to first learn the technology; teachers cannot help students with technical issues if they do not understand the software and/or hardware. Tips and guidelines throughout this text suggest ways for teachers to overcome this barrier, and resources are offered in chapter 9.

Time, always an issue for teachers, is an especially relevant challenge in content teaching and learning, especially with pressures to cover the curriculum, having to teach students research skills, and competing with other teachers for resources (Goldman, Cole, & Syer, 1999). The use of expert teacher or student groups that have mastered a concept or technology and can teach it can help with time issues. Additionally, resources such as Kids Click (http://www.kidsclick.org) give teachers a list of Web sites that have already been evaluated for use by students. Another useful resource is the "Kids' Search Engines" section of searchenginewatch.com, which describes search engines such as Ask Jeeves for Kids (http://www.askforkids.com) that are prefiltered or otherwise appropriate for students.

Learning to use and integrate technology with educational goals, especially specific content, does take time and effort. However, it can be made easier. Start with the essentials as presented in this book—an understanding of how students learn, what the goals of education are, what steps can be taken to help students achieve, and how technology can help. Then, by applying strategies mentioned throughout this book, learn more about what technology works in your specific contexts. One very effective and often overlooked resource is the school library media specialist, who is specially educated to support learning with technologies of all kinds.

GUIDELINES FOR SUPPORTING TECHNOLOGY-ENHANCED STUDENT CONTENT LEARNING

Content *teaching* is the focus of many teacher education programs, but more important is to understand how to make content *learning* most effective. The guidelines in this section focus on how to give all students opportunities to learn.

Designing Opportunities to Learn Content

All students can and do learn something, regardless of how they are taught. However, to focus that learning in productive ways and maximize learning gains, teachers can follow these guidelines:

Guideline #1: Incorporate principles of just-in-time learning. **Just-in-time (JIT) learning** is learning that occurs just when it is needed (Riel, 1998), but it is more planned than what educators call a "teachable moment," or a spontaneous opportunity to introduce a new concept or idea. As a complement to an ordered, standardized series of lessons that accomplish the curriculum, JIT learning delivers skills and information when students can best use, learn, and remember them. For example, an ELL who is working on reporting a historical event needs to know how to form and use the past tense of verbs, and JIT presentation of this grammatical concept will occur effectively during the broader task. When the teacher observes that the student needs this information, she can tutor the student, provide resources for the student to check, or assign another student to explain the concept. As another example, during the study of an abstract scientific concept in the textbook, some students might need a JIT lesson in finding the main ideas, particularly if their preferred learning style is visual or kinesthetic. The teacher can meet with the small group and teach a lesson on main ideas, have students use a computer program such as Tom Snyder's *Reading for Meaning* to practice finding main ideas, or assign class "reading experts" to work with those who need help.

Students do not often grasp the utility of a concept or the connection of ideas when they are first presented if there is not a true need to know. JIT learning necessitates careful observation by the teacher so that she can provide help and scaffolds when needed. It also requires teachers to have resources ready, or train students to access them, for potential areas of need, and to guide students in whatever way they need through the information.

Technology can support JIT learning and teaching in many ways; for example, the vast amount of information that is accessible in various formats and languages on the Internet means that ELLs and other students can find help on just about any issue. When the student asks the teacher for help with a grammar topic or needs a more simplified explanation of a science topic, the student can probably find something on the Web to help. However, the teacher's guidance is still central to ensuring that students find the information they need and use it in appropriate ways.

FROM THE CLASSROOM

Differentiation

This year at my school the staff has focused on differentiation of instruction to ensure all students reach the standards. All students are involved in the same goal, but how the teacher helps individual students reach the goal is different. Using differentiation in my class has helped more students master benchmarks versus having modified lessons for different students. My ELL students need to learn to write a persuasive paper—at the computer is a template that "guides" them through the process, prompting them with specific questions to answer in their paper. Other students may be working at their desk brainstorming, drafting, peer sharing [w]hile other students may be using a graphic organizer to organize the content of their writing. When lessons are modified—some students are then not necessarily working at reaching a standard. The technology available in the classroom helps develop differentiated learning opportunities. (Jean, sixth-grade teacher)

Guideline #2: Differentiate instruction. One of the chapter 5 tips recommends enriching the classroom environment through the use of materials that appeal to students' different senses and intelligences. From that discussion it is clear that students respond to different kinds of enrichment. **Differentiated instruction** is another way to provide enrichment for students' abilities, interests, and learning needs. In differentiated instruction, the goals and concepts are the same for all students, but the challenge varies so "all students are challenged and no students are frustrated" (Theroux, 2004, p. 2). According to Theroux (2004), teachers can differentiate instruction by giving students three to four different options in their work. She notes that some students will take different options at different times, depending on varying interests, subject-area ability or readiness, and learning preferences. Teachers can start out slowly by varying the content, process, product, or tool, or they can provide choices in any or all four at different stages of an activity.

Technology can help differentiate instruction (Tomlinson, 2001; Yatvin, 2004) by providing a variety of tools for different tasks at different times or for the same task by different students. For example, in a unit about bugs, one group of students may access information about how bugs communicate by using the videos and games in the Sidewalk Science program "Bugs" (Scholastic), while more proficient students might use a Web site such as http://insectzoo.msstate.edu/. Less proficient students might use another tool that is suited to their level. For all students, but particularly ELLs and students with diverse needs, differentiated instruction can provide opportunities to access the content and language they are learning, an essential component of learning. Read as one teacher describes differentiation at her school in From the Classroom: Differentiation on the previous page.

Guideline #3: Teach in a culturally responsive manner. Research shows that students whose lives are addressed and supported in classrooms learn better and achieve more. Teachers can make sure this happens by teaching in a *culturally responsive* manner. This means using materials that are **culturally relevant,** or that celebrate the lives and heritages of all students and reflect the contributions of all groups. Being culturally responsive empowers learners and makes learning meaningful for them, whether they are from another country, a different religion, or a minority group. For example, many groups throughout history have contributed to our current understandings of math, from the discovery of zero (see an overview at http://www-groups.dcs.st-and.ac.uk/~history/HistTopics/Zero.html) to contributions by women and people of many ethnicities (see http://www.ncrel.org/sdrs/areas/issues/educatrs/presrvce/pe3lk36.htm). Teachers can access culturally relevant information both on the Web and through software such as Culturegrams (http://www.culturegrams.com/). Teachers can also find lessons on the Web that suggest different ways to be more culturally responsive. Additionally, by connecting with families through software such as Parent Organizer (http://www.parentorganizer.com/) or Connect-Ed (Notification Technologies, Inc., http://www.notification.com/), teachers can find help in understanding and integrating learners' cultural resources.

Guideline #4: Adapt materials to be accessible for all students. Teachers can adapt, modify, and enhance materials in many ways to make the content more accessible to students. Adaptations can include:

a. Using graphic depiction
b. Outlining the text
c. Rewriting the text
d. Using audiotapes
e. Providing live demonstrations
f. Using alternate books (Echevarria & Graves, 2002)

However, it is important that adapted materials not sacrifice academic content for simplistic understandings. Adaptations allow ELLs, students with various physical impairments, and students with different learning preferences to have equitable chances to access the materials.

As Egbert (2005) notes, teachers do not have to make all of these changes themselves—they can enlist more proficient students to help, work in teacher groups and share materials, and find these materials on the Web.

Guideline #5: Balance content and tools. As Goldman et al. (1999) and many others have noticed, when computer technologies are adopted, learning the technology tools often takes precedence over learning the content. Teachers can help students find a balance between the two. For example, a student's first Power-Point presentation does not have to include audio and video. Read as two classroom teachers discuss balance in different ways in From the Classroom: Balance. In addition, make it easy for students to save their work; losing work that then has to be redone not only frustrates students but wastes considerable time and energy. Given the extra learning time that technology use might add to a project, plan more time for projects that involve technology, including technology down times and problems. Teachers can decide not to use electronic technologies in favor of content learning. However, striking a balance between the two often leads to achievement in both.

Figure 2.7 on page 50 lists the guidelines from this chapter.

FROM THE CLASSROOM

Balance

We have all heard the advantages and disadvantages of these tools. The concern I heard most often—how will they ever learn (math facts, spelling), students are too dependent on the tools and don't try on their own first. Teachers need to remember: What is the goal or objective of a lesson, how can the goal be reached—strategies/skills/tools needed to reach the goal, what support does a student need—scaffolding, language, drill. And, remember the assessment must be integrated in the learning. I prefer that my students first try to solve problems using their thinking power—then use the tools available—spell check, calculator, resources, each other, teacher. (Jean, sixth-grade teacher)

In regards to students using IRC [Internet Relay Chat] with friends, has anyone noticed a decline in students' abilities to write correctly with grammar and spelling? IRC has given rise to an entire new subculture language that kids are using for hours on end. I actually had a middle school student turn in homework with IRC lingo. To her, the word "for" is spelled "4," and that's how she turned in her paper. Is anyone else seeing evidence of this in the school setting? (Barbara, third-grade bilingual teacher)

How can the guidelines described here help Mr. Yates and the TC with the technology plan?

_____

_____

_____

FIGURE 2.7 Guidelines for Content Teaching

Suggestion	Ideas for Technology-Supported Implementation
Understand	Make overall learning goals and objectives clear. Present them in many ways—text, audio, graphics—and refer back to them during the process.
Guideline #1: Incorporate just-in-time learning.	Have mini-lessons ready to go on topics relevant to the lesson. Bookmark Web sites ahead of time.
Guideline #2: Differentiate instruction.	Vary content, process, product, and/or technologies to give students a variety of possible challenges.
Guideline #3: Teach in a culturally responsive manner.	Connect with parents to better understand students' home cultures. Send technology and the products of technology home to share with parents.
Guideline #4: Adapt materials.	Find, create, and share materials that have been modified to work with different ability levels but the same content. Set up a database by grade/topic/curricular goal that all teachers can access.
Guideline #5: Balance content and tools.	Use the simplest technology that serves the purpose when starting out. Add features as projects and activities warrant and extensions for those capable.

CONTENT LEARNING TECHNOLOGIES

Most teachers have a pretty good idea of how to teach content, but they may not understand as well how technology can help. Of course students can get facts and information from software and Web sites, but how does technology help content learning result in more than declarative knowledge? For one, it can "offer representations, visualizations, and interactions that really help students negotiate concepts and abstractions" (Goldman et al., 1999, p. 8). For example, students may understand that towns need people and that people need schools and so on. However, until they use the simulation SimTown (Maxis) to create their own towns and watch their towns succeed or fail, they may not understand how a complete town system really works.

In addition, students can obtain all kinds of raw data that do not have meaning until they transform the data in some way. For example, the National Center for Educational Statistics (nces.ed.gov) compiles data on education trends across the nation. Until students transform and apply the statistics to look at how the numbers are affecting their lives and communities, they may not understand the impact of demographics on their lives.

Many Web sites emphasize content learning, such as the Student Page of the global Cable News Network site (www.cnn.com), the U.S. National Aeronautics and Space Administration site (www.nasa.gov), and the Electronic Zoo (http://netvet.wustl.edu/e-zoo.htm; see Figure 2.8). In addition, professional organizations such as the National Council of Teachers of Mathematics, the National Science Teachers Association, and the International Reading Association suggest many useful sites for content learning.

Software programs such as Encarta (Microsoft) and Sammy's Science House (Edmark) can support content-based learning. Students can use office software such as PowerPoint, Excel, FrontPage

(Microsoft) and other multimedia development packages to compile and report their findings. The Tool CloseUp: Microsoft Word on page 53 describes how this common tool can play an important role in content learning.

ELLs can use these tools successfully if their use is *carefully planned* so that the language and content are made accessible to the students. Teachers can add external documents, as described in chapter 4, and provide any necessary organizers, prompts, or adaptations to make the content and language relevant and authentic.

For free office tools with many of the capabilities in the Office Suite, go to http://www.goffice.com or http://www.thinkfree.com.

A variety of bilingual software products may also help teacher confidence when using technology with ELLs. Software packages such as Bilingual Timeliner (Tom Snyder Productions), the I Spy/Veo, Veo Series from Scholastic, Decimal & Fraction Maze (Great Wave Software), MathKeys (The Learning Company), Usborne's Animated First 1,000 Words (Tom

FIGURE 2.8 The Electronic Zoo

Source: Used with permission of Washington University.

Snyder Productions), or Physics at Work (Videodiscovery) aim specifically at bilingual students in their content and skill learning. Other software packages such as Kid Pix (Broderbund) give students the option of using either English or Spanish but keeping icons consistent in both versions. In the classroom, teachers and students can also use native language-specific and bilingual Web sites as interactive tools for content learning. Find a list of additional Web sites in this chapter's Resources module on the Companion Website (http://www.prenhall.com/egbert).

ELL

EVALUATING TOOLS

New and "improved" content-focused tools for ELLs, special needs, and traditional students are introduced in the market all the time. These tools need to be carefully evaluated to justify the cost and to ensure they meet learning goals. Although having one teacher evaluate the tool is better than purchasing it without a review, it is better to use it in a classroom for its intended purpose to see how well it helps meet learning goals.

How should software and other tools be evaluated? Multitudes of Web sites and books suggest evaluation schemes and **usability tests** (an observation of the actual use of the product by a target user). Excellent resources can be obtained from ISTE (http://cnets.iste.org) and on Kathy Schrock's amazing Web site at http://kathyschrock.net/. Most of these resources suggest that tools must be evaluated according to the context in which they will be used. Because schools and programs differ widely, this means that evaluations should be adapted to each situation. In many cases this can work, but in others it is not feasible due to personnel, time, and budgetary constraints. Some software companies such as Tom Snyder Productions will lend software to teachers for a free 30–90-day trial, and time extensions are often granted.

The diversity of context and other situational features means that teachers and IT coordinators often use a general, premade form that has a broad fit with the school's purposes. In addition to the two mentioned above, another useful evaluation is enGauge Resources' *Resource Evaluation Form* provided by NCREL (http://www.ncrel.org; Figure 2.9 on page 52), and a short list of evaluation questions with examples can be found in Egbert (2005, pp. 26–31).

Teachers who need to evaluate software tools can also rely on others who have already done some of the work. Many software review sites exist, and a check of multiple sites might help

FIGURE 2.9 Part of enGauge's Resource Evaluation Form

Please circle the appropriate answer.

8. Are any additional software or plug-ins required for the site?   Yes   No
   Type:
9. Does the site appear stable? (does not freeze or crash)   Yes   No
10. The organization that created this site is readily identifiable.   Yes   No
11. Is this resource part of a larger Web site?   Yes   No
    If Yes, what is the URL?
12. Amount of text: ☐ Not Applicable

   1   2   3   4   5

   too little   too much

13. Ease of use: ☐ Not Applicable

   1   2   3   4   5

   too little   too much

14. Which 21st Century Skills are addressed? (Check all that apply.)

Digital-Age Literacy	Inventive Thinking	Effective Communication	High Productivity
☐ Basic, scientific, mathematical, and technological literacies.	☐ Adaptability/ability to manage complexity.	☐ Teaming, collaboration, and interpersonal skills.	☐ Ability to prioritize, plan, and manage for results.
☐ Visual and information literacies.	☐ Curiosity, creativity, and risk taking.	☐ Personal and social responsibility.	☐ Effective use of real-world tools.
☐ Cultural literacy and global awareness.	☐ Higher-order thinking and sound reasoning.	☐ Interactive communication.	☐ Relevant, high-quality products.

Source: Excerpted from *enGauge Resources: Resource Evaluation Form,* available online at http://www.ncrel.org/engauge/resource/resource/toolform.htm. Copyright © 2005 Learning Point Associates. Used with permission of the publisher.

teachers eliminate a software package from their list or decide to try it in their own classrooms. Free sites that can save time and money include:

- World Village's Schoolhouse Review (http://www.worldvillage.com/wv/school/html/scholrev.htm)
- California Learning Resource Network's outstanding searchable review database (http://clrn.org/search/)
- Inexpensive subscription sites such as Children's Technology Review (http://www.childrenssoftware.com/)

Some of these sites even suggest software that a school or program might not have considered. Also, to save time and energy, ask colleagues for their thoughts on software they have used. For content-area and technology-specific electronic lists that teachers can join, go to http://www.edwebproject.org/lists.html.

Table 2.1 presents software programs and Web site examples that can be used to teach a variety of content areas. Many more useful sites are listed in the learning activities section of this chapter. Integrated Learning Systems, which isolate and often decontextualize discrete content items to be learned, are not mentioned here because of their extreme expense and lack of flexibility.

TABLE 2.1 Tools for Content Learning

Tool	Location or Publisher	Objectives/Content
History Mystery	http://teacher.scholastic.com/histmyst/index.asp	Leads students through the problem-solving process while learning history content on a variety of topics.
Math Mysteries	Tom Snyder Productions	Students understand mathematical operations; understand the process of solving word problems; have fun doing math.
BER Collecting Data	http://www.edzone.net/%7Emwestern/BER/data.html	Provides links to fun and effective raw data sources; links to forums and activities for exploring raw data.
Multicultural Calendar	http://www.kidlink.org/KIDPROJ/MCC/	Provides data on holidays from all over the world in a searchable database.
Biography Maker	http://fno.org/bio/biomak2.htm	Helps students frame biographical information to create exciting and lively stories.
Musical Plates	http://www.k12science.org	This section of the CIESE Web site provides activities for turning science information into science knowledge.
Project Gutenberg	http://www.gutenberg.org/	Provides access to thousands of primary source texts; also includes audio books for those with visual impairments or who prefer to listen.
Lemonade Stand, Geometric Presupposer, Splish Splash Math	Sunburst	These and many other Sunburst content-based programs provide fun, context-based practice with concepts in basic numeracy, science, text-based literacy, and social studies.
Magic School Bus Series	Microsoft	Each CD provides facts and ideas on a different topic and allows students to practice and drill in fun ways.

Tool CloseUp: Microsoft Word

One advantage to using tools in the Microsoft Office Suite (Excel, PowerPoint, FrontPage, and Word) for content learning is that these tools are widely used in business and education and help is available in many formats. For example, an excellent beginning instructional guide can be found at http://www.utexas.edu/its/training/handouts/UTOPIA_WordGS/. Other resources include the tutorial at http://www.baycongroup.com/wlesson0.htm and Gookin's text *Word 2003 for Dummies* (2003, For Dummies). Another advantage is that Word files cross platforms with ease, making students' letters to the editor or pamphlets on home safety readable whether on a Mac or a PC. In addition, the menus and icons are consistent throughout the Office programs. For example, once a student understands that the icon 🖨 indicates "print" in Word, he will also be able to print in the other tools in the suite. (Take the quiz at http://www.sw/avriersb.qc.ca/english/edservices/pedresources/webquest/word_game/index. html to see how many of the icons you know.)

On the other hand, some educators feel that Word has too many options to learn and that students can become lost in the formatting to the detriment of learning goals. They also express concern about how student typing skills affect their work. However, as noted previously in this chapter, teachers and students do not need to use all the features of a program like Word to receive the benefits that it offers. And, with a little creativity, Word can be used for an amazing number of tasks.

Two of the features that make Word a valuable tool in classrooms are its editing and multimedia capabilities. Many research and anecdotal reports tell how students revise more with the computer than they do with paper and pencil. However, there is more to Word's editing capabilities. For example, using the commenting feature, teachers and peers can make comments on a student's paper that do not interfere with the original text. If multiple reviewers make comments, their names will appear with their comments. Mistakes in the text can be highlighted with color or font changes, or voice annotation can be used to make it easier for aural learners to understand.

To some people it may seem odd to call a word processing program multimedia. However, most word processors have gone far beyond this simple typing feature and make it easy to integrate graphics (including pictures, drawings, and charts), color, text, sound, and a variety of formats. (Of course, if the document is printed, the sound will not work.) Teachers can use a word processor to prepare different versions of documents that all students can use, for example, highlighting focal vocabulary for ELLs and others who need it, using sound for students who have hearing impairments, large text for students with visual impairments, and links to more advanced information for students capable of using it. Students can also use these features to make their reports interesting and accessible and to learn how to design appealing documents.

Word processors such as Microsoft Word, if integrated effectively into classroom practice, can help teachers and learners address the needs of diverse students and work toward all the learning goals. Additional examples of activities that are supported by the use of a word processor can be found throughout this book.

How do you use a word processor in your daily life? What additional features should you learn in order to use it in the ways noted in this CloseUp?

_____

_____

_____

_____

Tutorial

CW

To learn more about Microsoft Word, see the Microsoft Word tutorials in the Tutorials module on the Companion Website (http://www.prenhall.com/egbert).

FROM THE CLASSROOM

Content Tools

I'm locating Web sites for students and although it has taken me a long time to find some quality sites, I have finally found some that I can't wait to share . . . I found a cute site called Word Central. It has a lot of fun activities such as a rhyming dictionary, great kids' dictionary, games/activities, and message encoding/ decoding. Check it out at http://www.wordcentral.com/. Okay, one more. Kidshealth.com is awesome too. If you ever teach health or the human body, you've got to go here because there are cute videos, songs, and lots of informational articles for kids on all sorts of health-related issues: http://www.kidshealth.com/ kid/index.jsp.
(Jennie, first-grade teacher)

Read as one teacher describes her search for exciting content tools in From the Classroom: Content Tools.

In addition to effective content-based classroom learning, students need to participate in activities that help them to understand the foundations of technology use, including concepts of ethics.

What kinds of tools will help East Park High School reach its technology and learning goals? Why do you think so?

_____

_____

_____

LEARNING ACTIVITIES: CONTENT LEARNING

Integrating technology throughout the curriculum, the task that Mr. Yates and the Technology Committee have taken on, may seem like an overwhelming task. As described above, there are many technologies to help teachers present content. The problem is how to get started. McKenzie (2004b) believes that we can "invent curriculum rich lessons that take students half an hour but engage them in powerful thought with considerable skill." He says this can happen through "tight lesson design, no waste, no bother and no wandering about." He calls these short, structured, Web-based lessons "Slam Dunk Digital Lessons." Slam Dunks are tasks that focus on content learning through essential questions and Web-based resources. Teachers can integrate Slam Dunks into larger lessons or units (see http://fno.org/sept02/slamdunk.html for a brief, clear explanation) or use them as a starting point to develop lessons that integrate technology. A sample page of a lesson from Way Elementary is presented in Figure 2.10. The basic format consists of these six parts:

1. *The essential question and learning task:* The important question that students will have to work to answer, along with any other preview of the material and a picture if appropriate/ available.

2. *The information source:* A picture and information about the site(s) appropriate for your students that they will use to answer the essential question.

3. *The student activity:* What students will do with the information, typically completing some kind of graphic organizer using the links provided.

4. *The assessment activity:* The performance or product that will show what students understand.

5. *Enrichment activities:* A brief list of extra sites that have been checked for appropriateness.

6. *Teacher support materials:* Helpful hints, standards, instructions, and objectives.

For more details and examples, go to http:// questioning.org/.

McKenzie recommends building the lesson from the foundation of one or more content standards. The learning activities that follow adapt the basic Slam Dunk outline to demonstrate how digital tools can be used in different

FIGURE 2.10 Slam Dunk Lesson from Way Elementary

Animal Adaptations

1. The Question

How does climate and habitat affect an animal's physical and behavioral adaptations?

Next page

These materials and the HTML code behind them are © 2002 Way Elementary, all rights reserved.

Source: Used with permission of Bloomfield Hills Schools.

content areas to meet specific content standards. Each activity can be modified to make it effective for older or younger learners. As you read, think about the kind of content learning (declarative, structural, or procedural) each activity is designed to help students achieve.

Question: Why do we need to understand fractions?

Source(s): Beginning fractions, http://www.aaamath.com/ B/fra16_x2.htm

Activity: List all the ways that you use fractions during your day.

Assessment: Write a summary of your answers and share it with peers.

Enrichment:

- Hungry for Math, http://library.thinkquest.org/ J002328F/default.htm
- Identify with circles, http://www.visualfractions.com/EnterCircle.html
- Fresh Baked Fractions, http://www.funbrain.com/ fract/

Support: Understand commonly used fractions (Standard NM.NUM.PK-2.1).

Question: Which body system is the most important?

Source(s): Human Anatomy Online, http://www. innerbody.com/htm/body.html (Figure 2.11)

Activity: Chart the parts of the main body systems and their roles in the body.

Assessment: Write a brief position statement based on the data that answers the question "Which body system is the most important?"

Enrichment:

- Virtual Body, http://www.medtropolis.com/VBody.asp
- Interactive body, http://www.bbc.co.uk/science/ humanbody/
- Atlas of the Body, http://www.ama-assn.org/ ama/pub/category/7140.html

Support: Describe the basic structure and functions of the human body systems. Students will learn what the body systems are and the roles they play (Standard NPH-H.K–4.1, 5–8.1).

FIGURE 2.11 Human Anatomy Online

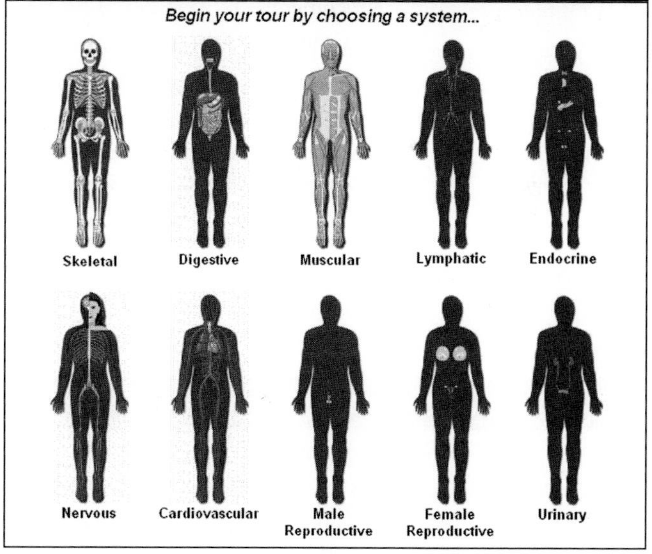

Begin your tour by choosing a system...

Skeletal   Digestive   Muscular   Lymphatic   Endocrine

Nervous   Cardiovascular   Male Reproductive   Female Reproductive   Urinary

Source: Images from Human Anatomy Online (www.innerbody.com) provided by INTELLIMED International Corporation.

Question: If you could no longer live on the earth, which planet in the solar system would you most want to live on?

Source(s): The Nine Planets (http://www.nineplanets.org/)

Activity: Complete a planet chart with average temperatures, length of days/years, atmospheric composition, and two other features of your choice.

Assessment: Present your argument to the class about which planet you would most want to live on.

Enrichment:

- Welcome to the Planets!, http://pds.jpl.nasa.gov/planets/welcome.htm
- Zoom Astronomy, http://www.enchantedlearning.com/subjects/astronomy/planets
- Comparing the Planets, http://www.nasm.si.edu/research/ceps/etp/ compare/etpcompare.html

Support: Students develop an understanding of objects in the sky. Students have to define what makes living on Earth good and how that definition changes as they look past the earth. They will learn or review the order of the planets in the solar system and some of their features (Standard NS.K–4.4, 5–8.4).

Question: If you had to eliminate one of the rights in the Bill of Rights, which would it be?

Source(s): *The Bill of Rights: Evolution of Personal Liberties* (CD-ROM from socialstudies.com)

Activity: Create a chart with pros and cons for each original amendment.

Assessment: Work in groups to choose one amendment to eliminate and defend your choice.

Enrichment:

- The National Archives, http://www.archives.gov/national_archives_experience/charters/bill_of_rights.html
- ACLU Student Rights, http://www.aclu.org/students/
- The Bill of Rights, http://www.billofrightsinstitute.org/

Support: What is the U.S. Constitution and why is it important (Standard NSS-C.K–4.3, 5–8.2, 9–12.2)?

The approach in this lesson involves the same content as a traditional overview of the Bill of Rights but requires students to understand the issues more deeply and to make an untraditional choice.

Question: Your school has money to purchase one piece of art by an American painter to display in the main hallway. Which piece of art should it be?

Source(s): Inventories of American Painting and Sculpture, http://americanart.si.edu/search/search_data.cfm

Activity: Choose five pieces of art from different genres. Create a table that includes the art's "message," its defining characteristics, and reasons why it should be displayed in the school.

Assessment: Peers from around the school vote on the choices.

Enrichment:

- Whitney Museum of American Art, http://www. whitney.org/
- National Gallery of Art (Figure 2.12), http://www.nga. gov/education/american/aasplash.htm

Support: Students know the differences among visual characteristics and purposes of art; students describe how different expressive features and organizational principles cause different responses (Standard NA-VA.K–4.2, 5–8.1, 9–12.2). As a follow-up, students can make interpretive versions of the artwork chosen.

Tasks like these that provide structure and appropriate resources and clearly meet standards might be the ideal tool for teachers who are just starting to integrate technology into their teaching. The tasks above are also useful to help students understand how to frame essential questions that include *why? how?* and *which?*

What implications does this section on learning activities have for the TC's technology plan?

FIGURE 2.12 American Art at the National Gallery

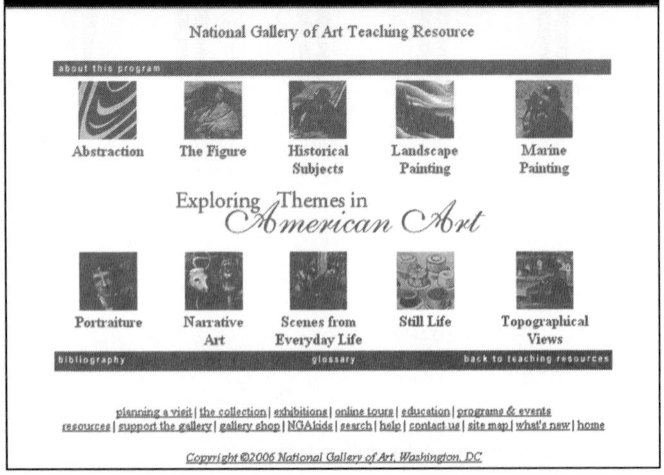

Source: Images © Board of Trustees, National Gallery of Art, Washington.

ASSESSING CONTENT LEARNING: SCORING GUIDES

Because content knowledge plays an important role in meeting other learning goals, teachers must assess content in ways that help them understand what students know and can do. As suggested in this chapter's learning activities section, students can be assessed through technology-supported summaries, retellings, and debates. Content knowledge can also be assessed through rubrics (chapter 3), tests (chapter 4), and a variety of performance assessments (chapter 6). The North Central Regional Educational Laboratory (NCREL) suggests that in addition to assessing students, teachers should evaluate their own instructional design and assessment process. To do so, they can employ scoring guides. **Scoring guides** are like rubrics, but they are used to evaluate learning in a broader sense than more local rubrics. The three functions of scoring guides are:

1. To help teachers and evaluators evaluate student learning in a relatively objective way based on predetermined standards

2. To identify and assess not only student learning but also instructional design

3. To serve as models for teachers in developing their own rubrics for a wide variety of assessment purposes. (NCREL, n.d.(b), p. 1)

NCREL provides a customizable scoring guide for the effective use of technology at http://www.ncrtec.org/tl/sgsp/overview.htm. Teachers can choose among 14 categories of student products and choose items from relevant checklists to construct their scoring guide. Figure 2.13 shows the first three sections of the scoring guide. More information on scoring guides can be found in the Assessment section of the Resources module on this text's Companion Website (http://www.prenhall.com/egbert).

What technologies should Mr. Yates's committee add to the plan to address student assessment? Why?

_____

_____

_____

FIGURE 2.13 Scoring Guide

	5	4	3	2	1	0	Comments
Standards/ Learning Objectives	Curriculum standards and learning objectives are specific and focused, intentionally driving the use of technology.		Curriculum standards and learning objectives are correlated to technology uses.		Curriculum standards and learning objectives are superficial uses of technology.	No demonstration of curriculum standards and learning objectives connected to the use of technology.	
Curriculum Linking with Technology Uses	Curriculum linking creates unique content learning benefits. Content learning experiences/benefits are extended and would be impaired or impossible without the use of technology.		Curriculum linking adapts or varies present student learning or work. Content learning experiences or benefits are enhanced but possible without the use of technology.		Curriculum linking provides topics " for technology skills or uses. Content learning incidental—student uses primarily to learn/practice technology skills.	Curriculum linking is incidental to technology use. Content learning not focused. Technology uses are mostly supplemental, or to provide fun/ motivation activities.	
Cognitive Tasks	Task requires synthesis and evaluation of information. Going beyond existing understanding to create own original position or product. Knowledge creation is expected.		Task requires analysis of information and/or putting together information from several sources to demonstrate an understanding of existing knowledge.		Task requires little analysis and is focused on simplistic tasks or concepts using a single source. Cookie-cutter, look-alike products are likely to develop.	The task has little relevance to content learning.	

Source: Excerpted from *Scoring Guide for Lesson Plans That Use Technology Resources,* available online at http://www.ncrtec.org/tl/sgsp/lpsg.htm. Copyright © 2001 Learning Point Associates and Bernajean Porter Consulting. Used with permission of Learning Point Associates.

SAMPLE LESSON: CONTENT LEARNING

Mr. Yates's committee has successfully completed a technology plan that meets the requirements of the funding. Before submitting the plan for approval, each member of the committee has been assigned a grade and content level for which to find or develop a sample lesson that meets the goals of the plan. These sample lessons are to accompany the technology plan through the approval process.

Mr. Yates must produce a plan for fifth- and sixth-grade science. As a result of a Web search, he finds the lesson "What Color Are Your Skittles?" from the Educators Desk Reference site (http://www.eduref.org/). The lesson is reproduced here.

WHAT COLOR ARE YOUR SKITTLES?

Submitted by: *Ellyn Bewes*

Grade Level: 5, 6

Subject(s):

- Computer Science
- Mathematics/Process Skills

Description: Students enter data into a spreadsheet to create a pie graph showing the percentage of colors found in a bag of Skittles.

Goals: Students will create and manipulate spreadsheets and graphs.

Objectives:

1. Students will create a spreadsheet to chart the different colors found in a package of Skittles.
2. Students will collect data, create appropriate charts, and use percentages to describe quantities.

Materials:

- 1 package of Skittles for each student
- computers with Microsoft Excel/access to the Internet
- floppy disks
- index cards
- What Color Are Your Skittles? Instruction Sheet

Procedure:

(Depending on class size and computer availability, teachers may choose to have students work individually or in pairs.)

Begin the lesson by distributing a bag of Skittles to each student, along with an index card. Have students look at their package of Skittles. Ask students, "How many different colors of Skittles are there? What percentage of each color do you think is in your bag?" Have students write their predictions on their index cards. "Now open your package of Skittles and tally the amounts of the different colors of Skittles." (Students can write the colors and numbers on the back of their index cards.)

After the results have been tallied, hand out an instruction sheet to each student. The instruction sheet provides step-by-step directions for creating a graph using Microsoft Excel. Students should be able to follow the instructions with minimal help, but the teacher should circulate around the room to answer students' questions. (The teacher can also encourage students to ask each other for help if the teacher is busy assisting another student.) When students have completed their graphs, they should print out a copy of their work. Students can compare their results to their earlier predictions.

Extension: Have students go to the Skittles Web site (http://www.skittles.com) to find out what percentage of each color is supposed to be in a package of Skittles—to see if their pie charts and percentages are similar to those advertised on the Web.

Assessment:
Collect students' completed work to check for accuracy.

Source: From HotChalk (www.HotChalk.com).

Mr. Yates uses a Lesson Analysis and Adaptation Worksheet (found in chapter 1 on page 33 and in the Lesson Planning Module on the Companion Website) to help him analyze the lesson. He concludes these things about the lesson:

- No standards are mentioned.
- The lesson requires students to use skills of data collection, estimating, counting, and data entry. There could certainly be more originality, a greater variety of language skills, and more integrated interaction. There is some scaffolding through the instruction sheet that gives step-by-step directions for completing the spreadsheet.
- Grouping arrangements could be included to differentiate the process. A clearer connection needs to be made between this lesson and students' lives outside school.
- The technology is used to support student content learning. Allowing for a variety of student products might help this issue and also differentiate by allowing students to show what they know in other ways.
- The variety of materials (Skittles, external document, computer, peers) means that ELLs and other students with diverse needs will likely be able to participate. However, the instruction sheet is only text and might be difficult for students with language barriers to understand and follow.
- The assessment is not sufficiently detailed and does not directly link to the objectives. It uses controlling feedback and does not leave room for students to show what they know in a variety of ways.

Mr. Yates believes that the idea of this technology-supported lesson is good but that it needs to focus more on students using 21st-century skills to learn content. Based on his analysis, he decides to make these changes before submitting the lesson:

1. Note relevant content area, language, and technology standards.
2. Include more skills and content. Students should work in groups so they communicate, and they should record their estimates, their actual count, and their process on a worksheet to include more language. At the end of the activity, students should also make a graph of the numbers from the Skittles Web site and compare their two graphs in text or visuals. This will require them to summarize and synthesize the information. More advanced students can also prepare a professional presentation based on their findings.
3. Hang the resulting graphs on the wall and let students peruse them. They can make notes on a worksheet of which bag of Skittles they would prefer the most, differences between how the graphs were made, and other ways they might present the information.
4. Provide visuals on the instruction sheet that show actual screens from the software so that students who need or prefer more visual orientation can access the information.
5. Provide more specific assessment and formative feedback. Mr. Yates will work with the students to develop a scoring guide that assesses not only student performance but their thoughts about the lesson in general and connections to their lives.

With these changes, Mr. Yates feels, this lesson will reflect the goals of the technology plan and provide evidence that the plan will work.

What other changes, if any, should Mr. Yates make to this lesson? Why?

_____

_____

_____

CHAPTER REVIEW

Key Points

- **Explain how content learning takes place.**

  Learning occurs when new information is attached to other information in the brain. If this information is isolated pieces of data, this process results in declarative knowledge. When declarative knowledge sorts into different webs of meaning, structural knowledge is the result. Procedural knowledge is the result of understanding connections among pieces of data. Procedural knowledge is the knowledge that allows students to take action. Teachers can and should support learners in every aspect of knowledge acquisition. Technology can help, but only if it is used wisely and arranged to fit the goals.

- **Explain the role of content learning in meeting other instructional goals.**

  Problem-solving, creativity, and other instructional goals depend, to an extent, on student mastery of content. However, content can also be learned through the process of reaching these goals.

- **Discuss guidelines and techniques for using technology in content learning and teaching.**

  Teachers must prepare their lessons in culturally responsive ways and use techniques such as differentiation and material adaptation to help all students access the content. They must also be flexible and observant enough to understand when students need a just-in-time lesson.

- **Analyze technologies that can be used to create opportunities for content learning for all students.**

  Teachers and students can employ a variety of electronic tools to support content learning, but they must also be aware of the content, nature, and viability of the tools that they use.

- **Describe and develop effective technology-enhanced content learning activities.**

  Effective content learning activities are those that consider students' backgrounds and needs, are designed on the basis of how students learn, and use technologies that are appropriate, relevant, and necessary.

- **Create appropriate assessments for technology-enhanced content learning activities.**
  In order to create appropriate assessments, teachers can evaluate the design of their instruction and their evaluation measures through the use of scoring guides.

Which information in this chapter is most valuable to you? Why? How will you use it in your teaching?

_____

_____

_____

CASE QUESTIONS REVIEW

Reread the case at the beginning of the chapter and review your answers. In light of what you learned during this chapter, how do your answers change? Note any changes below.

1. *What kind of hardware components should the committee choose? Why?*

_____

_____

_____

2. What kind of software and/or Internet access should the computers have? Why?

_____

_____

_____

3. How can the needs of ELLs and other students with special needs be addressed in the technology plan?

_____

_____

_____

4. How should the computers be assigned and laid out?

_____

_____

_____

5. Do you see any problems in the way the grant was awarded or how it will be implemented? If so, what are the problems?

_____

_____

_____

CHAPTER EXTENSIONS · · · · · · · · · · ·

For more information on school technology plans, see the resources from the Michigan Department of Education at http://www.techplan.org/ and the Tech Plans section of the Resources module on the Companion Website (http://www.prenhall.com/egbert). To answer any of the following questions online, go to the Chapter 2 Extensions module for this text's Companion Website.

Adapt · · · ·

Choose a lesson for your potential subject area and grade level from the lesson plan archives at Educators Desk Reference (http://www.eduref.org/). Use the Lesson Analysis and Adaptation Worksheet from chapter 1 on page 33 (also available on the Companion Website) to consider the lesson in the context of _content learning_. Use your responses to the worksheet to suggest general changes to the lesson based on your current or future students and context.

Practice · · · ·

1. _Describe content learning._ Review the lessons in the activities section of this chapter. For each lesson, tell which kind of knowledge each activity is designed to help students achieve (declarative, structural, or procedural).

2. *Evaluate software*. Choose a piece of software or a Web site and evaluate it for cultural responsiveness. Use these basic guidelines adapted from NWREL (2005) or develop a set of your own guidelines based on the literature:

   a. The software supports a climate of caring, respect, and the valuing of students' cultures.

   b. The software helps to build a bridge between academic learning and students' prior understanding, knowledge, native language, and values.

   c. The outcomes of software use help educators learn from and about their students' culture, language, and learning styles to make instruction more meaningful and relevant to their students' lives.

   d. Local knowledge, language, and culture are fully integrated into the software, not added on to it.

   e. Tasks provided or supported by the software are challenging, cooperative, and hands-on, with less emphasis on rote memorization and lecture formats.

3. *Obtain resources*. Search the Web for resources that you could access for JIT lessons that students in your classroom might need. Make a list of your findings to share with peers.

4. *Support strategies with technology*. Choose one or more strategies for content learning learned in your other classes and note how technology might make the process more efficient or effective. For example, you may have studied mnemonic devices. How could technology be used to support mnemonics?

5. *Create balance*. Find or use a technology-enhanced lesson for your grade level and content area. Analyze the lesson and describe how you will balance the need to learn the technology with the requirement to learn the content.

Explore • • •

1. *Adapt a model of knowledge*. Review the model in Figure 2.2. Using your content area, recreate the model with content-based declarative knowledge and a schema into which it could develop.

2. *Practice differentiating*. Choose one of the learning activities from this chapter and differentiate, creating choices for one of these elements: process, product, tool, or assessment. Explain why your change is effective and for what learners.

3. *Adapt an activity*. Choose one of the learning activities in the chapter. Adapt it *as little as possible* to make it work for older or younger learners or those who have different levels of skill or knowledge. Explain your changes.

4. *Reply to a teacher*. Look at the teachers' comments in this chapter's From the Classroom features. Choose one teacher's comment and write a reply.

5. *Create a lesson*. Choose a content area standard and develop a Slam Dunk lesson based on the framework presented in this chapter.

6. *Create a context-based software evaluation*. Explore a classroom or school context that you are familiar with. Develop an evaluation scheme for tools for that context.

7. *Review technology plans*. Find technology plans for other schools and districts on the Web by using one of the links that follow or doing a Web search. Examine the plans. What ideas can you see that you could use? What is missing?

   http://www.bham.wednet.edu/technology/2004-07TechPlan1-24.htm

   http://www.sabine.k12.la.us/mhs1/techplan.htm

   http://www.kent.k12.wa.us/ksd/DE/technology/tech_plan.html

8. *Research implementation*. Interview an IT coordinator for a school or district. Find out how their technology plan was implemented, what the pros and cons were, and what could be done differently.

9. *Adapt materials*. Briefly outline a technology-enhanced activity or lesson that you might use in your classroom. Review materials that you might use during the activity. Adapt the materials to make them accessible to: (a) students with less proficient English, (b) students with more advanced reading skills, and (c) students with a variety of prior knowledge and experience.

REFERENCES

Echevarria, J., & Graves, A. (2002). *Sheltered content instruction: Teaching English language learners with diverse abilities* (3rd ed.). Boston, MA: Allyn & Bacon.

Egbert, J. (2005). *CALL essentials: Principles and practice in CALL classrooms*. Alexandria, VA: TESOL.

Erlauer, L. (2003). *The brain-compatible classroom: Using what we know about learning to improve teaching*. Alexandria, VA: Association for Supervision and Curriculum Development.

Falk, B., & Blumenreich, M. (2005). *The power of questions: A guide to teacher and student research*. Portsmouth, NH: Heinemann.

Goldman, S., Cole, K., & Syer, C. (1999). *The Secretary's conference on educational technology—1999: The technology/content dilemma*. (ERIC Document Reproduction Service No. ED 452821).

Johnson, S. (2004). *Mind wide open: Your brain and the neuroscience of everyday life*. New York: Scribner.

Jonassen, D., & Wang, S. (1992). Acquiring structural knowledge from semantically structured hypertext. Proceedings of selected research and development presentations at the Convention of the Association for Educational Communications and Technology and sponsored by the Research and Theory Division. (ERIC Document Reproduction Service No. ED348000).

McKenzie, J. (1998). Creating technology enhanced student-centered learning environments. *From Now On, 7*(6).

McKenzie, J. (2004a, Summer). Five types of slam dunk lessons. *From Now On, 13*(9).

McKenzie, J. (2004b). Making good lessons quickly. Available: http://questioning.org/module2/quick.html.

NCREL (n.d.b). *Using scoring guides vs. rubrics*. Available: http://www.ncrtec.org/tl/sgsp/rubguide.htm.

New Horizons for Learning (2002). *Teaching and learning strategies*. Available: http://www.newhorizons.org.

Norman, D. (2004). *Emotional design: Why we love (or hate) everyday things*. New York: Basic Books.

NWREL (2005). *Culturally responsive practices for student success: A regional sampler*. Available from: http://www.nwrel.org/request/2005june/what.html.

Pearson, D., & Gallagher, M. (1983, July). The instruction of reading comprehension. *Contemporary Educational Psychology, 8*(3), 317–344.

Riel, M. (1998). *Education in the 21st century: Just-in-time learning or learning communities*. Paper prepared for the Challenges of the Next Millennium: Education and Development of Human Resources, 4th Annual Conference of the Emirates Center for Strategic Studies and Research, 137–160.

Theroux, P. (2004). *Differentiating instruction. Enhance learning with technology*. Available: http://members.shaw.ca/priscillatheroux/differentiating.html.

Tomlinson, C. (2001). *How to differentiate instruction in mixed-ability classrooms*. Alexandria, VA: ASCD.

Vygotsky, L. S. (1978). *Mind in society*. Cambridge, MA: Harvard University Press.

Wignall, E. (2006). *Media, minds, methods: Linking online instruction and media for maximum effect*. Paper presented at the 21st annual conference on Distance Teaching and Learning, May, 2006. Available: www.uwex.edu/disted/conference/Resource_library/proceedings/05-1898.pdf.

Williams, P. J. (2000, Spring). Design: The only methodology of technology? *Journal of Technology Education, 11*(2), 48–60.

Yatvin, J. (2004). *A room with a differentiated view: How to serve ALL children as individual learners*. Portsmouth, NH: Heinemann.

When we are in New Jersey, my mom likes the beach so much that we go to the beach almost every day we can. About the shortest time we go to the beach is about three hours and the longest time we go is about six and a half to seven hours.

Supporting Student Communication

Case: Geography Mystery

As you read the following case, pay attention to how and with whom the teacher plans for the students to communicate during their telecommunications project.

• •

Mr. Finley, a junior high school social studies teacher, is planning a telecommunications project for his seventh-grade students while they study the geography of the United States. His project will employ technology to support interaction among students at a distance from each other. Participating in this project will help students understand the use and importance of latitude and longitude and the role of geographical features in people's lives. It will also help the students to meet other content, language, and technology goals and standards.

During this project, Mr. Finley's class will work on geography mysteries via email with Ms. Stewart's sixth-grade class in a different state. Mr. Finley's students will work in teams of three students. Each team will choose a place somewhere in the United States. Team members will pretend that they were dropped unexpectedly in that particular place and need help figuring out the name of the place where they are located. They may choose a city, a landmark, the top of a mountain, or some other specific point for which they will figure out such details as the latitude, longitude, nearby geographic features, how the people in the area use the land, and mileage to nearby landmarks. They will send clues about their location in email messages to a team in Ms. Stewart's class, who will respond through email to try to discover where Mr. Finley's students are. A message from a team in Mr. Finley's class might look like this:

We are located near the capital of a state whose major industry is farming because of the large amount of volcanic soil. We are at the southern end of the largest wilderness area in the United States.

Ms. Stewart's students will use both online and offline resources to help make guesses and formulate questions to ask. A reply from the partner team in Ms. Stewart's class could be:

Are you in either Idaho or Washington? What is your elevation? Are you above the 45th parallel?

After Ms. Stewart's students guess the location correctly, they will make a map online at M. Weinelt's Online Map Creation site (www.aquarius.geomar.de/omc/), using latitude and longitude to show the location. The classes will then switch roles and Ms. Stewart's students will send clues to Mr. Finley's class.

Mr. Finley expects the project to take six weeks, during which time students in both classes will be studying different aspects of geography that will help them solve the mysteries. In addition, Mr. Finley has developed some scaffolds in the form of handouts to help students think about their group processes and to make good guesses. Mr. Finley also plans lessons on skills needed to communicate effectively, on email etiquette, on group work, and on logic and problem solving. Mr. Finley has done a similar telecommunications project with previous students and expects that his current students will work enthusiastically on this one.

As he makes copies of the starting instructions, which he will also explain orally to the students, Mr. Finley feels excited to begin the project, but he wonders if he has considered everything he needs to make this project a success.

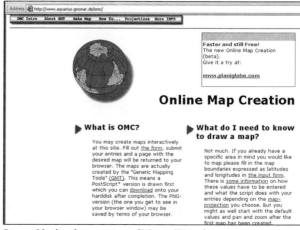

Source: Used with permission of Martin Weinelt.

• •

Answer these questions about the case. There are no right or wrong answers to this chapter preview—the goal is for you to respond before you read the chapter. Then, as you interact with the chapter contents, think about how your answers might change.

1. What learning benefits might the sixth- and seventh-grade students derive from participating in this telecommunications project?

_____

_____

_____

2. How can working with students at another school contribute to Mr. Finley's students' achievement?

_____

_____

_____

3. How did Mr. Finley approach the use of technology to meet his goals?

_____

_____

_____

4. *What other ways can Mr. Finley ensure the success of this telecommunications project?*

_____

_____

_____

Mr. Finley chose to have his students communicate with students in another school by email for the geography mystery project, but he could have chosen a variety of other participants and means of communication. It is important for teachers to understand the implications of the available choices to choose wisely. To this end, when you finish this chapter you will be able to:

- Define communication, collaboration, and related terms.
- Describe the communication process and explain how communication affects learning.
- Discuss guidelines and techniques for creating opportunities for technology-supported communication and collaboration.
- Analyze technologies that can be used to support communication, including MOOs, email, chat, blogs, and wikis.
- Describe and develop effective technology-enhanced communication activities.
- Create appropriate assessments for technology-enhanced communication tasks.

When you have completed this chapter, which NETS*T will you have addressed?

_____

_____

_____

• • • • **Meeting the Standards:** Communication • • • •

Guidelines for every content area include communication as an essential component for meeting national standards. For example, the education technology standards (NETS*S) address student mastery of technology communication tools, including being able to "interact, collaborate, and publish with peers, experts, and others," and "communicate information and ideas effectively to multiple audiences using a variety of media and formats." The national math standards have a complete section on math communication that emphasizes students "organizing and consolidating their mathematical thinking through communication" and being able to "communicate their mathematical thinking coherently"

(NM–COMM PK–12). Fine arts standards ask students to work together to develop improvisations; English focuses on communication skills, strategies, and applying language skills (4, 5, and 12); the first goal of the foreign language and ESL standards is communication; and even PE standards support the goal of communicating about health (NPH-H.5). In every area, communication is understood to be a foundation of learning, and technology can help students to communicate with a variety of audiences for a variety of purposes by connecting them both online and off. Some of the communication standards are mentioned in this chapter in the activities section.

Review the national or state standards for a content area that you will teach. How many of the standards address communication in some way? What kinds of connections do your students need to make to meet those standards? How do you think technology can help?

_____

_____

_____

As you read the rest of the chapter, look for ways to use technology to help your students communicate and make connections in the ways you outlined above. See national standards and your state standards for communication in the **Standards** module on this text's Companion Website.

CW⌐

• • • •

Technology-supported communication projects can be fun and effective learning experiences for students and teachers, but, as this chapter will show, preparation is necessary. For standards that guide communication and how technology is used to support them, see the Meeting the Standards feature.

OVERVIEW OF COMMUNICATION AND TECHNOLOGY IN K–12 CLASSROOMS

In keeping with the premise of this text, before discussing how technology supports communication it is important to understand what communication is and why it is an important learning goal.

What Is Communication?

Communication is a general term that implies the conveyance of information either one-way or through an exchange with two or more partners. Shirky (2003) identifies *three basic communication patterns*, also shown in Figure 3.1:

1. Point-to-point two-way (e.g., a two-person Internet chat or a phone conversation)
2. One-to-many outbound (e.g., a static Web site, a lecture, a TV show, a three-way phone conversation)
3. Many-to-many (e.g., a group discussion)

Learning takes place when the communication is based on true **social interaction**. Social interaction means that the communication is two-way, but it does not mean that participants are just giving each other information. Social interaction is communication with an **authentic audience** that shares some of the goals of the communication. It also includes an authentic task in which the answers are generally unknown by one or more (perhaps all!) participants. This kind of

FIGURE 3.1 Basic Communication Patterns

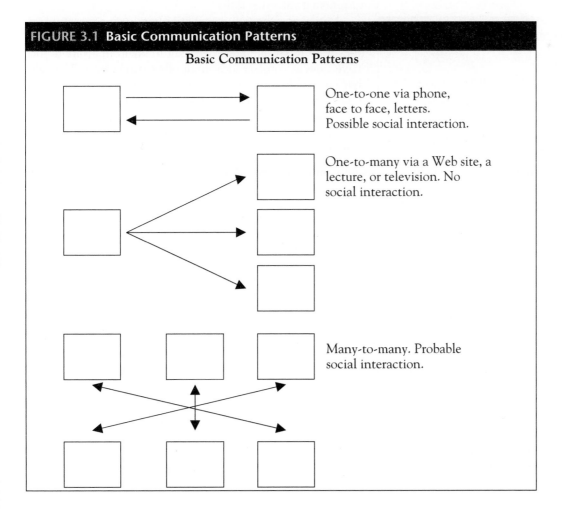

Basic Communication Patterns

One-to-one via phone, face to face, letters. Possible social interaction.

One-to-many via a Web site, a lecture, or television. No social interaction.

Many-to-many. Probable social interaction.

FIGURE 3.2 MSN Messenger

interaction requires interdependence and **negotiation of meaning**; in other words, during their communication participants ask for clarification, argue, challenge each other, and work toward common understanding. These features of communication can lead to effective learning by assisting students in understanding information and constructing knowledge with the help of others.

In fact, research shows that "social interactions play a fundamental role in knowledge apprehension and in skills acquisition as well as in socio-cognitive development" (Cesar, 1998). In other words, "any communicative act, be it verbal or nonverbal, which is apprehended by another, will alter that individual's perceptions, attitudes, beliefs, and motivations, even if ever so slightly" (Berger & Burgoon, 1995, p. 1).

This implies that, although educational software companies often advertise "interactive software," true social interaction cannot occur with a software program because it cannot offer original, authentic, creative feedback or meet the other requirements for social interaction. Social interaction can, however, occur *through* technology (e.g., directly between two or more people via email, a cell phone, or other communications technology), *around* technology (e.g., students discussing a problem posed by a software program), or *with the support of* technology (e.g., teacher and students interacting about a worksheet printed from a Web site).

Social interaction, in other words, occurs between people. The interaction can be **synchronous** (in real time during which participants take turns, such as during a phone call, face-to-face discussion, or chat) or **asynchronous** (not occurring at the same time, such as in an email conversation or letters—also known as "snail mail"). There are benefits and challenges for both types. For example, during synchronous communication in the popular MSN Messenger (Figure 3.2), learners can receive instant feedback, express themselves as ideas come to mind, and learn turn-taking and other skills.

During asynchronous communication, such as an email exchange, learners have more time to think about and format what they want to say and how they want to say it. In addition, they have time to consider ideas from other participants. They also have a record of the communication that they can refer to. For both types of student interaction to be successful, participants must learn and practice skills such as listening, speaking, writing, reading, and communicating nonverbally. A list of features of social interaction is presented in Figure 3.3.

FIGURE 3.3 Features of Social Interaction

- Is two-way
- Includes an authentic audience
- Can occur through, around, or with the support of technology
- Based on negotiation of meaning
- Offers authentic, creative feedback
- Synchronous or asynchronous
- Forms the basis for cooperation and collaboration

With whom do you interact socially on a daily basis? Why? With whom do K-12 students typically interact?

_____

_____

_____

What Is Collaboration?

One type of communication that involves two-way interaction is collaboration. **Collaboration** is social interaction in which participants must plan and accomplish something specific together. A more specific definition is provided by Coleman (2002), who defines collaboration as when "[m]ultiple interactions occur between two or more people for the transfer of complex information for some common goal over a specified period of time" (n.p.). Collaboration is a discovery process, with students bringing their strengths to bear on reaching an outcome together. According to Hofmann (2003), true collaboration is when "the success of the group is paramount and all individuals must contribute to that success." She adds that "no member of the group can be left behind and everyone within the group will do whatever it takes to reach the common goal" (n.p.). Clearly, good communication based in social interaction is central to collaboration.

What Is Cooperation?

Although both cooperation and collaboration require social interaction—and technology can support both—they are not exactly the same processes (Panitz, 1996). **Cooperation** generally implies that students have separate roles in a structured task and pool their data to a specific end, whereas collaboration means that students work together in different ways from the planning stage on. Both collaboration and cooperation are beneficial to student learning.

The Role of Technology in Communication

Technology can play a central role in learning through all forms of communication. Shirky (2003) claims that

> what is really revolutionary about the Internet is that it facilitates many-to-many two-way communication patterns. Prior to the Internet, the last technology that had any real effect on the way people sat down and talked together was the table. There was no technological mediation for group conversations. The closest we got was the conference call, which never really worked right—"Hello? Do I push this button now? Oh, shoot, I just hung up." It's not easy to set up a conference call, but it's very easy to email five of your friends and say "Hey, where are we going for pizza?" So ridiculously easy group forming is really news. (n.p.)

In addition, research shows that students are more task-attentive and positively collaborating around the computer than in non-computer-supported tasks (Svensson, 2000). Often, this is because the nature of the collaborative computer-based task is new, exciting, and requires different skills and language than previous tasks. It also might be because students feel that more individualized instruction and help are available. Research in these areas will continue to shed light on how and why collaboration and social communication lead to learning.

In classrooms, teachers and students often participate in a combination of the communication patterns and processes noted in Figure 3.1—most commonly simple one-way outbound communication in the format of a lecture or presentation—but sometimes in variations of cooperative or collaborative tasks. Creating tasks in which students interact socially can be challenging, but teachers need to understand how to promote social interaction through technology-supported communication tasks in order to help students achieve. The discussion of communication tasks in the next section will assist in that challenge. First read what two classroom teachers have to say about classroom interaction in From the Classroom: Classroom Interaction.

Is Mr. Finley's task cooperative or collaborative? Why do you think so? What kinds of interaction patterns does his mystery project support? Give examples.

_____

_____

_____

FROM THE CLASSROOM

Classroom Interaction

Students involved in group projects will have a positive experience with writing, reading, and speaking English when the emphasis is placed on the group versus on the individual. Students practice reading, writing, and speaking English through brainstorming of ideas. Through peer editing and revising students are involved in using/learning language. Using technology to locate information and publish group activities encourages careful use of reading strategies, following directions, creative thinking to solve problems, and respect and constructive behavior to accomplish a task. As the classroom setting becomes a group of students accustomed to sharing common interests and pursuits, mutual respect, trust, acceptance, responsibility, and self-evaluation will be fostered. These are lifelong skills needed to function productively in any society. (Jean, sixth-grade teacher)

While I think that cooperative learning has its place, I am not that enthralled with it. I disagree with always giving kids a specific job to do in a group activity. I think the student learns more from collaborative learning, when he or she is involved with the whole process. I like the idea better of all members sharing ideas to accomplish a task. I don't think all members of a cooperative learning team learn as much as they could because they are limited by their specific tasks. For example, how much learning does the timekeeper really get out of an activity when all he or she is doing is just keeping track of the time? Sure the timekeeper watches, but the timekeeper could be watching a demonstration in the front of the room and learn from observing. I think we want our kids to be actively involved. We want each one of them to be using as many senses as possible when learning. When we purposefully limit them to using only a few senses, I think we are shortchanging them. Collaborative learning, on the other hand, requires all students to be active participants in the learning. Students share in the total experience, and I feel much more learning can take place. I am not saying that cooperative learning does not have any place in the classroom. I think there are times when what we want to teach is accomplishing a task with each member of the group helping with just one role. In those cases I think cooperative learning is great. For the most part, however, my vote would be with collaborative learning. (Susan, fifth-grade teacher)

Characteristics of Effective Technology-Supported Communication Tasks

Like tasks in other chapters of this book, communication tasks span a wide range of structures and content. As noted previously, effective communication is based on social interaction. Other components of effective communication tasks include those summarized in Figure 3.4 and explained here.

FIGURE 3.4 Components of Technology-Supported Communication Tasks	
Component	**Focus**
Content	Based on curricular goals and student needs.
Time	Appropriate for all students to finish their task.
Communication technologies	Help all students access the interaction.
Participants	Knowledgeable audience that can work with students at their level.
Roles	Everyone has a part to contribute.
Intentional focus on learning	Task and pacing help students stay on task.

Content

The content of communication tasks and projects must be based on curricular goals and students' needs.

Time

Time is an important element and is also based on students' needs and on the task. Some classroom communications may take place very quickly, for example, giving instructions. Others, however, take longer, such as creating a joint bill to pass through the multischool student congress. Typically, the more people involved and the more communication required, the more time the task may take. Also, if new technologies must be learned, time must be allotted for students to do so. In addition, students need time to think before responding in order to have the benefits of communication (Kumpulainen & Wray, 2002), and some students may need more time to formulate their communication than others.

Communication technologies

Just as work toward other learning goals can take place without electronic technologies, so can communication. To support social interaction, communications tools should allow for "exploratory and argumentative talk" (Kumpulainen & Wray, 2002, p. 15). However, project participants outside the classroom may not be accessible in a timely manner without the use of electronic tools such as email or the telephone. Additionally, technology can make communication more accessible to learners with different physical abilities. For example, screen readers (discussed further in the Guidelines section of this chapter) that voice the text on a computer page can help students who do not see or read well to understand the content of a communication, and dictation software can help those who cannot type well to speak their messages while the computer translates them into text. Find more information on these assistive tools in the Accessibility and Special Education section of the Resources module of this text's Companion Website (http://www.prenhall.com/egbert).

Communication participants

There are a variety of people who can communicate with students. These include classmates and schoolmates (internal peers), peers from another school or area (external peers), parents, teachers, and content-area specialists (experts), and the general public. Lev Vygotsky (1962, 1978) and other researchers working in the sociocultural tradition show that participants are crucial to student success. These researchers posit that students learn by working through social interaction with the help of others on tasks that are slightly above their current level. Although the tasks could not be performed by the student alone, they are achievable with guidance and collaboration. Research in this area shows that what is learned with peers and others transfers to

other situations over the long term, even when students are later working individually (Cesar, 1998). Find more Vygotsky resources in the Learning Theories section of the Resources module of this text's Companion Website (http://www.prenhall.com/egbert).

Participant roles

As noted previously, communication tasks work effectively when everyone has a part to contribute to the whole. Roles can be structured and assigned by the teacher or they can be chosen less formally by students within their groups. Students can each be responsible for a certain part of the content—e.g., a different set of years in the life of a famous person—and/or a specific part of the process, such as typist, illustrator, editor, and so on.

Learning focus

Socializing, although certainly an important part of the communications process, will not help students learn content—students need to communicate about the concepts rather than just make conversation. Task structure and pacing can help students focus on the goals during tasks that require social interaction.

What form do these components of communication tasks take in Mr. Finley's project? Fill in this chart:

Element	Mr. Finley's Plan
Content	
Time	
Technologies	
Participants	
Roles	
Learning focus	

Student Benefits of Technology-Supported Communication

By communicating around or through technology in tasks with the characteristics listed above, students benefit in many ways. For those students who have access to relevant collaborators and technologies, benefits include

- Not being limited by the school day or the school confines
- Participating in individualized instruction
- Feeling more free to exchange ideas openly
- Being motivated to complete tasks (from Eisenberg, 1992)

As they interact and negotiate meaning with others during communication tasks, students gain in language and content by

- Having access to models and scaffolds
- Thinking critically and creatively about language and content
- Constructing meaning from joint experiences
- Solving problems with information from multiple sources
- Working with different points of view and different cultures
- Learning to communicate in new and different ways, including using politeness tactics, appropriate turn-taking, and taking and giving constructive feedback
- Working with an authentic audience
- Expressing thoughts during learning

In addition, students working in teams can receive additional benefits. For example, teams tend to be better at solving problems, have a higher level of commitment, and include more people who can help implement an idea or plan. During collaboration, students learn and use more communicative strategies (Kumpulainen & Wray, 2002). Moreover, teams are able to generate energy and

interest in new projects. Especially important is that groups can be significantly more effective at reaching a goal than individual students would be. Because teamwork can offer students a chance to work toward their strengths supported by these scaffolds, students with all kinds of barriers to learning can benefit. The role of technology is to connect all students with a variety of audiences and interactants so that they receive the maximum benefit from their communication.

Which of the above benefits would you expect Mr. Finley's students to get from his project? Why? Are there additional ways in which they might benefit?

_____

_____

_____

THE TECHNOLOGY-SUPPORTED COMMUNICATION PROCESS

The process of supporting communication with technology, like the content learning process described in chapter 2, includes the basic categories of planning, developing, and analysis/ evaluation. Following the steps in Table 3.1 can help teachers plan communication and collaboration activities effectively and efficiently.

Planning

During the *planning* stage, teachers should make sure that the process and outcomes are specific, relevant, and based on goals. Using objectives that state what the student will be able to do, to what extent, and in what way will assist in developing the rest of the lesson plan. For example, an objective that states, "The student will be able to describe five ways in which PCs and Macs differ" would

TABLE 3.1 Steps in Creating Technology-Supported Communication	
Planning	1. Choose the goals for the project.
	2. Choose the structure of the activity and other details.
	3. Review other projects for examples and explanations (e.g., those in the resources section of this chapter).
	4. Compile resources and models, check that the technology is available and works.
	5. Prepare ways to help students communicate by, for example, demonstrating how to use emoticons in email messages and using proper turn-taking manners. (For more on emoticons and the language of email, see the chapter 3 Resources module on the Companion Website.)
Development	1. Have students introduce themselves to their collaborators as necessary.
	2. As the project progresses, get copies of all student work, online and off.
	3. Communicate with teachers and other participants directly.
	4. Prepare updates and summaries as needed.
	5. Provide skills lessons as needed.
Analysis and evaluation	1. Thank audiences and/or participants.
	2. Help students to reflect, remember, and assess both good and bad aspects of the process and outcomes.
	3. Share results with participants and other stakeholders.
	4. Analyze overall project for successes, weaknesses, and changes needed.

Source: Adapted from Harris (1995) and 2Learn.ca Education Society of Canada (2005).

be more effective in helping focus the lesson than a very broad objective that states, "Students should understand computers." In addition to clear outcomes, the plan should include how and with whom students should interact. During the planning stage, teachers and students can decide whether technology is needed and if so, what kind of technology and how the chosen technology can meet the needs of students with different abilities. At this point, a review of other technology-supported communication projects might help teachers and students from forgetting something important that can make or break the activity.

During the planning stage the teacher should also find and evaluate potential participants and prepare them to understand the goals and responsibilities of the project. Many electronic lists and Web sites provide details of projects that teachers can join and allow teachers to post their own projects to find participants. iEARN (www.iearn.org) and Kidlink (www.kidlink.org) are two excellent project sites. Kidlink offers projects in many languages so that beginning English language learners can participate. Before they participate in the tasks, students should understand the writing conventions of their partners, especially if they are using a slightly different form of English (British English, for example). In addition, teachers should help students to figure out the language and content knowledge they need to grasp to communicate clearly and effectively during the project.

ELL

Development

The planning stage is the most crucial for creating a successful project, but the teacher's job does not end there. It is essential during the project *development* and implementation stage that the teacher observes students and makes changes in the project as necessary to meet student needs and curricular goals. Providing just-in-time skills lessons and coaching on team-building are also part of this stage.

Analysis

Analysis of the project should be conducted by all participants so that different perspectives are gained. Participants should also take part in the *evaluation* of the task process and product. Finally, the teacher must provide appropriate closure, such as whole group discussion, a summary, or a debriefing about group process. More information on the assessment of communication projects is included in the assessment section of this chapter.

What other steps in planning could Mr. Finley add to his project? What, if anything, did he neglect to do?

_____

_____

_____

Teachers and Technology-Supported Communication

The communication process, as outlined above, can pose any number of challenges for teachers and students, but teachers can make it easier by assuming different roles and giving their students opportunities to teach themselves and others. Technology-supported communication projects can be effective vehicles for providing such opportunities, as described here.

The teacher's role in communication projects

Teachers can take different roles in communication projects depending on the needs of their students. In some instances, for example, with younger or less-English-proficient students, the teacher may provide more help, resources, and structure and fewer truly collaborative tasks. In other projects the teacher may be more of an active facilitator in that she or he

ELL

- Provides structure through choices and limits
- Scaffolds and models
- Provides ongoing feedback

FIGURE 3.5 Roles for Teachers

1. The teacher encourages students to share and initiate.
2. The teacher scaffolds and strategizes with students.
3. The teacher assists in shaping the rules that help everyone participate and understand different perspectives.
4. The teacher paces the task according to student needs and acts as a member of the learning community.

- Addresses issues that come up with lessons on grammar or other skills
- Helps students to deal with any problems that arise

Some teachers may even act as "co-learners" in the task, collaborating with their students to construct meaning during a reciprocal experience. For example, teachers and students can co-learn while using Web-based resources to answer an essential question, as described in chapter 2. Because there is no "right" answer to the task, the teacher can work with students to decide "which is best" or "how it should be done."

Although teachers can take many roles, research shows that students are more willing to help and collaborate when the teacher is a facilitator rather than a guide or an all-knowing sage (Svensson, 2000). Kumpulainen and Wray (2002) outline four effective roles for the teacher in any project. These are shown in Figure 3.5.

The most important role for teachers in communication projects is to understand what their students need and to help them to meet the challenges of the task.

Which of the roles in Figure 3.5 best describe Mr. Finley's role(s) in the mystery project? Why do you think so?

_____

_____

_____

Challenges for teachers

Potential challenges for Mr. Finley and his students in completing his telecommunications project include:

- Dealing with technical difficulties and nonresponses from participants
- Planning around school breaks
- Making sure the distant partners understand the goals and procedures
- Handling inappropriate message content
- Providing just-in-time feedback and scaffolding

Group dynamics, or how people interact in a group, might also be an issue that Mr. Finley and his students must deal with, regardless of the type of interaction. For example, Kumpulainen and Wray (2002) point out that students' social status and other characteristics of group members might lead to breakdowns in participation and collaboration. The guidelines discussed in the next section suggest ways to overcome these barriers.

The more technology, distance, and participants involved in a communication project, the more challenges participants face in keeping the project going and making it an effective learning experience. That does not mean, however, that it is not worth the effort, but rather that careful planning and flexibility are necessary.

What should Mr. Finley do to avoid or meet some of these challenges?

_____

_____

_____

GUIDELINES FOR SUPPORTING COMMUNICATION WITH TECHNOLOGY

Designing Technology-Supported Communication Opportunities

Planning is crucial for the success of any communication project, regardless of how and whether it uses technology. Mr. Finley has chosen participants carefully, matched his project to standards and curriculum, and developed scaffolds to help his students succeed. Two other useful guidelines for planning include considering the context and making safety a primary focus.

Guideline #1: Consider the context. In the chapter's opening scenario, Mr. Finley has planned his task carefully. Among the many resources he will employ, he has decided to use Gaggle.net email as the most efficient way to give his students time to work on the project without having to learn a new technology. Gaggle.net is a Web-based email program to which teachers can control access and that they can set up to meet the needs of their specific students. Mr. Finley's students are familiar with Gaggle.net, and his classroom has a computer with the program set up for each team. For benefits of computer-based resources for students with special needs, see the Tool CloseUp: Assistive Support in Windows and Apple Operating Systems on page 76.

Mr. Finley did have other choices of tools, but he chose the most efficient for his physical context. In classrooms or schools that do not have reliable Internet access, participants still can access collaborators in other ways, such as through fax, phone, or letters, depending on the project timeline and the suitability of the technology to the project. If a classroom has only one computer, a project that is computer intensive for all students probably would not be efficient or effective.

Guideline #2: Safety first. The email tool that Mr. Finley chose (Gaggle.net) is one device that can help keep students safe in the context of the Geography Mystery project. Having children on the Internet is fraught with possible dangers, from accessing inappropriate Web sites to providing access to themselves; given only a child's name and general location, anyone can search the Web and obtain a map to the child's home. (For current statistics on Internet dangers and ideas about how to avoid them, see the excellent Enough is Enough site at http://enough.org/.) Three aspects of safety must be considered to ensure that students are not harmed during communication and collaboration projects.

1. *Classroom and school safety policy.* Many schools and districts have a safe use policy for the technology in their school. Students and parents must read and understand the issues and deal with them swiftly if the rules are broken. Teachers can model their rules on the "Rules for Online Safety" from the Safekids site (safekids.com). These rules for students include:
   - Never give out personal information or passwords, or send a picture without permission.
   - Tell adults if they come across information that makes them uncomfortable.
   - Do not meet online buddies without permission and a chaperone.
   - Do not respond to mean or uncomfortable messages.
   - Make rules with parents for going online.
   - Do not download anything without permission.
   - Do not hurt others or break the law.
   - Teach parents about the Internet.

   Samples of other acceptable use policies are provided by the Virginia Department of Education at http://www.pen.k12.va.us/VDOE/Technology/AUP/home.shtml#samples.

2. *Safe contexts.* There are two issues in providing a safe context—with whom students interact and about what. This aspect is easier to control in face-to-face communication projects, but even within the classroom students can be subjected to harassment, inappropriate interaction, and other types of harm. Teachers should choose participants with whom they are familiar and whom they have evaluated carefully as being able to carry out the project within the boundaries set.

3. *Safe tools.* The Internet can be a scary place, and open-ended software and access are fraught with financial, privacy, legal, and other potential problems. However, Mr. Finley felt that his project would work best by communicating with another class, so he chose Gaggle.net (see Figure 3.6). Gaggle minimizes risks to students by providing Web-based email access focused on

Tool CloseUp: Assistive Support in Windows and Apple Operating Systems

As technology improves, it becomes more accessible to everyone who needs to access it. Communication becomes possible even for severely challenged students. Formerly most assistive tools were add-ons or special purchases, but now a host of tools can be found on every new computer.

Mr. Finley's project can take advantage of many of these tools. For example, because Gaggle.net is Web based, students with visual impairments and those who learn best orally can use *screen readers* that turn text into speech to read the emails to them. Screen readers are built into most new operating systems. Windows XP includes Narrator, and Apple OS X includes the screen reader VoiceOver. For a list of other screen readers see the "list of screen readers" at wikipedia.org.

In addition, during the computer-supported project students with visual impairments can use the magnifier function built into the computer's accessibility features to make the text large enough for them to read comfortably. The user can choose the level of magnification and how the magnified items will appear. In Windows, the user can choose start>control panels and find the magnifier easily.

Students who have trouble typing can use the sticky keys function, which allows the user to press a keyboard command such as Shift or Control only once and have it stay active until pressing another command key. In addition, an onscreen keyboard can make it easier for some students to type. Other accessibility features contained in the computer's operating system are available as needed. Some of the options in Windows XP are shown here.

Accessibility Options

Keyboard | Sound | Display | Mouse | General

StickyKeys

Use StickyKeys if you want to use SHIFT, CTRL, ALT, or Windows logo key by pressing one key at a time.

☐ Use StickyKeys   [Settings]

FilterKeys

Use FilterKeys if you want Windows to ignore brief or repeated keystrokes, or slow the repeat rate.

☐ Use FilterKeys   [Settings]

ToggleKeys

Use ToggleKeys if you want to hear tones when pressing CAPS LOCK, NUM LOCK, and SCROLL LOCK.

☐ Use ToggleKeys   [Settings]

☐ Show extra keyboard help in programs

[OK]   [Cancel]   [Apply]

Find the accessibility options offered by the operating system on your computer and list them here. Which ones might help you use the computer more effectively?

_____

_____

_____

_____

Tutorial

CW

For more information on Assistive Support in Windows and Apple Operating Systems, see the Assistive Support in Windows and Apple Operating Systems in the Tutorials module on the Companion Website (http://www.prenhall.com/egbert).

classroom use. It filters all messages and provides access to a variety of administrators and other participants, and it includes message boards that are monitored for content and chat rooms just for the school. The teacher can review all messages, and the system sends the teacher messages that might have inappropriate content. In addition, teachers can develop a list of inappropriate words that the software monitors. Teachers have the power to deny student access to their account and can block **spam,** or unsolicited, unwanted, or inappropriate messages, from external domains. Mr. Finley felt that using Gaggle could help keep his students safe during the telecommunication project that he designed. He could also have chosen tools from a wide variety of student-safe offerings, including Kidmail (kidmail.net), www.epals.com, and other emailing options and filtering software such as NetNanny (http://www.netnanny.com/), so he could access and control what comes in and out of students' email boxes.

Read a classroom teacher's comments on the safety procedure at his school in From the Classroom: Safety.

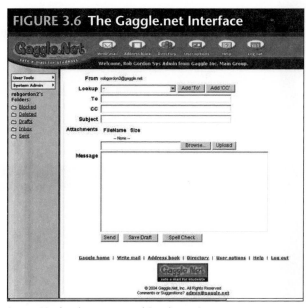

FIGURE 3.6 The Gaggle.net Interface

Source: Used with permission of Gaggle.net, Inc.

FROM THE CLASSROOM

Safety

Our students have to get a form signed by their parents allowing them to use the Internet. It also acts as a contract stating that the student will follow the school guidelines on Internet use. Furthermore, their core teacher has to sign the form, agreeing with the student and the parent that the student will use the Internet for appropriate, scholastic reasons. So in order for the student to have Internet use, not only does the parent have to sign the form but the student and the teacher as well. (Adrian, sixth-grade teacher)

Guideline #3: Teach group dynamics and team building skills. When students work face to face around or with the support of the computer they can use *pragmatic cues* such as facial expressions and gestures to help with understanding. It is sometimes difficult for students to work well in teams even when they do have these cues. When students work through the computer, these cues are absent, and therefore meaning has to rely solely on text. Lack of pragmatic cues can lead to miscommunication, misunderstanding, or worse, particularly if students from diverse backgrounds are participating. Therefore, students in all contexts need to develop or reflect on team building and group dynamics skills. In addition to clearly communicating the process and product expectations to students, teachers can help them learn to understand and work within groups by making sure that they can:

- State their views clearly, and provide constructive criticism.
- Listen to others and take criticism, intended or unintended.
- Evaluate information that affects both their individual contribution and the group product.
- Define their roles.
- Deal with dissent; ask about miscommunications or misunderstandings (conflict resolution).
- Use appropriate levels of politeness and language.
- Develop an effective self-evaluation process.

Scenarios, modeling, and role-plays can be effective tools for developing these skills.

Guideline #4: Provide students with a reason to listen. Teaching students to listen actively to each other is no easy task. However, if they do not develop this skill, time on task is lessened and learning is less successful. Often teachers assume that students will listen because they are expected to, but this does not always happen. A great project that does not require students to listen to each other wastes some of the most effective learning opportunities. For example, a group presentation aimed solely at getting a grade from the teacher typically isolates the rest of the class from the knowledge being presented, especially if the topic of the presentation is the same for the group before and the group after. Likewise, chats, online discussions, or even emails that are too long, too unstructured, or in which it is difficult to find the relevant information can also allow students not to listen. Students are more likely to listen actively if they have a good reason to do so, and project structures can give that reason. For example, teachers can provide "listening" handouts on which students have to record some of the information for future use, or assign students the role of presentation evaluator. In addition, authentic tasks in which outcomes are not all the same help students to listen. Figure 3.7 on page 78 presents a summary of these guidelines.

What did Mr. Finley do to get his students to listen to each other? What other structures can you think of to give students a reason to listen?

_____

_____

_____

FIGURE 3.7 Guidelines for Designing Opportunities for Communication

Guidelines	Explanation
Consider the context.	• Use technologies that work with the students, audience, and task.
Make safety a primary focus.	• Review the classroom and school safety policies. • Choose safe technologies and a safe audience. • Work with parents.
Teach group dynamics and team-building skills.	• Help students understand how to work effectively in groups with people of all kinds.
Provide students with a reason to listen.	• Provide opportunities for students to listen actively for important information. • Make the information crucial to their success.

COMMUNICATION TECHNOLOGIES

Guidelines like those above are useful for developing communication tasks, but the right tool is essential. Egbert (2005) notes, "Many educators believe that technology's capability to support communication and collaboration has changed the classroom more than any of its other capabilities. In fact, it is how educators make *use* of that capability that can change classroom goals, dynamics, turn-taking, interactions, audiences, atmosphere, and feedback and create a host of other learning opportunities" (pp. 53–54). One crucial aspect of effective use is a tool that fits the tasks that they are requiring of their students. There can be many such tools, from MS Word's commenting feature, with which the teacher and peers can communicate about a student's writing (Figure 3.8), to Yahoo! Messenger with Voice (Figure 3.9), through which students can communicate both in text and orally.

Shirky (2003) states, "The number of people writing tools to support or enhance group collaboration or communication [what he calls social software] is astonishing" (n.p.). This rapid growth attests not only to the value of social connections, but also to the importance of those connections to life and learning. Wikis and weblogs (described in Table 3.2) are some of the more recent developments in social software, but often the older (and sometimes simpler) tools such as tape recorders and basic email can provide what teacher and students need, and these tools can be more accessible to a variety of users.

FIGURE 3.8 MS Word Commenting

My Family

My family is not <u>vere</u> big. I have to <u>bruthers</u> and a sister and a mom and a dad and a dog. We live in a house. <u>Sumtims I fite with my bruthers but I still like them.</u> My sister is little. We all like to use computers.

Comment: Check your spelling here. Sometimes words don't look like they sound, right?

Comment: Can you tell us more about what your family likes to do?

Source: Reproduced with permission of Yahoo! Inc. © 2007 by Yahoo! Inc. Yahoo! and the Yahoo! logo are trademarks of Yahoo! Inc.

FIGURE 3.9 Yahoo! Messenger with Voice

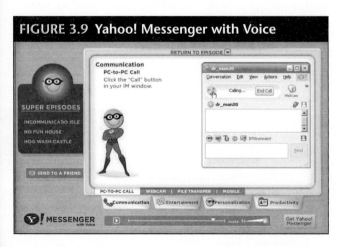

In addition to telephones and other communication technologies that are fairly ubiquitous, Table 3.2 describes tools that can facilitate communication *through* the computer. It is by no means an exhaustive list, but it includes many tools commonly used in schools. Where the software or Web site lists a specific grade level it has been included, but most of these tools can be adapted for a variety of student skills and levels. For more detailed descriptions of these tools, look them up in online dictionaries at http://webopedia.com and http://dict.die.net/email/.

Two-way interactive video and other communication technologies that are also used frequently for distance education or elearning are described in chapter 8.

TABLE 3.2 Examples of Communication Tools

Tool and Examples	Description	Sample Classroom Uses
MOO • Schmooze schmooze.hunter.cuny.edu (cross-cultural communication) • Digital Space Traveler www.digitalspace.com/traveler (any) • Mundo Hispano www.umsl.edu/moosproj/mundo.html	• Text- or graphics-based virtual worlds • Accessible by a large number of users simultaneously • Users type in words to "talk" to other users • Synchronous • Some have voice capabilities and include 3D and color graphics	*MOO visitors can:* • Converse with people from many different places • Collaborate on building new parts of the MOO • Play interactive games • Find resources and ideas A collaborative MOO treasure hunt can be fun!

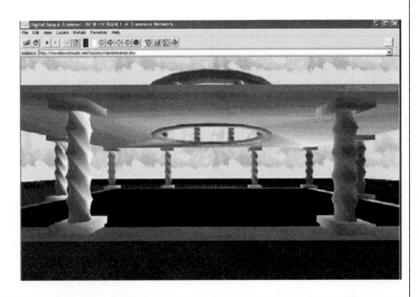

An Entrance to the Traveler's Network at Digital Space Traveler

Source: Used with permission of Bruce Damer.

Text chat/voice chat/instant messaging (IM) • MSN Messenger messenger.msn.com • Yahoo Messenger Messenger.yahoo.com • ICQ ("I Seek You") http://www.icq.com/	• Synchronous, interactive messaging • Does not typically lend itself well to intensive consideration of an issue or to use by learners who need more time • Available through cell phones, handhelds, and other types of hardware • Usually involves the use of a special "language" built of abbreviations (For more information, see the "text message abbreviations" entry in http://www.webopedia.com)	• Chat is useful when students can type well and the teacher wants everyone to have a chance to participate (and not be outshouted) • Voice chat can be useful for longer discussions of issues with collaborators at a distance • Computer video cameras can also be connected and used with chats for short demonstrations or sharing

continued

TOOLS

TABLE 3.2 Continued

Tool and Examples	Description	Sample Classroom Uses
Email (electronic mail) • Pine www.washington.edu/pine • Eudora www.eudora.com • Gaggle www.gaggle.net • Microsoft Outlook office.microsoft.com	• Sent asynchronously over the Internet • Requires the user to have the recipient's email address • For a discussion of netiquette, or rules for using email, see the Resources module on this chapter's Companion Website (http://www.prenhall.com/egbert)	• Email communication is useful for asynchronous conversation during tasks when participants need time to do something between messages • Email allows documents to be attached and shared
Electronic Discussion Forum and Courseware • Blackboard www.blackboard.com • Webworkzone Webworkzone.com • Daedalus Integrated Writing Environment www.daedalus.com • Yahoo groups groups.yahoo.com • Nicenet Nicenet.org (free)	• Asynchronous • Threaded so that replies and conversation turns are obvious • Discussions are included in most courseware packages • Often used in hybrid (face-to-face with distance components) and distance courses (described further in chapter 8)	• Students can have an ongoing conversation that they can access from any computer that has the software (usually just a Web browser) • Team spaces can provide a place for members to post tasks during the process and to discuss their ideas privately • The teacher and students can have a permanent record of the discussions

The Interface of Nicenet, a Free Web-Based Forum

Source: Used with permission of Nicenet.

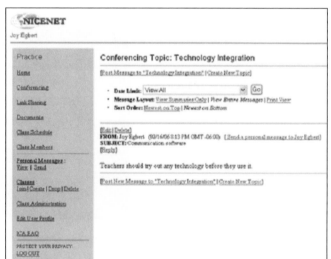

| Electronic list
See a list of education lists and electronic journals at www.edwebproject.org/lists.html | • Often known as a "listserv"
• Messages posted by users through their email arrive in the inbox of all users who subscribe to the list
• Asynchronous | • Students can communicate with experts by finding and joining a list to discuss a specific topic such as the Vietman War, polynomial equations, or the use of technology in education
• A list is a good way to disseminate a message to a large group of people |

TOOLS

TABLE 3.2 Continued

Tool and Examples	Description	Sample Classroom Uses
Weblog (Blog) • VisitMyClass www.visitmyclass.com • Blogger www.blogger.com	• Web site where users can add comments to the original content posted by an individual author • Only the author can modify or delete messages once they are posted • Typically used as an individual's personal journal • Asynchronous • Covers all range of subjects from the blog author's point of view	• Students can quickly and easily post messages, photos, and graphics and interact with others • Keep a class journal • Post handouts • Share with external stakeholders • Keep parents informed, especially if the blog has tools to "push" the information to subscribers' computers
Opening Screen at Blogger.com *Source:* Blogger logo © Google, Inc. Used with permission.		
Voice email • Talksender (download free from http://www.tucows.com/preview/164878 • Vemail http://www.nch.com.au./vemail/ • MailAmp http://www.mailamp.com/	• Allows the user to send a recorded audio message through the Internet	• Students with physical barriers to typing or who are still developing written skills can use voice email to communicate in the same way that others use email • Students can keep audio journals • Students can communicate with distant "voice" pals
Wiki • Wikipedia http://www.wikipedia.org/ • EvoWiki http://wiki.cotch.net/ (science topics)	• Asynchronous • Collection of work by any number of people, all of whom can modify the content	• Wikipedia is an Internet encyclopedia being built by users from all over the world • Students can add information to any topic • Students can understand topic views from many perspectives

Some of the tools listed in Table 3.2 are free (called **freeware**); others are shareware. **Shareware** is software that users can test, and if they decide to keep it they pay a small fee to the developer. Typically, freeware and shareware are created by individuals or small groups of developers. Other tools in the table are commercial products sold by software companies. They vary in how easy they are to use and what they can do. Commercial products are usually more sophisticated and have many more features, but that does not always make them better for classroom

TOOLS

Tool CloseUp: Asia Inspirer

As implied in this chapter, the designation of software as *communication* software characterizes how the software is *used*, not what it *contains*. Asia Inspirer (Tom Snyder Productions) has teams of students (or, alternatively, the whole class or a single team) traveling in contiguous countries throughout Asia to land in countries that have specific demographic, economic, and/or geographic features. The accompanying trip assignment image shows the features that one team must aim for. They are trying to land in countries that have the most tea and lumber and end up in a country with a specific population density on the last of their 10 moves.

Each student on the team has a different map of Asia that shows one or more of the features, and students must pool their information to travel to countries with the highest number of features to earn the most points from their travels. Student interaction is initiated not only by the need to cooperate on the facts but also on the need to figure out how they will cooperate at all. They have to negotiate turn-taking, leadership, and other roles in the group in addition to describing and answering questions about the countries on their maps. The level and amount of interaction is up to the team, and the maps provide scaffolding, so even limited-proficient language learners can join in easily. In addition, the teacher chooses the difficulty level, timer settings, and different configurations (head-to-head competition or team cooperation); this provides

slower learners or those who need more time or support with more opportunity to participate.

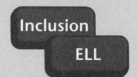

Source: Used with permission of Tom Synder Productions.

Asia Inspirer is designed for use in the one-computer classroom. Groups take turns inputting their moves while the rest of the groups are plotting their routes at their desks. In this way the objectives of learning Asian geography and economy and of collaborating are central, and the technology is used as support for goals.

Under what circumstances might a teacher choose to use a program with these features with the whole class? With teams? For a single team? Why?

_____

_____

_____

_____

use. As with any tool, teachers should check them carefully for characteristics that support effective and/or efficient learning before adopting them for classroom use.

Most teachers probably think of telecommunication tools as those mentioned in Table 3.2, but software packages can both directly and indirectly support communication. Even common software packages such as word processors can be used for collaboration; as noted in chapter 2 and above, the "comment" function in Microsoft Word allows learners to comment on one another's work in writing inside the document. Voice (oral) annotations are also possible and are a good alternative for students who do not type well, who have physical barriers, or whose written skills are not understandable.

In addition, much of the software from educational software companies such as Tom Snyder Productions (www.tomsnyder.com) is based on student collaboration. Packages such as the Inspirer (geography/social studies), Decisions, Decisions (government/social studies), and Fizz and Martina (math) series are aligned with content-area standards and have built-in mechanisms for collaboration. The teachers' guides that accompany these software packages also include ideas about how to make the collaboration work for all learners, including ELLs. Perhaps essential for some contexts, much of the Tom Snyder software is intended for students to work with as a class in the one-computer classroom. However, more important than *how* the software connects learners is *why* and *with whom* learners connect. Much content-based software guides students into predetermined conclusions, and teachers must take care to make sure that those conclusions are equitable and socially responsible. See the Tool CloseUp: Asia Inspirer on the previous page for more information about students interacting around the computer.

Choose a communication tool to investigate further. What features might be useful for the way you plan to teach? Why? Be creative in your thinking and response.

LEARNING ACTIVITIES: COMMUNICATION TASKS

Communication opportunities are mentioned throughout this book because learning results from the interaction that takes place during these opportunities, regardless of the task goal. Many of the activities in this book have a communication component. Although examples of telecommunications projects like Mr. Finley's abound, there are fewer examples of communication projects in which students work around and with the support of technologies, as in the Asia Inspirer example in the Tool CloseUp. However, in addition to the tools listed previously, Web sites and other Internet tools, such as the free tools on the Intel Education Thinking Tools Web site (http://www.intel.com), provide an amazing number and variety of opportunities for students to communicate around, with, *and* through technology.

This section presents examples of communication activities. Each of the examples described begins with a content-area standard as its goal. All examples also address the technology standard that students learn to communicate effectively with and to a variety of audiences. Audiences for the examples are included; an internal peer refers to a classmate or schoolmate, and an external peer is someone in another school, district, region, or country. Teachers are not included as participants in these examples because it is a given that much classroom communication will be aimed at or filtered through them.

In the activities, students work around, with the support of, and through the computer. As you read the activities, reflect on how the guidelines from this chapter might be applied in each case and which technologies from Table 3.2 starting on page 79 might be used to support the learning opportunities.

Standard: Physical Education—Demonstrate the ability to influence and support others in making positive health choices.	
Participants	**Activity**
Internal peers	Create and present a multimedia presentation for younger students about some aspect of health and fitness.
External peers	Through email, build an argument that uses online and offline resources to convince peers to try your favorite healthy recipe.
Experts (doctors)	Check WebMD.com or other sites for advice or information about a health issue and then discuss any questions, especially about the answers you found, on Ask a Doctor at http://www.mdadvice.com/ask/ask.htm. Use the findings to create a persuasive essay or letter to the editor.
General public	Develop Web pages that provide feedback about healthy eating, or create a survey that provides results about how healthy a particular diet is.

Which of these activities involve simple communication? Collaboration?

_____

_____

_____

Standard: Science—Students develop understanding of organisms and environments.	
Participants	**Activity**
Internal peers	Work together to build an electronic text on animal habitats. Present the text to students in other grade groups to help them prepare for a test.
External peers	Complete a series of science mysteries using the format that Mr. Finley developed. Use mystery animals from another region of the world as the subjects of the project.
Experts	Complete a habitat WebQuest, such as the one at http://questgarden.com/47/03/2/070226113229, and then have the products evaluated by local scientists or zoo personnel.
General public	Prepare the lesson on animal habitats located at http://school.discovery.com/lessonplans/programs/habitats/. Develop the Mystery Animals extension of the lesson and post the mysteries to the Web for others to guess.

Science Example: Mad Sci (http://www.madsci.org/)

In addition to features such as links, lessons, "random knowledge," the Visible Human tour, and lots of fun experiments, the Mad Sci site provides Ask-a-Scientist. Be sure that students understand the rules of use, published clearly on the site, before they pose questions to the experts. Students should also learn how to write succinct, pointed questions that experts can answer in a short amount of time. The people who run the site and its policies and procedures are clearly stated, making it easy for teachers to decide whether this is a safe site and how it can best be used. Use the information in "Setting Up an Ask the Expert Service" to create your own expert site.

Review Guideline #4 on page 77. What gives students a reason to listen during these activities? What group skills do they need in order to succeed?

_____

_____

_____

Participants	Activity
Internal peers External peers Experts General public	Work with internal peer teams using a worksheet and Web site such as those presented in Figure 3.10 from Education World to find out more about local democracy. Take one political organization or body (who serve as experts) to interview, or each team member can gather information on one aspect of each organization, by email, telephone, or face to face. Then create a report to share with the rest of the class. Build posters to hang in town so that the general public is also informed. Work with external peers to compare and contrast community decision makers across states, regions, and countries.

Standard: Social studies—Work together to promote the values and principles of American democracy.

FIGURE 3.10 Education World Internet Scavenger Hunt Democracy in Your Hometown

Name: _____

Directions: What do you know about people who make big decisions for a community? Explore the Web site provided below. Then read each statement and answer each question based on the information on the Web site. Three possible answers appear below each question. Circle the correct answer.

Web Resource: Hometown U.S.A http://www.pbs.org/democracy/inyourtown/hometown/index.html

1. Commuters are discussing how to spend the local transportation budget. Who will decide whether to spend the money on more buses or on better roads?

   police chief   governor   city council

2. A school is looking for a new principal. Who is responsible for finding and hiring the person who will do the best job?

   PTA   school board   mayor

Source: Reprinted with permission of Education World, Inc.

Social Studies Example: Voices of Youth (http://www.unicef.org/voy/)

Current discussions on this site supported by UNICEF
include "education for all," tsunami bracelets, and "what is your school like?", posted by students from around the world. The site includes Youth Digital Diaries to listen and add to, a one-minute video contest about international issues, and both research data and steps for action by students. Figure 3.11 presents opportunities offered on the Voice of Youth home page.

In what other ways could this social studies standard be met? How can technology help (or hinder) communication or collaboration centered on this standard?

_____

_____

_____

FIGURE 3.11 Voices of Youth

Source: Used with permission of UNICEF.

···

Standard: Math—Organize and consolidate mathematical thinking through communication. Communicate thinking coherently and clearly to peers, teachers, and others.	
Participants	**Activity**
Internal peers	Collaborate in groups around one computer as the teacher facilitates Fizz and Martina's Math Adventure (Tom Snyder Productions). Communicate answers and understandings as the work progresses.
External peers	Work on a math activity, such as The Cylinder Problem, at http://mathforum.org/ brap/wrap/elemlesson.html. Email understandings and questions to peers who are also studying this problem. Together, the groups come to solutions and conclusions.
Experts	Work with family members to perform the same calculations. Use the Family Math Activity provided by Math Forum at http://mathforum.org/brap/wrap/familymath.html.
General public	Write word problems and challenge members of the public to solve them, through email, a Web site, or public mail.

Math Example: The Globe Program Student Investigations (http://www. globe.gov/)

At this site, teachers and their students can join any number of collaborative student investigations with peers from around the world, submit reports and photos of their projects, and discover information from other projects.

What other math activities lend themselves well to collaboration and communication? List three, then add Web sites or other technologies that might enhance these activities for your grade level and curricular goals.

_____

_____

_____

···

Standard: English—Students adjust their use of spoken, written, and visual language to communicate effectively with a variety of audiences for different purposes.	
Participants	**Activity**
Internal peers External peers Experts General public	Write a persuasive essay collaboratively. Share the essay with internal and external peers for feedback and get help with content from experts during the process. Publish a hard copy of the paper at the school or a digital copy in an electronic forum for public consumption and response.

In what other ways can students communicate or collaborate around writing?

_____

_____

_____

Sandard: ESL—Use English to participate in social interaction.	

Participants	Activity
Internal peers	Work on a project using Tom Snyder Productions' Cultural Reporter books and templates. Conduct interviews, library research, and use other resources to find answers to a question about American culture.
External peers	Use the SchMOOze University MOO (described in Table 3.2) to meet and converse with peers from around the world.
Experts	Go to Dave's ESL Café (http://www.eslcafe.com/) to ask questions about grammar and other language and culture issues.
General public	Create an electronic forum using Blogger or another platform to discuss idioms, jargon, and colloquial speech from all over the United States. Ask follow-up questions to contributors and thank them for their participation.

ELL

What do teachers need to consider before asking ELLs to interact socially? Brainstorm a list of challenges with your peers.

_____

_____

_____

Multidisciplinary Example: iEARN (http://www.iearn.org/)

One of the most popular sites on the Web for "collaborative educational projects that both enhance learning and make a difference in the world," the International Education and Resource Network (I*EARN) provides three different types of opportunities for students and schools—to join an existing project, to develop a project relevant to their curriculum, or to join a learning circle. Projects span content and skill areas and include students from countries around the world. One ongoing project is the Art Miles Mural, in which students are attempting to create three miles of themed murals and capture a record in the *Guinness Book of World Records*. Other projects, on topics from folktales to funny videos and values to sports, incorporate every subject area and result in a product or exhibition that is shared with others. Figure 3.12 shows part of the amazing list of social studies projects underway.

Communicating in Limited Technology Contexts

Benefits of using the kinds of ready-made projects provided by I*EARN, described above, include the support that is available, such as tips for helping participants understand each other, software that is accessible for learners with slow Internet access, and offline work for students in limited technology contexts.

Of course, there are classrooms around the world that do not have access and cannot participate in the electronic portion of these amazing technology-enhanced projects. That does not mean that they are not valuable as interactants. Teachers and students

FIGURE 3.12 iEARN Social Studies Projects

Projects

Main
Creative/Language Arts
Science/Technology/Math
Culture and Society
Learning Circles
Alphabetical Project List
Search Project Database
Forum Tutorial

Social Studies

- **Against Scholar Dropout** -A place for students, parents, teachers and others responsible for education to think about the main problems in education.
- **Ancestor Photographs Project** - Create a world of past times making them as close to the contemporaries as possible.
- **Architecture and Living Spaces** - Student research the architecture and history of the houses, buildings and monuments of their town.
- **Atlas de la Diversidad** - A multi-media database of cultural products, created by the students, as the outcome of their learning.
- **Backtalk Journal: International News Magazine** - Students participate by contributing interviews of people, who play some kind of leadership role in service to sustainable development, for publication .
- **Breaking the Silence** - This project serves to raise awareness of issues pertaining to disease prevention in adolescents.
- **Breaking the Silence: The Trans-Atlantic Slave Trade Project** - Joining together in a serious examination of the legacy of the Trans-Atlantic Slave Trade (TST).
- **Bullying Project** - A collaborative attempt to address the issues of bullying, teasing and school violence.
- **Celebrations and Mournings** - A project to collect statements, pictures, poems and stories from children and their teachers about what they do when they are happy or sad.
- **Child Labour Project** - Youth collaboration in research and awareness-raising on the issues of child labour and exploitation.
- **Child Soldier Project** - This is a project where youth can bear witness to the issue of the child soldier and how it affects their lives, their families, their communities and their countries.
- **Cities Near the Sea** - Learning and working together by students

Source: Used with permission of iEARN-USA.

FROM THE CLASSROOM

Follow-Along

Last year I participated with my class in a wonderful Web-based project where a group of teachers registered as part of Iditarod. We shared general information about our classes: age, demographic, geographic location, etc. This information was posted in a list-serv. There were suggested activities and opportunities for classes to interact with one another as we researched the history of the Iditarod and followed the race itself in March. Each of my table groups picked a musher to follow through the race. They emailed the musher—all but one group received personal email responses from the musher. There are tons of resources that accompany the project, some submitted by teachers, others by the Web master. It connected the kids with real action following the daily postings of the Iditarod race. (Jennie, first-grade teacher)

need to reflect on how to communicate and collaborate with peers regardless of their access to electronic technologies.

Other Communication Projects

Some particularly powerful learning experiences based on communicating come from follow-alongs, in which classes interact with experts and adventurers around the world as they travel through space, bicycle around the world, compete in the Iditarod, or make discoveries along the Amazon River. For examples of these and other communication projects, teachers can conduct a Web search with the terms "student examples" and "telecommunications projects." This search will provide more responses than it is possible to review. To make the search more useful, add a content area, grade level, and other details to the search. Teachers do not necessarily need to develop projects from the ground up—there are plenty of project frameworks and examples for teachers to join or use in developing their own. Of course, teachers should give credit to the originator of the lesson or project and modify it to fit their specific contexts.

Read as a classroom teacher describes a follow-along in which her class participated in From the Classroom: Follow-Along.

Find a project (either online or one that you created) that fits the grade level and content area in which you will teach. Consider the content and technology standards and technology accessibility. Does this project meet the guidelines and incorporate the tips from this chapter? If not, what changes or additions would you make to have it do so?

_____

_____

_____

ASSESSING COMMUNICATION TASKS: RUBRICS

The wide variety of communication activities noted in the previous section, along with the diversity in student skills, goals, and needs in every classroom, indicate that student achievement during communication tasks should be assessed at different times in different ways. This section describes ways to assess student process and outcomes during communication tasks. Other assessments throughout this text may also be applicable to the assessment of communication tasks—as you read other chapters, keep this in mind.

Planning

In the planning stage, teachers can check on the effectiveness of the project design using the Lesson Analysis and Adaptation Worksheet (found at the end of chapter 1 and in the Lesson Planning module of the Companion Website).

Development

During the project, teachers can use **formative** assessment tools, or tools that help students understand their process and provide feedback to help them work better. Formative assessments include teacher observations. Teachers can make observations using personal digital assistants or other portable technologies in conjunction with checklists like the inclusion checklists from http://www.circleofinclusion.org/ or a teacher-made checklist that notes student progress toward individual goals. Student self-reports—for example, "a list of what I accomplished today" or "a question that came up today"—can also help to make sure that students are on task and that the project is moving toward the goals effectively.

Analysis

To make a **summative** evaluation, in other words, to assess outcomes or products, it is important to strike a balance between team outcome and individual accountability. Peer assessments, based on team participation or progress, are often useful for evaluating individual performance, and if the project consists of online segments, teachers can collect copies of the discussion and other participation examples. Another option for peers is to keep an "I did/he did/she did" list (McNinch, personal communication, 2005). Students list what each team member contributed to the project. The teacher can cross-reference the lists and observations and have a pretty good idea of what was done by whom and perhaps even what affected the group dynamics.

Rubrics are also useful to assess product and process. A rubric provides both criteria for evaluation and the performance levels that should be met. Rubrics also help students to understand what is expected of them throughout the project. Teachers can find many free rubric-makers and sample rubrics on the Web. Some guide the teacher through the whole rubric construction process (e.g., Rubistar, http://rubistar.4teachers.org/), and others supply different rubrics for different types of tasks (e.g., Teach-nology, http://teach-nology.com/web_tools/rubrics/). See Figure 3.13 for rubrics for a cooperative learning project. Even if teachers and students use these technologies, they still need to understand how and why to create assessment rubrics. Prentice Hall School Professional Development's Web site (www.phschool.com/professional_development/assessment/rubrics.html) sums up the following guidelines for rubric development:

1. Specify student behaviors that you will observe and judge in the performance assessment.
2. Identify dimensions of the key behaviors to be assessed. If the assessment tasks are complex, several dimensions of behaviors may have to be assessed.
3. Develop concrete examples of the behaviors that you will assess.
4. Decide what type of rubric will be used: one that evaluates the overall project, one that evaluates each piece of the project separately, a generic rubric that fits with any task, one created specifically for this task, or a combination.
5. Decide what kind of outcomes you will provide to students: checklists, points, comments, or some combination.
6. Develop standards of excellence, or criteria, for specified performance levels.
7. Decide who will score each performance assessment—the teacher, the students (either self-scoring or peer scoring), or an outside expert.
8. Share scoring specifications with other stakeholders in the assessment system—parents, teachers, and students. All stakeholders must understand the behaviors in the same way.

Rubrics are best understood by students when they have a hand in making them. Regardless of who makes the rubric, students must be able to access the criteria and have clear examples of performance levels throughout the project. For example, Mr. Finley provided handouts and mini-lessons during his project. He can use both the completed handouts and his observations to give students feedback on their progress. To measure the outcomes, Mr. Finley will develop a rubric with his students based on the objectives of the project. They will decide together that the important criteria for the project include providing well-written clues based on accurate data, asking good questions, arriving at the correct conclusions, using resources (including technology) appropriately, and making the map correctly. Mr. Finley will then work with the students to clarify each level of performance (excellent, good, fair, poor) and to help them use the rubric to assess their own performance.

Is this evaluation scheme appropriate for Mr. Finley's project? Why do you think so?

FIGURE 3.13 Cooperative Learning Project Rubric

Cooperative Learning Project Rubric A: Process

Name: _____

Date: _____

Class: _____

	Exceptional 4 points	Admirable 3 points	Acceptable 2 points	Amateur 1 point
Group Participation	All students enthusiastically participate	At least 3/4 of students actively participate	At least half the students confer or present ideas	Only one or two persons actively participate
Shared Responsibility	Responsibility for task is shared evenly	Responsibility is shared by most group members	Responsibility is shared by 1/2 the group members	Exclusive reliance on one person
Quality of Interaction	Excellent listening and leadership skills exhibited; students reflect awareness of others' views and opinions in their discussions	Students show adeptness in interacting; lively discussion centers on the task	Some ability to interact; attentive listening; some evidence of discussion or alternatives	Little interaction; very brief conversations; some students were disinterested or distracted
Roles Within Group	Each student assigned a clearly defined role; group members perform roles effectively	Each student assigned a role but roles not clearly defined or consistently adhered to	Students assigned roles but roles were not consistently adhered to	No effort made to assign roles to group members

Cooperative Learning Project Evaluation Form A: Process

Name: _____

Date: _____

Class: _____

	Exceptional 4 points	Admirable 3 points	Acceptable 2 points	Amateur 1 point
Group Participation				
Shared Responsibility				
Quality of Interaction				
Roles Within Group				

COMMENTS:

FIGURE 3.13 Continued

Cooperative Learning Project Rubric B: Outcome or Product

Name: _____

Date: _____

Class: _____

	Exceptional 4 points	Admirable 3 points	Acceptable 2 points	Amateur 1 point
Organization	Extremely well organized; logical format that was easy to follow; flowed smoothly from one idea to another and cleverly conveyed; the organization enhanced the effectiveness of the project	Presented in a thoughtful manner; there were signs of organization and most transitions were easy to follow, but at times ideas were unclear	Somewhat organized; ideas were not presented coherently and transitions were not always smooth, which at times distracted the audience	Choppy and confusing; format was difficult to follow; transitions of ideas were abrupt and seriously distracted the audience
Content Accuracy	Completely accurate; all facts were precise and explicit	Mostly accurate; a few inconsistencies or errors in information	Somewhat accurate; more than a few inconsistencies or errors in information	Completely inaccurate; the facts in this project were misleading to the audience
Research	Went above and beyond to research information; solicited material in addition to what was provided; brought in personal ideas and information to enhance project; and utilized more than eight types of resources to make project effective	Did a very good job of researching; utilized materials provided to their full potential; solicited more than six types of research to enhance project; at times took the initiative to find information outside of school	Used the material provided in an acceptable manner, but did not consult any additional resources	Did not utilize resources effectively; did little or no fact gathering on the topic
Creativity	Was extremely clever and presented with originality; a unique approach that truly enhanced the project	Was clever at times; thoughtfully and uniquely presented	Added a few original touches to enhance the project but did not incorporate it throughout	Little creative energy used during this project; was bland, predictable, and lacked "zip"
Presentation Mechanics	Was engaging, provocative, and captured the interest of the audience and maintained this throughout the entire presentation; great variety of visual aids and multimedia; visual aids were colorful and clear	Was well done and interesting to the audience; was presented in a unique manner and was very well organized; some use of visual aids	Was at times interesting and was presented clearly and precisely; was clever at times and was organized in a logical manner; limited variety of visual aids and visual aids were not colorful or clear	Was not organized effectively; was not easy to follow and did not keep the audience interested; no use of visual aids

continued

FIGURE 3.13 Continued

Cooperative Learning Project Evaluation Form B: Product

Name: _____

Date: _____

Class: _____

	Exceptional 4 points	Admirable 3 points	Acceptable 2 points	Amateur 1 point
Organization				
Content Accuracy				
Research				
Creativity				
Presentation Mechanics				

COMMENTS:

Source: © 2005 Pearson Education, Inc., publishing as Pearson Prentice Hall. Used by permission.

SAMPLE LESSON: COMMUNICATION

Mr. Finley's telecommunications project went very well, and he and his students are excited about trying another project. Mr. Finley decides to look at other communication-based lessons to find another project that might be appropriate for his students. The standards addressed by this lesson include math standards such as problem solving, reasoning, connections, and skills (statistics); content reading standards such as variety of sources, information access, and evaluation; and writing content standards.

The lesson Mr. Finley chose from the Educators Reference Desk (http://www.eduref.org/) is presented here.

MINI STUDY OF A STATE

Author: *Unknown*

Grade Level(s): 4, 5, 6, 7

Subject(s):

• Social Studies/State History

Objectives:
The students will learn to do research while comparing their state with one of the states of the U.S. They will be graded on information, drawing and art work, spelling and punctuation, and neatness.

Activities:
The students are given the following questions in a prepared booklet in which they write their answers. There is also room provided for them to draw the state flag, flower, tree, bird, and a map of the state.

1. Name of state:
2. Capital:
3. Is this state larger or smaller than (*******)?
4. Name all of the states, countries, or bodies of water that surround this state.
5. About how many people live in this state? Is that more or less than (*******)?
6. Name two prominent people that are from this state. Why are they famous?
7. What are the chief products of this state?
8. What kind of climate does this state have?
9. Tell about three things in this state that are very different from (*******).
10. Tell about three things in this state that are much the same as we have in (*******).
11. If you were traveling from_____, (******) to the capital of this state, how many miles would you drive?
12. How long would it take you to drive it if you drove 50 miles an hour?
13. These are facts about this state that I think are interesting . . .
14. I would like to live in this state because . . .
15. I would not like to live in this state because . . .
16. Make a pictorial graph of the population of your state and the state of (********).
17. When did it get its statehood?
18. Who is given credit for finding this state?
19. How did the U.S.A. get the land?
20. Tell three other historic things about your state.
21. Draw the state symbol and give an explanation.
22. What is the state motto?
23. What is the state's nickname?
24. Name three places to visit and tell about these places.

Mr. Finley completed a Lesson Analysis and Adaptation Worksheet (found in chapter 1 on page 33 and in the Lesson Planning module of the Companion Website) and concluded these things about the lesson:

- There are no standards mentioned, but learning about the geography of the states is part of the grade 7 standards.
- Some of the questions ask students to do more than memorize, but 21st-century skills and literacies could be incorporated more.
- No explicit resources are mentioned—a variety is needed.
- Links are made between students' home states and the states they are studying, and all students can actively search for information.
- There is no mention of technology use, but there are obvious ways to integrate it.
- A variety of resources, languages, and options is needed to meet the needs of diverse students.
- No assessment is included.

Mr. Finley likes the basic idea of this lesson and the variety of questions asked. However, based on his analysis and his knowledge of his students, he decides to make some small but important changes to the lesson. He wants to especially make sure that all students have access to the information. In addition to adding appropriate standards, he decides to make these changes based on his analysis:

- Provide students with prescreened resources at a variety of levels and in a variety of media to do the initial investigation of their state. In this way, all students will have information that they can access.

- Provide scaffolds such as formulas, worksheets, and experts to support student responses to the questions. In addition, students can choose to work in groups if they have a plan for completing the work.
- Incorporate seventh-grade keypals (electronic penpals) from each of the states under investigation who can verify and/or discuss responses to students. This telecommunications component will allow students to check the verity of their initial resources and gain different perspectives on some of the information they find.
- Vary the product, allowing students to produce a book, make a poster, or prepare a multimedia presentation. Doing so takes into consideration the variety of skills, abilities, and desires of his students.
- Ask the students to help develop process and product rubrics for the project.

With these changes, Mr. Finley feels that this lesson will help all his students meet many learning goals.

What other changes, if any, should Mr. Finley make to this lesson? Why?

_____

_____

_____

If students are safe and well prepared, communication around, through, and about computers can help them to achieve in a variety of ways. It can also support 21st-century skills such as critical thinking, the topic of chapter 4.

CHAPTER REVIEW

Key Points

- **Define communication, collaboration, and related terms.**

  The boundaries between communication, interaction, cooperation, and collaboration can be blurry. In the simplest sense, "communication" can be seen as the umbrella term. Communication can be one-way or two-way. Communication includes interaction, meaning give-and-take between participants. Interaction can be cooperative or collaborative, both of which require negotiation of meaning. Interaction can also be asynchronous or synchronous. Both types of interaction have advantages and disadvantages.

- **Describe the communication process and explain how communication affects learning.**

  The communication process includes planning, developing, and analysis/evaluation. Each step is important for communication tasks to be effective. This chapter has described the importance of social interaction to learning. Social interaction provides scaffolds for language and content, which help move students to new understandings. Benefits include exposure to new cultures, language uses, views of content, and the use of critical thinking skills.

- **Discuss guidelines and techniques for creating opportunities for technology-supported communication and collaboration.**

  Choosing the best technology for the task and making sure that students are safe while using the chosen tools are paramount objectives for successful projects. Most important for such projects is that tools can be used to facilitate the language and content acquisition of all students, from differently abled to differently motivated. In addition, teaching group dynamics and team-building skills and giving students reasons to listen help avoid communication breakdowns during projects that rely on communication. Fair, useful, and ongoing assessment facilitates students' understanding of their roles, their progress, and the effectiveness of the project. Careful planning that includes these strategies can support effective learning experiences.

- **Analyze technologies that can be used to support communication, including MOOs, email, chat, blogs, and wikis.**

  People probably think of communication tools as telephones, email, and other technologies that students can use to connect through. However, students can also connect around and with the support of technologies such as stand-alone software and Web sites. The technology must be appropriate for the goal, support the intended communication, and be accessible to all participants.

- **Describe and develop effective technology-enhanced communication activities.**

  Teachers can work with students to provide learning experiences that address the needs of a wide range of learners while addressing standards and curricular requirements by:
  - Using the planning, development, and evaluation processes outlined in the chapter
  - Keeping in mind student needs and the physical context
  - Focusing on crucial language and content goals

  This chapter's activity examples provide only a small sample of a very large set of interesting and fun projects that involve communication around, supported by, and through technology. The true scope of projects that include some kind of communication is beyond the ability of this book to address. Teachers can use existing resources and their own (and their students') knowledge and imagination in developing relevant tasks that achieve learning goals.

- **Create appropriate assessments for technology-enhanced communication tasks.**

  A wide range of tools is available for teachers to use in assessment. One tool that can help in a variety of contexts is a rubric-maker. In addition, ready-made rubrics and checklists are available across the Web. Understanding how to develop and use rubrics is an important step in creating appropriate assessments.

Which information in this chapter is most valuable to you? Why? How will you use it in your teaching?

_____

_____

_____

CASE QUESTIONS REVIEW

Reread the case at the beginning of the chapter and review your answers. In light of what you learned during this chapter, how do your answers change? Note any changes below.

1. *What learning benefits might the sixth- and seventh-grade students derive from participating in this telecommunications project?*

_____

_____

_____

2. *How can working with students at another school contribute to Mr. Finley's students' achievement?*

_____

_____

_____

3. *How did Mr. Finley approach the use of technology to meet his goals?*

_____

_____

_____

4. *Can you think of any other ways that Mr. Finley could ensure the success of this telecommunications project?*

_____

_____

_____

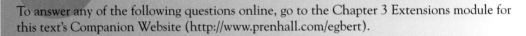

CHAPTER EXTENSIONS • • • • • • • • • • •

To answer any of the following questions online, go to the Chapter 3 Extensions module for this text's Companion Website (http://www.prenhall.com/egbert).

Adapt • • • •

Choose a lesson for your potential subject area and grade level from the lesson plan archives at Educators Desk Reference (http://www.eduref.org/). Use the Lesson Analysis and Adaptation Worksheet from chapter 1 on page 33 (also available in the Lesson Planning module of the Companion Website) to consider the lesson in the context of *communication*. Use your responses to the worksheet to suggest general changes to the lesson based on your current or future students and context.

Practice • • • •

1. *Integrate the standards.* Choose one or more of the activities in the chapter and note which technology standard(s) the tasks can help to meet.
2. *Improve an activity.* Choose a technology-supported activity example from the chapter and add details that would help to make it successful. For example, you may need to outline specific roles, choose a specific technology, or note an important safety tip.
3. *Think about learning.* Choose an activity from the chapter and explain how the communication might lead to learning. Say *what* students will learn, both what is obvious and less obvious.
4. *Create a rubric.* Create a rubric to assess both group process and individual participation for any of the example technology-supported tasks. Use one of the rubric generators listed in the assessment section of the chapter or develop your own.
5. *Reflect on language.* Use the chat abbreviations at http://www.webopedia.com/ to send a message to a friend, peer, or the instructor. Describe how this "language" differs from the classroom language that students must learn and use. How can you use this knowledge in your teaching?

Explore • • • • •

1. *Revise an activity.* Choose one of the learning activities in the chapter and adapt it for your content area and/or grade level. Add or change technology and change the existing audience as necessary. Briefly explain your changes.

2. *Assess.* Review the sample rubric in the assessment section of the chapter. Keeping the general structure and intent, change the question to evaluate a different activity.

3. *Create a project.* Choose a grade level and content area and create a telecommunications project following the guidelines from this chapter. Note what other ideas not mentioned in this chapter should be included, e.g., a different form of assessment or another type of technology.

4. *Explore a tool.* Choose a communication and/or collaboration tool and evaluate it for use by your current or potential students. Make a handout to help students use it effectively or a handout with guidelines for a project using the tool.

5. *Invent a tool.* Be imaginative—invent a tool that would meet the goals for collaboration without any of the challenges we currently experience. What would it look like and do?

REFERENCES

Berger, C., & Burgoon, M. (Eds.). (1995). *Commmunication and social influence processes.* East Lansing, MI: Michigan State University Press.

Cesar, M. (1998). Social interaction and mathematics learning. Nottingham, England: Centre for the Study of Mathematics Education. Retrieved from the World Wide Web on February 23, 2005: http://www.nottingham.ac.uk/csme/meas/papers/cesar.html.

Coleman, D. (2002, March). Levels of collaboration. *Collaborative strategies.* San Francisco, CA: Collaborative Strategies. Retrieved 4/15/05 from the World Wide Web: http://www.collaborate. com/ publication/newsletter/publications_newsletter_march02.html.

Egbert, J. (2005). *CALL Essentials: Principles and practice in CALL classrooms.* Alexandria, VA: TESOL.

Eisenberg, M. (1992). Networking: K-12. *ERIC Digest* ED354903. Retrieved 2/19/05 from http://www.ericdigests.org/1993/k-12.htm.

Harris, J. (1995). Organizing and facilitating telecollaborative projects. *The Computing Teacher, 22*(5), 66–69.

Hofmann, J. (2003). Creating collaboration. *Learning circuits.* Alexandria, VA: American Society for Training and Development. Retrieved February 23, 2005 from the World Wide Web: http:// www.learningcircuits.org/2003/sep2003/hofmann.htm.

Kumpulainen, K., & Wray, D. (Eds.). (2002). *Classroom interaction and social learning: From theory to practice.* New York: RoutledgeFalmer.

Panitz, T. (1996). A definition of collaborative vs. cooperative learning. *Deliberations on Learning and Teaching in Higher Education.* London, England: Educational and Development Unit, London Guildhall University. Retrieved 4/13/05 from http://www.city.londonmet.ac.uk/deliberations/ collab.learning/panitz2.html.

Shirky, C. (2003, April). *A group is its own worst enemy.* Presented at the O'Reilly Emerging Technology conference in Santa Clara, CA. Retrieved 2/20/05 from the World Wide Web: http:// www.shirky.com/writings/group_enemy.html.

Svensson, A. (2000). Computers in school: Socially isolating or a tool to promote collaboration? *Journal of Educational Computing Research, 22*(4), 437–453.

2Learn.ca Education Society. (2005). Explore or join projects@2Learn.ca. Retrieved 2/19/05 from www.2learn.ca/Projects/projectcentre/exjoproj.html.

Vygotsky, L. (1962). *Thought and language.* Cambridge, MA: MIT Press.

Vygotsky, L. (1978). *Mind in society.* Cambridge, MA: Harvard University Press.

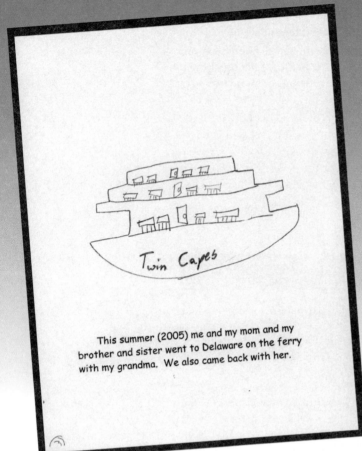

This summer (2005) me and my mom and my brother and sister went to Delaware on the ferry with my grandma. We also came back with her.

4

Supporting Student Critical Thinking

Case: Urban Legends

As you read the following scenario, note how the teacher guides the students to think critically about the information that they receive as a result of technology use.

••••••••••••••••••••••••••••

Mr. Andres's fourth-grade class was abuzz. The noise was coming from near one of the room's computers, where the teacher's aide and one of the students, David Perez, were involved in a discussion in front of the computer. Many of the other students in the class were gathered around listening and commenting. Mr. Andres approached the group to see why so many students seemed to be off the task he had assigned.

"What's up?" he asked as he approached the scene. One of the bystanders explained that David had received an email from his penpal in New York that contained some interesting news. Hmmm, thought Mr. Andres, I've read all the emails and didn't read something that I thought would cause such a stir. He asked David and the aide, "What's this all about?"

David exclaimed excitedly, "Janet is afraid to ride the subway to school any more! She says there are alligators in the sewers that could get into the subway! Is that cool or what?!"

"My," responded Mr. Andres. "Alligators in the sewers of New York? That's interesting." He remembered seeing the story in Janet's email. It was an urban legend, or a popularly believed story, that he had heard before. He had thought that Janet mentioned it as a joke to entertain David.

"Oh, yeah, well, it's true," replied David. "Janet read about it on the Internet. The story said that they were flushed down the toilet as babies by people who didn't want them as pets and now there's lots of them!"

"Ah," said Mr. Andres. "She saw it on the Internet."

Anna, another student, said, "It's not true, is it, Mr. Andres? Tell us!"

Other students chimed in. "Yah, tell us!" "What's up with that?!" "Is that for real?!" they exclaimed.

Then the teacher's aide broke in and said to Mr. Andres, "I've been trying to tell them it isn't true, but they won't listen!"

"Well," said Mr. Andres, "Maybe they need to find out for themselves whether there are alligators in New York's sewers. Sounds like a great project to me. Let's finish up what we're doing and then we'll talk about how we'll discover the truth."

At the end of the class, Mr. Andres had David explain the situation to the rest of the students. Mr. Andres asked how many students thought that there might be alligators under New York City, how many believed that there could not be, and how many weren't sure. Most of the students were not sure.

"How can we find out?" Mr. Andres asked the class.

The students brainstormed how they might find out whether there really were alligators in the sewers of New York City. After brainstorming, the students decided that they needed to read the original story on the Internet that Janet had written about, do some Internet and library research about alligators, discover online and offline resources for information about sewers, and find email contact information for some New York City officials to gather more data. When they had enough useful information from reliable sources, they would decide whether Janet really had a reason to fear.

Mr. Andres thought that this was a great opportunity for his students to develop critical thinking skills such as analysis, evaluation, interpretation, and explanation. At the same time, students would also enhance their technology skills by using a variety of tools; discover more about government agencies, reptiles, and big city life; and practice reading, writing, and other skills that were part of the fourth-grade curriculum.

• •

Answer these questions about the case. There are no right or wrong answers to this chapter preview—the goal is for you to respond before you read the chapter. Then, as you interact with the chapter contents, think about how your answers might change.

1. *What kinds of skills do David and his peers need to use to discover the answer to their question?*

   _____

   _____

   _____

2. *What support should Mr. Andres give to facilitate the students' critical thinking?*

   _____

   _____

   _____

3. *What should Mr. Andres's role be in teaching critical thinking skills?*

   _____

   _____

   _____

4. *What role will technology play in helping the students to think critically?*

   _____

   _____

   _____

Mr. Andres recognized an immediate opportunity to help his students learn and practice critical thinking skills. He made the choice knowing that he was deviating from his original unit plan, but he understands the importance of teachable moments, particularly when they focus on essential skills such as critical thinking. The goal of this chapter is to help you to understand the roles that teachers and technology can play in developing student critical thinking skills. After reading this chapter, you will be able to

- Define critical thinking.
- Understand the role of critical thinking in meeting other learning goals such as creativity and production.
- Discuss guidelines for using technology to encourage student critical thinking.
- Analyze technologies that can be used to support critical thinking, including strategy software to help students organize their thoughts, Web-based tools that both encourage and evaluate critical thinking, content software from companies such as Tom Snyder Productions, and content-free programs such as spreadsheets.
- Create effective technology-enhanced tasks to support critical thinking.
- Employ technology to assess student critical thinking.

When you have completed this chapter, which NETS*T will you have addressed?

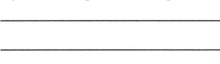

_____

_____

_____

The ideas, sample activities, and technology descriptions provided throughout this chapter will help you understand how to create and take advantage of opportunities to support student critical thinking with technology. To begin, see this chapter's Meeting the Standards for a discussion of critical thinking across the curriculum.

• • • • Meeting the Standards: Critical Thinking • • • •

Critical thinking is fundamental to learner achievement in all subject areas. The following standards represent only a part of the great number and variety of standards that students are expected to meet using critical thinking skills such as analyzing, evaluating, and assessing.

- _Music:_ Listen to, analyze, and describe music (NA-M.9–12.6).
- _Visual Arts:_ Reflect on and assess the characteristics and merits of their work and the work of others (NA-VA.K–4.5).
- _Dance:_ Identify possible aesthetic criteria for evaluating dance (NA-D.5–8.4).
- _Math:_ Analyze change in various contexts (NM-ALG.6–8.4).
- _English:_ Evaluate and synthesize data from a variety of sources. Participate as critical members of a variety of literacy communities (NL-English K–12.7/.11).

- _Health/PE:_ Analyze the influence of culture, media and technology, and other factors on health (NPH.K–4.4).
- _Science:_ Develop abilities necessary to do scientific inquiry (NS.5–8.1).
- _Social Studies:_ Evaluate rules and laws (NSS-C.K–4.1).
- _Technology:_ Evaluate and select new information resources and technological innovations based on the appropriateness for specific tasks (NETS*S).

Critical thinking is essential for students to lead productive lives. Facione (1990) argues that it is also necessary for societies to hang together, stating, "Being a free, responsible person means being able to make rational, unconstrained choices. A person who cannot think critically, cannot make rational choices. And, those without the ability to make rational choices should not be allowed to run free, for being irresponsible, they could easily be a danger to themselves and to the rest of us" (p. 13).

Do you agree with Facione's statement? Why or why not? Write your own statement about the importance of critical thinking.

_____

_____

_____

 Now read the rest of the chapter, starting with the overview of critical thinking, and see if any of your ideas change as you read. Explore the above standards in more detail in the Standards module on this text's Companion Website.

• • • •

OVERVIEW OF CRITICAL THINKING AND TECHNOLOGY IN K–12 CLASSROOMS

In order to implement technology use with a learning focus, teachers need to understand critical thinking before attempting to support it with technology.

What Is Critical Thinking?

Critical thinking skills refer to abilities to analyze, evaluate, infer, interpret, explain, and self-regulate (Facione, 1990; vanGelder, 2005). A simple way to define critical thinking is the ability to make good decisions and to clearly explain the foundation for those decisions. When using technology, being able to think critically allows one to:

- Judge the credibility of sources.
- Identify conclusions, reasons, and assumptions.
- Judge the quality of an argument, including the acceptability of its reasons, assumptions, and evidence.
- Develop and defend a position on an issue.
- Ask appropriate clarifying questions.
- Plan experiments and judge experimental designs.
- Define terms in a way appropriate for the context.
- Be open-minded.
- Try to be well-informed.
- Draw conclusions when warranted, but with caution. (Ennis, 1993, p. 180)

To some extent all humans, even very young children, continually think critically to analyze their world and to make sense of it. However, most people's skills are not as well developed as they could or should be. Sarason (2004) adds that schools are not the most productive learning environments for critical thinking, and that schools need to take a stronger focus on critical thinking.

Critical thinking is part of a group of cognitive abilities and personal characteristics called **higher order thinking skills** (HOTS). These skills also include creative thinking (chapter 5) and problem solving (chapter 6). This list of cognitive skills is based on the well-known *Bloom's Taxonomy of Educational Goals* (Bloom, 1956). Bloom's first three competencies—knowledge, comprehension, and application—are generally equated with the acquisition of declarative knowledge (discussed in chapter 2). The second three competencies—analysis, synthesis, and evaluation—are generally considered critical thinking or higher order skills. Figure 4.1 on page 102 presents an example of critical thinking skills from Bloom's taxonomy and the types of technology-enhanced tasks that might support them during Mr. Andres's class project. Anderson and Krathwohl (2001) recently revised Bloom's taxonomy to add a "metacognitive knowledge" category and to make it easier for teachers to design instruction that requires critical thinking. Excellent resources for using the revised taxonomy are available from Kurwongbah State School in Australia at http://www.kurwongbss.eq.edu.au/thinking/Bloom/blooms.htm. See the Learning Theories section of the Resources module of the Companion Website (http://www.prenhall.com/egbert) for more resources on Bloom's taxonomy and critical thinking.

Critical thinking has been central to education since the time of Socrates (469–399 B.C.E.). The focus of the Socratic method is to question students so that they come to justify their arguments; this teaching strategy is still used in many classrooms to foster critical thinking. One software program, Reason!Able (see this chapter's Tool CloseUp: Reason!Able), even has Socrates asking questions so that students can reflect on their work. Other critical thinking software provides tasks that require critical thinking and includes prompts to help students understand how to come to effective decisions. Regardless of the tool that students use to support their critical thinking, it is important to note the crucial role of critical thinking skills both in school and out. In fact, since Socrates, philosophers throughout history such as Plato, Francis Bacon, Rene

CW

FIGURE 4.1 Higher Order Thinking Skills from Bloom's Taxonomy		
Competence	**Skills Demonstrated**	**Sample Technology-Enhanced Tasks**
Analysis	• Seeing patterns. • Organize parts. • Recognize hidden meanings. • Identify components.	• Students brainstorm about the information they need and the questions they need to ask and make a chart using Inspiration software.
Synthesis	• Use old ideas to create new ones. • Generalize from given facts. • Relate knowledge from several areas. • Predict, draw conclusions.	• Students gather facts from electronic and paper resources about alligators, sewers, and New York and input them into a database. They arrange and study the data to suggest conclusions.
Evaluation	• Compare and discriminate between ideas. • Assess value of theories, presentations. • Make choices based on reasoned argument. • Verify value of evidence. • Recognize subjectivity.	• Students use the Reason!Able software described in the Tools CloseUp in this chapter to evaluate their argument and conclusions about alligators in the sewers before they present their argument to the class.

Source: From Benjamin S. Bloom, *Taxonomy of educational objectives.* Published by Allyn & Bacon, Boston, MA. Copyright © 1984 by Pearson Education. Adapted by permission of the publisher.

Descartes, William Graham Sumner, and John Dewey have emphasized the need for students to think critically about their world.

More specifically, Ellis (2002) notes that critical thinking is one foundation for learning, in part because all of the learning skills are interdependent and, as Paul (2004a) points out, "everything essential to education supports everything else essential to education" (p. 3). For example, as Mr. Andres's students consider how to decide whether they can believe everything they read on the Internet, they use a variety of skills to

- Understand basic content.
- Communicate among themselves and with others.
- Think creatively about resources.
- Assess the veracity of the information they come in contact with.
- Produce a well-supported conclusion.

In other words, they must think critically throughout the process as they develop other learning skills.

It is also clear that critical thinking "has applications in all areas of life and learning" (Facione, 1990, p. 4). Making a good decision about whether to buy a laptop or an iPod, and then which model, requires research, assessment, evaluation, and careful planning, just as deciding what to eat for dinner or how to spend free time does.

Although there may be discipline-specific skills, general critical thinking skills may apply across disciplines and content areas (Ennis, 1992; McPeck, 1992). For example, Facione (1990) notes that critical thinking skills test scores correlate positively with college GPA. Although this is not a *causal* relationship (in other words, the research does not show that effective critical thinking *causes* a high GPA), there appears to be something about students who can think critically that helps them succeed in college. In addition, the processes that students use to think critically appear to transfer or assist not only in the reading process but in general decision making. However, experts disagree to what extent this happens. Some researchers believe that much critical thinking is subject- or genre-specific (Moore, 2004). Nonetheless, all agree that it is crucial to help students hone their critical thinking abilities, and many believe that technology can help by providing support in ways outlined throughout this chapter (Jonassen, 2000).

In addition to the lessons presented in this chapter based on these ideas, other chapters of this book present ideas and activities that involve critical thinking either implicitly or explicitly. As you read through the text, see if you can find those examples. Now read what one classroom teacher says about the relationship between technology and higher order thinking in From the Classroom: Thinking Skills.

Critical Thinking and Media Literacy

Critical thinking, as defined in the previous section, is especially important because media, particularly television and computers, is increasingly prevalent in the lives of K–12 students. Students have always needed to have general **information literacy**, or "knowing when and why you need information, where to find it, and how to evaluate, use, and communicate it in an ethical manner" (CILIP, 2007). However, students who are faced with a bombardment of images, sounds, and text need to go beyond information literacy to interpret and assess (in other words, think critically about) information in new ways. In other words, they must be media literate.

In general **media literacy** means that students are able not only to comprehend what they read, hear, and see but also to evaluate and make good decisions about what media presents. There are many variations on how to support students in becoming media literate (Schwarz & Brown, 2005). For example, the Center for Media Literacy, the world's largest distributor of media education materials, recommends activities such as tracing racial images in the media throughout history, exploring how maps are constructed (and asking "Why does 'north' mean 'up'?"), and challenging gender stereotypes in TV comedies. These activities are crucial because learners of all ages watch TV, and even kindergartners use the computer and may have access to the Internet. Much of what learners read, see, and hear they believe verbatim and share as truth with others, as in this chapter's opening case. This occurs whether the message is intended as fact or not. To become more media literate, teachers and students need to learn and practice critical thinking skills that are directed at the ideologies, purveyors, and purposes behind their data sources. Most important, students must use the Internet responsibly and with the necessary skepticism; in particular, this includes investigative skills and the ability to judge the validity of information from Web sites.

Read what a classroom teacher has to say about getting started with media literacy in From the Classroom: Media Literacy.

There are many resources to help teachers and students to become media literate. One of the best is the Center for Media Literacy's free MediaLit Kit for K–12 Media Literacy (available from http://www.medialit.org/). The kit includes a clear, theory-based definition and outstanding lessons based on the five core concepts of media literacy. The lessons and handouts focus on students learning to ask these five "key questions":

1. Who created this message?
2. What creative techniques are used to attract my attention?
3. How might different people understand the message differently from me?
4. What values, lifestyles, and points of view are represented in, or omitted from, this message?
5. Why is this message being sent?

Another focus of the MediaLit Kit is the "Essential Questions for Teachers" that teachers should ask themselves:

1. Am I trying to tell the students what the message is? Or am I giving them the skills to determine what THEY think the message(s) might be?

FROM THE CLASSROOM
Thinking Skills

There are many activities young children need to be involved in before learning the ins and outs of working a computer. A good book on this topic is *Failure to Connect: How Computers Affect Our Children's Minds and What We Can Do About It*, by Jane M. Healy. All that said, computers can be extremely motivating and engaging. They can enhance our students' use of collaborative skills and problem-solving skills. These things are very powerful in helping people learn. So while the activities you are thinking of using don't directly match up to whatever test your students need to take, there are many computer activities that will involve many higher level thinking skills that will help our students learn, not only for THE TEST, but for life in general. (Susan, fifth-grade teacher)

FROM THE CLASSROOM
Media Literacy

Learning to recognize bias in any form of media is important, especially on the Internet where anyone can publish. When are students developmentally ready to recognize bias? This is a tough question and will vary for individual students. I think that [the] use of preselected Web sites for fifth and sixth graders is a logical step. This is a good age to point out why you, as the teacher, have selected certain sites for their validity and reliability. This can be contrasted with sites that don't meet the criteria. (Sally, fifth- and sixth-grade teacher)

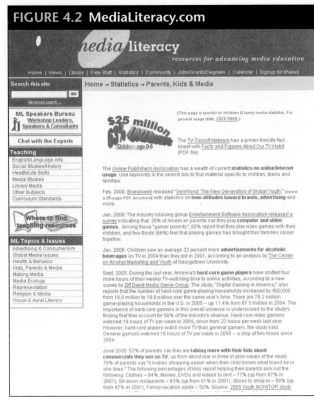

FIGURE 4.2 MediaLiteracy.com

Source: MediaLiteracy.com © 2007 by Susan Freas Rogers.

2. Have I let students know that I am open to accepting their interpretation, as long as it is well substantiated, or have I conveyed the message that my interpretation is the only correct view?

3. At the end of the lesson, are students likely to be more analytical? Or more cynical? (p. 11)

During the MediaLit lessons, students use technology to construct their own critically evaluated multimedia messages. The MediaLit Kit is an excellent resource both for teachers just beginning to explore media literacy and for those looking for additional pedagogically sound ideas and activities.

Another outstanding source of lessons, articles, and activities for K–12 is the Critical Evaluation Tools section of Kathy Schrock's Web site (http://school.discovery.com/ schrockguide/), as is the useful medialiteracy.com Web site (see Figure 4.2).

Characteristics of Effective Critical Thinking Tasks

There are many ways to help students become media-literate critical thinkers. In general, effective critical thinking tasks:

1. Take place in an environment that supports objection, questioning, and reasoning.

2. Address issues that are ill-structured and may not have a simple answer.

3. Do not involve rote learning.

4. Provide alternatives in product and solution.

5. Allow students to make decisions and see consequences.

6. Are supported by tools and resources from many perspectives.

7. Help students examine their reasoning processes.

Teachers who want to promote critical thinking can employ the terms in Figure 4.3 in their student objectives and assignments. For example, if the objective is for students to analyze their use of technology, the teacher can ask students to contrast, categorize, and/or compare. If the objective is for students to evaluate technology use in schools, the teacher might ask students to defend, justify, or predict.

Write three objectives for Mr. Andres's project that focus on the thinking skills that he might expect students to learn or practice while they research the alligator question. Use terms from the list in Figure 4.3.

_____

_____

_____

Student benefits of critical thinking

It should be clear from the previous discussion that good critical thinking skills affect students in many ways. Additional benefits that accrue to good critical thinkers include:

• Better grades (Facione, 1990)
• Independence
• Good decision making
• The ability to effect social change
• Becoming better readers, writers, speakers, and listeners

FIGURE 4.3 Critical Thinking Objectives

- *Application:* apply, choose, construct, classify, demonstrate, dramatize, employ, illustrate, interpret, manipulate, modify, operate, practice, schedule, sketch, show, solve, use, write
- *Analysis:* analyze, appraise, calculate, categorize, compare, contrast, criticize, differentiate, discriminate, distinguish, examine, experiment, investigate, question, separate, test
- *Synthesis:* arrange, assemble, collect, compose, construct, create, design, develop, devise, formulate, imagine, invent, manage, organize, plan, prepare, propose, set up, write
- *Evaluation:* appraise, argue, assess, attach, choose, compare, debate, decide, defend, estimate, evaluate, judge, justify, predict, rate, select, support, value, verify

Source: Adapted from Clark, 1999; Dalton and Smith, 1986; and Office Port, 2002.

- The ability to uncover bias and prejudice (Fowler, 1996)
- Willingness to stick with a task

Because critical thinking skills can be learned, all students, including those with different language and physical abilities and capabilities, have the potential to reap these benefits.

THE CRITICAL THINKING PROCESS

Although all students can benefit from critical thinking, no two people use the exact same skills or processes to think critically. However, teachers can present students with a general set of steps synthesized from the research literature that can serve as a basis for critical thinking. These steps are:

1. *Review* your content understanding/*clarify* the problem. Compile everything you know about the topic that you are working on. Try to include even small details. Figure out what other content knowledge you need to know to help examine all sides of the question and how to get that information.
2. *Analyze* the material. Organize the material into categories or groupings by finding relationships among the pieces. Decide which aspects are the most important. Weigh all sides.
3. *Synthesize* your answers about the material. Decide why it is significant, how it can be applied, what the implications are, which ideas do not seem to fit well into the explanation that you decided on.
4. *Evaluate* your decision-making process.

Students can use this process as a foundation for discovering what works best for them to come to rational decisions. As outlined in the following section, teachers play a central role in supporting students in this process.

Teachers and Critical Thinking

To support the critical thinking process with technology, teachers must first understand their roles and the challenges of working with learners who are developing their critical thinking skills. These issues are discussed here.

The teacher's role in critical thinking opportunities

Facione (1990) and other experts see the teacher's role in critical thinking as being a model, helping students to see the need for and excitement of being able to think critically. In modeling critical thinking, teachers should:

- Overtly and explicitly explain what they do and why.
- Encourage students to think for themselves.

- Be willing to admit and correct their own mistakes.
- Be sensitive to students' feelings, abilities, and goals and to what motivates them.
- Allow students to participate in democratic processes in the classroom.

By modeling self-questioning and other strategies, teachers can help students to understand what critical thinkers do.

Teachers can also decide to teach critical thinking skills directly and/or through content—both are appropriate in specific contexts. Techniques that teachers can use to support critical thinking are presented in Figure 4.4. Additional ideas are listed in the Guidelines section of this chapter.

FIGURE 4.4 Common Techniques to Support Critical Thinking

- Encourage students to find and use information from a variety of sources both online and offline.
- Provide support for information structuring (modeling with graphical organizers, for example).
- Assist students to compare information from different types of sources.
- Develop student debates.
- Allow students to reflect in different modes (e.g., writing, speaking, drawing).
- Help students make assumptions and values explicit.
- Use real experiences and materials.
- Involve students in creating and questioning assessments.

As Weiler (2004) notes, often students who are in a dualistic stage of intellectual development, in which they see everything as either right or wrong, will need a gradual introduction to the idea that not everything is so clear-cut. Rather than direct teaching of critical thinking, students can be led to understand this idea by encountering inexplicable or not easily answerable examples over time. For example, Mr. Andres in the chapter's opening case might ask his students to suggest what the sewers of New York might be like, and then to compare that to what they know about alligators' natural habitats. This might lead to a thoughtful consideration of whether alligators could really survive in New York sewers. The teacher's role in this case is to ask questions to support student movement toward more complex reasoning.

Challenges for teachers

As the process above implies, learning to think critically takes time, and it requires many examples and practice across a variety of contexts. The school library media specialist is an excellent source for resources and ideas for teaching all aspects of critical thinking.

ELL

However, teaching students to think critically is not always an easy task, and it may be made more difficult by having students from cultures that do not value or promote displays of critical thinking in children in the same way as schools in the United States do or believe that it is the role of the school to do so. As Ennis (1998) points out, critical thinking in itself is probably not culturally biased, but the instruction of critical thinking can be. Teachers need to understand their students' approaches to reasoning and objection and to teach critical thinking supported by technology in culturally responsive ways (as mentioned in chapter 2) by:

- Understanding and exploring what critical thinking means in other cultures
- Avoiding "invisibility, stereotyping, selectivity and imbalance, unreality, fragmentation and isolation, and language bias" (Abdal-Haqq, 1994) during the process, particularly in the tools used
- Taking into consideration the strengths and differences of students

What challenges might Mr. Andres face in supporting his students to think about alligators in New York sewers? How might he address these challenges?

_____

_____

_____

GUIDELINES FOR SUPPORTING STUDENT CRITICAL THINKING WITH TECHNOLOGY

Mr. Andres is on the right track by having his students think about how they can find the answers to their questions. There are other techniques that he can use to support their critical thinking; these are discussed in this section. As with all the goals outlined in this text, there are many things for teachers to think about when deciding how to support critical thinking. Many of the guidelines in other chapters also apply. The guidelines here are not specific only to critical thinking.

Designing Critical Thinking Opportunities

Guideline #1: Ask the right questions. Research in classrooms shows that teachers ask mostly display questions to discover whether students can repeat the information from the lesson and can explain it in their own words. However, to promote critical thinking and reasoning, students need to think about and answer "essential" questions that help them to meet universal standards for critical thinking such as *clarity, accuracy, precision, relevance, depth, breadth,* and *logic* (Paul, 2004a; Wiggins & McTighe, 1998). These standards are directly related to analysis, synthesis, and evaluation (and sometimes to application), discussed above as characteristics of effective critical thinking tasks. For example, questions about clarity (Can you give me an example of . . . ? What do you mean by . . . ?) ask students to apply their learning to their experience, and vice versa. Questions that focus on precision or specificity (Exactly how much . . . ? On what day and at what time did . . . ?) ask students to analyze the data more deeply. A question about breadth (How might _____ answer this question? What do you think _____ would say about this issue?) might also challenge students to synthesize.

Whichever set of standards or objectives teachers decide to use, it is important that the teacher support the critical thinking process by providing **scaffolds**, or structures and reinforcements that help guide learners toward independent critical thinking. Critical thinking does not mean negative thinking; therefore, questions should be "direct, clear, relevant, concrete, as unbiased as possible, specific, asked in a civil tone" (Petress, 2004, p. 462). Question formats and strategies for creating effective questions are provided by Kentucky Prism at http://www.kyprism.org, and see Cotton (2001) for both the research on questioning and strategies to make it work in classrooms. On the Web, find lists of questions that can lead to critical thinking by conducting a search on the term "critical thinking questions." Find more information in the 21st Century Literacies section of the Resources module of the Companion Website for this text (http://www.prenhall.com/egbert).

Guideline #2: Use tasks with appropriate levels of challenge. Mihalyi Csikszentmihalyi (1997) and other researchers have found that the relationship between skills that students possess and the challenge that a task presents is important to learning. For example, they discovered that students of high ability were often bored with their lessons and that the balance of challenge and skills could be used to predict students' attitudes toward their lessons. Their findings indicate that activities should be neither too challenging nor too easy for the student. Teachers can use observation, interview, and other assessments to determine the level of readiness for each student on specific tasks and with different content. Teachers can then use student readiness to change the challenge that students face in a task by:

- Changing the way students are grouped
- Introducing new technologies
- Changing the types of thinking tasks
- Varying the questions they ask
- Altering expectations of goals that can be met

Differentiation, a strategy for designing instruction that meets diverse students' needs (discussed in chapter 2), can help teachers to provide tasks with appropriate levels of challenge for students.

Guideline #3: Teach strategies. Supporting critical thinking by modeling and asking questions is useful but not enough for all students. Good critical thinkers use **metacognitive**

TOOLS

skills—in other words, they think about the process of their decision making. The actual teaching of metacognitive strategies can have an impact on when and if students use them. To help students think about their thinking, teachers can prompt the students to ask themselves:

- Did I have enough resources?
- Were the resources sufficiently varied and from authorities I can trust?
- Did I consider issues fairly?
- Do all the data support my decision?

For English language learners, this might mean teaching *how* to formulate and ask questions for clarity and specific information and to use relevant vocabulary words. One way this could happen is to have ELLs create interview questions and interact with an external audience via email. Through the interaction and feedback from their email partners, the students could learn whether their questions were clear and specific and the vocabulary appropriate.

FIGURE 4.5 Guidelines for Critical Thinking

Guideline	Example
Ask the right questions.	Can you give me an example of . . . ? What do you mean by . . . ? What do you think _____ would say about this issue?
Use tasks with appropriate levels of challenge.	Differentiate for different levels of students (see chapter 2 for more about differentiation). Give choices of tool, task, group.
Teach strategies.	Help students ask themselves questions about their learning processes.
Encourage curiosity.	Address and ask curious questions.

Guideline #4: Encourage curiosity. Why is the grass green? Why do I have to do geometry? Why are we at war? What are clouds made of? How do people choose what they will be when they grow up? Children ask these questions all the time, and these questions can lead to thinking critically about the world. However, in classroom settings they are often ignored, whether due to curricular, time, or other constraints. The Internet as a problem-solving and research tool (chapter 6) can contribute to teachers and learners finding answers together and evaluating those answers. However, if teachers stop learners from being curious, avoid their questions, or answer them unsatisfactorily, teachers can shut down the first step toward critical thinking.

A summary of these guidelines is presented in Figure 4.5.

Which of these guidelines is Mr. Andres following? How can he incorporate the others as he and his students develop their project?

_____

_____

_____

THE CRITICAL THINKING TECHNOLOGIES

What Are Critical Thinking Tools?

Critical thinking tools are those that support the critical thinking process. Critical thinking instruction does not *require* the use of electronic tools. However, many of the tools mentioned throughout this book can be used to support critical thinking, depending on the specific activity. For example, word processing can help students lay out their thoughts before a debate, and concept mapping software such as Inspiration (described in the chapter 7 Tool CloseUp) can help students to brainstorm and plan their ideas. Likewise, the Internet can supply information, and databases and spreadsheets can help students organize data for more critical review (see the Tool CloseUp: Microsoft Excel for examples).

This chapter presents tools that are specifically focused on building critical thinking skills. The following examples are categorized into:

- *Strategy software*—content-free and structured to support critical thinking skills with student-generated content.

Tool CloseUp: Microsoft Excel

Many content-free tools can be used effectively as part of critical thinking tasks. Tools in the Microsoft Office Suite can be considered "content-free." In other words, although they contain specific structures, the content that is entered into those structures is up to the user. Teachers are sometimes reluctant to introduce spreadsheets like Microsoft Excel to students because they perceive them as difficult to understand and use and because they think of them as tools for specific purposes. However, as with all powerful tools, students do not need to understand every feature or capability to use a spreadsheet effectively for a variety of tasks.

Students (and teachers) first need to understand what a spreadsheet is and what it can be used for. A **spreadsheet** is a table that consists of cells. Each cell contains a value, usually (but not always) in number form. After users input data into the cells, they can generate relationships between cells, called *formulas*. The formula is typed in the formula bar and indicates the values in the cells that are part of the formula and also the operations (e.g., addition, division) that will be performed using those values. Making a formula is most like using a calculator.

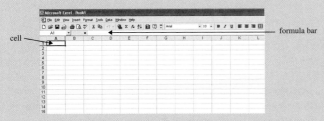

As a simple example, look at the accompanying screen. I want to add 2 (the value I enter in cell A1) and 2 (the value in B1). I click on the cell where I want the answer (C1). Then, I enter the formula "=Sum(A1:B1)" and when I press Enter, the answer, 4, appears in cell C1.

In spreadsheet software, several pages or sheets can be linked together, and the results of calculations can be made into graphs and charts with one click. Spreadsheets can be used to make all kinds of calculations, from the monthly payment on a car to converting Fahrenheit to Celsius temperatures. More important, spreadsheets help students turn data into information that can be used as the basis of critically made decisions. For example, i4c (www.internet4 classrooms.com/) shows teachers and students not only the basics of using Excel but also how to calculate the price of pizza per square inch and so decide if the snack is worth the money. Other tasks presented on this through Web site include calculating the cost of a trip by car (the same can be done for air travel and the results compared) and figuring out how much a student would weigh on another planet. With the additional training provided in tutorials across the Web, Excel and other spreadsheets can be used in an uncountable number of ways to support critical thinking. Another example of spreadsheet use in a critical thinking activity is provided in the lesson at the end of this chapter. While the tools presented in the Critical Thinking Technologies section of this chapter may be developed expressly for critical-thinking tasks, it is important for teachers to note ways that they can support critical thinking with software like Excel, which may already be available in their classrooms.

A note of caution: Younger students or students with motor disabilities may have difficulty using Excel or another spreadsheet program if their fine motor skills are not developed enough to designate the appropriate cells using the mouse. This can lead to frustration with the software. There are many possible solutions. For example, a larger mouse can be used, the zoom feature can make the cells appear larger, or the students can provide the contents and a more expert computer user can input the data.

For free spreadsheet software that works in the same manner as Excel, go to http://www.goffice.com or http://www.thinkfree.com.

How could Mr. Andres's students use a spreadsheet for their project? How do you use spreadsheets?

_____

_____

_____

_____

Tutorial

CW

Find more resources and links for spreadsheets in the Technology Tools module of the Companion Website (http://www.prenhall.com/egbert).

TOOLS

FROM THE CLASSROOM

Critical Thinking and Word Processing

[An article I read said that] one computer tool [that encourages students to think critically] is the word processor, because as students type, typographical, grammar or misspelled words are highlighted. Students should try to correct it themselves before looking at the suggestions by the computer. . . . this helps students become aware of their mistakes and make a conscious effort to avoid them in the future . . . I think that a conscious effort to avoid mistakes is probably going to take more than just seeing it highlighted as wrong on the computer. I think that some direct instruction or work related to those mistakes might be necessary to really help students critically think about what they did and why it wasn't right . . . because in my experience, the computer's tips aren't always all that helpful. Sometimes I even wonder if spell check helps me to be a critical thinker or a carefree writer who is reliant on the computer to make corrections for me. I'm certainly not dedicated enough to try and correct my mistakes before doing a spelling and grammar check. Can we expect our students to do this? (Jennie, first-grade teacher)

Inclusion

ELL

- *Content software*—content is predetermined and strategy use is emphasized. Students typically read the software content and work out answers to questions.

Many other tools in these categories exist; those described here are some of the most popular, inexpensive, and useful. First, read about what one teacher has to say about critical thinking and word processing in From the Classroom: Critical Thinking and Word Processing.

Strategy Software

CMap v.3.8 (IHMC, 2005)

This software is easy to learn and use for third grade and up. The user double-clicks on the screen and inputs text into the shape that appears. Users can change the colors of the graphics and text to show different categories of reasoning such as objections, reasons, and claims. A very useful feature allows users to put text on the connecting lines to show the reasoning behind the connections they made. Figure 4.6 is an example map of the argument for and against alligators in the New York City sewer system. Download this software free from http://cmap.ihmc.us/.

First Step KidSkills (Kid Tools Support System, 2003)

KidSkills is a free software package intended for students ages 7–13. Of the four sections, titled Getting Organized, Learning New Stuff, Doing Homework, and Doing Projects, the last has the greatest focus on critical thinking. This section has five activities: Project Planner, Getting Information, Big Picture Card, Working Together, and Project Evaluation. Each of the activities focuses on students combining information and printing or saving it in the form of a "card" or page. In the Project Planner exercise, students make a card that lists their question, topics for them to investigate, possible resources, and an evaluation of the resources (authority, fact, opinion, or don't know). There is also a Second Step available, and resources and tips for use are provided on the Kid Tools Web site. Although intended for use with learners with learning disabilities or emotional/ behavioral problems, it is useful for all children and simple enough for students with limited English proficiency to understand and use, particularly because all instructions are presented in text and audio.

Some teachers may find it too simple, but its simplicity is also part of its effectiveness. See Figure 4.7 on the next page for a resource plan for Mr. Andres's project in KidSkills Project Planner.

FIGURE 4.6 CMap Example

Source: Used with permission of Institute for Human & Machine Cognition.

Athena 2.4 (Wright State University)

Another free tool, Athena is powerful reasoning and argument mapping software intended for students in higher education but accessible to students in upper secondary. It is more difficult to learn and use than the other programs mentioned here, but it also has more capabilities. It does use the standard Microsoft icons, so many of the workings will be familiar to students who already use programs in the Office Suite. Available through http://www.athenasoft.org/.

The Argument Clinic (University of Northern Colorado)

This Web tool allows students to type in their argument, have it examined by experts, and receive a reply about the strength of the argument. UNC requests an email address and name to send their reply, so the teacher might want to be the "front man" for this activity. Available through http:// www.univnorthco.edu/philosophy/clinic.html.

Content Software

BrainCogs (Fablevision, 2002)

A CD-based strategy program, BrainCogs helps students to learn, reflect on, and use specific strategies across a variety of contexts. The software employs an imaginary rock band, the Rotten Green Peppers, to demonstrate the importance of and techniques for remembering, organizing information, prioritizing, shifting perspectives, and checking for mistakes. Although the focus is more on strategies to help students pass tests, the general strategy knowledge gained can transfer across subjects and tasks because it is not embedded in any specific content area (Bransford, Brown, & Cocking, 2000). The software is accompanied by a video, posters, and other resources that function as scaffolds for diverse learners. The exercises, in addition to being entertaining and fun, employ multimedia (sound, text, and graphics) in ways that make the content accessible to English language learners and native English speakers with diverse learning styles. Available through http://www.fablevision.com/.

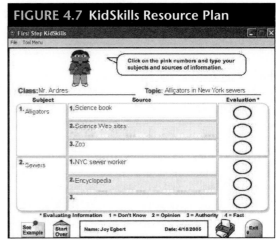

FIGURE 4.7 KidSkills Resource Plan

Source: Fitzgerald G., Koury, K., Peng, H., & Cepel, C. (2003). First Step KidSkills [Computer Software and CD]. Columbia, MO; University of Missouri. Funded in part of U.S. Department of Education Grant #H033271. Available: http://kidtools.missouri.edu.

Mission Critical (San Jose State University)

This Web tool provides information and quizzes on critical thinking. Although intended for college students, the quizzes are simple and well explained and could be used at a number of different grade levels with support from the teacher. The site addresses arguments, persuasion, fallacies, and many other aspects of logic and critical thinking. The site begins at http://www2.sjsu.edu/depts/itl/graphics/claims/claims.html.

WebLemur (LeBlanc, 2004)

Intended for college-level students, this site can also be useful for upper secondary, although it requires advanced reading skills. The program asks users to identify an argument, an explanation, or neither, to logically conclude a statement or paragraph, and to evaluate language used in arguments, the use of analogy, and causal arguments. It works in a simple multiple choice format, but it also provides review to support student choices. Teachers can pick and choose which parts are useful. The site is located at http://www.humanities.mcmaster.ca/~leblancj/weblemur/contents.html.

Choices, Choices: Taking Responsibility (Tom Snyder Productions)

Taking Responsibility helps students in grades K–4 work through a five-step critical thinking process:

1. Understand your situation.
2. Set goals.
3. Talk about your options.
4. Make a choice.
5. Think about the consequences.

Used on a single computer and facilitated by the teacher, the simulation in this software title provides a scenario in which two students have broken one of the teacher's possessions; however, no one else saw them. The class acts as the two students in the scenario. Through a series of decisions, the class must decide which actions to take and face the consequences of their decisions. There are 300 different ways that students can get through this software, so the consequences are not always clear-cut until they are presented to students. Figure 4.8 presents the Taking Responsibility goal-setting screen.

The software comes with many resources to help students think critically about the situations and their decisions and to assist the teacher in integrating literature, role-play, and other activities into the lesson. Each step of the simulation is presented in pictures, audio, and text, which helps ELLs and other students to access the information.

The Choices, Choices series includes a number of other titles. Tom Snyder Productions also provides a similar Decisions, Decisions series for older students.

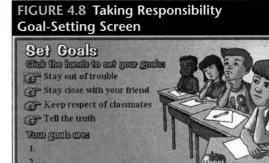

FIGURE 4.8 Taking Responsibility Goal-Setting Screen

Source: Used with permission of Tom Snyder Productions.

TOOLS

Tool CloseUp: Reason!Able

The Reason!Able software package provides scaffolds for students who are trying to answer a question or prove a claim. A screen shot for Mr. Andres's project using this software is shown here. On the left of the screen is Socrates, who asks questions about the claims, reasons, and objections that students input (he can be turned off). The user starts with a central claim—in this case, that there are alligators in New York City sewers. The user is then prompted to add one or more reasons and to include evidence that supports those reasons. The user is also prompted to add objections to the claim and to the reasons, and then to add any reasons to the objections. The interface is simple, clear, and easy to use. After all reasons and objections have been made, Socrates prompts the user to evaluate the reasons and objections. The user can see how the logic is working and where the weaknesses in the argument are. The evaluation prompting box is shown on the left of the screen.

This software would be great for whole class, small groups, and individual work in creating a reasonable argument. It is fun, colorful and icon-based, making it useful for ELLs and students with visually based learning needs.

A newer and a bit different version of the software, called Rationale, is now available from Austhink. Download a free preview version at http://www.austhink.com.

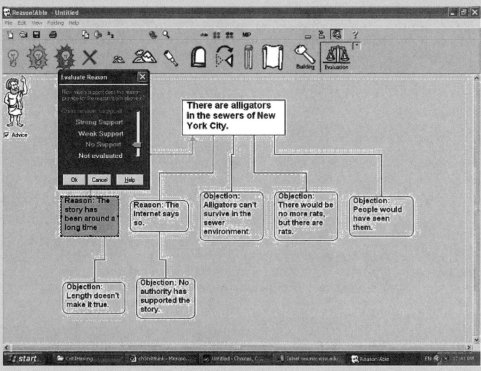

Source: Used with permission of Tim vanGelder.

In what other ways could Mr. Andres use this software for the project? What questions could he ask to help students look for more reasons and objections?

_____

_____

_____

Teachers who want to use this type of software should be aware that the choices that students are allowed to make within the software are preset and represent the views of the software author. Teachers and students must understand the limitations and biases of this software to use it in ways that demonstrate true critical thinking.

Tom Snyder Productions is located on the Web at http://www.tomsnyder.com/.

Other Options

There are a variety of other tool options for teachers and students to support critical thinking. Brainstorming and decision-tree software, strengths/weaknesses/opportunities/threats (SWOT) analysis packages, and Web-based content and question tools are available. Some of the best tools are free: these include Seeing Reason and Showing Evidence in Intel Education's suite of "Teaching Thinking Tools." In this chapter, the logic tool Reason!Able is highlighted in the Tool CloseUp: Reason!Able.

Whichever tools teachers decide to use, they need to remember that the tool should not create a barrier to students reaching the goal of effective critical thinking.

Read as one classroom teacher talks about the role of the Internet in critical thinking in From the Classroom: Critical Thinking and the Internet.

Which of the tools mentioned above might the students in Mr. Andres's class benefit from as they build their arguments about alligators in the sewers?

_____

_____

_____

FROM THE CLASSROOM

Critical Thinking and the Internet

I appreciate the fact that using the Internet can promote critical thinking because the students move from being passive learners to participants and collaborators in the creation of knowledge and meaning (Berge & Collins, 1995). The technology is empowering for students. . . . They seem to feel more control over what they are able to learn and this seems to be motivating! I wish I could figure out how to transfer that feeling to activities that are not suited for technology! (April, sixth-grade teacher)

TECHNOLOGY-SUPPORTED LEARNING ACTIVITIES: CRITICAL THINKING

As noted previously, instruction in critical thinking can be direct through the use of explicit instruction or indirect through modeling, describing, and explaining. The goal is to help learners understand clearly why they need to think critically and to give them feedback on how they do and how they can improve. Unfortunately, few software packages and Web sites, let alone textbooks, require critical thinking skills of students. Software that does support critical thinking, such as those packages and Web sites listed in the Tools section of this chapter, often require supplementing to help students understand and use them. Teachers can supplement these resources and facilitate critical thinking during activities by developing external documents. An **external document** is a kind of worksheet that can involve students in, for example, taking notes, outlining, highlighting, picking out critical information, summarizing, or practicing any of the skills that support critical thinking. An external document can also enhance students' access to critical thinking software or Web sites by providing language or content help. All kinds of external documents exist across the Internet in lesson plan databases, teacher's guides, and other educational sites to be shared and added to.

The goal for an external document is to overcome the weaknesses of the software. An external document should:

- Be based on current knowledge in the content area.
- Enhance interpersonal interaction.
- Provide higher order thinking tasks.
- Provide different ways for students to understand and respond.
- Enhance the learning that the software facilitates.
- Be an integral part of the activity.

L E A R N I N G   A C T I V I T I E S

- Make the information more authentic to students.
- Expose students to information in a different form.
- Give students more control.

Teachers can use the terms from Figure 4.3 on page 105 to help plan and create external documents. Like any other tool, external documents need to be clearly explained and modeled before students use them. To make documents more accessible to students with learning challenges and/or diverse learning styles, teachers can:

Inclusion

- Print instructions in a color different from the rest of the text.
- Provide oral instructions along with the written document.
- Provide visual aids when possible.
- Provide slightly different documents for students at different reading or content levels.
- Use large, clear print.

In this section, technology-enhanced lessons in critical thinking are supplemented by external documents to demonstrate how teachers can make do with the tools they have and also make the tools more effective. Each example provides an overview of the lesson procedure and the tools used and a sample external document that supports student critical thinking during the lesson. Specific grade levels are not mentioned, because the focus is on the principles behind the activities, and the tasks can be easily adapted for a variety of students. As you read, think about how each external document supports critical thinking and what additional documents might encourage student critical thinking in other ways.

FIGURE 4.9 Space Day Invention Resources

	Source 1	Source 2	Source 3
Complete citation			
Type of source			
Authors authority			
Author's purpose			
Contribution of this resource			

FIGURE 4.10 Space Day Invention Design Requirements

Requirement	Results	Meets guidelines? (Yes/no)	Evidence	Changes needed
Weight				
Capacity				
Power				
Gravity				
Health and Safety				

Science Example: Shooting for the Moon

Procedure:

1. The class reads *Space Day—Inventors Wanted* at the about.com site (http://childparenting. about.com/). The site gives students guidelines for designing and creating an item for astronauts to take into space.

2. The class uses a planning tool to decide how to address this task and to make a timeline for completion.

3. Students make teams and brainstorm their ideas in a word processing or graphics program. They list their resources and reasons for using each resource in the external document, a resource handout (Figure 4.9).

4. After they make a preliminary decision about their invention, they use the Space Day Invention external document handout (Figure 4.10) to analyze their choices.

5. Students complete a model of their invention, then use the Invention Justification external document (Figure 4.11) to plan the written explanation that will accompany their model.

The simple external documents in this case give students a foundation for thinking, a permanent record of their thinking, and assistance for thinking, speaking, and writing about their invention. The range of documents that can be created to facilitate this activity is large; the documents can also be adapted for different students. For example, documents intended for ELLs can include graphics and vocabulary explanations, and those for students with reading barriers can be set up online and read by an electronic text reader. When students finish their project, they can be asked to review their documents to reflect on their thinking processes.

What other documents might help students think critically during this task? Describe one or more.

_____

_____

_____

FIGURE 4.11 Invention Justification Handout

INVENTION JUSTIFICATION

Instructions: Answer the questions below. When you are finished create a summary of your answers that addresses all the questions.

1. In what ways is your invention compact and lightweight? Use examples and information to give evidence that it is. You might compare it to something that we use on earth.

2. What makes your invention easy for astronauts to use? Describe every way that it is easy to use. For examples, you might estimate how long it would take them to learn to use it or how much time and energy it might take.

3. How does your invention improve the astronauts' working or living conditions? Imagine that you are an astronaut being asked to use this item. Describe how it helps you.

Social Studies Example: Election Year Politics Debate

Procedure:

1. The class reads a variety of Internet sources, popular press, and opinion pieces to gather information to complete the Election Year Issues chart external document in Figure 4.12.
2. Students choose the issue they decide is most important according to the criteria given and use the Debate Planning document in Figure 4.13 on page 116 to organize their position.

FIGURE 4.12 Election Year Issues Chart

Which social problem is the most important?			
	Number and People Affected	Financial Cost	Other Costs
Racism			
Pollution			
Drugs			
Religion in Schools			
(write in your issue)			

FIGURE 4.13 Debate Planning Handout

Debate Planning

Claim	Evidence	Possible counter-claims

3. During the debate, students keep track of and summarize the arguments on a computer screen using Reason!Able software (described in this chapter's Tool CloseUp: Reason!Able).

4. After the debate, students try to come to a consensus using all their documentation for support.

The Issues chart helps students to focus on crucial aspects of the topic that they are thinking about. This type of grid can be used for almost any topic area. The debate planning handout is also a multiuse external document that can be employed in debate planning or discussion throughout the year in almost any subject area.

What issues might be more suitable for students at your grade level and content area to think about? Why?

_____

_____

_____

English Example: Critical Reading

Procedure:

1. After appropriate introduction by the teacher, students in groups of three read one of the three stories about the death of Malcolm X from Dan Kurland's Web site (http:// criticalreading.com/ malcolm.htm).

2. Student groups complete the Reading Analysis external document (Figure 4.14), which they would have used previously for other readings.

3. Student groups reconfigure, with one student from each of the initial three reading groups in a new group (known as **jigsaw learning**). In their new groups students compare the reports and understandings from their first group and summarize their analysis of all the readings.

4. Students go online to discover other discussions and reports on the death of Malcolm X and to make conclusions about the events and the sources that reported them.

FIGURE 4.14 Reading Analysis Worksheet

Instructions: Read the selection carefully. With your group, write answers to the questions. Use examples from the reading and other evidence to support your answers.

1. Choose the purpose of this selection from these three choices:

   a. To relate facts
   b. To persuade with appeal to reason or emotions
   c. To entertain (to affect peoples emotions)

2. Explain why you think this is the purpose. Use examples from the selection to support your idea.
3. Why did the author write this selection?
4. Where and by whom was it published?
5. List all the main ideas in this selection.
6. List any words that you do not know, and add a definition in your own words.
7. Write a short summary of the selection. Limit your summary to five sentences.
8. Decide if the information in this selection is well written. What makes you think so?
9. What are the selection's strengths and weaknesses?
10. What is your group's opinion about this selection? Does it seem fair, logical, true, effective, something else? Explain clearly why you think so and give evidence to support your ideas.

Reading is not only covered in English or language arts areas. Teachers in all subject areas need to help students evaluate sources and become more media literate, and external documents that help them to do so can be used across the curriculum.

What other kinds of documents or support might students need to help them think critically about what they read?

_____

_____

_____

Math Example: Write to Dr. Math

Procedure:

1. Throughout the semester, students choose a math problem that is giving them trouble. They complete the Dr. Math Questions worksheet (Figure 4.15, page 118) about that problem. The teacher helps students post their questions to the Write to Dr. Math Web site (http://mathforum.org/dr.math/).
2. Students use the answer from the experts to analyze their approach to the problem and to answer a similar problem.

Presenting a problem and their thought processes to an external audience helps students clarify, detail, and explain—supporting the development of critical thinking.

What other questions could help students work through the critical thinking process during this task?

_____

_____

_____

FIGURE 4.15 Dr. Math Questions

Write to Dr. Math

Instructions: Answer all of these questions as completely as possible to prepare to ask Dr. Math your question.

1. What is your question about?

   (Please be as specific as you can. Writing something too general, like *math* or *word problem* or *I need help* makes it likely that your question will be **ignored**.)

2. Write your question, with one specific example.

3. Tell us what you find most difficult or confusing about it.

4. Show us your work or thoughts on this question.

Source: Reproduced with permission from Drexel University. Copyright 2005 by The Math Forum @ Drexel. All rights reserved.

....

Art Example: Pictures in the Media

Procedure:

1. Students look at the use of art in advertisements on the Web. Students choose an advertisement about a familiar product.
2. Examining the art that accompanies the ad, students complete the Advertising Art document (Figure 4.16).
3. Students choose or create new art for the advertisement based on their answers.

Look back at the section earlier in the chapter about media literacy. What other questions might you ask students about advertising to help them think critically about it?

_____

_____

_____

External documents help make the technology resources more useful, more focused, and more thought-provoking. The combination of technology tools and external documents can lead to many opportunities for critical thinking.

FIGURE 4.16 Advertising Art

Instructions: Look at the art in your advertisement. Carefully consider your answers to these questions. Answer as completely as possible.

1. Describe the art objectively, including color selection, line direction, use of shadow and light, and other features. In other words, try not to use any opinion in your description.

2. In words, what do you think this picture is saying? Why do you think so? Give evidence and examples as support.

3. Is it an accurate representation of the product? How is it related to the product? Explain your answers clearly.

4. How do you think someone else would respond to the art in this ad? Think of several different people you know and project what effect the art might have on them.

5. What is the purpose of this art? What do the publishers of this ad hope to accomplish? Why do you think so?

6. What are the consequences of not knowing the influences that art can have on people?

ASSESSING CRITICAL THINKING WITH AND THROUGH TECHNOLOGY

Evaluating student work on external documents like those described in the previous section is one way to evaluate student progress in critical thinking. Student use of strategy and other critical thinking software tools can also aid in assessment. Many of the assessment means and tools mentioned throughout this text can assist teachers in evaluating the process and outcomes of student critical thinking.

Ennis (1993) provides several purposes for assessing critical thinking:

- Diagnosing students' level of critical thinking
- Giving students feedback about their skills
- Motivating students to improve their skills
- Informing teachers about the success of their instruction

Although critical thinking tests do exist, Ennis recommends that teachers make their own tests because the teacher-made tests will be a better fit for students and can be more open-ended (and thereby more comprehensive). He makes a logical argument that the use of multiple-choice tests that ask students for a brief written defense of their answers might be effective and efficient.

In addition, both content and thinking skills can be tested simultaneously. For example, asking students about the resources they used, Mr. Andres might ask:

Which is more believable? Circle one:

   a. The sewer worker investigates the alligators and says, "I've never seen one, so they don't exist."

   b. The mayor says, "Of course there are no alligators. I would know if there were."

   c. A and B are equally believable.

EXPLAIN YOUR REASON: _____

_____

_____

This format gives students who have credible interpretations for their answers credit for answering based on evidence. It can also eliminate some of the cultural and language differences that might otherwise interfere with a good assessment. For example, although the student might mark the multiple-choice part of the question incorrectly due to language misunderstandings or a slip of the hand, the teacher will be able to tell from the written explanation whether the student understands the question and is able to use thinking skills to think through and defend the answer. Students can complete this kind of test on the computer, avoiding problems with handwriting legibility.

Technology can aid teachers in developing tests of this sort. Test-making software abounds both from commercial publishers and nonprofit Web sites; however, few of the multiple-choice test creators also allow for short answers. An effective choice is to use a word processor to develop the test. The test can then be easily revised for future administrations. Teachers who have technical support and/or are proficient in Web page creation can also use an html editor such as Microsoft's FrontPage or Macromedia's Dream Weaver to create a Web-based test.

Facione (1990) adds that teachers should measure students' proficiency in using critical thinking skills for relevant activities. Measuring these skills is not easy, but observation over time, a criterion-referenced task, and/or talk-alouds by students during activities are some ways to do so. Self-assessments can also encourage student reflection on how well they have done. Teachers can use a personal digital assistant (PDA) such as a Palm Pilot or BlackBerry to quickly note and store observations and, if necessary, later transfer the notes into a desktop computer for editing and sharing.

Most important is to assess many situations using different methods to get the best idea of which critical-thinking skills students understand and to what degree they use them. For additional examples of measures, see the Critical Thinking assessments in the Assessment Library at Intel Education (http://www.intel.com/education).

SAMPLE LESSON: CRITICAL THINKING

After completing the Urban Legends project with his class, Mr. Andres realizes that his students need more instruction in and practice with critical thinking. He decides to create a project that will help his students gain these skills while addressing curricular goals related to nutrition and basic economics. He chooses a promising lesson from the Internet4Classrooms Technology Integrated Lesson Plans page (http://www.internet4classrooms.com/). The lesson is presented here.

FAST FOOD FUN

[Sample Spreadsheet] [Rubric]

Objective:

Use the Internet and spreadsheets to find calories and fat in a typical fast food meal.

Project Rubric:

Information on how this project will be graded.

Procedure:

Step One:

Decide which fast food restaurant you would like to visit. Click on that restaurant's Web site below.

McDonald's: http://www.mcdonalds.com/app_controller.nutrition.index1.html

Burger King: http://www.bk.com/

Wendy's: http://www.wendys.com/the_menu/nut_frame.html

Other Restaurants: http://www.nutritiondata.com/ (This site allows you to search many fast food restaurant sites.)

Once there, plan a meal with a sandwich, salad or other main dish, a side dish (french fries, etc.), a drink, and a dessert. For each item on your menu, record the total calories and the calories from fat.

Step Two:

Enter your data in an Excel spreadsheet. Click here to see a sample and directions for completing the spreadsheet. When you have finished your spreadsheet and charts, complete the handout and return here for the rest of the project directions. Compare your answers to at least one other student. In your notebook, record information about which restaurant they visited, what food they ate, and the nutritional content of that food.

Step Three:

Visit the United States Department of Agriculture to find out more about healthy eating guidelines: http://www.nal.usda.gov/fnic/dga/dguide95.html. Browse through this site and answer the questions on your handout.

Step Four:

Using Microsoft Word, type a three-paragraph report about your findings. Use the format for a one-page report.

Paragraph #1: Introduction including which restaurant you chose and the items on your menu.

Paragraph #2: Summarize your findings about your meal, including number of calories, percentage of fat, etc. Copy and paste one of your charts into your document as supporting evidence.

Paragraph #3: Compare and contrast your meal with another student. Use the information you recorded in step 2.

Paragraph #4: Use the information from the Department of Agriculture to evaluate your meal. How does your percentage of fat compare to the percentage recommended? What about other guidelines like eating fruits and vegetables? Have you planned a healthy meal? What changes might you make in your meal to make it healthier?

Source: Web Weavers Education Page. Copyright © 2000. Karen Work Richardson.

Mr. Andres read the lesson and the links to the lesson supplements carefully to make sure that students would meet the goals he requires. He completed a Lesson Analysis and Adaptation Worksheet (found in chapter 1 on page 33 and in the Lesson Planning module of the Companion Website) and concluded these things about the lesson:

- No standards are mentioned, but Mr. Andres can easily align the lesson with state and national standards.

- Students are asked to use some higher order thinking skills such as summarizing, but adding some essential questions might help focus even more on critical thinking. Students are also asked to work on communication and technology skills.

ELL

- Students have a choice of fast-food companies to focus on, but the materials are mostly online and text-based.
- Students have their own authentic task to accomplish. ELLs can choose the level of reading that works for them in the fast-food sites, but they may also need more scaffolding to collect the initial data.
- The technology supports access to a variety of resources and focal calculations that students must do to complete the task.
- The lesson includes an appropriate rubric, samples and scaffolds to help students use the spreadsheet, and both reading and writing components. However, all students are required to complete an essay, and no accommodations are made in the product requirement for students who reflect their learning better in other ways.

This lesson has many outstanding aspects. However, based on his analysis and his knowledge of his students, Mr. Andres decides to make some small but important changes to the lesson. He especially wants to make sure that the ELLs in his class will be able to participate fully. He decides to make these changes based on his analysis:

ELL

- Spell out the appropriate standards and curricular goals.
- Add additional resources such as charts, pamphlets, and other sources of information about fast food. Some of these will be in the first language of his ELLs.
- Include additional questions to help students think critically. For example, ask them to think about the resources they are using—would any bias be expected? Why or why not? What other resources would help them determine if they have factual information? Also ask them to take a position and argue whether people should eat fast food based on its nutritional value alone.
- Give students a choice of products. They may produce the essay or a poster, a multimedia presentation, a letter to a fast-food company, or an oral argument.

Mr. Andres thinks that this lesson supports critical thinking and other skills with technology well and will help his students be better consumers both of fast food and information.

What else would you add to this lesson to make it effective for your current or future students? What would you delete? Why?

_____

_____

_____

CHAPTER REVIEW

Key Points

- **Define critical thinking.**

  There are many different lists of the specific components of critical thinking, but in general experts agree that critical thinking is the process of providing clear, effective support for decisions.

- **Understand the role of critical thinking in meeting other learning goals such as creativity and production.**

  Teachers cannot teach their students all the content that they will use in their lives. They can, however, help them to become aware of and develop tools to deal with the decisions they will have to make in school and after. Learning to think critically will help students to become better communicators, problem solvers, producers, and creators and to use information wisely.

- **Discuss guidelines for using technology to encourage student critical thinking.**

  Techniques such as asking the right questions, using tasks with appropriate challenges, teaching thinking strategies, and encouraging curiosity facilitate more than critical thinking; they are good pedagogy across subjects and activities. Teachers do not need to search for tools to support critical thinking. There are plenty of free tools on the Web, and critical thinking can be supported by common tools such as word processors.

- **Analyze technologies that can be used to support critical thinking.**
  People do not often think of a word processor or spreadsheet as a critical-thinking tool, but when their use is focused on aspects of thinking, they can certainly support the process. Many electronic tools can be used to support critical thinking, but teachers must ensure that the tools do not create a barrier to students reaching the goal of effective critical thinking.

- **Create effective technology-enhanced tasks to support critical thinking.**
  Any task can have a critical thinking component if it is built into the task. Understanding how to promote critical thinking and doing so with external documents can turn ordinary technology-enhanced tasks into extraordinary student successes.

- **Employ technology to assess student critical thinking.**
  Multiple-choice tests in which students are asked to explain their reasons for their answers seem to be a logical and effective way to test not only content but thinking processes. However, this is only one way to assess critical thinking. Teachers need to employ observation, student self-reflection, and other assessments over time to gain a clear understanding of what students can do and how they can improve. Technology can help teachers prepare for and perform assessments.

Which information in this chapter is most valuable to you? Why? How will you use it in your teaching?

_____

_____

_____

CASE QUESTIONS REVIEW

Reread the case at the beginning of the chapter and review your answers. In light of what you learned during this chapter, how do your answers change? Note any changes below.

1. *What kinds of skills do David and his peers need to use to discover the answer to their question?*

_____

_____

_____

2. *What support should Mr. Andres give to facilitate the students' critical thinking?*

_____

_____

_____

3. *What should Mr. Andres's role be in teaching critical thinking skills?*

_____

_____

_____

4. *What role will technology play in helping the students to think critically?*

_____

_____

_____

CHAPTER EXTENSIONS • • • • • • • • • • • •

To answer any of the following questions online, go to the Chapter 4 Extensions module of this text's Companion Website (http://www.prenhall.com/egbert).

Adapt • • • • •

Choose a lesson for your potential subject area and grade level from the Internet4Classrooms page of Integrated Technology Lesson Plans (http://www.internet4classrooms.com/integ_tech_lessons.htm). Use the Lesson Analysis and Adaptation Worksheet from chapter 1 on page 33 (also available in the Lesson Planning module of the Companion Website) to consider the lesson in the context of *critical thinking*. Use your responses to the worksheet to suggest general changes to the lesson based on your current or future students and context.

Practice • • • • •

1. *Find out more.* Complete this WebQuest for teachers about Essential Questions: http://www.k12.hi.us/~dtisdell/webquest/ssessques.htm. What did you find out?
2. *Integrate the standards.* Choose one or more of the activities in the chapter and note which content and technology standard(s) the lesson can help to meet.
3. *Write a test question.* Review any of the tasks or activities in the chapter. Choose one, and write one test question that can assess students' critical thinking. Explain how your question assesses student thinking about content or language.
4. *Revise an external document.* Review the external documents presented in the chapter. Make improvements by editing or revising according to the goals for external documents. Justify your changes in writing.
5. *Review a tool.* Obtain one of the critical thinking tools discussed in this chapter and learn more about it. List 5 ways that you could use this tool effectively in your future classroom.

Explore • • • • •

1. *Revise an activity.* Choose one of the learning activities in the chapter and adapt it for your content area and/or grade level. Add or change technology. Change the existing document or create a new external document as necessary. Briefly explain your changes.
2. *Assess.* Review the sample test question in the assessment section of the chapter. Keeping the general structure and intent, change the question to evaluate the activity that you adapted for the previous question.
3. *Think about challenges.* Revisit a lesson that you have created. Think about and describe the challenges that students face during the lesson. Who might be bored? Who might feel too challenged? How can you adjust the lesson so that everyone feels the appropriate amount of challenge? How can technology help?
4. *Create a document.* Choose or create a technology-enhanced task or activity. Develop an external document that supports the use of critical thinking skills to accompany your activity. Justify your choices.

5. *Create questions*. Look at a reading, online or off, that you might use in your classroom. Discuss how the use of this reading might be improved by asking the right questions (what would they be?) and/or using critical thinking technologies.

6. *Develop a lesson on critical thinking*. Create a task or lesson to help students learn about the critical thinking process. Explain how your lesson meets this goal. Describe how your lesson could effectively use technology.

REFERENCES

Abdal-Haqq, I. (1994). *Culturally responsive curriculum*. ERIC Clearinghouse on Teaching and Teacher Education, Washington, D.C. ED370936. Available: http://www.ericdigests.org/1995-1/curriculum.htm.

Anderson, L. W., & Krathwohl, D. R. (Eds.). (2001). *A taxonomy for learning, teaching, and assessing: A revision of Bloom's taxonomy of educational objectives*. New York: Longman.

Bloom, B. S. (Ed.). (1956). *Taxonomy of educational objectives: The classification of educational goals: Handbook I, cognitive domain*. New York: Longmans, Green.

Bransford, J., Brown, A., & Cocking, R. (Eds.). (2000). *How people learn: Brain, mind, experience, and school*. Washington, D.C: National Academies Press.

CILIP (2007). *Information literacy: Definition*. www.cilip.org.uk/

Clark, D. (1999). *Learning domains or Bloom's taxonomy*. http://www.nwlink.com/~donclark/hrd/bloom.html.

Cotton, K. (2001). *Classroom questioning*. NWREL School Improvement Research Series, Close-Up #5. Available online: http://www.nwrel.org/scpd/sirs/3/cu5.html.

Csikszentmihalyi, M. (1997). Flow and education. *NAMTA Journal, 22*(2), 2–35.

Dalton, J., & Smith, D. (1986). Extending children's special abilities: Strategies for primary classrooms, pp. 36–37. Available: www.teachers.ash.org.au/researchskills/dalton.htm.

Ellis, D. (2002). *Becoming a master student* (10th ed.). Boston, MA: Houghton Mifflin.

Ennis, R. (1993). Critical thinking assessment. *Theory into Practice, 32*(3), 179–186.

Ennis, R. (1998, March). Is critical thinking culturally biased? *Teaching Philosophy, 21*(1), 15–33.

Ennis, R. (2002). *An outline of goals for a critical thinking curriculum and its assessment*. Available: http://faculty.ed.uiuc.edu/rhennis/outlinegoalsctcurassess3.html.

Ennis, R. H. (1992). The degree to which critical thinking is subject specific: Clarification and needed research. In S. Norris (Ed.), *The generalizability of critical thinking: Multiple perspectives on an educational ideal* (pp. 21–27). New York: Teachers College Press.

Facione, P. (1990). *Critical thinking: A statement of expert consensus for purposes of educational assessment and instruction: "The Delphi report."* Millbrae, CA: The California Academic Press. ED 315 423.

Fowler, B. (1996). *Critical thinking definitions*. Critical Thinking Across the Curriculum Project. Available: http://www.kcmetro.cc.mo.us/longview/ctac/definitions.htm.

Jonassen, D. (2000). *Computers as mindtools for school: Engaging critical thinking*. Upper Saddle River, NJ: Merrill/Prentice Hall.

McPeck, J. (1992). Thoughts on subject specificity. In S. Norris (Ed.), *The generalizability of critical thinking: Multiple perspectives on an educational ideal* (pp. 198–205). New York: Teachers College Press.

Moore, T. (2004). The critical thinking debate: How general are general thinking skills? *Higher Education Research and Development, 23*(1), 3–18.

Office Port (2002). *Bloom's taxonomy*. http://www.officeport.com/edu/blooms.htm.

Paul, R. (2004a). Critical thinking: Basic questions and answers. The critical thinking community. Dillon Beach, CA: Foundation for Critical Thinking. http://www.criticalthinking.org/aboutCT/CTquestionsAnswers.shtml.

Paul, R. (2004b). A draft statement of principles. The critical thinking community. Dillon Beach, CA: Foundation for Critical Thinking. Available: www.criticalthinking.org/about/nationalCouncil.shtml.

Petress, K. (2004). Critical thinking: An extended definition. *Education, 124*(3), 461–466.

Sarason, S. (2004). *And what do YOU mean by learning?* Portsmouth, NH: Heinemann.

Schwarz, G., & Brown, P. (Eds.). (2005). Media literacy: Transforming curriculum and teaching. *The 104th yearbook of the National Society for the Study of Education, Part 1*. Malden, MA: Blackwell.

vanGelder, T. (2005). Teaching critical thinking: Some lessons from cognitive science. *College Teaching 45*(1), 1–6.

Weiler, A. (2004). Information-seeking behavior in Generation Y students: Motivation, critical thinking, and learning theory. *The Journal of Academic Leadership, 31*(1), 46–53.

Wiggins, G., & McTighe, J. (1998). *Understanding by design.* Alexandria, VA: ASCD.

5 Supporting Student Creativity

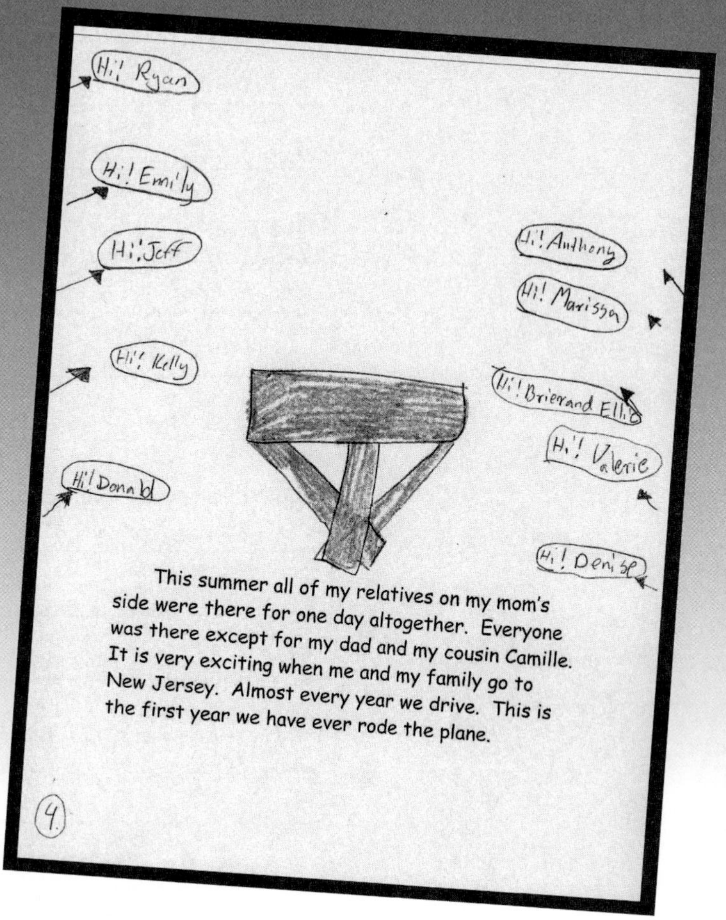

Inside the drawing (handwritten speech bubbles and text):

Hi! Ryan
Hi! Emily
Hi! Jeff
Hi! Kelly
Hi! Donna b.
Hi! Anthony
Hi! Marissa
Hi! Brier and Ellie
Hi! Valerie
Hi! Denise

This summer all of my relatives on my mom's side were there for one day altogether. Everyone was there except for my dad and my cousin Camille. It is very exciting when me and my family go to New Jersey. Almost every year we drive. This is the first year we have ever rode the plane.

④

Case: Circus Train

As you read the following scenario, think about how teachers and technology can support student creativity.

• •

The students in Pam Groves's first-grade class were excited about their circus project. Not only did they get to draw their own circus train cars on the computer, but also the completed train with all the students' pictures would be displayed for the whole school. Jamie Johnson had worked hard sketching her animal car on paper using crayons and a ruler as the teacher required. She had also learned how to use KidPix software from the student technology leader in her group. Earlier in the week she had started the computer rendering of her circus car. Now it was her group's computer center time again, and they were to finish drawing their train cars in KidPix following their sketches as carefully as they could.

Jamie had drawn a rectangle for the outside of her car and circles for the wheels. She had colored the car bright pink, her favorite color, and the wheels light blue. Now, looking at her sketch, she decided that the bars on the car looked much too zoo-like and that she would use windows and curtains instead in her KidPix version to make her animals feel more comfortable. She carefully drew squares for the windows and used the KidPix paintbrush tool to add colorful striped curtains. She was pleased with the result and was working on drawing a lion in one of the windows when Ms. Groves came by to check on the team's progress.

Ms. Groves looked at Jamie's sketch and then at the computer where her drawing was almost finished.

"What are these, Jamie?" asked Ms. Groves.

"Windows," said Jamie.

"But why are there windows? There are no windows in your sketch. And why are your wheels blue instead of black like they should be?" the teacher questioned.

"I wanted the animals to be comfortable. And they look better this way," Jamie explained.

"Yes, but it's not real," said Ms. Groves as she reached over and deleted the picture. "Now start again and do it right. You'll have to hurry if you're going to have your car displayed with all the rest."

• •

Answer these questions about the case. There are no right or wrong answers to this chapter preview—the goal is for you to respond before you read the chapter. Then, as you interact with the chapter contents, think about how your answers might change.

1. *What should Ms. Groves have done when she saw Jamie's colorful circus train car with windows? Why?*

    _____

    _____

    _____

2. *What role did Ms. Groves take in this project? What should the teacher's role be in enhancing student creativity?*

    _____

    _____

    _____

3. *What roles can technology play in enhancing and supporting student creativity?*

    _____

    _____

    _____

4. *What are some benefits that students might derive from using technology to support creativity? Are there any potential disadvantages?*

    _____

    _____

    _____

Ms. Groves missed an opportunity to support Jamie's creativity and to reinforce her creative thinking skills. Because she had a specific idea of how she wanted the finished product to look, Ms. Groves expected all the students to do it the "right way." The goal of this chapter is to help you understand that often there is no "right way," and that student creativity should be nurtured and encouraged. Technology can be used in many ways to meet this goal, particularly because it gives teachers and students options. This chapter addresses some of the ways that technology can help. After reading this chapter, you will be able to

- Define creativity.
- Understand the importance and benefits of creativity to life and learning.
- Discuss guidelines and technological tools for encouraging student creativity.
- Create effective technology-enhanced tasks to support creativity.
- Assess creativity and technology-enhanced creative tasks.

When you have completed this chapter, which NETS*T will you have addressed?

_____

_____

The chapter extensions at the end of the chapter will help you to practice and reflect on providing opportunities for student creativity. For standards that guide creativity and therefore the content of this chapter, see the Meeting the Standards feature.

• • • • Meeting the Standards: Creativity • • • •

It is curious how often people assume that creativity is relegated to subjects such as art and drama and overlook its importance in areas such as science, math, and social studies. People often ignore the fact that creative thinkers have established essential breakthroughs in knowledge in all areas—although their ideas may have been considered crazy at first. Of course, K–12 students are not expected to discover a new virus or found a new school of art, but they should be able to think creatively and to understand why it is important to do so.

Naturally, the standards for the fine arts mention creativity very clearly and often. For example:

NA-D.K.4.4 Applying and demonstrating critical and creative thinking skills in dance.

NA.VA.9–12.1 Students conceive of and create works of visual art.

In English students are also expected to create texts of different kinds. But how can math be creative? As explained in this chapter, creativity can be characterized as involving the ability to think

- *Flexibly*, or able to use many points of view
- *Fluently*, or able to generate many ideas
- *Originally*, or able to generate new ideas
- *Elaboratively*, or able to add details (Guilford, 1986; Torrance, 1974)

These abilities come into play in many ways in the subject areas. For example, in math, NM-NUM.6–8.1 says that students should be able to "work flexibly with fractions, decimals, and percents to solve problems." In NM.ALG.PK 2.2, meeting the standard to "use concrete, pictorial, and verbal representations to develop an understanding of invented and conventional symbolic notations" also takes creative thinking. Even NPH.K–12.7 requires that "a physically educated student understands that physical activity provides opportunities for enjoyment, challenge, self-expression, and social interaction."

In addition, deciding how citizens can take part in civic life (NSS-C.9–12.5), using technology tools to promote creativity (NT.K–12.3), and understanding science as a human endeavor (NS.K–4.7) all require creative thinking. In this age of high-stakes testing, creativity is often seen as a curricular "extra," but there are many compelling reasons, noted throughout this chapter, why it should be central. Clearly, thinking creatively is an important goal for teachers and students.

Explore the state standards for your content area and/or grade level. Which address creativity? How important do those standards make it seem? Why do you think so?

_____

_____

_____

cw See and explore your standards for creativity in the Standards module on this text's Companion Website.

OVERVIEW OF CREATIVITY AND TECHNOLOGY IN K–12 CLASSROOMS

Employing a learning focus to support creativity means that before decisions are made about technology use, the whys and hows of creativity are understood.

What Is Creativity?

There are many definitions of creativity. Which one is relevant depends on whether you are looking at the process, the outcome, or the goal, and which cultural and philosophic views you

FROM THE CLASSROOM:

Technology and Creativity

I try to look at my goals for using the computer. What am I trying to accomplish by using the computer? If it is just to give the students something fun to do, then I ask, can I stimulate their creativity and intellect in some other way? I read an article in the *New York Times* about a year or two ago by one of their technology writers who was all excited about teaching his 3-year-old to use the computer to work some kitchen software where they simulated making a cake. I personally thought this was a horrible use of the computer. His time would have been much better spent taking his 3-year-old into the REAL kitchen, putting the toddler on a stool, and making a REAL cake together. I think we need to look carefully at how and why we are using technology in our classrooms. While I feel that technology is great, and my students use it regularly, I think we want to make sure we are not using technology just to use technology. In addition to all the great things that technology can do, it can also limit creativity and learning. Kids will learn things much better if they can actually experience it through all their senses, rather than the limited number of senses that can be used when using the computer. So I think that we should make sure we have a valid reason for choosing the computer over real-life experiences. I think there are more and more kids nowadays that haven't had as many real-life experiences as kids from 20 years ago. They aren't out playing in the mud and making dams, or forts or whatever, because a lot of their time is spent on TV and video games. (Susan, fifth-grade teacher)

are taking. Generally, **creativity** can be defined as the creation of original ideas, processes, experiences, or objects. For example, inventions such as the computer and the printing press and paintings such as the *Mona Lisa* are creative endeavors. Creativity can also be described as the ability to see ordinary things differently. An often-cited example of this kind of creative thinking is the creation of Velcro, which arose from the observation of cockleburs clinging to clothes. The inventor, George deMestral, clearly was able to see a common item in a different and original way and was able to generate a clear, detailed idea that resulted in his million-dollar product. The developers of the iPod, the cell phone, and the YouTube Web site all employed creative thinking in the creation of their products.

Read what one teacher says about technology and creativity in From the Classroom: Technology and Creativity.

Creativity, or creative thinking differs from critical thinking (chapter 4) in that critical thinking involves the *evaluation* of whatever is created through the creative thinking process. In real life it is often difficult to separate creative thinking from critical thinking because they are closely related. For example, Rusbult (n.d.) suggests that putting a creative idea into practice without first evaluating it (i.e., thinking critically about it) could result in new problems, and therefore these two processes must go hand in hand. However, it is clear that critical and creative thinking should not happen at the exact *same* time for most people because criticism can create a barrier to creativity.

Research on creativity goes back a long way—the first formal study was conducted in 1869—and creativity was a topic of discussion and interest long before. In different cultures and disciplines creativity is described and investigated somewhat differently. However, many of the same findings hold true. Paul Torrance, considered a pioneer in creativity research, in his seminal book on creativity (published in 1962) noted as most important that stifling creativity (as the teacher in the opening scenario did) is dangerous both to the mental health and the educational and vocational achievement of children. Other researchers have found that teachers do tend to stifle creativity and focus more on solving close-ended problems that have only one correct answer. However, when teacher involvement in creativity is high, the creative achievement of students is also greater (Craft, 2001; Fasko 2000–2001). Research also shows that when appropriate creativity-enhancing processes are valued and supported by a "mentor," the results are markedly greater. This process can be supported beneficially by technology in ways outlined later in this chapter.

Fasko (2000–2001) reports the following findings in his review of the creativity research that teachers might consider:

- Some students are *assimilators*, or those who prefer to use known understandings to solve problems, and others are *explorers*, who like to find new solutions. A match between cognitive type and task leads to good problem solving. The variety of resources that the Internet provides can help teachers to create different types of tasks for different types of learners.

- Students find tasks more meaningful and so are more motivated when they choose their own tasks. This also applies to the products or outcomes of the tasks. For example, the teacher can provide a variety of WebQuests on the same topic from the WebQuest matrix at webquest.sdsu.edu and allow students to choose their specific topic, task, and creative outcome.

- A focus on *problem finding*, or being able to discern what a real problem is, is as important as one on creative problem solving. Technology can support problem finding in many ways, including by being used as a resource for world news and views, as an instrument to record survey information, or as a communication tool for brainstorming about problems.

Research also shows that creativity skills do not always transfer from one subject to another. This is because creativity can take on different looks in different subject areas, depending on the goals and values of that discipline. Therefore, creative thinking needs to be taught across disciplinary genres. In other words, creativity is not just a set of technical skills, but rather involves feelings, beliefs, knowledge, motivations, and disciplinary understanding. In addition, a creative idea can arrive in a "Eureka!" moment or be developed over time. It can be completely innovative, or it can be an incremental, original change to something that exists. In the accompanying photograph, Kirk works on developing an original piece of art in a paint program.

Although most creativity researchers believe that all humans have natural creative abilities, they also note that these abilities are rarely fully developed. This could be, as Plsek (1997) notes, because people have certain patterns in their minds that help them to recognize how certain problems can be solved. For example, if a person knows that electric devices do not work unless they are plugged in, when confronted with a device that is not working the person will probably first check whether the device is, in fact, plugged in. This use of previous knowledge will work until the person confronts a situation in which plugging in the device, or seeing that the device is already plugged in but does not work, does not lead to the desired outcome. Plsek suggests that people must break free from the habits of mind that are stored in memory in order to establish new (creative) patterns. Teaching creativity can help this to happen.

Russell Robinson

Creating using a paint program.

What habits of mind might Ms. Groves possess that led to her reaction to Jamie's creative drawing?

_____

_____

_____

Characteristics of effective creativity tasks

Figure 5.1 presents characteristics of an effective creativity task. There is no specific checklist for what a creativity task should contain. More important is what the task *does*. It should:

1. *Focus on content.* Although creative thinking can be taught and supported *through* lesson content or *as* lesson content, effective creative tasks are based on students' understanding of subject-area concepts. Like critical thinking and problem solving, creative thinking *cannot* occur without some content knowledge (Csikszentmihalyi, 1996). Therefore, a clear focus on content is the most important characteristic of effective tasks. Technology can support content learning in ways described in chapter 2, including supporting endless practice and helping students to connect ideas.

2. *Emphasize* **divergent thinking.** The task should encourage thinking that is out of the norm and goes in many different ways, rather than the typical **convergent thinking,** which emphasizes working quickly to get to *the* right answer and is typically used for information learning. In other words, tasks that encourage creativity are open-ended and have many possible solutions or outcomes. Four features of creativity, described in Meeting the Standards in this chapter, are often used to teach and

FIGURE 5.1 Characteristics of Effective Creativity Tasks	
Effective creativity tasks. . .	**For example. . .**
• Focus on content.	• Work from what students know.
• Emphasize divergent thinking.	• Let students hypothesize, experiment, suggest.
• Incorporate strategies.	• Make students aware of how creativity happens.
• Engage students.	• Use authentic content.
• Provide informational feedback.	• Help students understand their strengths and weaknesses.

measure divergent thinking: flexibility, fluency, originality, and elaboration. Ms. Groves in the opening case wanted Jamie to converge and did not support Jamie's divergent thinking. The result could be that Jamie would be careful not to diverge in the future.

3. *Incorporate creativity strategies.* Although first published in 1953, the book *Applied Imagination,* by Alex Osborn (1963), is still one of the most useful books for understanding what creativity is, why it is important, and how it can be nurtured. Osborn's list of more than 70 strategies to promote creative (divergent) thinking has been simplified throughout the creativity literature into eight categories. Tasks that ask students to be creative can include one or more of these strategies:

   - *Combine.* Blend two things that do not usually go together.
   - *Rearrange.* Try different sequences or layouts. Change parts with other things. Sort it differently.
   - *Adapt.* Look at other ways this can be used.
   - *Reverse.* Turn it upside down, inside out, front-side back. Change black to white and white to black. Choose the opposite.
   - *Substitute.* Find something else that could be a part of this or could do what this does.
   - *Modify.* Change the meaning, purpose, color, movement, sound, smell, form, or shape.
   - *Magnify.* Enlarge the size, the duration, the frequency; make smaller pieces into bigger segments.
   - *Minimize.* Decrease the size or strength; break it down into smaller pieces.

   These strategies can be used individually or with each other; they form the basis of the creative thinking techniques mentioned later in this chapter.

4. *Engage students.* Student engagement is also essential for tasks in which students are expected to think creatively. Typically, teachers can facilitate student engagement by using authentic content that students understand applies to their lives. The Internet is full of authentic content posted by and for students of the same age and with similar interests as yours. Check Egan's (2005) suggestions in the References module of the Companion Website for interesting ways to engage students' imaginations in content (http://www. prenhall.com/egbert).

5. *Employ informational rather than controlling feedback.* **Informational feedback** helps students to understand how their audience understands their work and what the strengths and weaknesses of their work are so that they can continue to assess themselves. **Controlling feedback,** which evaluates only how well students did compared to other students or to their previous work, can be threatening and disengaging for students (Starko, 1995). Jamie's reaction to Ms. Groves's controlling feedback might be to not try again.

Should Ms. Groves have incorporated more opportunities for creativity into the circus train project? Why or why not?

_____

_____

_____

Student benefits from creativity

Students who can think creatively can determine alternatives, solve problems (see chapter 6 for more information on problem solving), and avoid being what Lutus (2005) calls "lifelong idea consumers" who must consult others rather than working out problems themselves. Creative thinkers can also learn to make "original contributions to the store of human knowledge" (Lutus, 2005, p. 2) and can propose innovations that change their world. Creative students also tend to stay on task longer and therefore achieve more. In addition, creative thinkers can participate in mature risk taking, be flexible and adaptable, and read with greater engagement. Most important, students who can think creatively can have richer and more fulfilled lives (NCREL, 2004).

These benefits might seem abstract, and therefore not useful, to many students. How would you help your students understand the practical importance of creativity?

_____

_____

_____

THE CREATIVE THINKING PROCESS

Although the creativity literature focuses more on creative thinking strategies than on a specific process, there is some general agreement on the processes that help students become better creative thinkers. Keller-Mathers and Murdock (2002) suggest the following three-stage process for teachers to use in presenting lessons, based on Torrance's (1962) and other approaches:

Stage 1: Warm up. The purpose is to help students get excited about the activity, access prior knowledge, and understand what to expect. This stage is based on what students already know so that they can generate ideas rather than search for knowledge upon which to base ideas. This is particularly important for ELLs and other students who will be better prepared with the appropriate vocabulary and expectations when these connections are made.

ELL

Stage 2: Deepen expectations. During this stage, teachers lead students to become more aware of the challenge that they are facing and apply skills and strategies to deal with the challenge.

Stage 3: Extend the learning. Teachers help students to connect information to their lives, to experiment, and to diverge.

During the three lesson stages, students might employ some variation of the following steps, adapted from Plsek (1997):

- *Clarify* the focus, concept, or problem that requires new ways of thinking.
- *Review* the facts. Student prior knowledge is activated as they lay out the problem or idea in detail.
- *Identify* elements that could be modified. Content knowledge is called on as students apply new ideas to old.
- *Restate* the focus by suggesting modifications. Osborn's strategies (listed previously) are useful here, as are creativity techniques that fit the context.
- *Develop* the idea further to meet practical constraints; this requires critical thinking skills.
- *Test* it. Say it, create it, try it, and look at the results.

Figure 5.2 demonstrates the integration of the lesson stages and student creative thinking processes.

Black (1990a) provides a fun example using the idea that 1 + 1 does not always equal 2. He shows how, through the creative thinking process, students can come to understand that two insects of different genders, left alone, may come to equal many more than two; one dollop of blue paint added to one dollop of yellow will equal a new color entirely; one person's ideas added to another person's ideas can equal many new ideas; and one computer and one person together can equal all kinds of things. This example also demonstrates clear divergent thinking. Keller-Mathers and Murdock (2002) provide useful lessons that apply the stages of the creative thinking process. One of these lessons is reproduced in Figure 5.3 on page 134.

FIGURE 5.2 The Creative Thinking Process

Lesson stage	Student processes
Stage 1: Warm up	• Clarify • Review
Stage 2: Deepen expectations	• Identify • Restate
Stage 3: Extend the learning	• Develop • Test

FIGURE 5.3 Creative Thinking Process Lesson Example

Look At It Another Way Lesson

Content AND Creativity Objective

1. to identify and practice the key characteristics of Look At It Another Way by examining different perspectives
2. to promote incubation through the deliberate use of the three stages and strategies of the TIM.

Materials: kaleidoscopes, multiple examples of half of eight, pictures that can be viewed in more than one way (e.g., two faces/vase, old woman/young woman).

Warming Up

To get attention and heighten anticipation, have the room arranged in a different way before students come in (e.g., reverse back to front). To arouse curiosity about what is going to happen, have small kaleidoscopes out on every desk.

To provide focus and motivation, use the kaleidoscopes to encourage playfulness, and then begin a discussion about the characteristics and results of looking at things differently. Have students view the room through a kaleidoscope and describe what they see. Ask them *How do things look different? What do you notice that you didn't see before?* Discuss how familiar things begin to look different through the kaleidoscope.

Continue the warming up practice by showing a picture that can be viewed in more than one way (for example, the old woman/young woman perception drawing). Ask students: *What do you see? What else do you see? Who sees something different? How were you able to switch from one view to another? Was it easy or hard?*

Deepening Expectations

To make the transition into deepening expectations while sustaining motivation, begin a discussion on the various responses that are common when asked *What is half of eight?* Then ask students to dig deeper into this question and consider answers that require a different perspective. If you were playing a game of pool, for example, half of eight might represent half of the number eight ball. If you considered fractions, you might answer 4/8th. If you examined the question from the perspectives of the months of the year, the answer might be April. Have students draw, write, or state many perspectives to answer this question. Encourage surprising angles and uncommon views. Discuss how in viewing this differently youve taken somethin g that's familiar (half of eight is four) and made it strange by considering the various ways one might answer this question.

Extending the Learning

To facilitate incubation and continued thinking, encourage students to keep their kaleidoscopes with them for the rest of the day and to take them out at least three times to look around and remind themselves to look at things differently. Ask students to stop and consider a different perspective to situations or concerns that arise throughout the day. Continue students' thinking through a journaling activity where they observe, discuss, or reflect on looking at things differently by "making the strange familiar and making the familiar strange."

Source: Used with permission of Susan Keller-Mathers and Mary Murdock, Buffalo State.

How could technology be used to support this lesson?

_____

_____

_____

Teachers and Creativity

The teacher's role

Teachers may inadvertently stifle creativity in the push to complete the assigned curriculum (as seen in the opening case with Ms. Groves), but there is no reason why creativity cannot be an integral part of the curriculum. As with the other instructional goals and strategies described in this text, to truly support student creativity the teacher should structure activities according to curricular goals, standards, and students' knowledge and needs, and then provide relevant support as students work toward their own understandings.

In structuring creative activities, teachers can follow some general guidelines that apply to developing technology-supported critical and creative capacities in students of all ages. These include:

- Choose real objects and experiences over workbooks and textbooks in developing understanding whenever possible. For example, instead of a drawing of the inside of a frog, use a Web site that shows actual dissection photos, such as NetFrog (http://frog.edschool .virginia.edu//). Or, rather than using templates, used open-ended software such as a word processor for presentations, brochures, cards, and other products.

- Consistently allow for students' input into establishing the criteria for the evaluation of classroom activities, assignments, and behaviors. Let students describe the ways in which they should be evaluated, whether by computer-based test or multimedia-supported presentation.

- Choose to display students' work over commercially prepared displays. Allow students to decorate the classroom with important concepts and information presented in creative ways through the use of computer technologies.

- Consistently offer and encourage students to seek alternative ways of responding to structured art activities, fulfilling learning requirements, or completing a craft, project, or assignment. Make all kinds of technologies available so that students have choices in their responses. (Adapted from Saskatchewan Education, n.d., n.p.)

Creativity tasks are great for avoiding plagiarism (described in chapter 6) because individual responses are expected to be original and there is not one "right" way to complete such a task.

In addition, teachers need to ask good questions, as they do to reach many instructional goals. For creative thinking, teachers need to ask students questions that encourage them to be flexible, to think of more ideas, to expand on their ideas, and to think "out of the box."

Another role for teachers is to model creative thinking. To do so, teachers should:

- Be open-minded, encouraging students to follow their own thinking and not simply repeat what the teacher has said.

- Change their own position when the evidence warrants, being willing to admit a mistake.

- Consistently provide opportunities for students to select activities and assignments from a range of appropriate choices.

- Exhibit genuine interest, curiosity, and commitment to learning.

- Undertake the organization and preparation required to achieve learning goals.

- Seek imaginative, appropriate, and ethical solutions to problems.

- Be sensitive to others' feelings, level of knowledge, and degree of sophistication.

- Show sensitivity to the physical elements that contribute to a stimulating learning environment through the physical arrangements and displays they provide or facilitate.

- Allow for student participation in rule setting and decision making related to all aspects of learning, including assessment and evaluation. (Saskatchewan Education, n.d., p. 5)

Most important is that teachers learn how to teach playfully, which, as Renzulli and Callahan (1981) suggest, means working on creativity tasks right along with the students, suggesting "crazy" ideas, taking risks, using humor, and modeling their own creative thinking process. This helps all students to understand both the process and the outcomes of creativity.

What does Ms. Groves need to do to meet these guidelines?

_____

_____

_____

Challenges for Teachers in Creating Technology-Supported Opportunities for Creativity

Teachers can be challenged by any part of the creative thinking process, whether in developing their own abilities or working with students. However, two central barriers exist. First, as seen in the chapter case, school is often a place where creativity is not supported, having an individual thought is not encouraged by peers, and conformity is expected. It would be difficult to teach in a classroom without any rules or norms, but there can be different ways to conform that also allow creativity to flourish. The challenge for teachers is to find these ways.

A second challenge, mentioned at the end of the previous section, is for teachers to model creativity. This includes learning and using strategies and techniques, developing and using tasks that call for creative thinking, and exhibiting enjoyment and achievement in creativity. All teachers are creative in some ways; teachers need to discover these ways and build on them. The guidelines in the next section of this chapter provide some basic suggestions for how teachers might address both challenges.

GUIDELINES FOR SUPPORTING STUDENT CREATIVITY WITH TECHNOLOGY

The description of the teacher's role, task characteristics, and benefits of creative thinking presented in this chapter help teachers to understand the basics of creativity in classrooms. The following guidelines, while more practical, also present more in-depth information.

Designing Creativity Opportunities

Many classrooms are physically sterile, with commercially made visuals posted just so, rows of desks that do not move, and everything in its "correct" place. Such classrooms are often also psychologically sterile, with rules about cleanliness, orderliness, and what *must* get done rather than what *can be* done. According to Black (1990b) and to those who study brain-based theory (Clemons, 2005), positive psychological factors in the environment are most important in encouraging creativity. Black notes that people need their environments to be fun, honest, caring, sincere, flexible, supportive, encouraging, challenging, growth-oriented, free of politics, focused on learning, open to nonsuccess, free of manipulation, and free of "backstabbing" (1990b, p. 2). Ai-girl and Lai-chong (2004) and Craft (2001) agree, noting that learners need to be in an environment where they feel free to take risks; have opportunities to play with materials, information, and ideas; and have the time and feedback they need, whether individually or in groups. The following guidelines suggest ways to deal with these issues.

Guideline #1: Create an enriched environment. Features of the environment that can smother creativity include rewards, time pressures, overmonitoring, competition, restricted choice, and high-stakes evaluation. Environments that support creativity are those that create alternatives to these features and allow students to explore, cooperate, and pace themselves. An environment that supports creativity is also one that is rich with examples and opportunities; technology is particularly useful for providing a wide range of resources and choices. Moving desks around, taking a playful attitude, having students share their work with local and online peers, providing both quiet and group areas, and posting new ideas are some ways to enrich both the physical and psychological spaces in the classroom.

In addition, a creative environment must "feed the senses" by including visual, aural, kinesthetic, and other stimulation. Students can decorate, bring in something that smells different, play a variety of music, and use different group and physical arrangements to incite creativity. An environment that supports creativity in these ways also allows students with diverse abilities, language and cultural backgrounds, and content and language skills not only to access more easily what is happening in the classroom but perhaps also to participate more in creative tasks.

Guideline #2: Teach techniques. During the creative thinking process, an amazing number of specific techniques can be taught and used, many of which are based on Osborn's strategies discussed in the process section of this chapter. More than 200 techniques are described at

www.mycoted.com/creativity/techniques/index.php (Mycoted, 2004), and another useful list can be found at members. optus-net.com.au/%7Echarles57/Creative/ Techniques/index.html. Figure 5.4 presents just the "B" portion of the creativity techniques from mycoted.com. Most teachers will be familiar with brainstorming and browsing, but may be surprised to read about all of the other possible ways to teach creative thinking techniques. For example, "bug listing" is described as:

> simply a list of things that bug you! It should be personal and illuminate specific areas of need. Adams recommends keeping it fluent and flexible, remembering humorous and far-out bugs as well as common ones. He suggests that if you run out of bugs in under ten minutes, you are either suffering from a perceptual or emotional block or have life unusually under control! It may well be the most specific thinking you have ever done about precisely what small details in life bother you; if properly done, your bug list should spark ideas in your mind for inventions, ideas, possible changes, etc. (http://www.mycoted.com/Bug_Listing)

FIGURE 5.4 Creativity Techniques Starting with "B" from mycoted.com
B   • Backwards Forwards Planning   • Boundary Examination   • Boundary Relaxation   • BrainSketching   • Brainstorming   • Brainwriting   • Browsing   • Brutethink   • Bug Listing   • BulletProofing   • Bunches of Bananas

Source: Used with permission of Mycoted Ltd.

If students feel comfortable sharing, they could word-process and share their lists with peers, possibly sparking ideas in *their* minds, too.

Brainstorming is without doubt the most important technique for encouraging creative thinking, but it has to be done correctly in order to maximize its benefits. Rules for classic brainstorming include:

- Do not criticize any ideas during the brainstorming process. There will be time for this later.
- Generate as many ideas as possible. Do not worry whether they are practical or possible at this point.
- Do not stop to discuss the ideas—keep generating them for as long as possible.
- Try to piggyback on other ideas, generating still more ideas. Do not worry if they are only incrementally different.

Research has shown repeatedly that the more ideas a person generates, the better the chance that one of them will be new and useful (Renzulli & Callahan, 1981).

Fogler and LeBlanc (2005) provide a funny and useful list that shows the results of brainstorming. Some of their "suggested uses of old cars as equipment for a children's playground" include:

- Get on the roof and use the car as a slide.
- Take the seats out and use them as a bed to rest between activities.
- Teenagers could take the engine apart and try to put it back together.
- Make a garden by planting flowers inside.
- Use the tires to crawl through as an obstacle course.
- Take off the doors and use as a goal for hockey. (n.p)

Guideline #3: Let students show what they can do, rather than what they cannot. The high-stakes testing that is prevalent nationwide lets teachers know what their students cannot do; standardized tests cannot easily do more. Although tests can provide teachers with important information, they do not provide a whole picture of students' abilities. Allowing students to produce creatively builds on student successes and helps students to understand that they can think differently and still "pass." This idea is discussed further in the assessment section later in this chapter.

Guideline #4: Teach respect for ideas and people. When students fear criticism or are worried about competition, they may find it difficult to take risks and to be creative. This does not mean that classroom activities always have to be cooperative or that students should be taught to always agree with others, but teachers and their students can reflect on the reasons for treating people and ideas with respect and how this can be done. Working on respect also supports the team-building skills mentioned in other chapters in this book.

Figure 5.5 on page 138 presents the guidelines from this chapter.

TOOLS

FIGURE 5.5 Guidelines for Supporting Student Creativity

Suggestion	Example
Guideline #1: Create an enriched environment.	Set up desks in new arrangements; share student work on walls and other spaces.
Guideline #2: Teach creative thinking techniques.	%Teach students the "rules" for effective brainstorming and check that they abide by them.
Guideline #3: Let learners show what they can do.	Use assessments in addition to tests that allow students to show their creativity.
Guideline #4: Teach respect for ideas and people.	Make respect an overt part of every lesson; bring it to the forefront by addressing it directly.

Which of these guidelines did Ms. Groves meet? Which does she still need to work on?

_____

_____

_____

_____

_____

CREATIVITY TOOLS

Criticism can have a negative effect on creativity. Do computer tools also suppress creativity? Lutus (2005) suggests that they may when the user is "reduced to following a single behavioral pattern built into the program by its designers" (p. 3). Microsoft PowerPoint, in particular, has been criticized fairly often for allowing users to apply only prespecified formats (however, see the Tool CloseUp: Power-Point for benefits of using this software).

Cameron (2000) suggests that computers are taking away creativity in music and art, just as calculators might de-skill students in math, because they take away opportunities for students to work with other tools. However, creative learners and teachers can use these tools in ways that support and inspire creativity if they understand the options that the tools afford. That tools *might* work against creativity—for example, by providing preset formats and inserts that students cannot change or limiting what can be included on a page—means that teachers must ensure that the tools used enable students to do what they need to and want to do. It also calls attention to the idea that students need to develop skills and *then* use technology, not use technology as a replacement or shortcut. Cameron (2000) explains,

> in those fields where creativity is to be fostered, we must teach students that the ideas and content of their work must precede and supercede the implementation of the work. Technology helps them implement. Only their own creativity and thoughts can make their work original and worthwhile. (p. 6)

There are electronic tools that can support different strategies and parts of the creativity process. For example, videos that stretch the boundaries of what can happen can provide fodder for imagination. In addition, communication tools such as those described in chapter 3 allow students to exchange ideas and build on each other's creativity. Productivity tools (chapter 7) allow learners to put their ideas into practice and explain them to others. Critical thinking tools (chapter 4) help students to evaluate their creative process and products. Most important for the use of technology to support creativity is that teachers and students choose the one(s) that best help them express themselves. However, teachers who are daunted by the range of tools that can support creative thinking can invest in learning about one or two tools (for example, Inspiration and a good word processor) that can facilitate a large range of ideas and products.

Of course, as Cameron notes, being creative does not require electronic technologies. However, if technology can stir creative ideas, support their expression, facilitate and/or provide opportunities for creativity, and encourage the use of strategies and techniques, it can benefit the creative thinking process. The following creativity tools can be used effectively during one or more parts of the creative process. They are listed by type of tool and include a brief description of what it does followed by some possible classroom uses and specific examples.

Tool CloseUp: PowerPoint

Microsoft's PowerPoint presentation software allows teachers and students to create interactive, multimedia presentations containing text, graphics and photos, animation, audio, and video. PowerPoint is one of the most widely used software packages in the world not only because it often comes bundled with new computers but because it is easy to learn. It allows creative users to use it creatively and is limited in application only by the users' imaginations.

PowerPoint consists of a number of screens, or "slides," to which the user adds content and then links to other slides in a "slide show." The software includes templates for slide layouts and designs for students who need such scaffolding, but students can also work from scratch. Other tools in PowerPoint include online collaboration and broadcast, diagrams and charts, drawing tools, and notes pages.

In addition to presenting information to the class, the software can support teachers and diverse students in creative pursuits. For example, students or the teacher can use PowerPoint to create an action maze. In an action maze, the user receives information on the first screen and has to choose a response among several. The chosen response leads to more information and more choices, and so on.

Students can also use PowerPoint to make multimedia books for younger children, providing the story in a variety of modes (audio, text, and pictures) so that ELLs and other students with special needs can access the content.

ELL

In fact, PowerPoint is being used even with elementary students like those in Cara Bafile's project in which students created an oral history of their town (http://www.educationworld.com/a_curr/curr202 .shtml). Second graders are using it to create "Me Collages" that are literature related (http://iisme.org/etp/Elementary% 20Language%20 Art-Me%20Collage.pdf). At upper levels students are using PowerPoint for everything from science fair projects to public policy presentations (http:// www.big6.com/showenewsarticle.php?id=253).

However, a look across the Web shows that often the projects that students are asked to do with PowerPoint are very prescriptive, from font size to exact number of graphics. Having some guidelines does help many students to be on task and work with the content, but without room for creativity there will not be any.

What other ways can you think of to use PowerPoint to support creativity? Brainstorm and list as many as you can.

_____

_____

_____

Tutorial

CW

_____

gOffice (www.goffice.com), OpenOffice (http://www.openoffice.org/), and Thinkfree (www.thinkfree.com) include free alternatives for PowerPoint, and other presentation packages such as Hyperstudio have many of the same features as PowerPoint. Find tutorials for these and other tools that can support creativity in the Tutorials module of the Companion Website (http://www.prenhall.com/egbert).

Puzzles/Puzzlemakers

Description and uses

There are many kinds of puzzles, from jigsaws to math equations, and most require creative thinking to put together or solve. Jigsaw puzzles with content arranged in specific ways can be used as a fun warm-up activity or as a visual to assess student understanding. Puzzles are useful to promote interaction during group work, and creativity is definitely required to develop puzzles for others.

Examples:

- Creative Java Puzzles, http://www.enchantedmind.com/
- Jigsaw maker at http://www.shockwave.com/
- Content/jigsaw maker or bigjig, http://www.lenagames.com/bigjig.htm
- Primary Power Pack (Puzzle Power, Jigsaw Power) from Centron Software

There are also many crossword puzzle makers that encourage students to work creatively with language.

What else would you add to this list of puzzles that support creativity?

_____

_____

_____

Authoring Environments

Description and uses

These tools allow users to design and create software, Web sites, documents, and other products such as book reports and projects that include sound, graphics, animation, and video. A wide variety of classroom uses is possible, from designing a classroom Web site for parents to access to developing a system for interacting with peers around the world.

Examples:

- PowerPoint (www.microsoft.com) or other presentation software (www.goffice.com, www. thinkfree.com)
- Hyperstudio, for any multimedia project, www.hyperstudio.com
- Moodle, a course development tool, http://moodle.org/
- Arachnophilia, a Web development tool, http://www.arachnoid.com/arachnophilia/index.html
- Macromedia Director, multimedia authoring software, http://www.macromedia.com/software/director/?promoid=BIHT

There are many more tools for course, Web, multimedia, and MOO development, some of which are aimed at K–12 classrooms, and some of which require more technical skills. However, they all require creativity and allow users to determine the look and feel of their electronic environment.

What other resources would you add to this list?

_____

_____

_____

Video Editing Software

Description and uses

Video editing software can allow students the freedom to create amazing products. For example, students can create their own brief videos from photos or graphics, interpret a story or poem that they have written, or edit a performance.

Examples:

- iMovie, bundled with the Mac operating system and also available through http://www.apple.com
- MovieMaker, bundled with some of the Microsoft operating systems and available free elsewhere on the Web, www.microsoft.com
- CyberLink PowerDirector 4, http://www.cyberlink.com
- Adobe Premier Elements, http://www.adobe.com

Software is available for novice users who want to make videos for MP3 players or to post to Web logs (blogs).

What other resources would you add to this list?

_____

_____

_____

Thought Exercises

Description and uses

Thought exercises are problems from any field that usually require minimal content knowledge. They can be used to show transfer of creative thinking from one domain to another, as warm-up exercises, as free-time tasks, or to apply newly learned creative thinking techniques. Students could also use them as models to build their own exercises.

Examples:

- Robert Black's creativity challenges, www.cre8ng. com/CC/index.shtml
- Creative Mindxercises, http://www.mindbloom.net/

Figure 5.6a presents a list of some of Robert Black's creativity challenges, and Figure 5.6b shows the details of one of them.

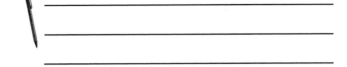

FIGURE 5.6a Robert Black's Creativity Challenges

Contents

1 - RAINBOW BY ANOTHER NAME
2 - No Matter How Often You Look
3 - Stories, stories, stories...tools for creativity
4 - What if-ing?
5 - Else-ing?
6 - From Smiles to Smirks to Laughs to Creativity
7 - It Won't Work!!!
8 - It Will Work if You Work It!!!
9 - Emotions Can Yield Creativity!!!
10 - Creativity and Creative Thinking Smell
11 - Creative Thinking Tastes Goooooooooood!!!????
12 - Creative Thinking Feeeeels Goooooooooood!!!????
13 - Creative Thinking Sounds Soooo Goooooooooood!!!????
14 - Creative Thinking Looks Soooo Goooooooooood!!!????
15 - Create With Just a Few Words
16 - 1,000 or More Words from Each Image
17 - Each Image Can Produce a 1.000 Words
18 - Combing Headlines for Fun
19 - Add Movement to Your Life and Challenges
20 - I'm Possible Not Impossible
21 - Think About Thinking
22 - Add Richness to Your Life Through More Color
23 - Collect Creative People and Learn from Them
24 - READ BACKWARDS . . . SDRAWKCAB DAER
25 - Make Your Own Stories
26 - Collecting Helps Us Be More Creative
27 - Switching Professions
28 - To Be More Creative Choose to Act More Creative
29 - Honoring Dr. E. Paul Torrance

Source: Used with permission of Robert Alan Black, alan@cre8ng.com, http://www.cre8ng.com.

FIGURE 5.6b Each Image Can Produce 1,000 Words from Robert Black's Creativity Challenges

MONDAY
Pick up a newspaper photograph and write at least 1,000 words about it. Just write. Your writing does not need to be grammatical or end up a gradable piece of writing. Simply write.

TUESDAY
Pick out a scene involving 2 or more people around you and write at least 1,000 words about it. Just write. Your writing does not need to be grammatical or end up a gradable piece of writing. Simply write.

WEDNESDAY
Pick up a magazine and randomly select a photograph or two and write at least 1,000 words about it or them. Just write. Your writing does not need to be grammatical or end up a gradable piece of writing. Simply write.

THURSDAY
Look through a children's picture book and write at least 1,000 words about any one or combination of the pictures or drawings. Just write. Your writing does not need to be grammatical or end up a gradable piece of writing. Simply write.

FRIDAY
Let your mind wander visually into your past. Once you see a scene or image that is powerful write at least 1,000 words about it. Just write. Your writing does not need to be grammatical or end up a gradable piece of writing.

Simply write.

The goal is to practice your abilities to communicate through words about images and to be creative in writing. If you are visually challenged use your 3rd eye to experience images of various types for each of the assignments.

Source: Used with permission of Robert Alan Black, alan@cre8ng.com, http://www.cre8ng.com.

TOOLS

Collaborative Idea Databases

Description and uses

A creativity pool is a database that gathers innovative ideas. Students can search for an idea under a specific topic or they can contribute their own.

Example: The Creativity Pool, http://www.creativitypool.com/

Idea/Object Generators

Description and uses

A generator, typically, randomly generates an idea or an object in some topic area. Using a generator can help students get an idea going, figure out what questions to ask, get their mind off a problem for a while, or relate to content in some creative way.

Examples:

There is a fairly comprehensive list of generators at http://generatorblog.blogspot.com/, but many of the generators are not appropriate for K–12 classrooms. Some of the more fun or interesting generators that may be used with K–12 students include:

- Generate your own painting, http://artpad.art.com/artpad/painter/
- Make-a-Flake (make your own snowflake), http://snowflakes.barkleyus.com/
- What animal are you? http://www.2on.com/
- The What-if inator by seventh sanctum generates all kinds of interesting and often wacky ideas, at http://www.seventhsanctum.com/generate.php?Genname=whatif
- Good Idea Generator software by managing-creativity.com

Another fun generator site is Ben and Jerry's, http://www.benjerry.com/fun_stuff/. Located at this site, "Ice Box Poetry" has magnetic words that students can arrange into poetry, and students can dress the "Virtual Snowman" in hundreds of ways.

What other creativity resources would you add to these lists?

_____

_____

_____

Graphics/Concept Mapping

Description and uses

Graphic organizer software is useful for all the goals mentioned in this book. During the creativity process, students can use it to generate and connect ideas, design, plan, and even evaluate.

Examples:

- The most popular are Inspiration and Kidspiration (http://www.inspiration.com/; see the Tool CloseUp in chapter 7 for more information).

Painting/Drawing

Description and uses

Most computers come preloaded with some type of paint program (on your PC, look under Programs—Accessories), and other more powerful programs are available commercially. Still others can be downloaded free from the Web (search, for example, http://www.freedownloads center.com/). Students can use paint software to create original art or to reconfigure photos and other graphics files.

Examples:

- Microsoft Paint, bundled with the Microsoft operating system
- MacPaint, bundled with older Macintoshes
- Paint Shop Pro, a professional paint package, http://www.corel.com
- Adobe Illustrator/Adobe Photoshop, http://www.adobe.com

Other software packages such as KidPix (see the Tool CloseUp later in this section) and Microsoft Word include painting and drawing tools.

Story Starters/Bookmaking/Publishing Software

Description and uses

These software types allow students to create stories and books, produce pamphlets and posters, and develop cards for all occasions. Although structured in some ways, most of these software packages are content free. They include audio, choices of graphics, and even a variety of languages, so English language learners can use them effectively, too. Students can create new holidays and cards to go with them, develop an ad campaign for a new invention, or write a book that presents history in a new way.

Examples:

- Storybook Weaver Deluxe 2004 (Riverdeep)
- Hollywood High and Hollywood (Grolier Interactive/Tom Snyder Productions)
- Publisher (Microsoft)
- Imagination Express (Edmark/Riverdeep)
- The PrintShop 22 (Broderbund)
- Any word processor

The teachers' guides for these software packages include ideas for assisting ELLs, students with physical disabilities, and other students with special needs to use them effectively.

Brainstorming Software

Description and uses

There are many brainstorming tools, most made for business, that support user idea generation. Students can use them to generate story starters, gather ideas to solve problems, discover names for the class pet, or any number of other tasks.

Examples:

- Brainstorming Toolbox, Infinite Innovations Ltd., http://www.brainstorming.co.uk
- Kidspiration/Inspiration, versatile software that can be used in many of these categories, http://www.inspiration.com

Figure 5.7 shows the Challenge Facts technique from Brainstorming Toolbox.

What other resources would you add to this section on creativity tools?

_____

_____

_____

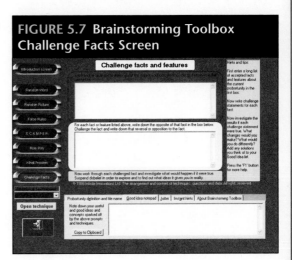

FIGURE 5.7 Brainstorming Toolbox Challenge Facts Screen

Source: Used with permission of Infinite Innovations Ltd.

Tools CloseUp: KidPix

KidPix Deluxe, by Broderbund, is a versatile tool that children (and adults!) of all ages can learn to use quickly and easily. The software allows the user to draw using a variety of electronic tools, including a paintbrush, pencil, crayon, and spray paint can. Features include more than 600 stamps that students can include in their creations; categories include animals, events, backgrounds, and many more. Students can add audio and text to their pictures and make a slide show or movie by adding their drawings to the slide show maker. Users can choose how unwanted items are deleted and a special sound for each type (e.g., dynamite blows up the item with a booming sound). This can sometimes make the destruction more fun than the creation, so teachers need to watch the use of this feature. Figure 5.8 shows the KidPix Deluxe interface and a partial drawing of a circus train car like the one Jamie was working on in the opening case.

Students can use KidPix to construct content-based slide shows and presentations, to illustrate a piece of music, to write books for younger students, and to experiment with color, sound, pattern, photos, and text. Examples and a list of great ideas to help students in grades K–6 be creative with KidPix across the content areas are provided by teacher Joyce Morris (2000) at http://www.uvm.edu/~jmorris/kidpix.html.

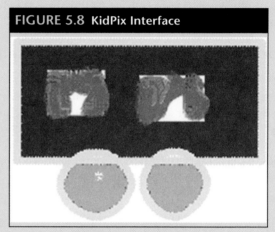

FIGURE 5.8 KidPix Interface

Source: Used with permission of Alpha Smart, LLC.

What other tools could enhance students' access to and expression of creative thinking skills? What assistive tools might be helpful for students with special needs?

_____

_____

_____

_____

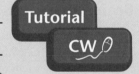

Tutorial

CW

Find KidPix tutorials and other information in the Tutorials module of the Companion Website (http://www.prenhall.com/egbert).

Students can use many of these tools merely by clicking, but there are also assistive tools for students who cannot type on a regular keyboard or who need graphics to understand key functions. **Overlay keyboards,** also known as concept keyboards, are flat input devices connected to a computer. An overlay is laid on the board to show what will happen when parts of the board are pressed (or, for students who cannot press, when they are touched lightly). Overlay keyboards can be used for foreign languages, for simple keyboard layouts, for larger keys, for graphical representations of the input, and for tactile or other assistance for students with visual impairments. See Figure 5.9 for an example of an overlay.

It is how the tool is used, not necessarily what it contains, that makes it a creativity tool. Paton (2002), among other ideas, recommends that students build Lego robots as a creativity exercise. In this chapter's opening case, Ms. Groves had her students use KidPix to draw their circus train cars. For more information on this tool, see this chapter's Tool CloseUp. Other creativity tools are listed in the learning activities section.

FIGURE 5.9 IntelliKeys USB with Overlays

Source: Image used courtesy of IntelliTools, Inc..

LEARNING ACTIVITIES: CREATIVITY

Many of the learning activities described in other chapters of this book require students to think in creative ways, but they do not have a specific focus on creativity. For example, the activity in chapter 4 during which students develop an invention combines production, communication, and creativity. However, no specific creative strategies or techniques were mentioned. The activities in this section are examples of different ways to model, practice, and/or use creative thinking during technology-enhanced tasks. Each content area example includes a goal and describes a specific creative thinking strategy or technique (although others may be included) and an appropriate tool. These examples can be modified for a variety of classrooms.

Math Example: What Would Pythagoras Say?

Goal: To show flexibility in mathematical understanding.

Technique: Analogical thinking. This technique asks students to transfer an idea from one context to another. For example, in learning addition, students might make an analogy such as, "It's like when you have a cookie and you really, really want two, and since you already have one you need to ask your mom for another one. You are adding one and one to have two cookies."

Activity and Tool: Students come up with analogies that Pythagoras might have used to explain his theory. They then use Crazy Talk software to animate Pythagoras' photo and make him explain the analogy. This activity also can be done in most other content areas. Figure 5.10 shows the Crazy Talk interface with Pythagoras chosen in the top right corner.

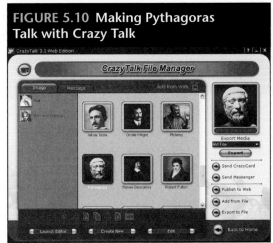

FIGURE 5.10 Making Pythagoras Talk with Crazy Talk

Source: Used with permission of Reallusion, Inc.

Vocational/Life Skills Example: Who Will You Be?

Goal: Use humor to understand college and career possibilities and to think about these options in different ways.

Technique: Rearrange/combine. Students use these strategies, described previously in the process section, to come up with innovative college programs.

Activity and Tool: Students use online college catalogs and put together courses that could lead to a degree in a profession not generally taught. For example, a job as a mermaid might require courses in oceanography, physical education (diving), botany, veterinary medicine, and organic nutrition, among others. Students can use tools such as Washington State University's online catalog at http://catalog.wsu.edu/. They can produce pamphlets for their programs using desktop publishing software.

English Example: Everything Old Is New Again

Goal: Conceptualize a modern version of a classic novel.

Technique: Storyboarding. This technique requires students to post their ideas in text or other visuals so that they can clearly reflect on what they have said and add to the ideas.

Activity and Tool: Students study a piece of classic literature and specify its attributes (plot, characters, etc.). They use a variety of strategies while brainstorming to change/adapt the attributes and write a modern version of the story. Students can brainstorm using a text chat program (see chapter 3 for more information on chatting) or Wimba Voice Board (http://www.horizonwimba.com/products/voicetools/) and use digital corkboard software to post and consider ideas (e.g., Corkboard from www.mycorkboard.com).

Social Studies Example: Alternative Pasts

Goal: To understand how events interact and how history is made.

Technique: Assumption dropping. Students list the assumptions associated with the events, and then explore what happens as they delete each of these assumptions individually or in combination. They would ask, for example, what if Paul Revere *couldnt* ride his horse? What if Japan *hadn't* bombed Pearl Harbor?

Activity and Tool: Students must come up with a plausible series of past events that would have changed history in some way and then carry forward the historical stream to the present. As they create their alternative history, they document and compare it to the actual events using Tom Snyder Production's Timeliner software (http://www.tomsnyder.com). This software is bilingual (English/Spanish) and comes with graphics and other visuals to make it accessible to diverse learners. The teacher's guide and Web site also provide scaffolds and ideas for using Timeliner across the curriculum.

Language Arts Example: Break the Code

FIGURE 5.11 Can You Break This Code?

Χαν ψου βρεακ τηισ χοδε?

Goal: Help students to understand patterns in language.

Technique: Modify. As mentioned previously, students use this strategy to change an item or idea by modifying the meaning, purpose, color, movement, sound, smell, form, or shape.

Activity and Tool: Students type a message using a word processor and then change it to a symbol font and see if others can "break" their code (adapted from James & Kerr, 1997, p. 28). Figure 5.11 has a sample coded message.

Music Example: What Is Music?

Goal: Demonstrate understanding of characteristics of musical genres by creating a parody.

Technique: Exploratory browsing. Students look through a series or collection of ideas or things looking for inspiration.

Activity and Tool: Students search one of the many online lyric databases (e.g., A-Z Lyrics Universe [azlyrics.com] or SoundTrack Lyrics [stlyrics.com]) to analyze songs from one or more musical genres. They define the attributes of that genre and then create their own parody using a popular song from the chosen genre. Different kinds of song parodies can be found in many places on the Web, including http://www.amiright.com/. Students must be aware, however, that parodies are satire, not fact.

Science Example: Home Sweet Home

Goal: Recognize the contributions to physical, social, and cultural environments made by residential buildings and work to enhance beneficial aspects.

Technique: Attribute listing. This technique requires students to identify the key features of something and then think of modifications.

Activity and Tool: Students create an ideal community based on balancing the needs of the environment with residents' social and cultural needs. They can use Community Construction Kit (Tom Snyder; http://www.tomsnyder.com) or SimTown (Maxis; http://www. maxis.com) to demonstrate their plans. The SimTown simulation will also provide feedback on whether the plan is viable or not.

Physical Education Example: Let's Pretend

Goal: To invent a new game.

Technique: Random input. Among a list of words, choose one randomly and try to use it.

Activity and Tool: Students write random words on index cards and mix them into a pile. Students take one (or more) card(s) from the pile and use the word(s) as a basis for developing a new game. They must lay out the rules in a word processor clearly enough so that other students can actually play the game. Students try it, then the creators revise it and submit it to the Physical Education Lesson Plan Page at http://members.tripod.com/~pazz/lesson.html.

There is really no end to the ways that creative thinking can be supported in classrooms and in the ways that technology can support and enhance creativity.

Based on your chapter reading, how do you think Ms. Groves could have made better use of the KidPix program with her class?

_____

_____

_____

ASSESSING LEARNER CREATIVITY

More than 200 standardized instruments exist that measure creativity, but most are not useful for everyday assessment. This is because they often need to be evaluated by experts, there is some cost attached, and they can require expertise to administer. However, there are ways for teachers to assess creativity. Most of the literature on assessing creativity suggests three types of assessment: (1) tests of knowledge and skills, (2) performance assessments to evaluate the process, and (3) personal communication and observation to understand both process and product.

First, because content knowledge is essential for creativity, assessing students' knowledge base is crucial for understanding why and how they use creative thinking skills. Content assessments are discussed in chapter 2.

Second, in order to use performance assessments that are authentic tasks, Mau (1997) notes that clear assessment criteria are necessary. Guilford (1986) and Torrance (1974) propose as criteria the four aspects of divergent thinking mentioned several times in this chapter:

- Fluency (number of ideas)
- Flexibility (variety of ideas)
- Originality (new or unusual ideas)
- Elaboration (adding detail to ideas)

Renzulli & Callahan (1981) support the idea that students should be assessed on these aspects during an authentic task, adding that "unless we reward [students] for the sheer quantity of ideas that they produce, they may never get beyond the ordinary and the obvious."

These aspects of creativity can form the basis of a rating scale. Teachers can, for example, provide a rubric that asks students to generate a certain number of ideas, explain how they came to their ideas, and provide a rationale for their final choices. Students can respond in reflective journals. Another option for an elementary rubric is presented in Figure 5.12 on page 148.

Checklists, in which teachers or students check off criteria when they are met, can also help students to move through the process. Students can self-evaluate according to their performance on the checklist items. Figure 5.13 on page 148 presents a middle school creativity checklist from Intel Education.

FIGURE 5.12 Elementary Creativity Fluency Rubric from Intel Education

Elementary Creativity Fluency Rubric

Use this rubric to assess students' ability to generate numerous possible ideas and solutions to problems.

4	3	2	1
I can think of lots of different ideas.	I can think of some ideas.	With help, I can think of some ideas.	I have a hard time coming up with ideas.
I can look at things from several different points of view.	I can look at things from more than one point of view.	I need help to see things from different points of view.	I usually can only see things from one point of view.
When I see a problem, I can think of several different solutions.	When I see a problem, I can think of more than one solution.	With help, I can think of more than one solution to a problem.	I can usually only think of one solution to a problem.
I can think of many ways to reach a goal.	I can think of more than one way to reach a goal.	With help, I can think of more than one way to reach a goal.	I can usually only think of one way to reach a goal.

Source: Used with permission of Intel Corporation.

FIGURE 5.13 Creativity Checklist from Intel Education

Middle School Creativity Evaluation Checklist

Use the following checklist when observing and assessing students' ability to evaluate the value and quality of their ideas.

Choosing Projects

☐ Considers resources when choosing projects
☐ Considers time when choosing projects
☐ Considers available support when choosing projects
☐ Considers skills when choosing projects
☐ Chooses challenging projects

Determining Quality

☐ Uses rubrics, scoring guides, and checklists to guide work
☐ Creates rubrics, scoring guides, and checklists to guide work
☐ Compares work with exemplars to judge quality
☐ Solicits feedback from peers and experts on quality of work

Communication

☐ Gives good reasons why a particular project was selected
☐ Clearly and thoroughly describes why features of project are examples of excellent work

Source: Used with permission of Intel Corporation.

Craft (2001) notes that assessment of creativity should be left to teachers rather than to a set of predetermined criteria, because teachers can use observation and data records to determine what is creative for each child. Personal communication between students can also be valuable for assessment and for creativity; students who assess another's creative process and product may benefit from looking at the ideas of their peers. Electronic portfolios, discussed in chapter 8, may also be an effective way of assessing creativity because they allow students to store and reflect on a variety of artifacts and show progress and change over time.

However teachers choose to assess creativity and creative tasks, the assessment needs to take place across disciplines to account for the disciplinary bases of creativity that may not transfer across subject areas. Now read as one teacher questions the use of technology in assessment in From the Classroom: Technology and Assessment on page 150.

SAMPLE LESSON: CREATIVITY

A teacher at the high school in Ms. Groves's district, Ms. Farelli, supports her students in thinking out of the box, imagining, and developing their creativity in many different activities throughout the day. She often adapts lesson plans found on the about.com site, particularly their inventors site, to take her students through the stages of the creativity process and to practice a variety of strategies. One of her (and the students') favorite lessons helps students find and create solutions to classroom problems.

ACTIVITY: PRACTICING INVENTIVE THINKING WITH THE CLASS

Mary Bellis, 2007

http://inventors.about.com/od/lessonplans/a/creativity_3.htm

Before your students begin to find their own problems and create unique inventions or innovations to solve them, you can assist them by taking them through some of the steps as a group.

Finding the Problem

Let the class list problems in their own classroom that need solving. Use the "brainstorming" technique. Perhaps your students never have a pencil ready, as it is either missing or broken when it is time to do an assignment (a great brainstorming project would be to solve that problem). Select one problem for the class to solve using the following steps:

- Find several problems.
- Select one to work on.
- Analyze the situation.
- Think of many, varied, and unusual ways of solving the problem.

List the possibilities. Be sure to allow even the silliest possible solution, as creative thinking must have a positive, accepting environment in order to flourish.

Finding a Solution

- Select one or more possible solutions to work on. You may want to divide into groups if the class elects to work on several of the ideas.
- Improve and refine the idea(s).
- Share the class or individual solution(s)/invention(s) for solving the class problem.

Source: ©2007 by Bellis (http://inventors.about.com/od/lessonplans/a/creativity_3.htm). Used with permission of About, Inc. which can be found online at www.about.com. All rights reserved.

Ms. Farelli has used the Lesson Analysis and Adaptation Worksheet to help her explore the lesson. She concluded that these changes make this lesson more effective:

- Although standards for the lesson are not mentioned, she focuses on general creativity standards across content areas.
- Some of her students are more hesitant to participate than others, so she gives students the choice to brainstorm in small groups, either face to face or anonymously on the computer. This provides a scaffold for students who need it and gives all students more chances to participate. This also allows students more chances to communicate and use other skills.

FROM THE CLASSROOM

Technology and Assessment

I also can see the benefit of using the computer to support assessment, as well as to prepare it. Performing assessment is a bit troublesome for me as well. I think that for certain things, such as the state driver's license exam, the computer tests are probably a lot more efficient because they get so many more people tested in the same amount of time, with little preparation for the people administering the test . . . I do question the ability of the computer to accurately assess or measure, as it can only do what it is programmed to do. Students and kids are way more creative and spontaneous than any software program! Also, we have to ask the question if using the computer to perform the assessment would be an authentic measurement. Was instruction and content similar to the form of the assessment? I'm also concerned that some teachers might use computers to perform assessments without taking into consideration the importance to adapt or accommodate the diverse needs of their students. Perhaps some students are ELLs, or others have a learning disability. How will the computer treat them? (Jennie, first-grade teacher)

The use of the computer as an assessment tool has revealed many limitations so far. But the major benefit of a computer assessment tool might be that it can provide students expanded opportunities to represent their abilities. For example, students can freely express their abilities by using audio/video tools if they are well trained in the use of technology. In addition, once a certain assessment tool is made, it can be semi-permanently used. And the performance information of students can be easily stored. (Keun, teacher educator)

- Ms. Farelli provides a handout with instructions for students to follow as she explains the task, and she will have students model so that everyone understands. This supports ELLs and other students with special needs in accessing the instructions and participating.

- Student groups are asked to support their solutions with a PowerPoint presentation, a poster, or another product that clearly explains their solution.

- For those students who need help finding resources to support their solutions, she provides some general resources.

- No assessment is mentioned in the lesson, but Ms. Farelli observes and questions as the groups work. She notes who is participating and who is not, how the groups interact, and what roles students take in the process. She intervenes where necessary, so that each student has input. Finally, she will listen to the culminating discussions and wrap up with a give-and-take about creativity with the students.

Ms. Farelli does not give grades for this lesson, but she does provide each student with comments about both their process and outcomes. She believes that the changes she will make to this lesson will make students more active, support their learning more clearly, and make the lesson memorable so that students will use what they learn.

In what other ways could Ms. Farelli change this lesson to make it even more effective for her students?

_____

_____

_____

Like the other learning goals addressed in this text, creativity is important to the lives of teachers and students. Although creativity cannot be taught per se, its development can be supported in an enriched, respectful environment that values creative thought. Creativity, as you will see in chapters 6 and 7, is an especially crucial attribute for students to become effective critical thinkers and problem solvers.

CHAPTER REVIEW

Key Points

- **Define creativity.**
  This chapter defined creativity as the creation of original ideas, processes, experiences, or objects, or the ability to see ordinary things differently. However, these are relatively simplistic explanations of a complex phenomenon. Researchers are just beginning to understand the biological, social, cultural, and environmental foundations of creativity.

- **Understand the importance and benefits of creativity to life and learning.**
  There are both psychological and more practical reasons for students to be creative thinkers. From helping students to find meaning in their learning to meeting standards to making students highly employable, creative thinking skills are in demand in almost every arena. More important, they are needed for quality of life before, during, and outside of school.

- **Discuss guidelines and technological tools for encouraging student creativity.**

  Although humans may be biologically predisposed to creativity, most people have not developed their creative potential. Teachers can help their students in this process by creating an enriched environment, direct teaching of creative thinking techniques, letting learners show what they can do, and teaching students respect for ideas and people. Tools that can enhance creative thinking and the development of creative thinking skills range from the word processor to brainstorming programs. Most important is that teachers use tools that are appropriate for what students are expected to do. Teachers also can be creative in the selection of such tools.

- **Create effective technology-enhanced tasks to support creativity.**

  Effective creativity tasks consider students' content knowledge, use convergent but emphasize divergent thinking, incorporate creative thinking strategies, engage students in tasks that have meaning for them, and provide informational feedback so that students understand their progress.

- **Assess creativity and technology-enhanced creative tasks.**

  Creativity and creative tasks should be assessed in at least three ways–through content testing, performance assessment, and personal communication. The format of these assessments can vary, but specific criteria should be used and formative feedback should be one outcome.

Which information in this chapter is most valuable to you? Why? How will you use it in your teaching?

_____

_____

_____

CASE QUESTIONS REVIEW

Reread the case at the beginning of the chapter and review your answers. In light of what you learned during this chapter, how do your answers change? Note any changes below.

1. *What should Ms. Groves have done when she saw Jamie's colorful circus train car with windows? Why?*

   _____

   _____

   _____

2. *What role did Ms. Groves take in this project? What should the teacher's role be in enhancing student creativity?*

   _____

   _____

   _____

3. *What roles can technology play in enhancing and supporting student creativity?*

   _____

   _____

   _____

4. *What are some benefits that students might derive from using technology to support creativity? Are there any potential disadvantages?*

_____

_____

_____

CHAPTER EXTENSIONS • • • • • • • • • • • •

To answer any of the following questions online, go to the chapter 5 Extensions module of this text's Companion Website (http://www.prenhall.com/egbert.).

Adapt • • • •

Choose a technology-enhanced lesson for any subject area and grade level from the lesson plans at Teachers.Net lessons (http://www.teachers.net/cgi-bin/lessons/sort.cgi?searchterm=Computer). Use the Lesson Analysis and Adaptation Worksheet from chapter 1 on page 33 (also available in the Lesson Planning module of the Companion Website) to consider the lesson in the context of *creativity.* Use your responses to the worksheet to suggest general changes to the lesson based on your current or future students and context.

Practice • • • •

1. *Test a tool.* Choose one of the tools mentioned in this chapter. Try it out, and then describe how you might use it to support creativity for a diverse student population.
2. *Brainstorm ideas.* Write down as many ways as you can think of how to help students develop an ongoing respect for people and ideas in your classroom.
3. *Create an assessment.* Develop a rubric with specific criteria that address creativity for one of the activity examples in this chapter.

Explore • • • •

1. *Integrate creativity in a lesson.* Review a lesson that you have written recently. Describe opportunities for creativity that are included in the lesson. If there are none, describe how you might include such opportunities and how you might support them with technology.
2. *Think about creative teaching.* Pick a content area and theme (e.g., science and the water cycle), and brainstorm as many innovative ways to present it as you can. Then, brainstorm ways that technology can help you present your theme.
3. *Match techniques and tools.* Look at some of the creative thinking techniques from the technique Web sites mentioned in the chapter. Choose 5 techniques that sound useful for your current or future students and your teaching context. Make a T-chart, listing on one side a brief description of the technique, and on the other side an electronic tool that might help you and/or your students to learn and practice that technique. An example is shown here.

Technique	Tool
Example: Brainstorming	Text chat

REFERENCES

Ai-girl, T., & Lai-chong, L. (2004). *Creativity for teachers*. New York: Marshall Cavendish Academic.

Black, R. (1990a). But we can't allow 25 different answers to the same question in our classrooms! *Cre8v Thoughts Newsletter #12*. Available: http://www.cre8ng.com/newsletter/news12.shtml.

Black, R. (1990b). Establishing environments for creativity. *Cre8v Thoughts Newsletter #14*. Available: http://www.cre8ng.com/newsletter/news14.shtml.

Cameron, S. (2000). *Technology in the creative classroom*. ED441260.

Clemons, S. (2005, January). Encouraging creativity in online courses. *International Journal of Instructional Technology and Distance Learning, 2*(1). http://www.itdl.org/Journal/Jan_05/article05.htm.

Craft, A. (2001). *An analysis of research and literature on creativity and education*. Report prepared for the Qualifications and Curriculum Authority, UK. Available: http://www.ncaction.org.uk/creativity/creativity_report.pdf.

Csikszentmihalyi, M. (1996). *Creativity: Flow and the psychology of discovery and invention*. New York: HarperCollins.

Egan, K. (2005). *An imaginative approach to teaching*. San Francisco, CA: Jossey-Bass.

Fasko, D. (2000–2001). Education and creativity. *Creativity Research Journal, 13*(3–4), 317–327.

Fogler, H., & LeBlanc, S. (2005). Suggested uses of old cars as equipment for a children's playground. Available: http://www.engin.umich.edu/~cre/probsolv/strategy/mag-minify.htm.

Guilford, J. (1986). *Creative talents: Their nature, use and development*. Buffalo, NY: Bearly.

James, F., & Kerr, A. (1997). *Creative computing: Essential and imaginative activities using information technology with children from five to eleven years*. Dunstable, UK: Belair.

Keller-Mathers, S., & Murdock, M. (2002). Teaching the content of creativity using the Torrance Incubation Model: Eyes wide open to the possibilities of learning. *Celebrating Creativity Newsletter* (National Association for Gifted Children), *13*(2), 3–4, 7–9 (electronic version: www.buffalostate.edu/orgs/cbir/readingroom/html/TIMc-02.html.

Lutus, P. (2005). Creative problem solving. Available: http://www.arachnoid.com/lutusp/crashcourse.html.

Mau, R. (1997, December). The role of assessment in developing creativity. *REACT, 2*(7). Available from http://eduweb.nie.edu.sg/REACTOld/1997/2.7.html.

Morris, J. (2000). *KidPix Resources*. Available: http://www.uvm.edu/~jmorris/kidpix.html.

Mycoted. (2004). Classic brainstorming. Available: http://www.mycoted.com/creativity/techniques/classic.php.

North Central Regional Educational Laboratory (NCREL). (2004). 21st century skills: Creativity. Available: http://www.ncrel.org/engauge/skills/invent4.htm.

Osborn, A. (1963). *Applied imagination: Principles and procedures of creative problem-solving* (3rd ed.). New York: Charles Scribner's Sons.

Paton, B. (2002). Children and creativity resources. Available: members.optusnet.com.au/%7Echarles57/Creative/Children/index.html.

Plsek, P. (1997). *Creativity, innovation, and quality*. Chicago: Irwin.

Renzulli, J., & Callahan, C. (1981). Developing creativity training exercises. In J. Gowan, J. Khatena, & E. P. Torrance (Eds.), *Creativity: Its educational implications* (2nd ed.). Dubuque, IA: Kendall/Hunt.

Rusbult, C. (n.d.). Creating thinking. ASA Science Education. Available: www.asa3.org/ASA/education/think/creative.htm.

Saskatchewan Education. (n.d). *Understanding the common essential learnings*. Regina, SK: Author.

Starko, A. (1995). *Creativity in the classroom: Schools of curious delight*. White Plains, NY: Longman.

Torrance, E. P. (1962). *Guiding creative talent*. Englewood Cliffs, NJ: Prentice-Hall.

Torrance, E. P. (1974). *Torrance tests of creative thinking*. Lexington, MA: Ginn.

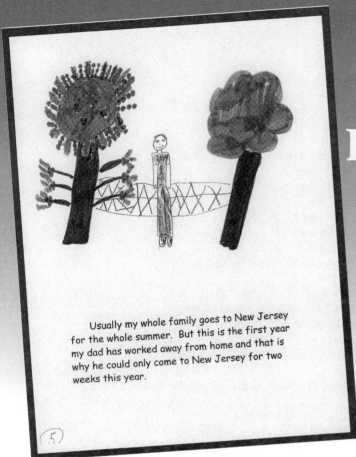

Usually my whole family goes to New Jersey for the whole summer. But this is the first year my dad has worked away from home and that is why he could only come to New Jersey for two weeks this year.

(5)

6

Supporting Student Problem Solving

Case: The Big Question

As you read the following scenario, note how the teacher guides the students during the inquiry process.

• •

A major discount retailer wants to build a giant new superstore in the small rural town where Ms. Lee teaches eighth-grade social studies. Ms. Lee's students have been exposed to picketers, mailers, publicly posted flyers, and letters in the local newspaper both supporting and opposing the superstore. On one side, some local small businesspeople are worried that they will be put out of business by the giant, and other town citizens are concerned that their way of life will be ruined by extra traffic, noise, pollution, and low-paying jobs. Others who oppose the superstore complain that the low wages that the store pays will mean fewer good jobs in town. On the other side, the Chamber of Commerce, some educators, and other citizens anticipate more revenue to pay for schools and roads, and some people are looking forward to having a nearby place to shop and save money.

Ms. Lee's students are also divided on the issue, echoing the partisan arguments of their parents and friends. Her students tell her that they would like to know the "real story." Ms. Lee decides that this is an excellent opportunity for students to study a large range of economic, political, and social issues that directly impact them and their families. Ms. Lee agrees to plan a project for the students to help the town solve the dilemma over whether the superstore is in the best interests of the town. During the project she will focus on problem solving and inquiry and use technology to support both.

• •

Answer these questions about the case. There are no right or wrong answers—the goal is for you to respond before you read the chapter. Then, as you interact with the chapter contents, think about how your answers might change.

1. *What prior content and language knowledge do the students need to solve this problem?*

_____

_____

_____

2. *What process should the students follow to find a solution to the problem?*

_____

_____

_____

3. *What should Ms. Lee's role in the project be?*

_____

_____

_____

4. *What role can technology play in helping the students to solve their problem?*

_____

_____

_____

Ms. Lee understands that this issue is important for her students to understand, and that it also presents a learning experience that will help them gain in content knowledge, language, and skills. The goal of this chapter is to help you to understand how teachers and technology can support student problem solving. After reading this chapter, you will be able to

- Define problem solving and inquiry.
- Understand the interaction between problem solving and other instructional goals.
- Discuss guidelines and technologies for encouraging effective student problem solving.
- Create and adapt effective technology-enhanced tasks to support problem solving.
- Assess student technology-supported problem solving.

When you have completed this chapter, which NETS*T will you have addressed?

_____

_____

_____

Like critical and creative thinking, problem solving is not an easy thing to teach. However, educators believe it is crucially important that students gain these skills. The standards that support this goal in every content area demonstrate the significance of problem solving. See the Meeting the Standards feature on the next page for an overview of these standards.

• • • • **Meeting the Standards:** Problem Solving • • • •

Across content areas, the standards address problem solving in the form of being able to improvise, decide, inquire, and research. For example:

- NA.T.K–12.2 Acting by assuming roles and interacting in improvisations.
- NL-Eng.K–12.7 Students conduct research on issues and interests by generating ideas and questions and by posing problems.
- NM-NUM.6–8.3 Develop, analyze, and explain methods for solving problems involving proportions, such as scaling and finding equivalent ratios.
- NPH.H.K–4.6 Demonstrate the ability to apply a decision-making process to health issues and problems.
- NS.K–4.1 As a result of activities, students should develop abilities necessary to do scientific inquiry.

- NT.K–12.6
  a. Students use technology resources for solving problems and making informed decisions.
  b. Students employ technology in the development of strategies for solving problems in the real world.

These are only samples; there are many more standards in each area that emphasize inquiry and problem solving. In fact, the national math standards and the national science standards are premised almost completely on problem solving and inquiry. According to the literature, however, these areas are often overlooked or addressed superficially in classrooms, and in some subject areas, are not attended to at all.

Check your state standards in the Standards section of the Resources module of the Companion Website. How do they address problem solving?

_____

_____

_____

CW

• • • •

OVERVIEW OF PROBLEM SOLVING AND INQUIRY IN K–12 CLASSROOMS

In keeping with a learning focus, this chapter first discusses problem solving and inquiry to provide a basis from which teachers can provide support for these goals with technology.

What Is Problem Solving?

Whereas production is a process that focuses on an end-product, **problem solving** is a process that centers on a *problem*. Students apply critical and creative thinking skills to prior knowledge during the problem solving process. The end result of problem solving is typically some kind of decision, in other words, choosing a solution and then evaluating it.

There are two general kinds of problems. **Close-ended** problems are those with known solutions to which students can apply a process similar to one that they have already used. For example, if a student understands the single-digit process in adding 2 plus 2 to make 4, she most likely will be able to solve a problem that asks her to add 1 plus 1. **Open-ended** or **loosely structured** problems, on the other hand, are those with many or unknown solutions rather than one correct answer. These types of problems require the ability to apply a variety of strategies and knowledge to finding a solution. For example, an open-ended problem statement might read:

• •

A politician has just discovered information showing that a statement he made to the public earlier in the week was incorrect. If he corrects himself he will look like a fool, but if he doesn't and someone finds out the truth, he will be in trouble. What should he do or say about this?

Obviously, there is no simple answer to this question, and there is a lot of information to consider.

Many textbooks, teachers, and tests present or ask for only the *results* of problem solving and not the whole *process* that students must go through in thinking about how to arrive at a viable solution. As a result, according to the literature, most people use their personal understandings to try to solve open-ended problems, but the bias of limited experience makes it hard for people to understand the trade-offs or contradictions that these problems present. To solve such problems, students need to be able to use both problem-solving skills and an effective inquiry process.

What Is Inquiry?

Inquiry in education is also sometimes called *research, investigation,* or *guided discovery*. During inquiry, students ask questions and then search for answers to those questions. In doing so, they come to new understandings in content and language. Although inquiry is an instructional strategy in itself, it is also a central component of problem solving when students apply their new understandings to the problem at hand. Each question that the problem raises must be addressed by thorough and systematic investigation to arrive at a well-grounded solution. Therefore, the term "problem solving" can be considered to include inquiry.

Mansilla and Gardner (1997) note that inquiry must occur through "multiple domains and symbol systems" (p. 1). This means that, for students to understand both the question and ways of looking at the answer(s), resources such as historical accounts, literature, art, and eyewitness experiences must be used. In addition, each resource must be examined in light of what each different type of material contributes to the solution. **Critical literacy**, or reading beyond the text, then, is a fundamental aspect of inquiry and so of problem solving. For critical literacy resources, see the 21st Century Literacies section in the Resources module of the Companion Website (http://www .prenhall.com/egbert).

What Is Problem-Based Learning?

Problem-based learning (PBL) is a teaching approach that combines critical thinking, problem-solving skills, and inquiry as students explore real-world problems. It is based on unstructured, complex, and authentic problems that are often presented as part of a project. PBL addresses many of the learning goals, including communication, creativity, and often production.

Research is being conducted in every area from business to education to see how we solve problems, what guides us, what information we have and use during problem solving, and how we can become more efficient problem solvers. There are competing theories of how people learn to and do solve problems, and much more research needs to be done. However, we do know several things. First, problem solving can depend on the context, the participants, and the stakeholders. In addition, studies show that content appears to be *covered* better by "traditional" instruction, but students *retain* better after problem solving. PBL has been found effective at teaching content *and* problem solving, and the use of technology makes those gains even higher (Stites, 1998). Research clearly shows that the more parts of a problem there are, the less successful students will be at solving it. However, effective scaffolding can help to reduce student cognitive overload (Blosser, 1988). Discover technology that can provide scaffolds in Tool CloseUp: Microsoft Student on page 158.

The PBL literature points out that both content knowledge and problem-solving skills are necessary to arrive at solutions, but individual differences among students affect their success, too. For example, field-independent students in general do better than field-dependent students in tasks. In addition, students from some cultures will not be familiar with this kind of learning, and others may not have the language to work with it. Teachers must consider all of these ideas and challenges in supporting student problem solving.

Is the problem that Ms. Lee's students want to solve an open-ended or close-ended problem? Why do you think so? What difference does it make?

_____

_____

_____

T O O L S

Tool CloseUp: Microsoft Student

There are many tools that can support parts of the problem-solving process if the teacher has the time and desire to find and evaluate them. Many of these are described in the Tools section of this chapter. Microsoft Student provides many of these supports in one software package, saving teachers time and effort (but not money—the package costs about $70).

Student features four main tools that serve a variety of purposes. These include:

- *Encarta Premium.* Much more than an electronic encyclopedia, this tool contains 300 video clips, 66,000 articles, over 25,000 photos, an atlas, the-saurus, dictionary, and sound and music clips. It also includes Encarta Kids with content for younger learners. This is a very thorough resource for inquiry about thousands of topics and a good place to start gathering information on a project.

- *Math tools.* The math tools include an online graphing calculator, an equation library, and homework help. Students can use these tools not only for solving math problems but for graphing information to support problems in other areas.

- *Learning essentials.* This section includes tutorials for the Microsoft Office Suite, writing tutorials, and templates for writing in different genres. Students can get support for presenting their inquiry and problem-solving projects.

Student has additional features such as foreign language tools, but more important than what it has is what it can do. First, Student can help support students during inquiry by providing resources in a variety of modes. By providing information in formats from audio to video, Student makes it possible for ELLs and students with different learning preferences to access the content.

Inclusion

ELL

Second, tutorials such as that showing how to make diagrams in Microsoft Word can help students to organize, synthesize, and present information during PBL. In the same way, templates can assist students in preparing and presenting their problem solutions. Other tools scaffold student learning during PBL and make it possible for students with different language backgrounds to communicate. Another benefit is that, because the tools are bundled, students know where to go to find what they need.

There are problems with the software. For example, it runs only on the Microsoft operating system, and teachers need to spend time learning the tools to understand how best to use them with students. In spite of this, Student is a powerful software package that can support effective problem solving and inquiry in K-12 classrooms.

Based on the description of Student, what other characteristics of PBL does it support? Would you try this software? Why or why not?

_____

_____

_____

Tutorial

CW

Find tutorials for Microsoft Student in the Tutorials module of the Companion Website (http://www.prenhall.com/egbert).

Characteristics of effective technology-enhanced problem-based learning tasks

PBL tasks share many of the same characteristics of other tasks in this book, but some are specific to PBL. Generally, PBL tasks:

- Involve learners in gaining and organizing knowledge of content. Inspiration and other concept-mapping software is useful for this.
- Help learners link school activities to life, providing the "why" for doing the activity.
- Give students control of their learning.
- Have built-in and just-in-time scaffolding to help students. Tutorials are available all over the Web for content, language, and technology help.
- Are fun and interesting.
- Contain specific objectives for students to meet along the way to a larger goal.
- Have guidance for the use of tools, especially computer technologies.
- Include communication and collaboration (tools described in chapter 3).
- Emphasize the process and the content.
- Are central to the curriculum, not peripheral or time fillers.
- Lead to additional content learning.
- Have a measurable, although not necessarily *correct*, outcome.

More specifically, PBL tasks:

- Use a problem that "appeals to human desire for resolution/stasis/harmony" and "sets up need for and context of learning which follows" (IMSA, 2005, p. 2).
- Help students understand the range of problem-solving mechanisms available.
- Focus on the merits of the question, the concepts involved, and student research plans.
- Provide opportunities for students to examine the *process* of getting the answer (for example, looking back at the arguments).
- Lead to additional "transfer" problems that use the knowledge gained in a different context.

Not every task necessarily exhibits all of these characteristics completely, but these lists can serve as guidelines for creating and evaluating tasks. Figure 6.1 shows an Educator's Desk Reference Lesson plan that includes many of these features that can be supported by technology. Can you pick them out? Can you see where technology might best fit in this lesson?

FIGURE 6.1 Justice Lesson Plan

Justice

Melanie McCool

Grade Level(s): 7, 8, 9, 10, 11, 12

Subject(s): Social Studies/U.S. Government

Overview: This lesson will allow students to experience brainstorming and open-ended questioning strategies and research to develop a better understanding of the justice system.

Purpose: To provide an opportunity for students to discuss both strengths and weaknesses of the court system in providing equal justice for all and to identify factors that cause these weaknesses and recommend solutions.

Objectives: As a result of this activity:

1. The student will investigate the criminal justice system.
2. The student will analyze the 7 Articles to the Constitution.
3. The student will develop problem-solving and critical-thinking skills.

Activities and Procedures:

1. Students take attitudinal survey.

continued

FIGURE 6.1 Continued

2. Brainstorm "Equal Justice for All" motto on Supreme Court Building. Students write their opinions of what the motto means:

   a. Show picture of symbol of justice.
   b. Ask: What is the meaning of the symbol?
   c. Why is the woman blindfolded?
   d. What does the scale stand for?

3. Constitution Search: Point out "establish justice" as purpose outlined in Preamble. Have students search the Constitution to find ways this purpose is carried out. (Use only the 7 Articles to the Constitution.)

4. Guest: Invite a local trial court judge to discuss the organization of the court system.

5. Guest: Invite an attorney to visit. Raise questions about appeal, time involved in ajudication, and fairness of the system.

Tying It All Together:

1. Students complete attitudinal survey and discuss.

2. After the visit from a local trial court judge have students construct a diagram of the applicable federal and state courts for their jurisdiction. Debrief: Does the flow chart indicate an effort to provide "equal justice?" Ask for suggestions to improve the system.

3. Encourage all students to share the results of this activity with their parents/guardians.

4. Use this activity to introduce the first unit or lesson.

Attitudinal Survey

Instructions: For each of the following statements, circle the one that corresponds most closely with your opinion.

Key: SA=Strongly Agree / A=Agree / U=Undecided/ D=Disagree / SD=Strongly Disagree

1. In a court of law, the defendant is always treated justly. SA A U D SD

2. Trial by jury should be abolished. SA A U D SD

3. A person is always considered innocent until proven guilty. SA A U D SD

4. The more money you have, the more likely you are to be proven innocent. SA A U D SD

5. Everyone should be required to serve on a jury at least once in his life. SA A U D SD

6. Courts are too lenient with criminals. SA A U D SD

7. People who have low IQ's should not be allowed to serve on juries. SA A U D SD

8. In the United States, every defendant who requests a jury trial is actually tried by his peers. SA A U D SD

9. All judges should be elected by the people they serve. SA A U D SD

10. People who do not agree with the outcome of their trial should only be allowed to appeal their case one time. SA A U D SD

11. The news media should be allowed to cover all trials without restriction because the Constitution guarantees the right of freedom of the press. SA A U D SD

12. Courts usually see that justice is served. SA A U D SD

13. People charged with serious crimes should not be allowed out on bail. SA A U D SD

14. Most trials should take place without a judge since his role is only to umpire the proceedings. SA A U D SD

15. The judicial system in the United States is probably the best system which has ever been developed. SA A U D SD

Source: http://www.eduref.org/cgi-bin/printlessons.cgi/Virtual/Lessons/Social_Studies/US_Government/ GOV0022.html

How can Ms. Lee create her project to include these important elements? Where should she start? How can technology help in her planning?

_____

_____

_____

Student benefits of problem solving

There are many potential benefits of using PBL in classrooms at all levels; however, the benefits depend on how well this strategy is employed. With effective PBL, students can become more engaged in their learning and empowered to become more autonomous in classroom work. This, in turn, may lead to improved attitudes about the classroom and thus to other gains such as increased abilities for social-problem solving (Elias & Tobias, 1996). Students can gain a deeper understanding of concepts, acquire skills necessary in the real world, and transfer skills to become independent and self-directed learners and thinkers outside of school. For example, when students are encouraged to practice using problem-solving skills across a variety of situations they gain experience in discovering not only different methods but which method to apply to what kind of problem. Furthermore, students can become more confident when their self-esteem and grade does not depend only on the specific answer that the teacher wants. In addition, during the problem-solving process students can develop better critical and creative thinking skills.

Students can also develop better language skills (both knowledge and communication) through problems that require a high level of interaction with others (Dooly, 2005). This is important for all learners, but especially for ELLs and others who do not have grade-level lan-guage skills. For students who may not understand the language or content or a specific question, the focus on process gives them more opportunities to access information and express their knowledge.

ELL

The problem-solving process

The use of PBL requires different processes for students and teachers. The teacher's process involves careful planning. There are many ways for this to happen, but a general outline that can be adapted includes the following steps:

1. After students bring up a question, put it in the greater context of a problem to solve (using the format of an essential question; see chapter 4) and decide what the outcome should be—a recommendation, a summary, a process?
2. Develop objectives that represent both the goal and the specific content, language, and skills toward which students will work.
3. List background information and possible materials and content that will need to be addressed. Get access to materials and tools and prepare resource lists if necessary.
4. Write the specific problem. Make sure students know what their role is and what they are expected to do. Then go back and check that the problem and task meet the objectives and characteristics of effective PBL. Reevaluate materials and tools.
5. Develop scaffolds that will be needed.
6. Evaluate and prepare to meet individual students' needs for language, assistive tools, content review, and thinking skills and strategies.
7. Present the problem to students, assess their understanding, and provide appropriate feedback as they plan and carry out their process.

These steps are summarized in Figure 6.2.

The student process focuses more on the specific problem-solving task. PBL sources list different terms to describe each step, but the process is more or less the same. Students:

1. *Define and frame the problem:* Describe it, recognize what is being asked for, look at it from all sides, and say why they need to solve it.
2. *Plan:* Present prior knowledge that affects the problem, decide what further information and concepts are needed, and map what resources will be consulted and why.
3. *Inquire:* Gather and analyze the data, build and test hypotheses.

FIGURE 6.2 Steps in Planning a PBL Task

Step	Example
1. Contextualize the question.	Ask, "What is the question here? What should we do about it?"
2. Develop objectives.	Figure out the goal and the skills the task will meet.
3. Review background.	Explore materials and tools that focus on the problem.
4. Write the problem.	Be specific about student roles and responsibilities.
5. Develop scaffolds.	Create documents, mini-lessons, and other helps.
6. Evaluate student needs.	Review students' current level of knowledge and skills.
7. Implement.	Provide clear instructions and ongoing observation and feedback.

FIGURE 6.3 Student Problem-Solving Process

Step	Example
1. Define and frame the problem.	Determine what the problem is and why it is important to address.
2. Plan.	Decide how to address the problem.
3. Inquire.	Gather data and come to some conclusions.
4. Look back.	Review and evaluate the conclusions.

4. *Look back:* Review and evaluate the process and content. Ask "What do I understand from this result? What does it tell me?"

These steps are summarized in Figure 6.3.

Problem-solving strategies that teachers can demonstrate, model, and teach directly include trial and error, process of elimination, making a model, using a formula, acting out the problem, using graphics or drawing the problem, discovering patterns, and simplifying the problem (e.g., rewording, changing the setting, dividing it into simpler tasks). Even the popular KWL (Know, Want to Know, Learned) chart can help students frame questions. A KWL for Ms. Lee's superstore project might look like the one in Figure 6.4. Find out more about these strategies at http://literacy.kent.edu/eureka/strategies/discuss-prob.html.

Wilson, Fernandez, and Hadaway (1993) recommend a procedure for teaching problem solving in groups that involves the use of a Planning Board, a Representation Board, and a Doing Board. Using these tools, students post, discuss, and reflect on their joint problem-solving process using visual cues that they create. This helps students focus on both their process and the content.

Throughout the teacher and student processes, participants should continue to examine cultural, emotional, intellectual, and other possible barriers to problem solving.

FIGURE 6.4 KWL Chart

Topic	What I Know	What I Want to Know	What I Learned
The economy of our town			
The political process for new businesses			
How other towns like ours have been affected by superstores			
The impact of many low-paying jobs			
Noise, pollution, and traffic caused by superstores			
Benefits of having local shopping alternatives			

Teachers and Problem Solving

The teacher's role in PBL

During the teacher's process of creating the problem context, the teacher must consider what levels of authenticity, complexity, uncertainty, and self-direction students can access and work within. Gordon (1998) breaks loosely structured problems into three general types with increasing levels of these aspects. He explains:

1. *Academic challenges*. An academic challenge is student work structured as a problem arising directly from an area of study. It is used primarily to promote greater understanding of selected subject matter. The academic challenge is crafted by transforming existing curricular material into a problem format.

2. *Scenario challenges*. These challenges cast students in real-life roles and ask them to perform these roles in the context of a reality-based or fictional scenario.

3. *Real-life problems*. These are actual problems in need of real solutions by real people or organizations. They involve students directly and deeply in the exploration of an area of study. And the solutions have the potential for actual implementation at the classroom, school, community, regional, national, or global level. (p. 3)

To demonstrate the application of this simple categorization, the learning activities presented later in this chapter follow this outline.

As discussed in other chapters in this book, during student work the teacher's role can vary from director to shepherd, but when the teacher is a co-learner rather than a taskmaster, learners become experts. An often-used term for the teacher's role in the literature about problem solving is "coach." As a coach, the teacher works to facilitate thinking skills and process, including working out group dynamics, keeping students on task and making sure they are participating, assessing their progress and process, and adjusting levels of challenge as students need change. Teachers can provide hints and resources and work on a gradual release of responsibility to learners.

What level of inquiry/problem solving might be most effective for Ms. Lee's class? Why do you think so?

_____

_____

_____

Challenges for teachers

For many teachers, the roles suggested above are easier said than done. To use a PBL approach, teachers must break out of the content-dissemination mode and help their students to do the same. Even when this happens, in many classrooms students have been trained to think that problem solving is getting the one right answer (Wilson et al., 1993), and it takes time, practice, and patience for them to understand otherwise. Some teachers feel that they are obligated to cover too much in the curriculum to spend time on PBL or that using real-world problems does not mesh well with the content, materials, and context of the classroom. However, as Gordon (1998) notes, "whether it's a relatively simple matter of deciding what to eat for breakfast or a more complex one such as figuring out how to reduce pollution in one's community, in life we make decisions and do things that have concrete results. Very few of us do worksheets" (p. 2). He adds that not every aspect of students' schoolwork needs to be real, but that connections should be made from the classroom to the real world.

In addition, many standardized district and statewide tests do not measure process, so students do not want to spend time on it. However, we can overcome this thinking by demonstrating to students the ways in which they need to solve problems every day and how these strategies may transfer to testing situations. Furthermore, PBL tasks and projects may take longer to develop and assess than traditional instruction. However, teachers can start slowly by helping students practice PBL in controlled environments with structure, then gradually release them to working independently. Gordon's framework presented above can assist teachers in this effort, and the guidelines in this chapter also address some of these challenges.

GUIDELINES FOR TECHNOLOGY-SUPPORTED PROBLEM SOLVING

Obviously, PBL is more than simply giving students a problem and asking them to solve it. The following guidelines describe other issues in PBL.

Designing Problem-Solving Opportunities

In the opening scenario, Ms. Lee has chosen to address a problem that has no simple correct answer, in which people are very partisan, and in which a variety of resources, not all reliable, are addressed. To help her students work through some of the challenges of solving this problem, she will review and list resources, create scaffolds, and gather appropriate materials and tools. The guidelines described here will assist her in developing the PBL opportunity.

Guideline #1: Integrate reading and writing. Although an important part of solving problems, discussion alone is not enough for students to develop and practice problem-solving skills. Effective problem solving and inquiry require students to think clearly and deeply about content, language, and process. Reading and writing tasks can encourage students to take time to think about these issues and to contextualize their thinking practice. They can also provide vehicles for teachers to understand student progress and to provide concrete feedback. Students who have strengths in these areas will be encouraged and those who need help can learn from their stronger partners, just as those who have strengths in speaking can model for and assist their peers during discussion. Even in courses that do not stress reading and writing, integrating these skills into tasks and projects can promote successful learning.

How can Ms. Lee integrate reading and writing into the superstore project?

_____

_____

_____

Guideline #2: Avoid plagiarism. The Internet is a great resource for student inquiry and problem solving. However, when students read and write using Internet resources, they often cut and paste directly from the source. Sometimes this is an innocent mistake; students may be uneducated about the use of resources, perhaps they come from a culture where the concept of ownership is completely different than in the United States, or maybe their language skills are weak and they want to be able to express themselves better. In either case, two strategies can help avoid plagiarism:

- The teacher must teach directly about plagiarism and copyright issues. Strategies including helping students learn how to cite sources, paraphrase, summarize, and restate.
- The teacher must be as familiar as possible with the resources that students will use and check for plagiarism when it is suspected.

To do so, the teacher can enter a sentence or phrase into any Web browser with quote marks around it and if the entry is exact, the original source will come up in the browser window. Essay checkers such as Turnitin (http://turnitin.com/) are also available online that will check a passage or an entire essay. See the Technology Tools module of the Companion Website (http://www.prenhall.com/egbert) for more information on copyright and plagiarism, and read From the Classroom: Research and Plagiarism, in which one teacher describes how she uses elements of Microsoft Researcher.

Guideline #3: Do not do what students can do. Teaching, and particularly teaching with technology, is often a difficult job, due in part to the time it takes teachers to prepare effective learning experiences. Planning, developing, directing, and assessing do not have to be solely the teacher's domain, however. Students should take on many of these responsibilities, and at the same time gain in problem-solving, language, content, critical thinking, creativity, and other crucial skills. Teachers do not always need to click the mouse, write on the whiteboard, decide criteria for a rubric, develop questions, decorate the classroom, or perform many classroom and learning tasks. Students can take ownership and feel responsibility. Although it is often difficult for teachers to give up some of their power, the benefits of having more time and shared responsibility can be transformational. Teachers can train themselves to ask, "Is this something students can do?"

What responsibilities for planning the superstore project can Ms. Lee give her students?

_____

_____

_____

Guideline #4: Make mistakes okay. Problem solving often involves coming to dead ends, having to revisit data and reformulate ideas, and working with uncertainty. For students used to striving for correct answers and looking to the teacher as a final authority, the messiness of problem solving can be disconcerting, frustrating, and even scary. Teachers need to create environments of acceptance where reasoned, even if wrong, answers are recognized, acknowledged, and given appropriate feedback by the teacher and peers. In this chapter's superstore case, Ms. Lee already knows that her students come to the task with a variety of beliefs and information. In working with students' prior knowledge, she can model how to be supportive of students' faulty ideas and suggestions. She can also ask positive questions to get the students thinking about what they still need to know and how they can come to know it. She can both encourage and directly teach her students to be supportive of mistakes and trials as part of their team-building and leadership skills.

In addition, teachers need to help students to understand that even a well-reasoned argument or answer can meet with opposition. Students must not feel that they have made a bad decision just because everyone else, particularly the teacher, does not agree. Teachers should model for students that they are part of the learning process and they are impartial as to the outcome when the student's position has been well defended.

A summary of these guidelines is presented in Figure 6.5.

FROM THE CLASSROOM
Research and Plagiarism

We've been working on summaries all year and the idea that copying word for word is plagiarism. When they come to me (sixth grade) they continue to struggle with putting things in their own words so (Encarta) Researcher not only provides a visual (a reference in APA format) that this is someone else's work, but allows me to see the information they used to create their report as Researcher is an electronic filing system. It's as if students were printing out the information and keeping it in a file that they will use to create their report. But instead of having them print everything as they go to each individual site they can copy and paste until later. When they finish their research they come back to their file, decide what information they want to use, and can print it out all at once. This has made it easier for me because the students turn this in with their report. So I would say it not only allows students to learn goals of summarizing, interpreting, or synthesizing, it helps me to address them in greater depth and it's easier on me! (April, middle school teacher)

FIGURE 6.5 Guidelines for Problem Solving

Suggestion	Example
Guideline #1: Integrate reading and writing.	Add content-based literature and a text-based product.
Guideline #2: Avoid plagiarism.	Teach explicitly about plagiarism and copyright.
Guideline #3: Do not do what students can do.	Let students develop the problem, search for resources, and design assessments.
Guideline #4: Make mistakes okay.	Teach students how to accept mistakes and use formative (constructive) criticism.

PROBLEM-SOLVING AND INQUIRY TECHNOLOGIES

As with all the goals in this book, the focus of technology in problem solving is not on the technology itself but on the learning experiences that the technology affords. Different tools exist to support different parts of the process. Some are as simple as handouts that students can print and complete, others as complex as modeling and visualization software. Many software tools that support problem solving are made for experts in the field and are very difficult to learn and use. Examples of these more complicated programs include many types of computer-aided design software, advanced authoring tools, and complex expert systems. There are few software tools for K–12 students that address the problem-solving process directly and completely, but the The Factory and other inexpensive programs from Sunburst Technologies, one-computer classroom packages by Tom Snyder Productions, Where in the World? series by Broderbund, and the Jump-start series by Knowledge Adventure provide examples of software that comes close.

Simple inquiry tools that help students perform their investigations during PBL are much more prevalent. The standard word processor, database, concept mapping/graphics and spreadsheet software can all assist students in answering questions and organizing and presenting data, but there are other tools more specifically designed to support inquiry. The Microsoft Encarta suite (which includes Encarta Researcher and other software) is commonly used to support inquiry. Additional software programs that can be used within the PBL framework are mentioned in other chapters in this text. These programs, such as the Tom Snyder Productions programs mentioned above and in chapter 2, address the overlapping goals of collaboration, production, critical thinking, creativity, and problem solving. Interestingly, even video games might be used as problem-solving tools. Many of these games require users to puzzle out directions, to find missing artifacts, or to follow clues that are increasingly difficult to find and understand. A great place for teachers to start understanding how to support problem solving with technology is Intel Education's "It's a Wild Ride" and other free thinking tools and resources on the http://www.intel.com/education/ Web site.

The following section presents brief descriptions of tools that can support the PBL process. The examples are divided into stand-alone tools that can be used on one or more desktops and Web-based tools.

Stand-Alone Tools

Example 1: Fizz and Martina (Tom Snyder Productions)

Students help Fizz and Martina, animated characters in this software, to solve problems by figuring out which data is relevant, performing appropriate calculations, and presenting their solutions. The five titles in this series are perfect for a one-computer classroom. Each software package combines computer-based video, easy navigation, and handouts and other resources as scaffolds. This software is useful in classrooms with ELLs because of the combination of visual, audio, and text-based reinforcement of input. It is also accessible to students with physical disabilities because it can run on one computer; students do not have to actually perform the mouse clicks to run the software themselves.

This software is much more than math. It includes a lot of language, focuses on cooperation and collaboration in teams, and promotes critical thinking as part of problem solving. Equally important, it helps students to communicate mathematical ideas orally and in writing. See Figure 6.6 for the "getting started" screen from Fizz and Martina to view some of the choices that teachers and students have in using this package.

Example 2: I Spy Treasure Hunt, I Spy School Days, I Spy Spooky Mansion (Scholastic)

The language in these fun simulations consists of isolated, discrete words and phrases, making these programs useful for word study but not for overall concept learning. School Days, for example, focuses on both objects and words related to school. However, students work on extrapolation, trial and error, process of elimination, and other problem-solving strategies. It is difficult to get students away from the computer once they start working on any of the simulations in this series. Each software package has several separate hunts with a large number of riddles that, when solved, allow the user to put together a map or other clues to find the surprise at the end. Some of the riddles involve simply finding an item on the screen, but others require more thought such as figuring out an alternative representation for

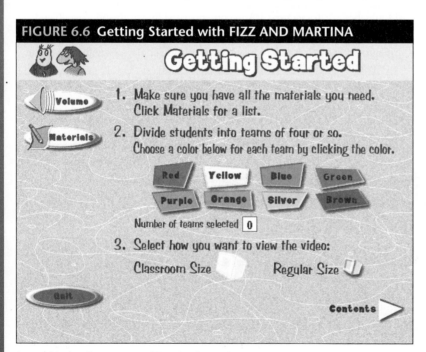

FIGURE 6.6 Getting Started with FIZZ AND MARTINA

Source: Used with permission of Tom Snyder Productions.

the item sought or using a process of elimination to figure out where to find it. All of the riddles are presented in both text and audio and can be repeated as many times as the student requires, making it easier for language learners, less literate students, and students with varied learning preferences to access the information. Younger students can also work with older students or an aide for close support so that students are focused.

There are many more software packages like these that can be part of a PBL task. See the Technology Tools module of the Companion Website for titles and publishers (http://www .prenhall.com/egbert).

I Spy used alone does not fit all the characteristics of problem-based learning. What can teachers do to make sure that software such as I Spy includes more of the characteristics of PBL?

_____

_____

_____

Example 3: Science Court (Tom Snyder Productions)

Twelve different titles in this series present humorous court cases that students must help to resolve. Whether the focus is on the water cycle, soil, or gravity, students use animated computer-based video, hands-on science activities, and group work to learn and practice science and the inquiry process. As students work toward solving the case, they examine not only the facts but also their reasoning processes. Like Fizz and Martina and much of TSP's software, Science Court uses multimedia and can be used in the one-computer classroom (as described in chapter 2), making it accessible to diverse students. Figure 6.7 presents a team question from Science Court's "Living Things" title to demonstrate some of the scaffolding available in the program.

Example 4: Geographic Information Systems (GIS)

The use of GIS to track threatened species, map hazardous waste or wetlands in the community, or propose solutions for other environmental problems supports student "spatial literacy and geographic competence" (Baker, 2005, n.p.), in addition to experimental and inquiry techniques, understanding of scale and resolution, and verification skills. Popular desktop-based GIS that students can access include Geodesy and ArcVoyager; many Web-based versions also exist, including the Student Data Mapper at http://kangis.org/ mapping/sdm/. GIS is not necessarily an easy tool to learn or use, but it can lead to real-world involvement and language, concept, and thinking skills development.

Example 5: The Adventures of Jasper Woodbury (Vanderbilt University)

The Jasper series is actually video-disc–based rather than CD-based and consists of a series of 12 adventures. Each adventure presents a challenge that students must solve using math, science, social studies, literature, and history. It presents the data in natural settings and presents authentic, collaborative problems to be solved.

Web-Based Tools

Many technology-enhanced lessons and tools on the Web come premade. In other words, they were created for someone else's students and context. Teachers must adapt these tools to fit their own teaching styles,

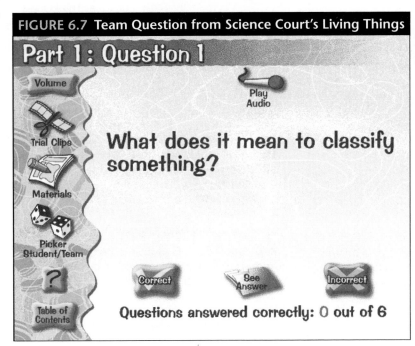

FIGURE 6.7 Team Question from Science Court's Living Things

Source: Used with permission of Tom Snyder Productions.

student needs, goals, resources, and contextual variables. Teachers must learn to modify these resources to make them their own and help them to work effectively in their unique teaching situation. With this in mind, teachers can take advantages of the great ideas in the Web-based tools described below.

Example 1: WebQuest

A WebQuest is a Web-based inquiry activity that is highly structured in a preset format. Most teachers are aware of WebQuests—a Web search finds them mentioned in every state, subject area, and grade level, and they are popular topics at conferences and workshops. Created by Bernie Dodge and Tom March in 1995 (see http://webquest.sdsu.edu/), this activity has proliferated wildly.

Each WebQuest has six parts. The Quest starts with an introduction to excite student interest. The task description then explains to students the purpose of the Quest and what the outcome will be. Next, the process includes clear steps and the scaffolds, including resources, that students will need to accomplish the steps. The evaluation section provides rubrics and assessment guidelines, and the conclusion section provides closure. Finally, the teacher section includes hints and tips for other teachers to use the WebQuest.

Advantages to using WebQuests as inquiry and problem-solving tools include:

- Students are focused on a specific topic and content and have a great deal of scaffolding.
- Students focus on using information rather than looking for it, because resources are preselected.
- Students use collaboration, critical thinking, and other important skills to complete their Quest.

FROM THE CLASSROOM

WebQuests

I evaluated a WebQuest for middle elementary (third–fourth grades), although it seems a little complicated for that age group. The quest divides students into groups and each person in the group is given a role to play (a botanist, museum curator, ethnobotanist, etc.). The task is for students to find out how plants were used for medicinal purposes in the Southwest many years ago. Students then present their findings, in a format that they can give to a national museum. Weird. It was a little complicated and not well done. I liked the topic and thought it was interesting, but a lot of work would need to be done to modify it so that all students could participate. (Jennie, first-grade teacher)

Teachers across the United States have reported significant successes for students participating in Quests. However, because Quests can be created and posted by anyone, many found on the Web do not meet standards for inquiry and do not allow students autonomy to work in authentic settings and to solve problems. Teachers who want to use a WebQuest to meet specific goals should examine carefully both the content and the process of the Quest to make sure that they offer real problems as discussed in this chapter. A matrix of wonderful Quests that have been evaluated as outstanding by experts is available at http://Webquest.sdsu.edu/matrix.html. Read what two teachers have to say about WebQuests in From the Classroom: WebQuests.

Although very popular, WebQuests are also very structured. This is fine for students who have not moved to more open-ended problems, but to support a higher level of student thinking, independence, and concept learning, teachers can have students work in teams to build a ThinkQuest (http://www.thinkquest.org/) or employ Web Inquiry Projects, the topic of this chapter's Tool CloseUp.

Example 2: Virtual Field Trips

Virtual field trips are great for concept learning, especially for students who need extra support from photos, text, animation, video, and audio. Content for field trips includes virtual walks through museums, underwater explorations, house tours, and much more. However, the format of virtual field trips ranges from simple postcard-like displays to interactive video simulations, and teachers must review the sites before using them to make sure that they meet needs and goals. Many field trips are available from Tramline Virtual Field Trips at http://www.field-trips.org/trips.htm. Other virtual trips can be found by searching "virtual field trips" on the Web. Tramline has also developed field trip generator software called TourMaker that is inexpensive and helps the user create fun trips, which is a problem-solving/creativity/critical thinking exercise in itself.

Example 3: Raw Data Sites

Raw data sites abound on the Web, from the U.S. Census to the National Climatic Data Center, from databases full of language data to the Library of Congress. These sites can be used for content learning and other learning goals. Some amazing sites can be found where students can collect their own data. These include sites like John Walker's (2003) Your Sky (www.fourmilab.to/yoursky) and Water on the Web (2005, waterontheweb.org). When working with raw data students have to draw their own conclusions based on evidence. This is another important problem-solving skill. Note that teachers must supervise and verify that data being entered for students across the world is accurate or the usefulness of these sites is diminished.

Tool CloseUp: Web Inquiry Projects

Web Inquiry Project (WIP) scaffolds were created to support guided and open inquiry, rather than the very structured inquiry included in WebQuests. WIPs consider that each discipline may have its own understanding and specific processes for inquiry, and so WIPs provide authentic, real-world problems in a discipline; examples are available at http://edweb.sdsu.edu/wip/examples.htm. WIPs require students to make use of uninterpreted data in their area available from a variety of online resources.

Like Gordon (1998), mentioned previously, Molebash and Dodge (2003) and others discuss WIPs by looking at their level of inquiry based on how much students are scaffolded during the task. In other words, they determine the level of the WIP by looking at how students are provided with the problem, procedure, and/or solution. For example, at the "lowest" level of inquiry are close-ended problems to which there is a known and specific answer. At the highest level, students pose the questions and design and select the procedures through which to examine them. WIPs are aimed at the higher levels of inquiry.

The WIP framework provides teachers with six stages through which to lead students in developing their projects: hook, focus, methodology, resources, tools, and defend. Definitions of the stages and WIPs templates can be found at http://edweb.sdsu.edu/wip/. An example is presented in Figure 6.8 to show the focus and presentation of the WIP.

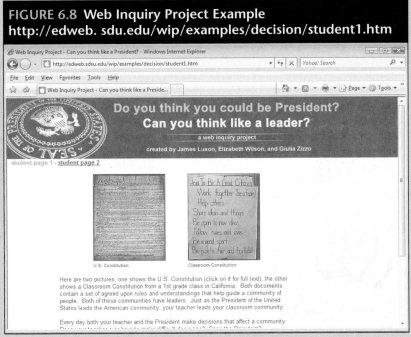

FIGURE 6.8 Web Inquiry Project Example
http://edweb. sdu.edu/wip/examples/decision/student1.htm

Source: Used with permission of San Diego State University.

How could Ms. Lee use WIP to help her students with their project?

_____

_____

_____

_____

Find tutorials for WIP in the Tutorials module of the Companion Website (http://www.prenhall.com/egbert).

T O O L S

FIGURE 6.9 Land of Fill from NASA

Source: Used with permission of NASA.

Example 4: Filamentality

Filamentality (http://www.kn.pacbell.com/wired/fil/index.html) presents an open-ended problem with a lot of scaffolding. Students and/or teachers start with a goal and then create a Web site in one of five formats that range in level of inquiry and problem solving from treasure hunts to WebQuests. The site provides lots of help and hints for those who need it, including "Mentality Tips" to help accomplish goals. It is free and easy to use, making it accessible to any teacher (or student) with an Internet connection.

Example 5: Problem Sites

Many education sites offer opportunities for students to solve problems. Some focus on language (e.g., why do we say "when pigs fly"?) or global history (e.g., what's the real story behind Tut's tomb?). "Someone in Time" allows students to guess the identity of different people in history. These problems range in level from very structured, academic problems to real-world unsolved mysteries.

The NASA SciFiles present problems in a format similar to WebQuests at http://whyfiles.larc.nasa.gov/. In other parts of the Web site there are video cases, quizzes, and tools for problem solving. See Figure 6.9 for the introduction to The Land of Fill problem from the Why? Files.

One of the most fun and effective problem-solving sites is Verizon's Superthinkers at http://www.superpages.com/ enlightenme/superthinkers/pages/. In addition to the Internet Learning Tutor, Mental Market, Kids' Camp, lesson plans and other resources, the site hosts the Peetnik Mysteries. These problem-solving cases feature a narrative story line about a mystery in town that Penelope Peetnik, of the Problem-Solvers Agency, needs help to solve. A variety of resources that students must consult are included on the site.

There is an amazing number of tools, both stand-alone and Web-based, to support problem solving and inquiry, but no tool can provide all the features that meet the needs of all students. Most important in tool choice is that it meets the language, content, and skills goals of the project and students and that there is a caring and supportive teacher guiding the students in their choice and use of the tool.

Teacher Tools

There are many Web sites addressed specifically to teachers who are concerned that they are not familiar enough with PBL or that they do not have the tools to implement this instructional strategy. The Cycle of Inquiry by the Bay Area School Reform Collaborative is one such site. It provides documents, ideas, and how-to video at http://www.springboardschools.org/tools_resources/coi.html. Another great help is From Now On at http://www.fno.org/toolbox.html, which provides specific suggestions for how to integrate technology and inquiry. Perhaps the most thorough site is University of Illinois' Inquiry Page (http://inquiry.uiuc.edu/). It contains inquiry plans with examples, definitions and articles, and even a mailing list. Any of these resources would be a good place to start for teachers interested in PBL and inquiry.

Inclusion

For teachers developing their own tools, Learning in Motion provides free software that allows teachers to add sign language support at www.learn.motion.com/deaf/ index.html.

Which of these tools, if any, could Ms. Lee use in the superstore project? How could she use them?

_____

_____

_____

LEARNING ACTIVITIES: PROBLEM SOLVING AND INQUIRY

In addition to using the tools described in the previous section to teach problem solving and inquiry, teachers can develop their own problems according to the guidelines throughout this chapter. Gordon's (1998) scheme of problem-solving levels—academic, scenario, and real life—is a simple and useful one. Teachers can refer to it to make sure that they are providing appropriate structure and guidance and helping students become independent thinkers and learners. This section uses Gordon's levels to demonstrate the variety of problem-solving and inquiry activities in which students can participate. Each example is presented with the question/problem to be answered or solved, a suggestion of a process that students might follow, and some of the possible electronic tools that might help students to solve the problem.

Academic problems

Example 1: What Will Harry Do?

Problem: At the end of the chapter, Harry Potter is faced with a decision to make. What will he do?

Process: Discuss the choices and consequences. Choose the most likely, based on past experience and an understanding of the story line. Make a short video to present the solution. Test it against Harry's decision and evaluate both the proposed solution and the real one.

Tools: Video camera and video editing software.

Example 2: Treasure Hunt

Problem: Students need resources to learn about the Civil War.

Process: Teacher provides a set of 10 questions to find specific resources online.

Tools: Web browser.

Example 3: Problem of the Week

Problem: Students should solve the math problem of the week.

Process: Students simplify the problem, write out their solution, post it to the site for feedback, then revise as necessary.

Tools: Current problems from the Math Forum@Drexel, http://mathforum.org/pow/ (see Figure 6.10 for an example).

Scenarios

Example 1: World's Best Problem Solver

Problem: You are a member of a committee that is going to give a prestigious international award for the world's best problem solver. You must nominate someone and defend your position to the committee, as the other committee members must do.

Process: Consult and list possible nominees. Use the process of elimination to determine possible nominees. Research the nominees using several different resources. Weigh the evidence and make a choice. Prepare a statement and support.

Tools: Biography.com has over 25,000 biographies, and Infoplease (infoplease.com) and the Biographical Dictionary (http://www.s9.com/) provide biographies divided into categories for easy searching.

FIGURE 6.10 Problem of the Week

math fundamentals
problem of the week

Print This Problem

Zelma's ZIP Code* - posted May 9, 2005

(Mentor group at work)

Zelma noticed something unusual about her ZIP Code: each consecutive pair of digits is the product of two one-digit numbers.

For example, look at this four-digit number: 1564.

$$15 = 5 * 3$$
$$56 = 7 * 8$$
$$64 = 8 * 8$$

Zelma's ZIP Code contains the digits 2, 3, 4, 6, and 7, exactly once each.

What is Zelma's 5-digit ZIP Code?

Be sure to explain your strategy and show how you know you are right. Include any observations about products or digits that helped you solve the problem.

Just for fun, do you know where Zelma lives?

Extra: Arrange all the digits 1 through 9 similarly, so that each consecutive pair of digits is the product of two one-digit numbers. Include any observations that helped you solve the problem.

Learn About Our Scoring System

Meet the mentors of this puzzle:
Western Oregon University Spring 2005

Source: Reproduced with permission from Drexel University, Copyright 2005 by The Math Forum @ Drexel. All rights reserved.

Example 2: Curator

Problem: Students are a committee of curators deciding what to hang in a new community art center. They have access to any painting in the world but can only hang 15 pieces in their preset space. Their goals are to enrich art appreciation in the community, make a name for their museum, and make money.

Process: Students frame the problem, research and review art from around the world, consider characteristics of the community and other relevant factors, choose their pieces, and lay them out for presentation to the community.

Tools: Art museum Web sites, books, and field trips for research and painting clips; computer-aided design, graphics, or word processing software to lay out the gallery for viewing.

Example 3: A New National Anthem

Problem: Congress has decided that the national anthem is too difficult to remember and sing and wants to adopt a new, easier song before the next Congress convenes. They want input from musicians across the United States. Students play the roles of musicians of all types.

Process: Students define the problem (e.g., is it that "The Star-Spangled Banner" is too difficult or that Congress needs to be convinced that it is not?). They either research and choose new songs or research and defend the current national anthem. They prepare presentations for members of Congress.

Tools: Music sites and software, information sites on the national anthem.

Real-life problems

Example 1: Racism in School

Problem: There have been several incidents in our school recently that seem to have been racially motivated. The principal is asking students to consider how to make our school a safe learning environment for all students.

Process: Determine what is being asked—the principal wants help. Explore the incidents and related issues. Weigh the pros and cons of different solutions. Prepare solutions to present to the principal.

Tools: Web sites and other resources about racism and solutions, graphic organizers to organize the information, word processor or presentation software for results. Find excellent free tools for teachers and students at the Southern Poverty Law Center's Teaching Tolerance Web site at www.tolerance.org.

Example 2: Homelessness vs. Education

Problem: The state legislature is asking for public input on the next budget. Because of a projected deficit, political leaders are deciding which social programs, including education and funding for the homeless, should be cut and to what extent. They are interested in hearing about the effects of these programs on participants and on where cuts could most effectively be made.

Process: Decide what the question is (e.g., how to deal with the deficit? How to cut education or funding for the homeless? Which programs are more important? Something else?). Perform a cost-benefit analysis using state data. Collect other data by interviewing and researching. Propose and weigh different solution schemes and propose a suggestion. Use feedback to improve or revise.

Tools: Spreadsheet for calculations, word processor for written solution, various Web sites and databases for costs, electronic discussion list or email for interviews.

Example 3: Cleaning Up

Problem: Visitors and residents in our town have been complaining about the smell from the university's experimental cattle farms drifting across the highway to restaurants and stores in the shopping center across the street. They claim that it makes both eating and shopping unpleasant and that something must be done.

Process: Conduct onsite interviews and investigation. Determine the source of the odor. Measure times and places where the odor is discernible. Test a variety of solutions. Choose the most effective solution and write a proposal supported by a poster for evidence.

Tools: Encarta and other oneline and offline sources of information on cows, farming, odor; database to organize and record data; word processing and presentation software for describing the solution.

These activities can all be adapted and different tools and processes used. As stated previously, the focus must be both on the content to be learned and the skills to be practiced and acquired. More problem-solving activity suggestions and examples can be found at Judy Harris's site at http://www.2learn.ca/Projects/Together/Structures.html.

ASSESSING LEARNER PROBLEM SOLVING AND INQUIRY

Many of the assessments described in other chapters of this text, for example, rubrics, performance assessments, observation, and student self-reflection, can also be employed to assess problem solving and inquiry. However, Gordon (1998) says that problem-solving tasks also should be judged against "real-world standards of quality" (p. 2). Most experts on problem solving and inquiry agree that schools need to get away from testing that does not involve showing process or allowing students to problem solve; rather, teachers should evaluate problem-solving tasks as if they were someone in the real-world context of the problem. For example, if students are studying an environmental issue, teachers can evaluate their work throughout the project from the standpoint of someone in the field, being careful that their own biases do not cloud their judgment on controversial issues. Rubrics, multiple-choice tests, and other assessment tools mentioned in other chapters of this text should account for the multiple outcomes that are possible in content, language, and skills learning. Figure 6.11 shows a high school rubric for problem solving that can be used to assess students' current levels or be used as an evaluation of progress over time. Figure 6.12 on page 174 presents one for elementary classrooms. These resources can be used as models for assessing problem-solving skills in a variety of tasks.

FIGURE 6.11 High School Problem-Solving Assessment from Intel Education

High School Reasoning Checklist

This checklist can be used by students or teachers to assess reasoning skills.

Forming and Supporting Opinions
- ☐ Values well-reasoned opinions
- ☐ Puts forth effort necessary to form good opinions
- ☐ Focuses on validity of argument rather than personal feelings
- ☐ Recognizes subtle manipulations of facts used to persuade
- ☐ Identifies own assumptions
- ☐ Identifies assumptions of others

Drawing Conclusions
- ☐ Uses personal experiences and knowledge to make inferences and draw conclusions
- ☐ Uses thorough understanding of systems within topic to make inferences and draw conclusions
- ☐ Draws conclusions that add meaning and insight

Logical Thinking
- ☐ Uses deductive reasoning to make generalizations
- ☐ Uses inductive reasoning to understand unfamiliar concepts
- ☐ Uses "If . . . then . . ." statements to draw conclusions about relationships

Determining Cause and Effect
- ☐ Describes multiple cause-and-effect relationships in a system
- ☐ Differentiates between causation and correlation
- ☐ Creates detailed visual representations of inter-related systems that show causes and effects

Communication
- ☐ Uses appropriate subject-area language to explain conclusions and reasoning
- ☐ Uses language of logical thinking to explain conclusions and reasoning

Source: Used with permission of Intel Corporation.

FIGURE 6.12 Elementary Problem-Solving Assessment

Elementary Identifying and Describing Problems Rubric

	4	3	2	1
Anticipating Problems	I think ahead and guess what problems might be coming in a project in time to prevent them.	Sometimes I can think ahead and guess what problems I might have in time to avoid them.	With help, I can tell what problems there might be.	I have a hard time knowing when there is going to be a problem.
Monitoring Processes	When things are not going well on a project, I pay attention to what's happening and figure out where the problem is.	When things aren't going well, I figure out what the problem is.	I need help to figure out what a problem is.	I do not try to figure out what is going wrong.
	I am always looking at how things are going on a project and thinking of ways to make things go better.	I pay attention to how things are going so I can fix problems as they happen.	I usually expect others to notice problems while I'm working and help me fix them.	I do not notice problems while I am working unless someone points them out to me.
Choosing Solutions	I take a lot of time to think about a problem before I try to solve it.	I think about a problem before I start solving it.	If someone reminds me, I think about a problem before I solve it.	I usually just start right in solving a problem without thinking about it.
	I think of as many solutions as I can before I choose one.	I think of more than one solution before I choose one.	With help, I think of more than one solution.	I usually try the first solution I think of.

Source: Used with permission of Intel Corporation.

In addition to the techniques mentioned above, Wilson et al. (1993) suggest keeping a weekly problem-solving notebook, in which students record problem solutions, strategies they used, similarities with other problems, extensions of the problem, and an investigation of one or more of the extensions. Although the authors' focus is on math, using this notebook to assess students' location and progress in problem solving could be very effective.

What are some specific ways that Ms. Lee should plan to assess the process and progress of her students during the superstore project?

_____

_____

_____

SAMPLE LESSON: PROBLEM SOLVING

After they complete their research on the topic, Ms. Lee's students will create a Web site focusing on the superstore issue. They will use the site to collect additional information and opinions. However, before they start Ms. Lee wants to reinforce concepts about fair use and copyright. She finds a lesson that might work at PBS's Teacher Source (www.pbs.org).

INTELLECTUAL PROPERTY IN THE DIGITAL AGE

Grade Level: 4–8, 9–12

Subject: Technology, Arts, Current Events

Introduction: Many people share the misconception that information found on the Internet is free and for all to use without permission. However, by collecting many images, sounds, and readings when creating a Web site you may be violating a person's intellectual property (IP) or copyright.

1. Begin this lesson by introducing your students to the concepts of intellectual property and copyright to your students.

Definitions:

- *Intellectual property* represents the property of your mind or intellect. Types of intellectual property include patents, trademarks, designs, confidential information/trade secrets, copyright, circuit layout rights, plant breeder's rights, etc.

- *Copyright* protects the original expression of ideas, not the ideas themselves. It is free and automatically safeguards your original works of art, literature, music, films, broadcasts and computer programs from copying and certain other uses.

2. Explore these questions with your students: How are the two concepts similar and different? What are the various types of intellectual property? Why do laws protecting IP exist? How has the revolution in communications technology over the past decade complicated issues surrounding IP?

   You and your students may want to use these resources for more information:

- NewsHour Online: Copyrighting in the Digital Age
  http://www.pbs.org/newshour/media/digital_copyright/cases.html

- Crash Course in Copyright
  http://www.utsystem.edu/OGC/IntellectualProperty/ cprtindx.htm

- Intellectual Property on the Web
  http://digitalenterprise.org/ip/ip.html

- *Web and Software Development: A Legal Guide* by Stephen Fishman; *Digital Copyright: Protecting Intellectual Property on the Internet* by Jessica Litman

Source: © 2007 Public Broadcasting Service. Used with permission.

Ms. Lee likes to see that the lesson provides a guideline but is not too prescriptive of what students should do. She uses the Lesson Analysis and Adaptation Worksheet (found in chapter 1 on page 33 and in the Lesson Planning module of the Companion Website) to figure out what she needs to do to make this lesson work for her students. She decides to make these adaptations based on her analysis:

- Because there are no standards or objectives, she will add these. She particularly wants to focus on the NETS*S that recommend that students understand and practice responsible uses of technology and that they use technology resources for solving problems.

- Rather than just answer questions, Ms. Lee will ask her students to research some answers and compare them with what classmates found. Then she will ask them to develop a set of guidelines, in their choice of medium, for the class to refer to when they are using online resources. This addition will support student inquiry, communication, critical thinking, production, and creativity along with content learning and problem solving.

- Ms. Lee will brainstorm with students the possible subquestions that will help them answer the questions in the lesson. She will assign each student dyad to find information on one subquestion, keeping the students active and each making a contribution.

- Technology is used as a tool in this lesson and helps students discover a variety of viewpoints and resources. However, to make sure that all students can access the resources, she will add both print and electronic references at a variety of levels for students to choose from.

- Ms. Lee will use the guidelines that students create as part of her assessment, and she will continue to observe how well her students follow the guidelines as they create their Web pages for the superstore project.

Ms. Lee believes that, with the additions she will make, this lesson will support the objectives and provide her students with practice in many skill areas.

What else would you add to this lesson to make it effective for your current or future students? What would you delete? Why?

_____

_____

_____

CHAPTER REVIEW

Key Points

- **Define problem solving and inquiry.**

  The element that distinguishes problem-solving or problem-based learning from other strategies is that the focal point is a problem that students must work toward solving. A proposed solution is typically the outcome of problem solving. During the inquiry part of the process, students ask questions and then search for answers to those questions.

- **Understand the interaction between problem solving and other instructional goals.**

  Although inquiry is also an important instructional strategy and can stand alone, it is also a central component of problem solving because students must ask questions and investigate the answers to solve the problem. In addition, students apply critical and creative thinking skills to prior knowledge during the problem-solving process, and they communicate, collaborate, and often produce some kind of concrete artifact.

- **Discuss guidelines and tools for encouraging effective student problem solving.**

  It is often difficult for teachers to not do what students can do, but empowering students in this way can lead to a string of benefits. Other guidelines, such as avoiding plagiarism, integrating reading and writing, and making it okay for students to make mistakes, keep the problem-solving process on track. Tools to assist in this process range from word processing to specially designed inquiry tools.

- **Create and adapt effective technology-enhanced tasks to support problem solving.**

  Teachers can design their own tasks following guidelines from any number of sources, but they can also find ready-made problems in books, on the Web, and in some software packages. Teachers who do design their own have plenty of resources available to help. A key to task development is connecting classroom learning to the world outside of the classroom.

- **Assess student technology-supported problem solving.**

  In many ways the assessment of problem-solving and inquiry tasks is similar to the assessment of other goals in this text. Matching goals and objectives to assessment and ensuring that students receive formative feedback throughout the process will make success more likely.

What information in this chapter is most useful to you? Why? How will you use it in your teaching?

_____

_____

_____

CASE QUESTIONS REVIEW

Reread the case at the beginning of the chapter and review your answers. In light of what you learned during this chapter, how do your answers change? Note any changes here.

1. **What prior content and language knowledge do the students need to solve this problem?**

_____

_____

_____

2. **What process should the students follow to find a solution to the problem?**

_____

_____

_____

3. **What should Ms. Lee's role in the project be?**

_____

_____

_____

4. **What role can technology play in helping the students to solve their problem?**

_____

_____

_____

CHAPTER EXTENSIONS • • • • • • • • • • •

To answer any of the following questions online, go to the Chapter 6 Extensions module of this text's Companion Website (http://www.prenhall.com/egbert).

Adapt • • • •

Choose a lesson for your potential subject area and grade level from the Internet4Classrooms page of Integrated Technology Lesson Plans (http://www.internet4classrooms.com/integ_tech_lessons.htm). Use the Lesson Analysis and Adaptation Worksheet from chapter 1 on page 33 (also available on the Lesson Planning module of the Companion Website) to consider the lesson in the context of problem solving. Use your responses to the worksheet to suggest general changes to the lesson based on your current or future students and context.

Practice • • • •

1. *Determine tool levels.* Apply Gordon's three-level scheme to the tools listed in this chapter. Which level would each tool be appropriate for? Why?

2. *Review a tool.* Review one of the tools described in the chapter, including tools to spot plagiarism. Explain how it addresses problem solving and inquiry and how you might integrate it into your current or future classroom.

3. *Practice planning.* Review the sample activities in this chapter. Choose three, and describe how you could integrate reading and writing into the activities to promote effective problem solving.

Explore • • • • •

1. *Create an activity.* Outline a WebQuest, ThinkQuest, WIP, or other inquiry or problem-solving activity. Describe each stage briefly but clearly.

2. *Create a standards-based task.* Choose a national or state standard for your subject area and grade level. Write a problem based on that standard following the characteristics described in the chapter, and then evaluate the problem using the characteristics of effective tasks.

3. *Turn theory into practice.* Use the adapted Figure 6.2 on page 161 to develop a classroom lesson based on the PBL process. On the chart below, fill in the "Lesson" column with ideas for each step.

Step	Example	Lesson
1. Contextualize the question.	Ask, "What is the question here? What should we do about it?"	
2. Develop objectives.	Figure out the goal and the skills the task will meet.	
3. Review background.	Explore materials and tools that focus on the problem.	
4. Write the problem.	Be specific about student roles and responsibilities.	
5. Develop scaffolds.	Create documents, mini-lessons, and other helps.	
6. Evaluate student needs.	Review students' current level of knowledge and skills.	
7. Implement.	Provide clear instructions and ongoing observation and feedback.	

REFERENCES

Baker, T. (2005). *The history and application of GIS in education.* KANGIS: K12 GIS Community. Available from http://kangis.org/learning/ed_docs/gisNed1.cfm.

Blosser, P. (1988). *Teaching problem solving—secondary school science.* ERIC/SMEAC Science Education Digest No. 2.

Dooly, M. (2005, March/April). The Internet and language teaching: A sure way to interculturality? *ESL Magazine, 44,* 8–10.

Elias, M., & Tobias, S. (1996). *Social problem solving: Interventions in the schools.* New York: Guilford Press.

Gordon, R. (1998, January). Balancing real-world problems with real-world results. *Phi Delta Kappan, 79*(5), 390–393. [electronic version]

IMSA (2005). *How does PBL compare with other instructional approaches?* Available: http://www2.imsa.edu/programs/pbln/tutorials/intro/intro7.php.

Mansilla, V., & Gardner, H. (1997, January). Of disciplines and kinds of understanding. *Phi Delta Kappan, 78*(5), 381–386. [electronic version]

Molebash, P., & Dodge, B. (2003). Kickstarting inquiry with WebQuests and web inquiry projects. *Social Education, 671*(3), 158–162.

Stites, R. (1998). What does research say about outcomes from project-based learning? Evaluation of project-based learning: The Multimedia project. Available: http://pblmm.k12.ca.us/PBLGuide/pblresch.htm.

Wilson, J., Fernandez, M., & Hadaway, N. (1993). Mathematical problem solving. In P. Wilson (Ed.), *Research ideas for the classroom: High school mathematics*. New York: Macmillan.

This year for the first time I got to go crabbing. It is very fun! Every year I go to the beach a lot, but this year was different because we couldn't go to the beach until about the first week and a half we were there. We were there for five weeks.

7

Supporting Student Production

Case: See You on TV!

As you read the following scenario, note both the processes in which students are involved and the products that they generate.

Students in Ms. Farber's fifth-grade class are working on a media literacy unit that will help them to become more critical consumers of media. Ms. Farber has incorporated standards-based content and language goals across the unit and has planned carefully so that all students are active participants in their learning.

Part of the unit is a five-stage project focusing on one area of media—television advertising—with the goal of producing infomercials, or long commercials. In order to focus their infomercials, students first researched and then designed new products that they believe they can sell to other fifth graders (an authentic audience) using persuasive techniques (Stage 1). With the use of graphics software and copyright-free clip art from the Internet, student teams have developed a three-dimensional model and a one-paragraph description of their products for use in their 5-minute commercials (Stage 2). Teams are currently in the process of writing scripts using both print and electronic resources (Stage 3). Each team must spell-check its script and check it against both the project grading rubric and an "infomercial checklist" before asking another team and then Ms. Farber to evaluate it. As the unit progresses, readings, class discussions, skills-based lessons, and other exercises and activities inform the students' understanding of media literacy and the development of student products.

During script development, Ms. Farber observes one team reviewing sample infomercials using the VCR, members of different teams using two of the three class computers to do research, and most of the students working with great animation on their scripts around their desks. Because each team is required to gather feedback from at least one other team about their script, she also sees a lot of intergroup interaction.

In future classes, when the scripts are drafted and have passed evaluation by another team and Ms. Farber, they will go into production (Stage 4). This stage requires the most advanced technology use. Students will prepare whatever scenery and props they need and use one of the school's digital cameras to film their segment. Students will then use either iMovie (Apple) or Avid Free DV (Avid) video editing software to edit their infomercial, add any text, and burn it (save it) to a digital video disk (DVD) (Stage 5).

Final versions of the infomercials will be shown to the other fifth-grade classes, who will provide feedback on which products they would buy and why. After the project teams debrief, students will turn in an explanation of the assignment and a reflection on the different processes they experienced and ideas and skills they learned. They will include any questions they still have about any aspect of the project or unit.

• •

Answer these questions about the case. There are no right or wrong answers—the goal is for you to respond before you read the chapter. Then, as you interact with the chapter contents, think about how your answers might change.

1. *What are some learning benefits that students might derive from creating this product?*

_____

_____

_____

2. *What aspects of the process seem to be most important to student achievement toward the goals? Why do you think so?*

_____

_____

_____

3. *What is the teacher's role in this project?*

_____

_____

_____

4. *What role does the technology play?*

_____

_____

_____

Ms. Farber has chosen a specific process and product for the student media literacy project, but there are many other choices that she might have made. The goal of this chapter is to help you to understand the range of choices for student production by exploring why production is important to student learning and the many ways in which production can be supported effectively with technology. After reading this chapter you will be able to

- Define production.
- Describe the benefits of student production for learning.
- Explain the role of process in production.
- Discuss guidelines for supporting student technology-enhanced production.

- Describe technologies for supporting student production.
- Evaluate and develop pedagogically sound technology-enhanced production activities.
- Design appropriate assessments for technology-enhanced process and product.

When you have completed this chapter, which NETS*T will you have addressed?

_____

_____

_____

The sample activities, tools, and student products presented in this chapter will help you understand how to apply the standards described in this chapter and address the learning goals for student production. For standards that guide production and therefore the content of this chapter, see the Meeting the Standards feature.

• • • **Meeting the Standards:** Standards That Guide Production • • •

Production is mentioned in the standards in every content area and also in the national standards for English language learners (Goal 2.2). The words "compose" (NA-M.5–8.4, NA-M.9–12.4), "design" (NA-M.9–12.3), "create" (NA-M.PK–12.1, NA-D.K–4.7, NL-ENG.K–12.6, NM-GEO.PK–2.3), "model" (NM-ALG.PK–2.3), "develop" (NPH-H.5–8.6), and "report" (NSS-G.K–12.1) are used to indicate that an important aspect of student learning across the content areas involves student products such as musical scores, written descriptions, models, multimedia presentations, posters, and role-plays. In science and social studies, as in math, music, and English, teachers and students are expected to use the production process to learn. In addition, the third goal of the National Educational Technology Foundation Standards for All Students (NETS*S) requires that "Students use technology tools to enhance learning, increase productivity, and promote creativity" (National Academies of Science, NT.K–13.3). It also states that "Students use productivity tools to collaborate in constructing technology-enhanced models, prepare publications, and produce other creative works." Production projects also meet many of the other standards because they involve understanding, communicating, collaborating, and other learning goals.

How do your state standards address student production? Find terms that your standards use that indicate production as a goal.

_____

_____

_____

 See your state standards for production in the Standards module of this text's Companion Website (http://www.prenhall.com/egbert).

• • • •

OVERVIEW OF TECHNOLOGY-SUPPORTED PRODUCTION IN K–12 CLASSROOMS

In order to support production effectively, teachers must understand why production is important and how it occurs.

What Is Production?

Production is a form of learning whereby students create a **product,** or a concrete artifact that is the focus of learning. Production is one kind of project-based learning; production can be seen as the process, and the product is typically the end result. There are many kinds of tasks used in classrooms, but not all of them result in a tangible product. For example, some tasks lead to new understandings, a discussion, or an action. In production projects, both the impetus and outcome of learning are a material object. In other words, a tangible, manipulable outcome is the driving force behind the development of each stage of the production project.

Products can take many forms, for example, a slide show, photographs, three-dimensional objects, or a portfolio (discussed further in chapter 8). They can range from essays to multimedia presentations to more elaborate productions like the infomercials that Ms. Farber's students are creating. Good products are the result of communication, collaboration, creativity, and other student goals discussed in this book. Production is also a valuable activity in itself, particularly if the products are based in curriculum standards and support language and content learning. Read as a teacher describes projects in her classroom in From the Classroom: Projects.

Because it is a relatively new teaching strategy for many classrooms and contains many elements of other strategies, and because it is hard to measure, there is not yet a great deal of research on project-based learning or production per se. However, the theoretical support for project-based learning goes back to Dewey's idea (1938) of learning by doing, and the components of production have received a great deal of attention in the literature. Learning goals that can be included in the production process are widely supported in the literature as leading to gains in student achievement; for example, *collaboration* (discussed in chapter 3), *problem solving* (chapter 6), and *critical thinking* (chapter 4). In addition, **active learning**, or learning activities in which students do and think about what they do, has been found to be more useful for students than inert knowledge transfer (i.e., lecture). Active learning is more likely to be remembered and applied (Thomas, 2000). In addition, as noted in several other chapters in this text, the literature shows that "learning is maximized if the context for learning resembles the real-life context in which the to-be-learned material will be used" (Thomas, 2000, p. 7). This means that authentic activities that are meaningful in students' lives support student achievement. For one tool that can support student production, see the Tool CloseUp: Quandary on page 184.

Overall, research exploring the use of project-based learning shows that students gain in subject matter, in skills and strategies worked on as part of the project, in problem solving with groups and other work behaviors, and in attendance and attitude (George Lucas Foundation, 2005; San Mateo County Office of Education, 2001; Thomas, 2000). More important for some stakeholders in the educational process, some evaluations of project-based learning show student gains of more than 10% on statewide skills assessments (San Mateo County Office of Education, 2001).

Characteristics of effective production tasks

There is no one accepted model of project-based learning. In fact, it is implemented in so many different ways in classrooms that the distinctions between it and other learning activities are often blurred. The results of production activities can span the range from highly structured and prescribed outcomes, such as a written dialog with five lines that must contain certain vocabulary and grammatical items, to a very loosely controlled outcome, such as some type of new invention. During highly structured projects, students are provided with a clearly defined outcome, which they attempt to reproduce to the teacher's specifications; in loosely controlled projects, students are given a general area in which to produce and have many choices in the forms and features of their products.

Review the project in the opening scenario. On the continuum from highly structured and prescribed to loosely controlled, where do you think it lies? Why do you think so?

_____

_____

_____

FROM THE CLASSROOM

Projects

I use a lot of projects as a means to teach concepts. This approach works for me, because I can have the same basic thing that all kids are doing, but adjust expectations or requirements depending on students' various abilities. I feel that the projects give the kids problems to solve and help encourage critical thinking. I also think projects on the computer that require students to make an end product really encourage this as well. The computer projects have been great for my ELLs. (Susan, fifth-grade teacher)

T O O L S

Tool CloseUp: Quandary

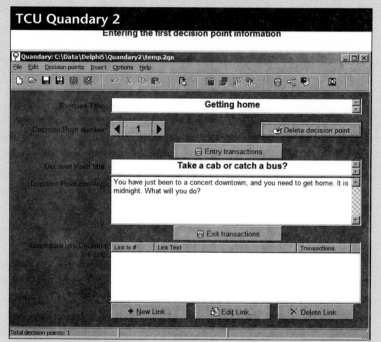

TCU Quandary 1

Source: Used with permission of Half-Baked Software, Inc.

clear framework for students who need more structure and scaffolding. The Quandary interface shows exactly where to place the elements on each page of the maze. Producing action mazes with Quandary allows students to learn actively, to focus on the content rather than the technology, and to develop products that can be used by authentic audiences around the world. Working in teams, students can learn and practice communication, collaboration, and creativity skills and provide a learning tool for other students.

Quandary is shareware, so teachers can download and test its basic features before deciding to buy a license. To

TCU Quandary 2
Entering the first decision point information

Source: Used with permission of Half-Baked Software, Inc.

The figure above shows a Web-based action maze. It was made with Quandary, a software package from Half-Baked Software that helps users create action mazes, surveys, and other branching learning exercises. The authors describe Quandary in this way:

> A Quandary exercise consists of a large number of *Decision Points*. These are like nodes in a tree. Each decision point represents a situation in the "adventure," or a position in the maze. The user reads the information at the decision point and then chooses from a range of alternative courses of action by clicking on a link.
>
> Each time the user makes a choice, he or she moves to another decision point and is faced with a new situation. In this way, the user moves through the adventure, or maze, and may eventually find a solution or reach a dead end. As the author, your job is to create the series of decision points and link them together. Quandary should make this process easy for you. (http://www.halfbakedsoftware.com/quandary/version_2/tutorial/tutorial.htm)

Other tools, for example, PowerPoint and Hyperstudio, can support learners in making action mazes. However, Quandary provides more focused and powerful tools in a

help make that decision, view examples of a range of Quandary uses at http://www.halfbakedsoftware.com/quandary/version_2/examples/.

Try out one of the action maze examples linked to the Quandary home page. What ideas do you have for using it to support production and other learning goals with your current or future students?

_____

_____

_____

_____

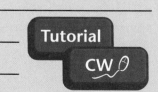

Find tutorials for Quandary in the Tutorials module of the Companion Website (http://www.prenhall.com/egbert).

The flexibility involved in creating production tasks means that teachers with different philosophies of teaching and learning can take advantage of production as a strategy. In the educational literature on production, characteristics of an effective production task generally include those in Figure 7.1

How well does Ms. Farber's infomercial project display the characteristics noted in Figure 7.1? Explain why you think so.

_____

_____

_____

FIGURE 7.1 Production Task Characteristics
1. It is developed over time.
2. It involves more than one discipline.
3. It includes student choices.
4. It deals with authentic (real-world) issues.
5. Students receive help and scaffolding (support) from a variety of sources.
6. Assessment is ongoing from many sources, including the students themselves.

Source: Adapted from Bazeli, 1997; Blumenfeld et al., 1991; San Mateo County Office of Education, 2001.

Student benefits of production

Production can serve as a motivator by engaging students in the process of their learning. Production also allows students some leeway to work in ways that they prefer, helps them to develop real-world skills, and develops their abilities to communicate and collaborate with others. Most important for production projects, students are motivated by producing a tangible outcome. Like other types of group projects, well-planned production projects can result in the following student gains:

- Individual and group/social responsibility
- Planning, critical thinking, reasoning, and creativity
- Strong communication skills, both for interpersonal and presentation needs
- Cross-cultural understanding
- Visualizing and decision making
- Knowing how and when to use technology and choosing the most appropriate tool for the task (George Lucas Foundation, 2005)

Production projects can also benefit a wide range of students. For example, these projects can support the skills and abilities of English language learners. Production offers all students opportunities to communicate in a variety of modes (e.g., speaking, drawing, gesturing), to receive language and content input in a variety of modes (e.g., graphics, video, listening), and to use different learning styles (e.g., hands-on, visual, aural) during the production process. This helps ELLs to receive input in English that is comprehensible, to work in ways that they understand, and to play a role in the project regardless of their language fluency. Project-based learning also helps less-motivated students to "engage in and persist at" learning activities (Blumenfeld et al., 1991).

In addition, the variety of tasks that are part of the production process, described in the following section, makes it easier to integrate students with different physical, social, and psychological abilities. Students can play roles that most suit their needs and aptitudes.

ELL

Inclusion

Which of the benefits listed above would you expect Ms. Farber's students to gain from the project? Why?

_____

_____

_____

THE PRODUCTION PROCESS

What Is the Production Process?

Producing facilitates learning in many ways, but creating a product is not enough to promote effective learning. The **production process** is crucial to learning as students work to understand

and make decisions about the product. During a production project, students may go through a process like the one presented in Table 7.1. The three main stages are *planning, development,* and *evaluation*. These stages are similar to those used in other learning activities, but the focus here is on a product.

Stage	Focus	Steps and Activities
TABLE 7.1 The Student Production Process		
Planning	*Preproduction*	1. Understand the project goals, objectives, and evaluation criteria. 2. Understand the overall project plan stages. 3. Research the product. 4. Understand the audience. 5. Outline ideas for the product and a plan for getting there.
Development	*Production*	6. Students create their product.
Evaluation	*Postproduction*	7. Students and other stakeholders assess the product and process.

The preproduction stage

In the preproduction or planning stage, students may help the teacher to uncover the features of a good product and develop rubrics and other evaluations to guide both process and product. Students construct a schematic that lays out in different ways the various steps in the project. They then conduct initial research, include finding information from print and electronic sources and evaluating existing products (if any). Students can also conduct interviews and plan other interactions with their intended audience. Students brainstorm, draw, discuss, demonstrate, and create a draft plan that includes roles for team members, tools needed, and a plausible timeline for each step. They use feedback from the teacher and other stakeholders to revise their plans as necessary.

The production stage

During the production or development stage, students engage in direct creation, including designing, making models of their products, and performing the other tasks outlined in their plan. Teams use feedback from audience members and other stakeholders and the rubric criteria to form their product.

The postproduction stage

During postproduction, or the evaluation stage, students reflect on feedback from their audience and on the process and product. They debrief, or discuss and reflect, individually, in teams, or as a class.

The production process is not linear; rather, it is iterative in that students can repeat previous stages at any time as needed. In other words, if they find that they need to do additional planning or replanning during the production stage, they can do so.

What other steps or activities could be included in this process? How do these additions make the process more effective?

Teachers and Production

The teacher's role in production projects

The teacher plays a crucial role in the success of production projects. It takes skill to plan well and keep the process running smoothly. The teacher's role in projects can range from a very directive to a more facilitative role, depending on student level and abilities and the project goals. Teachers need to provide guidelines and models for what the product should be, not necessarily so that students can copy them exactly, but so that they realize what is expected and why. To keep students most active, teacher planning should include ways to have students make their own decisions and work closely with each other. The teacher can help students to identify roles and/or to disseminate them, provide clear goals and benchmarks, model both the language and content needed for the project, and provide ongoing feedback and skills lessons as students require them. However, not all students can work so autonomously and it is often difficult for teachers to loosen control; in these cases, a more structured project with a very specific product can be used.

What role(s) does Ms. Farber play in the infomercial project? What makes you think so? Is this effective? Why or why not?

_____

_____

_____

Challenges for teachers

In addition to the challenges of developing good projects, teachers may face school, community, and classroom obstacles to developing production projects. For example, projects often take time that standardized testing schedules or a rigid curriculum do not permit. Some teachers (or administrators) cannot abide noisy classrooms or relinquishing control to students. Another challenge for teachers is to understand how to provide enough scaffolding, or assistance, as students need it without interfering too much; they might also have to learn new technologies and learn how to assess the process and the product. All these challenges can be overcome with time and practice. The guidelines, tools, and resources mentioned in the next section can help teachers understand how to avoid or work through these challenges.

Which of these obstacles seems the most likely to challenge you in your future or current teaching? Why do you think so? What ideas do you have for overcoming these challenges?

_____

_____

_____

GUIDELINES FOR SUPPORTING STUDENT PRODUCTION

Guidelines for Designing Production Opportunities

In the chapter's opening scenario, Ms. Farber has carefully planned the project so that students understand the process and understand that the technology is secondary in importance to the content and goals of the project. Students are active learners; they make decisions, ask questions, write dialog, draw, direct, suggest, critique, and disagree. Students have the opportunity to play many different roles. Students who are not as competent in one area, for example, students whose language proficiency is not at grade level or those who have difficulty performing certain tasks, have the opportunity to work in other areas. However, the work of all students is valued and none of the students is exempt from working toward the final goal. By requiring that learners ask each other for help and evaluate one another's work, Ms. Farber is providing frameworks of support (scaffolding) and guiding learners to use valuable resources (their peers). Read as another teacher describes using roles in her classroom in From the Classroom: Roles.

FROM THE CLASSROOM

Roles

I have used the strategy of assigning roles to students for group work. I've used it in the middle school and with adults. You may choose to play a smaller part in this and list the different roles on the board: time keeper, recorder, etc., and have students decide who will do what in their group. Assigning roles also eliminates the possibility of hitch-hikers, students who just go along with everything and don't contribute. For younger students I would have jobs assigned at random or make smaller groups with fewer roles. Just simplify it and it will still be successful. Rotating also helps everyone participate in the different types of roles available, which you can alter according to your lesson plans and expected outcomes. (Gabriela, second-grade teacher)

Ms. Farber has clearly put a lot of thought into how the media project should be accomplished. She has planned carefully to give students opportunities not only to produce but to get the most out of the process. Some of the guidelines for designing effective production projects that she followed are discussed here.

Guideline #1: Focus on process. Ms. Farber has put a clear focus on process. This is important because often while creating projects, learners may get caught up in the graphics and other "fun" parts of production and lose some of the project's opportunities for learning. Teachers must ensure that the task is devised so that students focus on the use of the language and content that are to be learned and used. Like Ms. Farber in the opening scenario, designing opportunities means:

- Establishing both language and content goals that students understand
- Involving students in the evaluation of content and process
- Helping all students be actively involved in every aspect of the project

To help students get the most out of the process, Ms. Farber has assigned the teams roles for each stage of the infomercial project. Her students are familiar with these roles because they have used them before. Each stage has a Technology Operator, an Editor, a Team Liaison, and an Idea Generator. Team members redistribute the roles for each stage of the project so that all students have a chance to work to their strengths and also improve on their weaknesses. At each stage, Ms. Farber, the school technology coordinator, and the library media specialist work with an expert group (one member of each team) in a form of "cascade learning" to train students who are playing the role of Technology Operator. In different stages, for example, the Technology Operator is responsible for Internet searching, the digital camera, the editing software, and word processing. In each stage a different student is the Editor, who is responsible for both editing text documents and completing project paperwork. A third team member, who serves as the Team Liaison, works with other students and the teacher as a representative of the team, and an Idea Generator leads the development of the different stages of the project.

By focusing on all students being actively involved with content and language, Ms. Farber can assist learners in completing a process that will meet their goals and result in a useful product. Ms. Farber has found that her ELL students, although not at grade level in reading and writing, are very successful at learning and teaching the technologies, generating ideas, and working as Liaison. She encourages them to take on the role of Editor in the last stage of the project when they are familiar with the vocabulary, ideas, and tasks involved in the project. In this way, she is helping them work from their strengths to developing their weaknesses while still holding them accountable for each part of the task.

ELL

What other roles could students in this project play? What would be an appropriate role for a monolingual Spanish-speaking student? What about a student with dyslexia?

_____

_____

_____

Guideline #2: Use an authentic audience. Research on student production shows that students work harder when their work will be viewed by others. However, publishing student products for only the teacher to view generally is not enough to support this kind of motivation and effort. Instead, learners need an audience that is external to the immediate classroom and that cares about and has knowledge of the product, because such an audience will provide useful, authentic, and effective feedback. The audience should also be able to engage in interaction around both the process and the product and should clearly understand their roles in the project. Finding such an audience can be a difficult task, but it is one that students and teacher can share. For example, students might suggest that their reports on the first Gulf War be read by veterans of that conflict. The teacher can ask for volunteers from a veterans' electronic list or a local veterans organization. Remember that providing student products to an authentic audience in the public sector, for example, on a Web site that has open access, means that safety and other issues must be considered (these issues are discussed in chapter 3).

What additional authentic audiences could Ms. Farber use for the infomercial project? How could these audiences be contacted? What guidelines would you give the audience members?

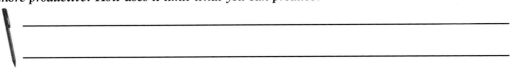

Guideline #3: Teach the tools. It is important that students understand how to use the computer tools that might help them in their production process (see Table 7.2 in the next section for tools). Students do not need to understand every component of the program, but the salient features that support their current process should be clear. This information, like all important content, should be presented in a variety of ways for all learners to access the instructions: graphically, orally, and in written form, at a minimum. ELLs and other students who may need extra help to understand have more chance to comprehend when the information is presented in many ways. Multimodal presentation also addresses the different student learning preferences present in every classroom.

Ms. Farber decided to use expert groups to teach the technologies that her students need for their projects, such as video editing, word processing, disk burning, graphics, and downloading or copying clip art from the Internet. She teaches a subset of the students and they, as experts, teach other students in the class. Because each stage of the project requires different skills and tools, all students have a chance both to be the expert and to learn about different technologies from their peers. Students might see this as just another part of the project, but Ms. Farber knows the power that students feel when they are allowed to be experts and how teaching others leads to greater learning.

To deal with her challenge to learn the technologies for each stage of the infomercial project, Ms. Farber has called on part of her support network in the school, the information technology coordinator and library media specialist, to teach her and each group's current Technology Operator. This way, she learns as the students learn rather than trying to figure out multiple tools herself before the project begins.

Guideline #4: Understand the tools. It is important that students know not only how to use the tools but also that they understand the opportunities that each tool affords. To this end, teachers and learners can brainstorm the kinds of tasks that can be accomplished with tools such as a database program, a word processor, or a graphical organizer. For example, if students were to produce a newspaper, they would need to understand that graphical organizer software could help them brainstorm and lay out a process, but it could not help to format the newspaper in the way that a word processing or desktop publishing program could. Teachers and their students can consider how the use of the tools limits or structures what they can produce, and they can continue to add to the list over time so that students use tools that provide them the most effective opportunities for producing content and language.

Think of a computer tool that you use frequently. In what ways does the tool help you to be more productive? How does it limit what you can produce?

Guideline #5: Scaffold experiences for all learners. Some students, such as ELLs and students with disabilities, may need extra time, help, and modeling while working on projects. To facilitate their understanding, teachers can present information about project instructions, goals, and outcomes in a variety of modes (written, oral, visual), as described previously. Presenting guidelines and tasks in multiple modes provides opportunities for English language learners and those with special needs to receive content and language input in a variety of ways and helps to support comprehension; it also addresses the needs of students who prefer to learn in diverse ways.

In addition, as in any effective learning experience, projects should start with learners' knowledge in content, language, and technology and build from there. Ms. Farber provided scaffolds by breaking up the task into logical stages; encouraging students to use a variety of resources in different modes such as writing, graphics, and oral language; and providing examples and models during the process.

In what other ways could Ms. Farber provide scaffolds for her students during this project?

FIGURE 7.2 Guidelines for Designing Production Opportunities
1. Focus on process.
2. Use an authentic audience.
3. Teach the tools.
4. Understand the tools.
5. Scaffold experiences for all learners.

Figure 7.2 presents a summary of the guidelines for designing production opportunities.

TECHNOLOGIES FOR SUPPORTING PRODUCTION

What Are Productivity Tools?

Ms. Farber's students used a variety of tools in creating their media projects, all of which were suited to a particular stage or process. **Productivity tools** are those that maximize or extend students' ability to create products and to solve problems. They also "expand opportunities for expression" (Male, 1997, p. viii), which is an important principle for learning. With productivity tools, students can construct models, publish, plan and organize, map concepts, generate materials, collect data, and develop and present their work. Electronic productivity tools include hardware such as digital cameras and video recorders and many different kinds of software. Many teachers are familiar with at least some of the commonly used productivity software packages in Table 7.2.

It is important to note that the production process does not inherently require the use of technology. Rather, technology is used as it fits into the plan and makes the process more effective and/or more efficient. In developing activities that result in a student product, teachers and students should reflect on *why* they might use technology during the process. As discussed earlier in this book, if the technology does not make the teaching and learning more effective or more efficient, other tools should be considered.

There are many more examples in each category of production tools, including some that are made specifically for different student grade and ability levels. Different schools and classrooms may have entirely different sets of these tools, but they work in similar ways. The tools presented in Table 7.2 do not *necessarily* make learner products better or more creative, but they can be more professional and easier to share with others. Some research shows that learners are encouraged to produce more while using such tools. The more output students produce, the more opportunities they have to learn both content and language.

Student examples

Student iMovie products in a number of content areas can be found on the Springfield, Illinois, school district Web site at http://www.springfield.k12.il.us/movie/. Art, English, math, science, music, and social studies projects are represented. The site also includes tips from teachers, including using iMovie in the science classroom and making commercials with iMovie.

Some interesting high school projects using PowerPoint in a variety of content areas, along with hints and tips on using PowerPoint in the classroom, are found on Jerry Taylor's PowerPoint Projects (2000) page. Others from the same Greece, New York, school district can be found at http://www.greece.k12.ny.us/webworld2000/projects.htm.

Tools for teachers

Productivity tools also provide opportunities for teachers. All of the technologies mentioned in Table 7.2, along with grading programs and worksheet and puzzle-making software, assist teachers in creating products to use in their classes and in being more effective in their instruction (see chapter 9 for more on teacher tools).

TABLE 7.2 Examples of Productivity Software

Tool and Examples	Description	Sample Classroom Uses
Word processor: Microsoft Word, Word Perfect, Appleworks, Text Edit, OpenOffice Write	Used to create, edit, format, and print documents, most commonly text documents.	Students produce letters, essays, reports, and reflections. Can be used to format newsletters, create simple stories, and format handouts.
Database: Access, OpenOffice Base	Stores and organizes information; an electronic filing system in which users can search for and report on specific aspects of the information.	Students can use a database to input information collected from surveys, to make phone lists of class members, to make schedules, or to save data over time.
Spreadsheet: Excel, OpenOffice Calc	Organizes and relates information based on mathematical formulas; used in grade books and other applications where calculations are needed. Users can also make graphs and charts from the data.	Students can produce graphs and charts to support their presentations, make mathematical calculations on data, and keep records of their grades during the semester.
Desktop publisher: Printshop 22, Microsoft Publisher	Like a word processor but typically includes more templates, more powerful graphics capabilities, and greater freedom of layout.	Students can produce pamphlets, newspapers with photos, posters, bumper stickers, and almost anything that uses graphics and text.
Authoring software: Hot Potatoes (Half-Baked Software), Hyperstudio (Roger Wagner), Quandary	Also called authorware, these programs are typically more open-ended and more powerful than presentation software. They allow users to create software applications.	Students can produce action mazes, electronic quizzes, and multimedia presentations in addition to talking books, electronic portfolios, and interactive games.
Presentation packages: PowerPoint, KidPix, OpenOffice Impress	Allows the user to create slide shows that include sound, graphics, and text. These can range from simple to highly choreographed.	Students can produce narrated stories, multimedia presentations, action mazes, and simple slides.
HTML editors or Web page makers: Composer, FrontPage, Nvu	These programs allow the user to make documents for the World Wide Web.	Students can produce WebQuests, school information pages, electronic resumes.
Bookmaking software: Storybook Weaver Deluxe 2004 (Riverdeep) or the Edmark/Riverdeep Imagination Express series	These software programs are preformatted as books to which students can add graphics, text, and sound. The format provides scaffolds for students.	Students produce electronic books of any length and can include narrative text and sound, music, and even moving elements.
Video and video editing: iMovie, Avid, Microsoft Movie Maker, Visual Communicator	Video editing software allows the user to manipulate video images, including editing and moving frames and adding text and other special effects.	Students can produce short or long music videos or commercials, document some aspect of school life, support a presentation, or tell a video story.
Graphical organizer software: Kidspiration, Inspiration (See the Tool CloseUp feature for more information on this software program)	These programs support users in constructing concept maps and organizers of all kinds.	Among many other uses, students can use this software to brainstorm before reading a text, to plan or outline a task, and to categorize sets of items.

Overcoming challenges

With all the guidelines to follow and possible challenges to face, teachers might find creating and using production projects supported by technology overwhelming at this point. However, if teachers build on standards for content and language learning, focus on the process, provide effective scaffolds, and encourage the *principled use of technology* (in other words, grounded in research, standards, and effective practice), they can create an almost limitless number of possibilities for projects that can be effective learning experiences. In addition to those presented in the following section, activities in other chapters throughout this text also support production.

LEARNING ACTIVITIES: PRODUCTION PROJECTS

The production projects described here are not addressed to specific grade or language levels—those for which they are appropriate is a choice that the teacher, knowing her students well, can make. Instead, the multidisciplinary activities are grouped initially by the content area that is most central to the project. Sample emphases for goals in both content and language are provided for each project; these are the focus of task development and tool use. After the product is presented, the examples in each content area are divided into one of three technology categories. Examples in each content area include

- One that employs *basic technologies* (those that involve simple or few features that are generic across many tools)
- One that uses relatively *more sophisticated technologies* (those that require additional features or multiple tools or are relatively new)
- One that could use *advanced technologies* (those that require more in-depth knowledge of the tool or tools that are more complicated)

This format demonstrates that production is not a result of the technology used, but that the technology use is based on the task goals and structure.

The project descriptions do not state the teacher's role, the challenges that teachers may face, how scaffolding should be done, or specific name brands for each project. Think about these aspects as you read the project descriptions, and be prepared to answer the question at the end of this section.

●●●

English

1. Content and language goals: Culture, media, adjective use, descriptive writing

Product: Movie flyer

Basic technologies: Word processor or simple graphics program

Students complete the following process:

- Review movie flyers and advertisements.
- Choose a theme for a movie that they would like to see.
- Develop text about their movie that fits with the genre.
- Use a word processor to type their text and use appropriate fonts and styles, leaving room for any photos or graphics.
- Add fonts/graphics.
- Work with other students to review and revise their poster.

Students can produce very inventive products in this project. Follow up by posting the flyers around the room and letting students comment on which movies they might like to see and why.

2. Content and language goals: Genres, elements of story, peer editing

Product: Digital montage

Sophisticated technologies: Word processor, simple authoring program, presentation program, digital camera (optional)

Students work in cooperative groups to:

- Develop themes or stories in a chosen genre.

- Develop auto-play presentations with graphics, sound, and text.
- Edit with peers.
- Share with the intended audience.

These tools permit a fairly basic montage, typically slide by slide. Classes of younger children often make a very authentic audience for this activity.

3. Content and language goals: Summary, dialog, culture, text comprehension

Product: Five-minute movie trailer

Advanced technologies: Word processor, digital editor, CD burner and software, digital cameras/ video recorders

Students work together to:

- Create the script for a five-minute movie based on a book they have read.
- Develop costumes and scenery as needed.
- Film the movie.
- Edit the movie and burn it to a CD or DVD.
- Share the movie with the intended audience.

The moviemaking/video editing software seems to be a sophisticated technology, but it is actually easy to use—it can be expensive, however, and many people tend to associate expensive technologies with higher levels of technical skill. Avid DV, mentioned in the opening case, is free video editing software for the PC, as is iMovie for Macintosh computers. This activity is an excellent assessment and provides a different take on postreading activities.

....

Social studies

1. Content and language goals: Idioms, slang, humor, current events/politics

Product: Magnets and bumper stickers

Basic technologies: Word processing software with magnet or bumper sticker paper

After researching and discussing a current event and related language, students:

- Develop a slogan or saying, explain the meaning and purpose of the slogan.
- Revise based on classmates' or others' comments.
- Type their sayings into a word processor and print.
- Display for an appropriate audience.

Even students with less advanced English proficiency can come up with some witty and thoughtful sayings for this activity. Other content areas can also make use of this kind of task. See Figure 7.3 for an example of a bumper sticker that questions the "top-down" view of maps and globes.

2. Content and language goals: Reporting, five W's (who, what, where, when, and why), historical facts, extrapolation

Product: Simple newsletter for a historical organization

Sophisticated technologies: Desktop publishing software, Web search engines, scanner

Creating a newsletter is a common activity in many classes in which students:

- Collect historical information from both electronic and print resources.
- Type their articles using a word processor.
- Include whatever graphics are necessary, using a scanner if available.
- Edit, headline, and lay out the articles.
- Print, copy, and deliver the newsletter to relevant readers.

Simple newsletters are often the most interesting. This activity includes many different roles that can assist ELLs and other students who need extra time or feedback to complete their tasks.

3. Content and language goals: Reported speech and other genres, current events, humor, titles

Product: A newspaper, complete with political commentary, cartoons, features, and ads

FIGURE 7.3 Sample Bumper Sticker

Why is *North* "up"?

Let's look at the world in new ways.

ELL

FIGURE 7.4 Student Product

Peru

By: Johanna

Read and learn about Peru by using the links.

You can find interesting facts about the country and it's people.

- *Learn about Peru's <u>government</u>. How is it the same?*
- *Read about the <u>people</u>. What do they do for work?*
- *See a <u>physical</u> and <u>political</u> map.*
- *What does Peru sell? Look at it's <u>economy</u>.*
- *Read about a <u>famous person</u> in Peru.*
- *Learn about Peru's <u>history</u>.*
- *Back to <u>Latin America home page</u>.*

Source: Used with permission of Kent School District.

Advanced technologies: Depends on content, but a desktop publishing package, graphics package, word processor, digital image editing software, and others could be used

Students

- Create and assign job responsibilities.
- Collect historical information from print, electronic, and human resources.
- Create their part of the newspaper using appropriate technology.
- Work with team members to revise and improve their work.
- Edit; write headlines, captions, bylines; and design the layout.
- Print, copy, and deliver; solicit feedback.

Students can publish more than one issue during a semester, or use the one issue as a springboard for additional projects and discussion. Roles can change during the additional issues as students learn and become more comfortable with different language and tasks.

Social Studies Sample: Latin America Projects

Sixth-grade students in Washington State's Kent School District present their Latin American projects at http://www.kent .k12.wa.us/. The products are simply designed examples of research that the students did to explore countries in Latin America. Figure 7.4 presents an example of one student's product.

....

Science

1. Content and language goals: Descriptive language, inventions

Product: New invention

Basic technologies: Word processing, paint program (optional)

During a unit on inventors, learners:

- Design a new invention that they would like to use.
- Type a clear and complete description of the invention.
- Have another student try to draw their invention from the description.
- Revise.
- Post so that other students can try to draw it.
- Compile the drawings and descriptions into a catalog.

This activity allows learners to write as much or as little as they can and practice process writing while focusing on science content. The catalog can be used for a variety of follow-up activities, such as writing stories about the new inventions, calculating costs of making the product, and so on.

2. Content and language goals: Patents, inventions, persuasive language, descriptive language

Product: Patent application

Sophisticated technologies: Desktop publishing software, graphics software, scanner

In teams, students:

- Explain their inventions clearly in text, comparing them to existing inventions as necessary.
- Draw their inventions, scan, and import their pictures to their application document.
- Complete a patent application form.

- Receive feedback from evaluators (e.g., local experts, the teacher, other students) who decide which should be awarded patents and which need more work and why.
- Revise.

Students can have roles that help them to perform their project tasks.

3. Content and language goals: Instructions, imperatives, inventions, and inventors

Product: A WebQuest

Advanced technologies: An electronic encyclopedia, word processing and graphics software, HTML editor, or Web page creation software

After working with WebQuests, student teams:

- Review criteria for WebQuests.
- Download appropriate templates from Bernie Dodge's WebQuest site at http://webquest .sdsu.edu (see Figure 7.5).
- Develop a plan for creating a science WebQuest.
- Design each section, using and including appropriate resources.
- Complete and post their WebQuests for evaluation.

Student teams can also choose one segment of a whole-class WebQuest project to work on, or they can improve a WebQuest that they have participated in.

FIGURE 7.5 Part of a Generic WebQuest Template

Put the Title of the Lesson Here

A WebQuest for _____th Grade   Put some interesting graphic
(Put Subject Here)   representing the content here

Designed by Put Your Name Here

Put Your E-mail Address Here

Introduction | Task | Process | Evaluation | Conclusion |
Credits | Teacher Page

Introduction

This document should be written with the student as the intended audience. Write a short paragraph here to introduce the activity or lesson to the students. If there is a role or scenario involved (e.g., "You are a detective trying to identify the mysterious poet.") then here is where you'll set the stage. If there's no motivational intro like that, use this section to provide a short advance organizer or overview.

Remember that the purpose of this section is to both prepare and hook the reader. It is also in this section that you'll communicate the Big Question (Essential Question, Guiding Question) that the whole WebQuest is centered around.

Task

Describe crisply and clearly what the end result of the learners' activities will be. The task could be a:

- problem or mystery to be solved;
- position to be formulated and defended;
- product to be designed;
- complexity to be analyzed;
- personal insight to be articulated;
- summary to be created;
- persuasive message or journalistic account to be crafted;
- a creative work, or
- anything that requires the learners to process and transform the information they've gathered.

If the final product involves using some tool (e.g., HyperStudio, the Web, video), mention it here.

Source: Used with permission of Bernie Dodge, San Diego State University.

FIGURE 7.6 Examples from the Clean Communities Project

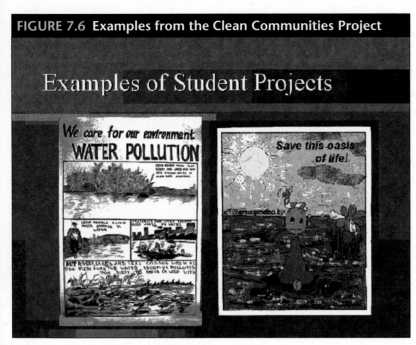

Source: Used with permission of iEARN-USA.

Science Sample: International Clean Communities Project

In one science-based project, secondary students in Belarus and the United States worked together online and traveled to work face to face to understand waste management around the world and increase communication between these countries about environmental issues. One outcome from their project was student-made posters addressing their concerns. Figure 7.6 presents examples of the posters produced by the students.

Math

1. Content and language goals: Connectors, story writing, discussion, word problems

Product: Action mazes

Basic technologies: Presentation software or a word processor (can also be done in HTML or with an authoring program)

In an action maze, students must solve math puzzles and choose the correct answer to follow a story line. To make their own action mazes, in collaborative groups, students:

- Decide on a math focus, content topic, and layout for their maze.
- Write the text and decide how it will branch at decision points.
- Find or create necessary graphics.
- Create the maze in an authoring program (refer to Table 7.2 on page 191 for suggestions).
- Share it with peers.

Producing and using action mazes (Egbert, 1995; Healey, 2002; Holmes, 2002) can facilitate discussion, collaboration, and creativity in both the creators and the users.

2. Content and language goals: Question formation, percentage, graphs, reporting

Product: Peer survey

Sophisticated technologies: Spreadsheet

Students choose an issue that is important to them and:

- Design a survey to gather student opinions.
- Interview peers or other target audience.
- Use a spreadsheet to calculate results and make graphs.
- Present the results to the administration or other authentic audience.

Students can propose a new traffic light in front of the school, additions to the cafeteria offerings, or new books for the school library while working on math content and language.

3. Content and language goals: Area, house vocabulary, measurement

Product: House design

Advanced technologies: A computer-aided design program

The teacher assigns a specific total house area, and students:

- Brainstorm and/or research the kinds of rooms and their relative sizes that people might want in a home.
- Work with the CAD program to create their house to the specifications.
- Revise to meet the total house area given.
- Present the house plan to an authentic audience.

By creating and producing with other students who have different backgrounds and ideas, learners improve their content knowledge and language abilities while also increasing their cultural capital.

Student Sample: Math Tessellations
Teachers and elementary school students in grades 4 and 5 at Fairland Elementary in Maryland present examples of student products across content areas at http://www.towson.edu/csme/mctp/StudentProjects/FairlandHomePage.html. From tessellations to tall tales, this site has a great variety of interesting products. The site also provides project outlines for teachers to use in developing similar projects. Figure 7.7 presents one of the student tessellations.

Production projects can also be designed to address specific topics and language areas. Following are examples of language skills and vocational skills learning.

·····································

Language skills

1. Content and language goals: Vocabulary, definitions, spelling

Product: Puzzle

Basic technologies: A puzzlemaker program

Students use the vocabulary under study and:

- Choose a puzzle type.
- Create the puzzle text (typically clues or definitions for each word).
- Create the puzzle.
- Share it with peers.

Students are active when the teacher allows them to take responsibility for their learning, including creating opportunities for practice and assessment.

2. Content and language goals: Story elements, sentence formation, cohesive devices

Product: A book

Sophisticated technologies: A book publishing program

Students work with a given topic or develop one of their own into a book. Students:

- Complete a storyboard with text and possible graphics (a sample storyboard is shown in Figure 7.8).
- Revise for grammar and surface features.
- Create the title, text, and graphics in the software.
- Edit as necessary.

Students can share their books with parents or students in another class or grade level. Using software available for different technical levels and language abilities can make this project easy and structured.

3. Content and language goals: Question and statement formation, explaining

Product: Interactive quizzes

Advanced technologies: A Web page composer program or another authoring/authorable software package

Working alone or in groups, students:

- Choose the format, questions, and answers for their quiz and decide on the type of feedback to be provided.
- Create their quiz.
- Give their quiz and take those that other students have made to study for the teacher's version.

Like the simpler puzzlemaker, the products in this project help students study, practice, and review. They can also reinforce correct answers and help learners to understand plausible mistakes.

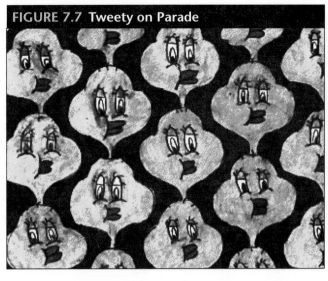

FIGURE 7.7 Tweety on Parade

Source: Used with permission of the Center for Science & Mathematics Education, Towson University.

FIGURE 7.8 A Sample Storyboard

Visual:	Visual:	Visual:
Text:	Text:	Text:
Visual:	Visual:	Visual:
Text:	Text:	Text:

LEARNING ACTIVITIES

FIGURE 7.9 A Sample Student Business Card

Jicela Cortez, Lawyer
Civil Rights and Immigration
Cortez Law Firm
Los Angeles, CA

"Bilingual and Honest"

Vocational skills (community/business)

1. Content and language goals: Occupations, small talk, future verb tense

Product: Business cards

Basic technologies: Simple word processor

Students prepare for their possible futures and:

- Think about what they might like to be when they are older.
- Decide on the company and location where they want to work (authentic or fictitious).
- Design a business card with their name and work information and print on precut business card stock (see an example in Figure 7.9).
- Role-play their business selves and hand out business cards to their peers.

This project is great for English language learners because it does not require much text and it provides practice in small talk.

2. Content and language goals: Résumé content, book characters, business language, past tense, formatting

Product: Résumé

Sophisticated technologies: Advanced word processing features or desktop publishing program

In this multidisciplinary project, students:

- Answer questions on a character or author's life. The questions require them to discover information typically required for résumés.
- Create their character's résumé using a word processor.
- Compare to the work of others who have chosen the same character, or check with someone who knows the character.
- Revise the résumé.
- Present their character to the class.

This activity facilitates extensive interaction among students and helps students to understand elements of resumes and of literature.

3. Content and language goals: Question formation, business register, surveying, calculating

Product: A business (bake sale), including business cards, a survey, a schedule, advertisements

Advanced technologies: Spreadsheet, advanced word processing features, graphics package

Students, with members of the school parent or student organization:

- Decide on business type and create and distribute roles to each student.
- Make business cards.
- Create a survey asking students at the school their preferences (for favorite bake-sale cookie types or whatever the business will be).
- Enter the numbers into a spreadsheet and calculate percentages.
- Decide on what will be sold and when, how advertising will be done, and other issues.
- Create the advertising and the product.
- Sell it.
- Measure their success by comparing survey results to actual sales.

As long as schools have bake sales, they can be used for learning purposes. In this activity, all students have many choices of how to work, which supports diverse abilities and skills.

Adapting Activities

The steps presented in each project are suggestions and can be adapted in many ways. Some of these activities can also be done using nonelectronic technologies such as pencil and paper. However, in most cases the use of technology adds to the process by giving the products a professional appearance and giving students more time and more resources for creating and learning. For a closer look at one of these tools, see Tool CloseUp: Inspiration. In addition, teaching learners through and about technologies can help them accomplish many language and content goals while also learning valuable technology skills.

ELL

LEARNING ACTIVITIES

Tool CloseUp: Inspiration

One tool that teachers and students commonly use during the planning process, whether the product is an essay or a five-story architectural wonder, is Inspiration (Inspiration Software). This tool provides a very visual way to create graphic organizers with text, symbols, and graphics. This tool is effective for many ELLs because even the toolbars are visual (iconic). In addition, the text in the graphic organizers that students develop can be converted to outline form, helping students understand the relationship between text and graphic, providing the information in an alternative format for students who prefer it, and supporting their writing. There is also a version of Inspiration developed for younger children called Kidspiration that is widely used to support all the learning goals in this text. The accompanying figure shows an organizer for part of Ms. Farber's infomercial project.

ELL

Download a free 30-day trial of this software at www.inspiration.com.

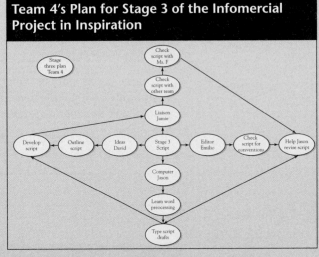

Team 4's Plan for Stage 3 of the Infomercial Project in Inspiration

Source: Diagram created in Inspiration® by Inspiration Software®, Inc.

Inspiration has been mentioned throughout this text as a tool to support all the learning goals. What are the advantages to having such a tool? The disadvantages?

_____

_____

_____

_____

Tutorial

CW

Find Inspiration and Kidspiration examples and tutorials in the Tutorials module of the Companion Website (http://www.prenhall.com/egbert).

The examples above are only a few of the activities that facilitate production, and thereby content and language learning. There are others throughout this text and more examples can be found all over the Web. Teachers who want to design their own effective production activities should keep in mind the principles and standards from chapter 1 and also reflect on the process that students will use as they produce. All of the projects can be adapted to use different technologies and to work in different contexts. Even the most sophisticated products can often be completed with basic technologies, although the products will be different in some ways. These examples also illustrate what great products can come from simple technologies and how goals can be met effectively through production.

Choose one or more of the examples above and describe what you think would be the appropriate role for the teacher, the challenges that teachers may face, how scaffolding should be done, and specific technologies that might be useful in developing the product.

_____

_____

_____

ASSESSING PRODUCTION PROJECTS

Evaluating production projects can be different from evaluating other kinds of projects in that one major outcome is tangible; however, it is similar in that both process and product must be evaluated to provide a true understanding of the learning that has occurred. Evaluating the process and product means that teacher and students must be involved in ongoing assessment throughout the project. During the infomercial project in the opening case, Ms. Farber uses observation of student teams as a crucial part of assessment. She has also included assessment by student peers in the other fifth-grade classes. In addition, student explanations and reflections on their learning provide information necessary to assess both the process and the product. Ms. Farber will use the rubric that the class constructed to evaluate the final products.

Teachers and students can use one, more than one, or all of these assessments for project-based learning, and include any of the following:

- *Team activity reports*—These can be written or oral, individual or group, and explain what the group and/or individual has been doing and what help they need to continue. One team activity report for Ms. Farber's project was the infomercial checklist, as seen in Figure 7.10. Notice that this assessment helps students to practice language, in this case past and present tense. ELLs and others who need to work on basic language skills are supported by the simple language used in this assessment.

- *Peer teamwork reports*—Students report on how the collaborative process is working, where it breaks down, and what they are learning by working with their team. These reports can take any number of forms; Figure 7.11 shows one possibility for Ms. Farber's project. Other sample group rubrics can be found on the NALD Web site at http://www.nald.ca/ CLR/btg/ed/evaluation/ groupwork.htm.

- *Self-assessment*—Students can be asked to describe their progress and outcomes according to the rubric criteria, or they can be asked to reflect on how well and in what ways they participated in their group. For Ms. Farber's project, students could be asked in which role they performed the best, in which they achieved the most, which role was most difficult and why, and which they preferred. This information will help students

FIGURE 7.10 Infomercial Checklist

Infomercial Checklist

We have completed these tasks for our infomercial:

___ Made a plan

___ Considered our audience

___ Reviewed models

___ Wrote the script

___ Checked our sources

___ Edited the script

___ Checked the script with another team

___ Filmed our infomercial

___ Edited our infomercial

Our infomercial:

___ Is about 5 minutes long

___ Shows the product

___ Uses advertising language

___ Uses good grammar

___ Is exciting

assess their strengths and weaknesses and Ms. Farber to plan future projects.

- *Teams assess each other*—This can be formal or more informal and based on general criteria or on whatever teams find to comment on. During the infomercial project, the teams assessed each other informally based on what they saw as strengths and weaknesses in the scripts. Some teams commented on the interest that the script generated, others how well written it was, and yet others how clearly the product was described.

- *Outside stakeholders*—External reviewers can create their own criteria for the product or use criteria provided by the teacher. For example, the other fifth-grade students who watched Ms. Farber's class projects commented on whether or not they would use the product promoted in the infomercial and why.

These assessments can take place orally, in written form, or both. Students, such as some ELLs who are unable to respond in these formats, can draw pictures or present their information in other ways.

FIGURE 7.11 Teamwork Report for Infomercial Project

Teamwork Report—Stage 2

In my group I:

1. Listened actively	Usually	Sometimes	Never
2. Asked questions	Usually	Sometimes	Never
3. Gave ideas	Usually	Sometimes	Never
4. Agreed or disagreed	Usually	Sometimes	Never

By working with my group, I can do something that I could not do before:

In group work I still need to improve on this:

Do a Web search for sample student projects/products in your content area and/or grade level. What interesting products did you find? Note the product(s) and location(s) here for further reference.

_____

_____

_____

SAMPLE LESSON: PRODUCTION

With sufficient scaffolding, time, and feedback, Ms. Farber's students were able to produce infomercials that demonstrated their understanding of persuasive techniques used in the media. During the project Ms. Farber's students were enthusiastically engaged. Ms. Farber wants to try another project with a relevant product. This time, she wants to focus on some of her curricular math goals. She searches the Web for good ideas and comes up with an idea by teachers Tom Scavo and Byron Petraroja from LessonPlanZ.com. Their detailed description made this math lesson sound like an effective and fun way to meet the standards (http://mathforum.org/trscavo/statistics.html). She copies down the plan's outline:

ADVENTURES IN STATISTICS

Problem: Are the areas of classrooms in the sixth grade larger, on the average, than the areas of the fifth-grade classrooms?

Procedure:

- Students hypothesize what they think the answer to this question might be and document their responses.
- Discuss the practical applications of the ultimate findings.

- Talk about the length and width of the classroom and how to go about measuring it. Estimate these measures by sight and write down the estimates for future reference. Discuss what is meant by the area of the room and then compute using the above length and width estimates.

- Working in pairs, all students measure the length and width of the classroom. First one student from each team measures while the other records, and then they switch roles, measuring again. Record the two sets of measurements on data sheets. When all the teams have completed the measurement task, write the data on the blackboard and compare. Note discrepancies between the measurement pairs. Take again those that cannot be attributed to measurement or round-off error.

- Arrange for the students to measure each of the fifth- and sixth-grade classrooms in the school with the same procedure followed earlier.

- Convert the data to common units and then use calculators to compute the area. Make sure students accompany all answers with appropriate units.

- Examine the data.

- Line graph the data. Then change the line graphs to bar graphs. Examine the graph data.

- Repeat the above lessons for number of students and compare the area to the number of students.

- Compute the average area of fifth- and sixth-grade classrooms and the average number of students, showing student work. Then compute average area per student.

- Prepare a presentation of the data (they invited the principal), each student team taking a different part.

Source: Reproduced with permission from Drexel University, Copyright 2005 by The Math Forum @ Drexel. All rights reserved.

Ms. Farber can instantly see that students will be active and focused on an authentic task, and she likes that many scaffolds are provided in the form of teacher mini-lessons and worksheets. She decides to analyze the lesson with the Lesson Analysis and Adaptation Worksheet (found in chapter 1 on page 33 and in the Lesson Planning module of the Companion Website) to see ways in which the lesson might be improved. As a result of her analysis she decides to use this lesson, but to change it in the following ways:

1. Add the standards and curricular goals that apply. She sees that, in addition to math content standards, the lesson can help students meet goals for communication, problem solving, critical thinking, and even creativity in their final product. In addition, the lesson addresses a variety of literacies (technological, mathematical, visual) and student learning preferences.

Inclusion

2. Add additional resources. Instead of just their meter sticks, students can use a pedometer, a measuring tape, or another rule of their choice to measure. Ms. Farber will also make the computers available for students who want or need to use a spreadsheet to calculate, a word processor or drawing program to make their charts and diagrams, and presentation or other software to produce their final product. These choices help address the needs of a variety of students, from those who need more structure and support to more independent, gifted students.

3. Add more choices for the final product. Students can use the data to argue for or against any of the reasons they gave at the start of the lesson for the practical application of the lesson. For example, one group might create an action maze to help future students carry out the same calculations, while another might write a letter to the school board about overcrowding at their school.

4. Spell out specific assessments. Ms. Farber will observe her students, check their written work, and use a rubric to evaluate their final product. She will also ask the students to write a self-reflection of their process and product, and determine whether their final products should become part of their grade-level portfolios.

Ms. Farber believes that, with these changes, this lesson will be accessible to all of her students and that all of her students will have the opportunity to achieve the intended goals.

S A M P L E   L E S S O N

What else would you add to this lesson to make it effective for your current or future students? What would you delete? Why?

_____

_____

_____

CHAPTER REVIEW

Key Points

- **Define production.**

  Production is the development, through a process, of a tangible, manipulable outcome (a product). The product is the impetus behind the development of each stage of the production project.

- **Describe the benefits of student production for learning.**

  The benefits of student production for learning include student gains not only in language and content but also in social skills, critical thinking and planning, communication, cultural knowledge, and evaluation.

- **Explain the role of process in production.**

  The production process is a carefully designed process and crucial for the success of the project. Planning, development, and evaluation are three general stages in the production process.

- **Discuss guidelines for supporting student technology-enhanced production.**

  Teachers need to focus on the process, provide authentic audiences to view student work, understand and teach the tools, and provide scaffolds for students. In addition, the teacher's role varies from project director to project guide depending on the structure and goals of the project. Research supports the use of production for student learning, although there are challenges for teachers, students, and administrators in designing and carrying out production projects.

- **Describe technologies for supporting student production.**

  Tools such as word processors, spreadsheets, draw programs, and presentation software can support production. The use of production tools alone, however, does not result in learning. As noted above, production projects must be carefully planned so that they meet both content and language objectives and support other learning goals.

- **Evaluate and develop pedagogically sound technology-enhanced production activities.**

  A wide range of products can fit a variety of goals; the role of technology is to support the goals, not to determine them. Teachers and students have a range of choices in meeting production goals. Most important, production can facilitate the achievement of all students, regardless of language background, learning preference, or physical ability. Examples of both teacher and student products and the results of their creative processes are easily accessible on the World Wide Web. A review of some of these Web sites can inspire teachers and learners to integrate and use production tools in their teaching and learning and serve as models for product development.

- **Design appropriate assessments for technology-enhanced process and product.**

  Just as there is a huge range of production projects, there is a great variety of assessments that teachers and students can use to assess them. Most important is that both process and product are evaluated, and that students are involved in the assessments.

Which information in this chapter is most valuable to you? Why? How will you use it in your teaching?

_____

_____

_____

CASE QUESTIONS REVIEW

Reread the case at the beginning of the chapter and review your answers. In light of what you learned during this chapter, how do your answers change? Note any changes below.

1. *What are some learning benefits that students might derive from creating this product?*

   _____

   _____

   _____

2. *What aspects of the process seem to be most important to student achievement toward the goals? Why do you think so?*

   _____

   _____

   _____

3. *What is the teacher's role in this project?*

   _____

   _____

   _____

4. *What role does the technology play?*

   _____

   _____

   _____

CHAPTER EXTENSIONS • • • • • • • • • • •

To answer these questions online, go to the chapter 7 section of the Extensions module of this text's Companion Website (http://www.prenhall.com/egbert).

Adapt • • • •

Choose a lesson for your potential subject area and grade level from the technology-enhanced lesson plan archive at KidzOnline (http://www.kidzonline.org/LessonPlans/). Use the Lesson Analysis and Adaptation Worksheet from chapter 1 on page 33 (also available on the Lesson Planning module of the Companion Website) to consider the lesson in the context of *production*. Use your responses to the worksheet to suggest general changes to the lesson based on your current or future students and context.

Practice • • • •

1. *Write objectives for a technology-enhanced project.* Write specific content and language objectives for Ms. Farber's project. Share them with a peer and revise them as necessary. Use the "objectives" table from chapter 1 as needed.

2. *Create student roles.* Review the learning activity examples in this chapter. Choose three of the projects and suggest what roles you might create for students and who an authentic audience could be for each of the three projects.

3. *Assess technology-enhanced learning.* Choose one or more of the learning activity examples from the chapter and develop an assessment plan. Address who will be assessed, when, in what categories, based on what criteria. Also suggest how you would generate an overall assessment for the project.

Explore • • • •

1. *Create a production handout for students.* On paper, use graphics, text, and any other modes you can to outline for your students a production project that you might use in your class. Include information that explains to students the content and process of the task. Add a brief description of how the task process will be accessible to all students, regardless of language proficiency, content knowledge, or physical abilities.

2. *Create a quick reference for production software or hardware.* One way to learn a piece of software or a technology is to make a reference to help someone else. Choose a piece of software or hardware that you might use in the production process in your classroom (see Table 7.2 for tool ideas). Explore your choice, examining the features and learning about the opportunities that it offers. Then create an explanation for students on how to use it. Be sure to make your reference appropriate for diverse learners.

3. *Examine a production project.* Choose a production project from a text, Web site, or other resource that is relevant to your current or future teaching context. Explain how the project you choose meets the guidelines and provides the opportunities mentioned throughout this chapter. Describe how it might be adapted to better meet the needs of all students and to use technology more effectively.

4. *Create a production project.* Review your content area standards and any other relevant standards. Choose a topic that works within these standards and other curricular requirements for your state or region and develop a technology-enhanced project around it.

REFERENCES

Bazeli, M. (1997). Visual productions and student learning. ERIC 408969

Blumenfeld, P., Soloway, E., Marx, R., Krajcik, J., Guzdial, M., & Palincsar, A. (1991). Motivating project-based learning: Sustaining the doing, supporting the learning. *Educational Psychologist, 26*(3/4), 369–398.

Dewey, J. (1938). *Experience and education.* New York: Collier Books.

Egbert, J. (1995). Electronic action mazes: Tools for language learning. *CAELL Journal, 6*(3), 9–12.

George Lucas Foundation. (2005). *Instructional module: Project-based learning.* Retrieved June 30, 2007, from the World Wide Web: http://www.edutopia.org/projectbasedlearning.

Healey, D. (2002). *Teaching and learning in the digital world: Interactive Web pages: Action Mazes.* Retrieved February 11, 2005, from the World Wide Web: http://oregonstate.edu/~healeyd/ups/actionmaze.html.

Holmes, M. (2002). *Action mazes.* Retrieved from the World Wide Web, February 11, 2005: http://www.englishlearner.com/llady/actmaze1.htm.

Male, M. (1997). *Technology for inclusion* (3rd ed.). Boston, MA: Allyn & Bacon.

San Mateo County Office of Education. (2001). The multimedia project: Project-based learning with Multimedia. Retrieved February 11, 2005, from the World Wide Web: http://pblmm.k12.ca.us.

Thomas, J. (2000). *A review of research on project-based learning.* San Rafael, CA: Autodesk Foundation.

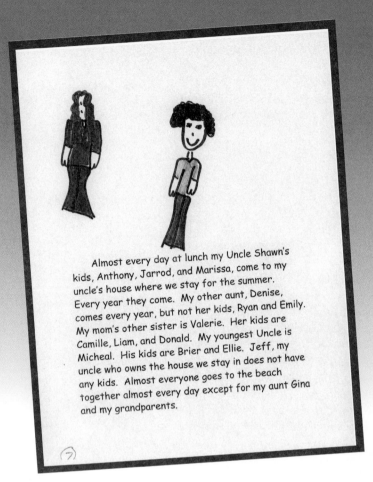

Almost every day at lunch my Uncle Shawn's kids, Anthony, Jarrod, and Marissa, come to my uncle's house where we stay for the summer. Every year they come. My other aunt, Denise, comes every year, but not her kids, Ryan and Emily. My mom's other sister is Valerie. Her kids are Camille, Liam, and Donald. My youngest Uncle is Micheal. His kids are Brier and Ellie. Jeff, my uncle who owns the house we stay in does not have any kids. Almost everyone goes to the beach together almost every day except for my aunt Gina and my grandparents.

(7)

Case: Long Way to Go

As you read the following scenario, note potential benefits and drawbacks of using technology to help students learn when they are physically separated from the teacher.

• •

Jim Sanderson, the science teacher at Wedmore High School, is concerned that his four advanced students are not getting the courses that they need for college preparation. He wants to offer Advanced Placement (AP) courses, but because of the school's rural location, small student body, and lack of resources, offering such courses is not feasible. Jim recently came across an article in a teaching journal about electronic learning (eLearning), instruction that uses technology to enhance learning, often when the teacher and students are not in the same location. The article noted districts that are partnering via video conferencing and other technologies to make it possible for students in schools like his to get the courses they need. Jim is excited about the idea of joining with other schools to offer AP science courses, and he has decided to learn more about it.

Jim discovers through his research that his district is part of the statewide K–12 telecommunications system that connects all of the districts in the state. He also learns that the technology class at his school is already using video conferencing technologies to meet with students in different locations. He sends a message out on an electronic discussion list for science teachers and receives replies from other teachers in rural districts around his state who are interested in collaborating on AP courses. Jim decides to develop a proposal to create at least one online shared AP course and present it to the principal as soon as possible.

• •

Answer these questions about the case. There are no right or wrong answers to this chapter preview—the goal is for you to respond before you read the chapter. Then, as you interact with the chapter contents, think about how your answers might change.

1. *What other information does Jim need before he writes his proposal?*

   _____

   _____

   _____

2. *What are some potential benefits of eLearning?*

   _____

   _____

   _____

3. *What are some potential disadvantages of eLearning?*

   _____

   _____

   _____

4. *How could Jim most easily teach and assess students who are at a distance from him?*

   _____

   _____

   _____

5. *If you were Jim's principal, how would you react to this proposal? Why?*

   _____

   _____

   _____

Like many other teachers wanting to serve their students better, Jim is excited about the prospects that eLearning can offer his students, but he has just begun to understand what it involves. eLearning, particularly learning that takes place completely online, often requires students and teachers to have different skills and understandings than face-to-face classroom learning does. In addition, student needs are different in some ways, and to be effective, the techniques, approaches, and technologies used might also have to change. Teachers who may want to use aspects of eLearning need to be aware of the essentials before they get started. To this end, when you finish this chapter, you will be able to:

- Explain eLearning and how it can help meet learning goals.
- Discuss guidelines for creating eLearning opportunities.
- Describe eLearning tools.
- Develop and evaluate effective technology-enhanced eLearning activities.
- Create appropriate assessments for technology-enhanced eLearning activities.

When you have completed this chapter, which NETS*T will you have addressed?

_____

_____

_____

Although the process may be somewhat different, the standards that address eLearning are not different from those that guide all student learning. For more on these standards, see Meeting the Standards: eLearning.

• • • • Meeting the Standards: eLearning • • • •

Although many states and organizations are developing standards for distance education, a widely accepted set does not yet exist. Rather, distance educators agree that eLearning should support content standards and state learning goals in the same ways that traditional classroom learning does. In addition, participating in distance learning can help students meet many of the NETS-S standards such as using technology tools to collaborate, communicate, solve problems, and inquire. The National Education Association (NEA, 2006) has put together some guidelines for eLearning that, used along with standards and other curricular guidelines, can help focus the design of eLearning opportunities. These guidelines include:

1. **Curriculum**—Online curricular offerings should be challenging, relevant, and aligned with appropriate national, state, and/or district standards for student learning.

2. **Instructional Design**—Online courses should be informed by and reflect the most current research on learning theory. They should be designed to take advantage of the special circumstances, requirements, and opportunities of the online learning environment and support the development of 21st-century learning skills.

3. **Teacher Quality**—Teachers should be skilled in the subject matter, learning theory, technologies, and teaching pedagogies appropriate for the content area and the online environment.

4. **Student Roles**—Students should be actively engaged in the learning process and interact on a regular basis with the teacher and online classmates in the course.

5. **Assessment**—Assessment should be authentic, formative, and regular, providing opportunities for students to reflect on their own learning and work quality during the course. End-of-course assessments should give students the opportunity to demonstrate appropriate skills and understandings that reflect mastery of the course content.

6. **Management and Support Systems**—The course should be managed to ensure effective student and school participation. Support systems should provide resources to teachers, students, and parents comparable to those provided by face-to-face courses, as well as special support necessitated by the unique circumstances of the online environment.

7. **Technological Infrastructure**—Finally, the technical infrastructure supporting the online course should provide the necessary tools for instruction and interactivity. The technology behind the course should work reliably, simply, and economically. Technical assistance should be available whenever needed by students or teachers.

Source: Used with permission of NEA.

More specific guidelines are being developed, but for now teachers can think about how eLearning might better help them meet curricular goals and student needs. If eLearning cannot meet these goals and needs, then a different instructional strategy should be used.

In what situations might eLearning not be the best solution? Why do you think so?

_____

_____

_____

 See your state standards for eLearning in the Standards section of the Resources module of this text's Companion Website (http://www.prenhall.com/egbert).

• • • •

OVERVIEW OF eLEARNING IN K–12 CLASSROOMS

What Is eLearning?

Because learning through or with the aid of technology like the Internet is a relatively new phenomenon, there are many terms to describe it and few consistent understandings of what these terms mean. For example, common terms to describe some or all aspects of learning through technology include *distance education, distributed learning, open learning, online education, virtual classrooms,* and *eLearning.* Clearly, eLearning is not a learning goal per se but rather a structure or context for technology-supported learning through which content, communication, critical thinking, creativity, problem solving, and production can all take place. For this book, the term **eLearning** (short for electronic learning) means that the learning environment:

- Is enhanced with digital technologies, particularly but not necessarily computer-mediated communication software (CMC, described in chapter 3)
- Involves learning situations where interaction between the student and instructor is **mediated,** or bridged by technology, in some way
- Uses technology in an ongoing and consistent way, not in isolated events
- Is learner-centered
- Focuses on students with instructor and student with student interaction
- Uses a wide variety of resources

According to this definition, eLearning can occur in contexts such as

- A face-to-face (f2f) classroom in an online chat
- Video conferencing
- A virtual school that is completely online (for examples, see the Idaho Virtual Academy, www.idahova.org/—a lesson provided by K–12, Inc. is shown in Figure 8.1; Florida Virtual School, www.flvs.net/; or www.class.com)
- Situations that combine these options (see the U.S. government's Star Schools at www.ed.gov/)

All of these examples fit the definition of eLearning in this chapter.

A combination of face-to-face and electronic learning can be referred to as **blended, hybrid,** or **mixed-mode** environments. Generally, in blended contexts f2f time is partly given over to eLearning experiences. These optimal environments allow teachers to blend the best of f2f and online learning. Abate (2004) explains, "The traditional face-to-face elementary classroom imparts the social contact that children need to guide their learning while the online, or Web-based, learning environment offers flexibility and opportunities not possible in a traditional classroom. To create a learning environment using both modes to enhance the learning experiences of the students would provide the greatest benefit" (p. 1). Cavanaugh, Gillan, Kromrey, Hess, and Blomeyer (2004) note that blending f2f and eLearning results in higher quality achievement and a higher number of students who complete the course successfully. Figure 8.2 on page 210 presents online projects that could be integrated into a blended learning environment.

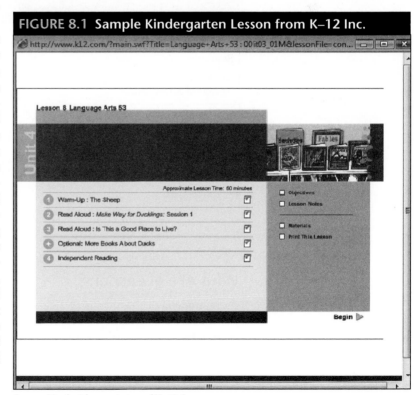

FIGURE 8.1 Sample Kindergarten Lesson from K–12 Inc.

Source: Used with permission of K–12, Inc.

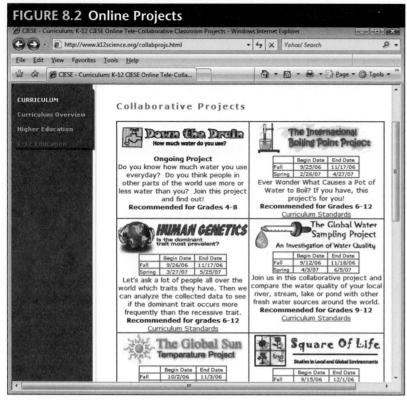

FIGURE 8.2 Online Projects

Source: http://stevens.edu/ciese/collabprojs.html

As in most instructional contexts, three general components interact to comprise eLearning:

1. *Instructional and learning strategies,* such as collaboration, reflection, problem solving, communication
2. *Pedagogical models or constructs,* which indicate how learning takes place
3. *Learning technologies,* including everything from Web sites to communication software and digital cameras (Dabbagh & Bannan-Ritland, 2005)

However, there can also be crucial differences between traditional learning in f2f classrooms and eLearning; for example, Dabbagh and Bannan-Ritland (2005) contrast the characteristics of traditional and Web-based learning as outlined in Table 8.1.

Have you ever participated in eLearning? Of what kind? Why do you think eLearning was used? How effective was it? Why?

_____

_____

_____

TABLE 8.1 Characteristics of the Web as a Learning Environment versus Those of Traditional Learning Environments

Traditional Learning Environments	Web-Based Learning Environment
Bounded	Unbounded
Real time	Time shifts: asynchronous communications and accelerated cycles
Instructor controlled	Decentralized control
Linear	Hypermedia: multidimensional space, linked navigation, multimedia
Juried, edited sources	Unfiltered searchability
Stable information sources	Dynamic, real-time information
Familiar technology	Continuously evolving technology

Note: Data from *Why the Web? Linkages,* by M. Chambers, 1997. Paper presented at The Potential of the Web, Institute for Distance Education, University of Maryland University College, Adelphi, MD.
Source: Dabbagh & Bannan-Ritland (2005).

Who Are eLearners?

Today, students of all kinds are participating in distance learning through a variety of eLearning opportunities. According to the U.S. Department of Education, 36% of school districts and 9% of all public schools have 328,000 students enrolled in some kind of eLearning. High-poverty districts are among the most ardent supporters of using eLearning to provide services that the district cannot otherwise afford to provide to students, as in the opening scenario (Setzer & Greene, 2005).

Most K–12 eLearners access their online courses from their schools, which often provide onsite help for eLearners. However, home learners, homebound learners, juvenile detainees, alternative school attendees, and school dropouts also use eLearning resources. eLearning is flexible enough to meet their needs for easy access and alternative curricula. Although the majority of eLearners are in high schools, even younger children are taking part in eLearning tasks in their classrooms. Schools generally provide eLearning for advanced study and remediation, but many schools and districts are also making a systematic effort to use eLearning in reforming what they do across their classrooms. For example, second graders are communicating regularly through email with experts about class content, and ninth graders are working with students in other countries through the Internet to understand culture.

Because distance education at the K–12 level is just developing, the full results of these changes will not be available for some time. However, preliminary research shows that, done well, eLearning environments can be effective for K–12 learners (see, for example, Moore & Koble, 1997; Zucker & Kozma, 2003). Because eLearning concepts and understandings change rapidly and the research cannot keep up, Conceicao and Drummond (2005) suggest that the best place to find out about eLearning in K–12 contexts is to look at Web sites that provide examples of how eLearning is taking place.

Contexts for eLearning

Many eLearning tasks and courses are interactive multimedia explorations among a variety of participants. However, some eLearning formats still replicate the isolating, one-way correspondence course. There is no one set format or way to conduct eLearning, but what it should not (and usually cannot) be is traditional teaching moved to a new medium. For example, in a text-based electronic forum, if the teacher monopolizes the discussion (the equivalent of offline lecture), it is easy enough for students to ignore her postings.

The use of technology for eLearning makes it imperative that teachers rethink how they teach and investigate what the new mediums afford (Tallent-Runnels et al., 2006). Such reassessment is necessary because during eLearning, communication can take place synchronously (at the same time) or asynchronously (at different times), and participants can be in a variety of spaces and places. The variety in these instructional features calls for a variety of approaches, as seen in the three scenarios that follow.

Scenario One—Videoconferencing

The teacher and students at four different sites videoconference twice per week for an hour each session. Students find materials on the course Web site, use online chat to work in teams to collaborate on assignments, and receive help from teachers at their local school site when they have questions and concerns. They fax their assignments or post them to their Web site for evaluation, and they each have an office visit with the teacher by phone once per month.

Scenario Two—Online Course

In a completely Web-based course, students who never meet their instructor f2f go into their course space in an online learning environment such as WebCT (WebCT.com) and find instructions for the current assignment. As they proceed through the assignment, they interact with other students and the teacher asynchronously through the discussion forum. They can ask for help and feedback, post comments and Web site URLs, and participate in an analysis of the topic at hand. They also send and receive emails with the teacher and consult the online resources available in the course space, including rubrics for the activities. After they turn in (fax, email, or post) the final draft of their assignments, they receive comments and a grade in a virtual space online that is only seen by them. Figure 8.3 on page 212 shows the interface of one electronic forum where an ELL student and teacher are discussing weather as part of a unit on creativity. In the threaded discussion shown, the comments are inset to show the order in which the comments were input and whether they are new messages or replies to a previous message.

ELL

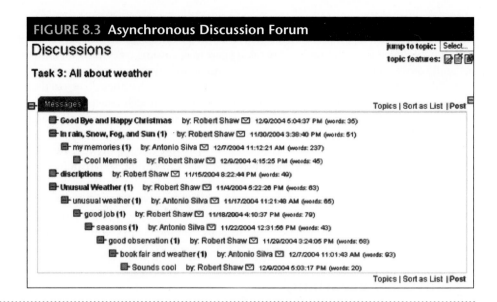

FIGURE 8.3 Asynchronous Discussion Forum

Scenario Three—Blended Learning

In an example of a hybrid or blended course, students in advanced high school science are released from two class periods each week to work on individual projects. They keep in touch with the other students and the teacher about their projects using an electronic forum where they post information about their progress.

As discussed in chapter 3, students could participate in other eLearning activities including communicating with external experts, accessing remote resources, mentoring and tutoring students at other sites, and working in projects where students collaborate with external peers or other audiences. There are many variations on eLearning, but all must comply with standards and guidelines for effective teaching. Blomeyer (2002) notes that the most important understanding that teachers and administrators must have about eLearning is:

> In the final analysis, eLearning isn't about digital technologies any more than classroom teaching is about chalkboards. eLearning is about people and about using technology systems to support constructive social interactions, including human learning. (p. 5)

Which eLearning context might best suit Jim's students' needs? Why?

_____

_____

_____

Characteristics of effective eLearning tasks

Small but critical differences exist between tasks in face-to-face classrooms and in online contexts. For example, Jackson (2004) contrasts content-high and process-high tasks that occur during eLearning. **Content-high tasks,** the most common in face-to-face instruction, are one-way resource dumps from instructor to student with little interaction. If this occurs during eLearning, students may drop the task or not do well because of the lack of support.

Process-high tasks, on the other hand, acknowledge the importance of interaction and communication among students and instructors before, during, and after the task. Employing process-high tasks is a principle emphasized throughout this text to support all learning goals and is especially important for online learning experiences (Tallent-Runnels et al., 2006). However, even process-high online activities lack the kind of student gestures, facial expressions, and other feedback that allow teachers to "read" how their students are doing. Teachers in f2f contexts find this type of feedback essential during process-high tasks and must learn either to do without it or obtain it in another manner during online courses. To address this potential problem, effective eLearning tasks must have carefully designed opportunities for interaction. In addition, teachers can help students learn to convey their intentions through the use of text color and size (e.g., ALL CAPS MEANS SHOUTING), format (e.g., use italics for emphasis), and emoticons, or text-based emotion icons (find a complete definition and a list of emoticons at the What is . . . site at http://whatis.techtarget.com/).

In addition, effective eLearning tasks employ multimedia rather than one medium. If the interaction during eLearning is solely in writing it can pose a barrier to language learners and other students with different reading and writing abilities. To overcome this barrier, accompany instructions sent in an email message with a recording of the message and/or attach a handout with graphics.

To be effective, tasks must also be diverse and have clear instructions so that students are not bored or confused before they begin. To avoid confusion, effective eLearning tasks should include ways for students to:

- Receive reinforcement.
- Review or repeat any part of the task.
- Ask for help or remediation for parts of the task that are not clear or are too challenging.

This is relatively easier to do in blended contexts because the teacher can interact f2f with students and understand their needs more readily.

Finally, because students typically work more independently when involved in eLearning tasks, extra time may be needed to complete tasks. Therefore, build flexibility into the assignment ahead of time. Characteristics of effective eLearning tasks are summarized in Figure 8.4.

FIGURE 8.4 Characteristics of Effective eLearning Tasks

Effective eLearning tasks:

- Are process-high rather than content-high.
- Include carefully designed opportunities for interaction.
- Offer help and instructions in a variety of media.
- Include diverse tasks and clear instructions.
- Are flexible.

Student benefits from eLearning

Students can derive a number of benefits from participating in effective eLearning tasks. A *Teacher's Guide to Distance Learning,* published online by the Florida Center for Instructional Technology (http://fcit.coedu.usf.edu/distance), suggests that eLearning can have the following benefits for students:

- *Flexibility/control.* When students participate in true eLearning, they have more control over their learning. They can choose the pace, site, and format of their learning. Students in many eLearning situations can also choose what they wear to learn.

- *Responsibility.* During eLearning, students are required to become active, responsible learners. To be successful, students must develop skills in working independently, in asking for help, and in interacting with fewer nonverbal cues from other participants.

- *Exposure.* Often, eLearning exposes students to resources, people, and interactions that may not occur in traditional f2f tasks or environments. This idea was outlined in chapter 3 and throughout this book.

- *Interaction.* During eLearning, students learn technology and have more opportunities to interact with teachers than in traditional classrooms. Shy students, those with limited language skills, and those with physical limitations can often have more time and more access to the interactions because they can read and respond at their own pace.

- *Anonymity/equity.* When students are online, cultural, physical, and other personal attributes are not focal and are often invisible during interaction. The online format can be more equitable for students with noticeable speaking differences, physical disabilities, and other characteristics that might present barriers in f2f interactions.

- *Convenience.* eLearning opportunities come in all shapes and sizes. While some require attendance or a starting date at specific times, others allow teachers and students to set their own schedules.

Overall, research shows no significant difference in student achievement between good f2f instruction and eLearning. In other words, if done well, both can work toward student achievement. However, in a way the comparison is a false one—students do different kinds of tasks during eLearning and they learn in different ways, and therefore it is important to offer a variety of options for learning, including face-to-face time. Researchers are looking into these outcomes more closely to see which factors promote what kind of achievement for which students. For example, according to an analysis of the research on distance learning, Cavanaugh et al. (2004) concluded that:

> Students in virtual schools showed greater improvement than their conventional school counterparts in critical thinking, researching, using computers, learning independently, problem-solving, creative thinking, decision-making and time management. (p. 5)

School and district eLearning benefits

In addition to student benefits, eLearning also has benefits for schools and districts. According to the National Education Technology Plan (Office of Educational Technology, 2004),

> A perennial problem for schools, teachers and students is that textbooks are increasingly expensive, quickly outdated and physically cumbersome. A move away from reliance on textbooks to the use of multimedia or online information (digital content) offers many advantages, including cost savings, increased efficiency, improved accessibility, and enhancing learning opportunities in a format that engages today's web-savvy students. (n.p.)

These are benefits that cannot be overlooked in this age of shrinking funding, teacher shortages, and increased accountability. Of course, there are also disadvantages to eLearning.

Disadvantages of eLearning

The disadvantages of eLearning, like the benefits, vary by context. These include, for example:

- Teachers might find it difficult to meet all learners' needs in a completely online course since some need more structure or f2f interaction than exists in eLearning contexts.
- Learners at a distance from the teacher might not have support for technical problems.
- Students who do not have access to technology outside of school may not have the option to participate.
- Teamwork is more complicated in online contexts because the typical classroom immediacy of contact is mediated by access to and use of the technology.
- If information and resources are not carefully chosen, the learner can be overwhelmed with the amount of information available online.
- The often huge number of discussion postings and assignments for teachers to check in completely online classes might prevent students from getting the direct, immediate feedback that they need.

Figure 8.5 summarizes some of the benefits and disadvantages of eLearning.

In spite of these difficulties, adding eLearning to f2f courses, such as integrating a discussion board or class blog, for example, can enhance effective learning. As Cavanaugh et al. (2004) note, "the importance of knowledge about effective virtual schooling cannot be overstated" (p. 22). They include knowledge by teachers and students but also by the "broader educational community" who can contribute to the experiences.

Read two teachers' description of their thoughts about eLearning in From the Classroom: eLearning on the next page.

Review Figure 8.5. In your opinion, do the benefits of eLearning outweigh the disadvantages? Why or why not?

_____

_____

_____

FIGURE 8.5 Benefits and Disadvantages of eLearning

Benefits	Disadvantages
Provides students with flexibility/control	Might be harder for teachers to meet student needs at a distance.
Builds responsibility	Technology glitches must be solved by students.
Exposes students to new resources, people, and interactions	Some students do not have access outside of school.
Provides equity through anonymity	Teamwork is more complicated online.
Is convenient	Students may have to wait for feedback.
Cost savings, efficiency, and improved accessibility in schools and districts	The amount of written data can be overwhelming for students.
Engages students	The amount of written work to evaluate and respond to may be overwhelming for teachers.

eLearning Processes

The benefits from eLearning will accrue if participants pay careful attention to the processes involved. These include:

- The teacher's (or instructional designer's) process of creating eLearning opportunities
- The student's process in taking those opportunities

According to Bowman (1999), teachers and instructional designers generally use the following process to create and implement successful eLearning experiences:

- *Plan*—assess the learners and the technology.
- *Design*—develop learning objectives that advance content to [achieve] desired learning outcomes.
- *Develop*—match learning objectives to media using multiple strategies to engage creativity (e.g., lecture, text, audio, video, case study, team projects, practical exercises and individual assignments, interactive problem solving, student-to-student interaction).
- *Implement and evaluate*—use iterative (repeating) design so activities can be improved and updated easily. (n.p.)

During eLearning tasks, students must:

- Understand the assignment.
- Learn the technology to a level sufficient to complete the task(s).
- Interact with the online community to build understandings.
- Complete the assignments and related assessments.

Depending on the goals of the eLearning course, students will also use processes to solve problems, communicate, produce, and meet other learning goals.

Teachers and eLearning

Teachers must often learn new skills and take on new responsibilities in eLearning environments. Davis and Roblyer (2005) note that online instructors, while sharing the need for good communication and organization skills with f2f teachers, also require a different set of skills. These include:

- Planning for asynchronous or other distant interaction
- Organizing detailed tasks and instructions
- Using presentation skills specific to eLearning environments
- Using questioning strategies for different (often unseen) students
- Involving students across different sites

These needs might require that the instructor learn new technologies and teaching strategies, as described in the following section.

The teacher's role

There are cases where electronic instruction consists of lectures posted online, but these are not *good* examples of eLearning. The teacher's role in eLearning is to be a *facilitator*, making sure that students are engaged in working toward learning goals. In this role, teachers can:

- Build rapport with students by meeting with them f2f or working on a personal basis at the start.
- Encourage eLearners by addressing feedback to them by name, and guide them in finding their own answers.
- Make sure students are spending their time effectively, not spending a disproportionate amount of time on assignments but working efficiently toward the course or task objectives.

FROM THE CLASSROOM

eLearning

Technology and machines have become such an integral part of our lives. There are certainly consequences—both good and bad—that are a result of this. You are probably all familiar with the many online educational classrooms/schools there are now. It just fascinates me when I go to some of their Web sites and browse through what a typical "school day" is for elementary and high school students who stay at home and learn via the computer/online courses. I think a balance is best. I can't imagine how those student graduates of Internet schools negotiate people and peer skills. (Jennie, first-grade teacher).

It's easier to see another angle or point of view when you don't have those emotional cues in your face! (April, middle school teacher)

- Divide classes into discussion groups. More than six members in a group tends to isolate at least one member. Fewer tends to shut down the group in the event two members become unavailable (Jackson, 2004).
- Require individuals to identify their discussion posts clearly. Also require groups to summarize their group discussions so that students do not need to read every posting.
- Create a presence in the course or task. Let students know that the teacher is observing and is available.

Above all, teachers must be able to promote successful interaction during eLearning.

Challenges for teachers in creating eLearning opportunities

There are barriers that teachers may face when first using eLearning. For example, the technology chosen for the course can get in the way of instruction because it mediates in ways that prevent teachers from receiving and providing visual cues or instant feedback. Therefore, teachers and course designers must make instruction direct and concise. They must also take into consideration:

- The difficulty for students of reading extensive text on a monitor
- The time it takes students to type their responses
- The pace and amount of information such as video clips, discussion postings, and Web-based data

To work around these challenges, during course design teachers can work with an instructional designer, a technology specialist, the library media specialist, and even students.

Once the course or task is designed, teachers can and should partner with the students' on-site teachers and counselors. To see an example of teachers partnering with others, take the online tour of Virtual High School at www.govhs.org/website.nsf.

What can Jim suggest that will help teachers of the proposed AP classes overcome barriers to effective eLearning?

_____

_____

_____

GUIDELINES FOR SUPPORTING STUDENT eLEARNING

This chapter has shown that eLearning is not entirely different from f2f learning, nor does it require completely different teaching skills. Likewise, the guidelines in this section apply to all learning contexts, but take on particular importance in eLearning contexts, whether hybrid or fully online.

Guidelines for Designing eLearning Opportunities

Four guidelines for building effective, interactive eLearning opportunities are presented here.

Guideline #1: Build community. Whether participating in a Web-based course or a technology-enhanced homework assignment, students need to know that they are not alone and that others are working toward the same goals. It is important that students identify themselves as members of the learning community whether they are face-to-face with other students or in a virtual online classroom. Strategies for building community include encouraging all students to participate, providing support for group work, connecting learning to students' lives as a group, and incorporating team-building exercises into tasks. Community can also be built using strategies such as all participants using others' names when they are interacting online, posting profiles (and possibly photos) that help learners choose group members and get to know more about each other, and having online chats to give learners a chance to work together in real time.

Guideline #2: Consider the hidden curriculum. In any curriculum, there are elements that are not explicitly taught (i.e., they are "hidden"). These include values, relationships, societal norms, and expectations. These are essential elements that students are expected to learn. eLearning also has its hidden curriculum, such as the cultural and social impacts of eLearning. Questions for teachers to answer that address this **hidden curriculum** include:

- Who benefits from the way information is being presented?
- What dominant ideology, explicit or implicit, is being espoused?
- What is credit being given for in the course? Participation? Writing well? Citing the course texts?
- What kind of student will succeed or fail in this context?
- How is technology valued?
- Who should be allowed to participate in this eLearning experience?

This last question arises from the economic impact of courses that are offered for a fee. Find more information about the hidden curriculum of 21st-century schools by playing the simulation Hyddyn at www.people.coe.ilstu.edu/rpriegle/mysted/.

What aspects of the hidden curriculum might Jim need to be aware of as he creates his AP science course?

_____

_____

_____

Guideline #3: *Organize ahead of time.* Bowman (1999) notes that a Web site that accompanies eLearning opportunities and provides the following can help students and teachers work more efficiently and effectively. This site should include:

- One-stop location for up-to-the-minute course announcements, materials, assignments, etc. Digitized information is also easily modified and maintained.
- Resource and access capabilities for all students.
- A way to display and receive resources which may otherwise be difficult to assemble or locate, such as samples of assignments (good and bad with reasons why), or hot links to Web sites used for course assignments (for example, analyses of corporate annual reports).
- Online archive of course slides, graphics, digitized video, for student retrieval and study on their own time.
- Digitized multimedia that illustrate course concepts, especially those that are interactive. (n.p.)

By organizing ahead of time and creating a Web site with all the essential information and tools, teachers will have more time to dedicate to the important interactions necessary to the success of eLearning.

Guideline #4: *Give clear instructions.* Part of organizing eLearning is clarifying what students need to do and how they should do it. Because students are generally not in the same room as the teacher and typically cannot ask questions on the spot, the instructions for eLearning tasks need to be very explicit and models, if available, should be accessible to students. This seems easier than it really is—classroom teachers usually rely on being able to "read" their students to clarify and add to instructions, and it takes practice to write good instructions that do not need further explanation.

Table 8.2 on page 218 presents general guidelines for writing clear instructions.

Figure 8.6 on page 218 summarizes the guidelines for eLearning.

How can Jim make sure that the course he is proposing follows these guidelines?

_____

_____

_____

TABLE 8.2 Guidelines for Writing Instructions

- Use titles and subtitles for each section of the instructions (e.g., "Instructions for posting to the discussion," "Posting a new message," "Posting a reply."
- If students have different roles or tasks, write separate, well-labeled instructions for each.
- Start each instruction with a command word (also known as an imperative verb). For example: "*List* three alternatives," "*Click* on this link," "*Summarize* the comments."
- Try not to combine instructional steps. For example, the instruction "Write a 50-word description using your personal vocabulary words and post it to the discussion in the task 1 thread" should be broken into two steps—one to write and one to post.
- Write for the reading and skill level of your audience. Provide examples and models where appropriate.
- Avoid long lists of instructions. Break lists of more than 10 steps into two or more sets of instructions.
- Clearly instruct the student what to do when the task is complete. Note what the next task is and where to find the instructions.

FIGURE 8.6 Guidelines for eLearning

Guideline #1: Build community.	Help students find common interests and goals and interact in productive ways.
Guideline #2: Consider hidden curriculum.	Reflect on the impacts of what is taught and how.
Guideline #3: Organize ahead of time.	Lay out the documents and information that students will need.
Guideline #4: Give clear instructions.	Put everything in writing and/or graphics that you might say or show to embellish the same instructions in a f2f context.

eLEARNING TOOLS

Because eLearning occurs in so many configurations and contexts, many different tools, alone or in combination, are used. Electronic tools for eLearning can include any of the tools mentioned throughout this text (CD-ROMs, videos, and so on). From printed materials such as textbooks and handouts to simple audio material such as audiocassettes to the latest computer technologies, almost any tool can be integrated into eLearning. However, most eLearning contexts currently include interactive technologies such as the World Wide Web, email, and video technologies. It is not within the scope of this text to discuss how to use all the tools that are used for eLearning, but the annotated collection presented in this section can help teachers begin an investigation of common eLearning tools. Most of the tool Web sites include tutorials and other support for new users.

In addition to an Internet connection, a Web browser (e.g., Netscape, Internet Explorer, Mozilla, Safari) with add-ons (i.e., mini-applications or **plug-ins**) will help students listen to audio, see video, and compose and send email. Other tools that can be used during hybrid and online classes include the following.

1. Learning environments

Learning environments provide online or "virtual" places to interact and post course content. Some environments are commercially produced, others are free. Some are **authorable,** or able to be changed by users, while others cannot be changed. Many commercial environments come with preset content; others allow the use of **homegrown** (locally produced) content. Each tool has specific strengths and weaknesses that can best be found by using it in context (most offer a demonstration version and technical assistance for evaluation purposes).

Some popular learning environments are listed here. They typically include some preset features such as asynchronous threaded discussion, internal email, document and link posting, and synchronous chat capabilities. For less structured environments, see authorable platforms later in this section.

Commercial environments

- Blackboard and WebCT (www.webct.com)
- eClassroom (www.eclassroom.com)

- Idaho Virtual Campus (http://ivccourses.ed.uidaho.edu)
- Sitescape/Webworkzone (www.sitescape.com)
- Nicenet (www.nicenet.org; free for teachers)

For an overview of one of these tools, see the Tool CloseUp: Internet Classroom Assistant on page 220.

MOOs and other free virtual spaces

MOOs can also function as learning environments where students can go to practice what they learned face to face, interact with other students in different locations, or hold class meetings. For more information on MOOs visit Rachel's Super MOO list of educational MOOs at http://moolist.yeehaw.net/edu.html. Some of the more popular MOOs used for online learning include:

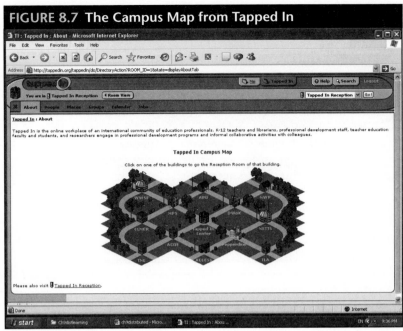

FIGURE 8.7 The Campus Map from Tapped In

Source: Copyright SRI International. Tapped In is a registered trademark of SRI International.

- Tapped In (tappedin.org; see Figure 8.7 for the campus map that shows some of the places users can go). Teachers can use classrooms here for group meetings.
- Diversity University (www.marshall.edu/commdis/moo)
- Digital Space Traveler (www.digitalspace.com/traveler/). Users of this space can discuss with others who appear as graphical characters on their computer screens.

Authoring platforms

These eLearning environments can be integrated into a second-grade class to allow students to post their electronic work or a tenth-grade math class that is completely online. Some of the most popular authorable eLearning environments, or those that can be changed by teachers and/or students, include:

- Macromedia Breeze/eLearning Studio (www.macromedia.com)
- Moodle (www.moodle.org; free of charge)
- Mambo (www.mamboserver.com; free of charge)
- Sakai (http://sakaiproject.org/; free of charge)

Figure 8.8 shows the Moodle interface developed for a high school history course. Because Moodle is authorable, the look and content can change from course to course.

To compare many of these eLearning platforms and environments, go to edutools at www.edutools.info/course/index.jsp. A more complete list of environments can be found at www.ncsa.uiuc.edu/~jfile/learnenv/.

2. Quiz and assessment tools

Many online assessment tools are listed throughout this book and on the Companion Website (http://www.prenhall.com/egbert). A large number of quiz and survey tools are available to conduct pre- and postassessments with students both online and off. For example:

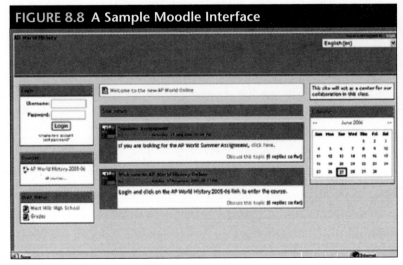

FIGURE 8.8 A Sample Moodle Interface

Source: Used with permission of Moodle.

Nicenet.org, part of the California Community Colocation Project, provides a free learning environment called the Internet Classroom Assistant (ICA) to members of non-profit organizations. Teachers can use the features of the ICA to support both online and hybrid courses.

The ICA is easy for teachers and students to learn and use. It has a simple interface and includes many of the features mentioned previously: conferencing (discussion), email, link sharing, and space for teachers to post assignments and documents. The screen shot here shows the ICA interface. The accompanying main menu appears on each page of a course and allows teachers and students to navigate through sections of the course easily. The "class administration" link is only for teachers.

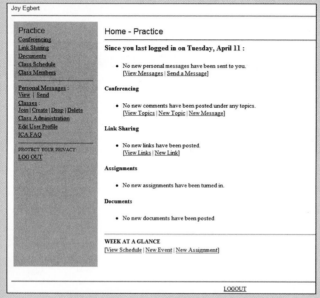

Source: Used with permission of Nicenet.

Teachers have a variety of choices in administering a course within this environment.

A search for "nicenet" in a Web browser brings up a large number of Web sites with suggestions and instructions that can assist teachers and learners in using ICA. For example, teacher Peggy Maslow's page on www.teachersnetwork.org provides instructional ideas and some cautions. In

Source: Used with permission of Nicenet.

Source: Used with permission of Nicenet.

addition, many examples of teacher uses of ICA are described in detail. McKeand (www2.selu.edu/) even provides sample student comments about ICA use:

> Using www.nicenet.org is very easy for me to check my homework and also to receive my teacher's comments about my homework. Another is that if I am in home doing my homework and if I am concerned about something I just write to my teacher asking about it, and she right away can advise me.
>
> —FA
>
> One of the best things is that I can read my classmates work. I don't need to print it. Also, I can give opinions. It is a good way to learn. . . . Schedule in Nicenet is clear. We know when we must do something. . . . It is a good way to save paper.
>
> —CV

Teachers can begin to use this simple but powerful tool by signing up for an account and exploring its features one at a time.

What are the benefits for Jim of proposing that his course use the ICA? What might be some disadvantages, evidenced in the student excerpts above?

Link to a tutorial from the Tutorials module of the Companion Website (http://www.prenhall.com/egbert).

- QuestionMark (www.questionmark.com). QuestionMark can be integrated into some commercial learning environments and provides quizzes, surveys, and tests.
- QuizRocket (www.learningware.com/quizrocket/). A free trial allows teacher to create multiple choice, sequencing, matching, true or false, short answer, and branching surveys and quizzes.
- Quizstar and Rubistar (www.4teachers. org). Create quizzes and rubrics easily with these free tools.
- Advanced Surveys (www.advancedsurvey.com/surveys/). After creating an account, surveys can be published to the Web for all kinds of data-gathering purposes.

3. Video and audio conferencing tools and resources

Not typically as comprehensive as learning environments, conferencing tools allow students to meet and discuss as part of hybrid and completely online classes. For example, third graders learning about space can call a scientist at NASA for free, or middle school students in an online course can hold a videoconference with peers in Germany to compare ideas about important world problems. Usually these resources provide some combination of video, audio, and/or text capabilities, and many are free. Telephony software, or software that allows the user to make telephone calls over the Internet, is currently becoming very popular. Examples of free conferencing and telephony software include:

- Netmeeting 3 (www.microsoft.com/windows/NetMeeting/Features/default.ASP)
- CUSeeMe (www.cuworld.com)
- MSN Messenger with Video and/or Voice (imagine-msn.com)
- Yahoo Messenger (http://messenger.yahoo.com)
- iChat (www.apple.com)
- Skype (www.skype.com)

To get started with videoconferencing, check out the PacBell videoconferencing guide at www.kn.pacbell.com/.

4. Digital libraries

Students and teachers can take advantage of digital libraries in hybrid and online courses. These libraries contain everything from raw data to online texts. Examples include:

- Digital Video Library from United Streaming (www.unitedstreaming.com/)
- Library of Congress (www.loc.gov/index.html)
- NASA Astrophysics Data System(http://adswww.harvard.edu/)
- Project Gutenberg (www.gutenberg.org/)
- Visible Human Project (www.nlm.nih.gov/research/visible/visible_human.html)

Find more resources for both teacher and student use in the digital libraries section of www.itcnetwork.org/.

5. Web page hosts

All of the following Web sites host personal Web space for free, although some do require registration. Instructors and students in eLearning courses can create Web pages to share their ideas and work, whether they are in different locations or in the same classroom. There are many more providers across the Web than are listed here.

- Geocities (www.geocities.com)
- Quia (www.quia.com/)
- FreeSite.com (www.thefreesite.com/Free_Web_Space/)
- Bravenet.com (www.bravenet.com)
- Blogger (www.blogger.com)
- TeacherWeb (http://teacherweb.com)
- SchoolNotes (www.schoolnotes.com/)
- Tripod (www.tripod.lycos.com)

T O O L S

Tool CloseUp: iPods and Handhelds

Podcasting

Handheld electronic devices of all kinds are beginning to find a place in eLearning. In fact, the term "M-learning" (mobile learning) has been coined to describe learning with portable hardware and software (Clyde, 2004). From cell phones that take pictures and allow Web surfing to Palm handheld computers, the use of small handheld devices is taking off in K–12 classrooms as teachers begin to realize their potential.

Podcasting

According to Lucas (2005), creative teachers are using iPods (Apple), or small digital MP3 players, in a variety of situations to engage students. One use is for **podcasts**, or online radio shows. Students can record the show on a computer, convert it to the appropriate format (called MP3) and upload it to the Web. Other users can download and listen to the shows on their iPods or other devices that use the MP3 format. Using detachable microphones and other iPod add-ons, students can record interviews and other audio information, from history lessons to explanations of mathematical functions. Lucas claims that even third graders are easily integrating iPods into their daily schoolwork. One school in Washington State is using MP3 players to send assignments home so that parents of English language learners can listen and respond with their children. The accompanying figure presents another blended class that is using podcasts to learn about history in effective and innovative ways.

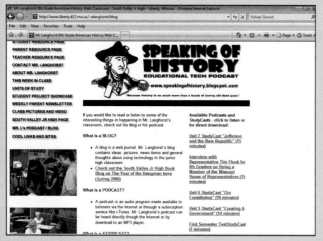

Source: Used with permission of Eric Langhorst, Liberty Public Schools.

Approximately 10,000 podcasts are posted around the world (Tumulty & Locke, 2005). Many of them can be found listed at www.ipodder.org/. For those interested in podcasting, a good entry site is http://learninginhand .com/podcasting/. For educational uses and how-tos, check the site's find.html and links.html.

Handhelds

Whereas an iPod is really a listening device, handheld computers can do much more. The K12 Handhelds Web site (www.k12handhelds.com/101list.php) lists 101 educational uses for a handheld computer. Some of them are shown in the screen shot here.

Source: Courtesy of K12 Handhelds, Inc.

Research shows that when students take handhelds home, they experience achievement gains. They not only learn the technology better, but the use of handheld computers also allows students to discover the content material at their own pace and ability level (see http:// kathyschrock.net/power/ for research).

Kathy Schrock's Power in the Palm of Your Hand Web site is one among many that provides ideas, resources, and research on handhelds and demonstrates their growing use. For example, teachers can send programs and information to students, and students can use the handheld to organize

continued

Tool CloseUp: Continued

Russell Robinson

and transform the data in many of the same ways they might use a desktop computer. However, a handheld is portable, underscoring the goal of eLearning anytime, anywhere. The student in the accompanying photo is working on a writing assignment on his handheld computer.

A concern with the growing use of handheld computers is how the use connects to learning standards and goals. To enhance learning, schools must provide teachers and students with the technical and curricular support to use the tools well. In addition, educational stakeholders must understand, value, and support the use of technology. For information about funding, using handheld devices in classrooms, classroom management with handhelds, and many other "tips and tricks," visit the thorough and useful page by Midge Frazel at www.midgefrazel.net/pda.html.

How could Jim use podcasting or handheld activities to enhance the eLearning courses that he is proposing?

_____

_____

_____

_____

Tutorial
CW

Find podcasting tutorials in the Tutorials module of the Companion Website (http://www.prenhall.com/egbert).

6. Content-based learning sites

Content-based Web sites, along with content-based stand-alone software packages, are mentioned throughout this text and can be integrated into both hybrid and online classes at all grade levels. Here are some useful sites:

- National Geographic Kids' Network (www.nationalgeographic.com/education/)
- i*earn Learning Circles (www.iearn.org/circles/ lcguide/)
- WebCurrents from Learners online (www.learnersonline.com/weekly/index.htm)
- Library of Congress learning page (http://lcweb2. loc.gov/ammem/ndlpedu/)

7. Software archives

These online storage places for software offer free or very cheap downloads for education software that can be integrated into eLearning contexts. Not all of it is the best, and teachers need to review their selections carefully.

- Tucows (www.tucows.com)
- WinSite (www.winsite.com)
- download.com (home and education; www.download.com/)
- ZDNet (teaching tools; http://downloads-zdnet.com)

FIGURE 8.9 eLearning Tools

Tool	Examples
Learning environments	MOOs, commercial environments, authorable platforms
Quiz and assessment tools	Surveys, rubric makers, quiz makers
Video and audio	Conferencing and telephony software
Digital libraries	Video and text compilations
Content-based learning resources	Lesson archives, activity sites, resource pages, software packages
Software archives	Shareware and freeware

One of the best sources on the Internet for online learning resources is e-Learning Centre's School e-Learning Showcase at www.e-learningcentre.co.uk/. Figure 8.9 summarizes some of the tools available for eLearning. Other tools are gaining popularity as eLearning flourishes. See the Tool CloseUp: iPods and Handhelds for more information.

How can Jim choose the most effective tools for his AP science class among all of the tools that exist? What features should he look for in the tools that he proposes?

_____

_____

_____

LEARNING ACTIVITIES: ELEARNING

As noted throughout this book, it is not the tool that makes the difference, but how it is used. This is also true for eLearning. Throughout this text, eLearning activities such as epals, virtual field trips, ask the expert, and technology-supported communications have already been mentioned. Like other parts of this chapter, this section looks at the differences between hypothetical face-to-face (f2f) contexts and eLearning opportunities. It describes what an instructional feature or task might look like as part of an eLearning context. The features and tasks described here could be part of a hybrid or an online course. The green text signals adaptations for eLearning. All of the links can be found in the Web Links module of this chapter's Companion Website (http:// www.prenhall.com/egbert).

Feature: Instructions

F2f: The teacher says, "Do exercise 5 on page 6. Ask me if you have any questions."

eLearning: Written instructions say,

Step 1. Read the instructions for exercise 5 on page 6.

Step 2. Answer the question in no more than a paragraph using complete sentences.

Step 3. Post your answer in the Unit 1 discussion thread in the class discussion forum.

If you have questions, email your online buddy for help. This assignment is due by 3 pm on Thursday.

For eLearning, the instructions must not only be more precise, but in writing them the teacher must also try to predict what questions students might ask.

Feature: Lesson presentation

F2f: The teacher gives a lecture about creating how-to (process) essays and points out the important features.

eLearning: The instructor has students read examples from the course Web site and How Stuff Works (www.howstuffworks.com). Students then go to the online forum and discuss the important characteristics they see in process essays. Together they create a features checklist for process essays they will write.

In the online environment, this task becomes much more learner-centered.

Feature: Lesson presentation

F2f: The teacher leads a discussion based on drawings of how the Internet works from the textbook's technology section.

eLearning: Students work in teams to complete one or more of the Peter Packet missions in Cisco's Packetville at www.cisco.com/. (See Figure 8.10 for the introduction screen.) Using external documents such as questionnaires and graphic organizers posted to their course site by the teacher, students record important information as they discover it. They post their findings to the discussion area of the course site for other students to review.

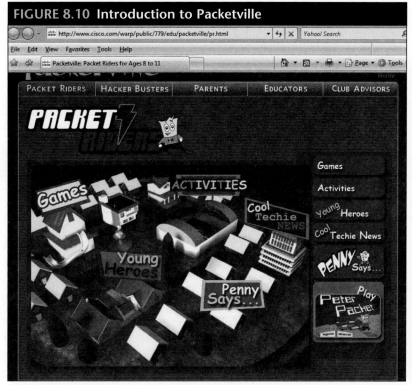

FIGURE 8.10 Introduction to Packetville

Source: These materials have been reproduced by Prentice Hall Inc. with the permission of Cisco Systems, Inc. Copyright © 2005 Cisco Systems, Inc. All rights reserved.

The addition of online resources not only pushes students to be more independent learners but also addresses the needs of students with different learning preferences.

Task: Propose solutions for how to end world poverty

F2f: Students read texts about world poverty and discuss solutions with classmates.

eLearning: Through the United Nation's Millenium Development site (www.un.org/), students work with information and people from all over the world to investigate, understand, and work toward solutions for world poverty.

With eLearning integrated into the course, students can receive information directly from those involved in the issue, which broadens not only their audience but also their potential understanding.

Task: Prepare to study sharks

F2f: Teacher asks students to look at pictures of sharks in their text and brainstorm a list of what they understand about sharks from the photos.

eLearning: Students watch the shark videos from Nova Online at www.pbs.org/ and brainstorm a list of what they understand about sharks from the videos.

The online videos provide a more authentic glimpse of sharks and allow students to produce more language and content than the still photos from the book.

Students can learn without participating in eLearning. However, it is clear from these simple examples that, although eLearning might require more advanced planning and reassessment of important teaching skills, electronic resources and technologies can help teachers to change, in powerful ways, the focus of learning from teachers to students.

What changes do you see when eLearning is added in the examples above? Are there any changes that are not beneficial? If so, explain.

_____

_____

_____

ASSESSING eLEARNING

eLearning requires different options for assessment because, particularly in Web-based courses, the instructor cannot always observe students. Tests, quizzes, surveys, and other standard evaluations can be constructed and implemented with the tools noted above and in other chapters. However, as in traditional classrooms, these assessment tools do not provide the whole picture of student progress and achievement. Portfolios are one solution to this problem.

Overview of Portfolios

A **portfolio** is a purposeful, reflective collection of student work. *Purposeful* means that it is not a folder that contains everything students have done, but rather it is a focused compilation of student work that is developed with guidelines from both the teacher and the student. Traditional portfolios help students set learning goals, encourage students to reflect on their growth and achievement, serve as a basis for communication with parents and other stakeholders, and allow teachers to see how students are performing and plan to address gaps. There are many types of portfolios. Two common types are:

- Showcase—Students display only their best work.
- Developmental—Students show their progress over time.

In each case, the binding element is student reflection. Many excellent texts describe the use of portfolios to assess student progress and achievement; see the Assessment section on the Resources module of the Companion Website for suggestions (http://www.prenhall.com/egbert).

ePortfolios

ePortfolios are portfolios that are kept in an electronic format (video, audio, computer-based). There are many reasons to use ePortfolios. In addition to the benefits mentioned above, ePortfolios are easy to store and access. They require students to develop multimedia skills that support the NETS standards. In addition, they can include sound, video, graphics, and photos, allowing students to demonstrate their learning in multiple ways.

The steps for developing ePortfolios are the same as for paper-based portfolios, except that ePortfolios require a technological aspect. The general steps that teachers and students can take are outlined below (adapted from Barrett, 2000a, 2000b; Chamberlain, 2001; Niguidula, 2002):

1. *Identify the purpose of the portfolio.* Is it to showcase students' outstanding work, to show progress, to share with stakeholders, to demonstrate mastery, or something else?

2. *Identify the desired learner outcomes.* These should be based on national, state, or local standards and curricular requirements and include learner goals.

3. *Identify the hardware and software resources available and the technology skills of the students and teachers.* Barrett (2005) provides examples of commercial portfolio software and other tools such as PowerPoint (Microsoft) that can be used in ePortfolio development.

4. *Identify the primary audience for the portfolio.* The audience could include a college registrar, a future employer, a parent, or peers, for example. Choose a format—Web-based, CD-ROM, video—that the audience will most likely have access to. Chamberlain (2001) notes that teachers are required to obtain permission from students' legal guardians before posting student work online. She provides sample permission letters at www.electricteacher.com.

5. *Determine content.* Teachers and students can develop a checklist of required content, including the sequencing of the information.

6. *Gather, organize, and format the materials.* Students should be required to include reflections on each piece and on the entire portfolio. Figure 8.11 shows a page from a sixth-grade social studies ePortfolio.

7. *Evaluate and update as necessary.* Software such as SuperSchool Portfolio Assessment Kit (SuperSchool Software), Hyperstudio (Roger Wagner), Grady Profile (Aurbach), and even Microsoft Word can be used to provide templates for students to enter work samples and other relevant material. ePortfolios can be evaluated by rubrics that assess each step of the process (see chapter 3 for a discussion of rubrics) and that focus on meeting the standards or on other qualities deemed important, such as collaboration and participation. A sample rubric is shown in Figure 8.12.

Other examples using a variety of tools can be found in the electronic portfolio samples section of www.forsyth.k12.ga.us/ and http://dragonnet.hkis.edu.hk/. More links can be found in the Resources module of the Companion Website for this chapter (http://www.prenhall.com/egbert).

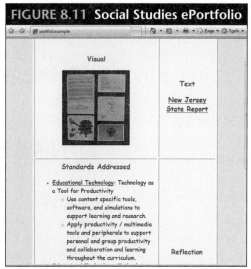

FIGURE 8.11 Social Studies ePortfolio

Source: Used with permission of Maunawili Elementary, Kailua, Hawaii.

Should Jim plan to use ePortfolios in his AP science class? What would the advantages be? The disadvantages?

_____

_____

_____

FIGURE 8.12 ePortfolio Rubric Sample

Electronic Portfolio Scoring Rubric				
	Missed the Mark! 5 pts.	**Getting Close!** 10 pts.	**Right On Target!** 15 pts.	**Bulls Eye!!!** 17 pts.
Title Card:	Design is inappropriate	Design could be neater or might be inappropriate	Design is attractive and colorful	Design is attractive, colorful, and shows creativity.
Mechanics:	Spelling and punctuation errors are distracting.	Spelling and punctuation errors are evident.	Errors in spelling and punctuation are minor and few.	There are NO errors in spelling or punctuation.
Buttons:	The student project card contains 4 or less buttons that link to projects.	The student project card contains 5 or 6 buttons that link to projects.	The student project card contains 7 buttons that link to projects.	The student project card contains 8 buttons that link to projects.
Sounds:	Many sounds are inappropriate and/or distract from the stack.	Some sounds are inappropriate and/or distract from the stack.	Sounds are of high quality and are appropriate.	The sounds enhance the quality of the stack.
Content of project reflections:	Few reflections include: the program used and the main skills learned.	Some reflections include: the program used and the main skills learned.	All reflections include: the program used and the main skills learned.	All reflections include: the program used and a detailed account of all skills learned.
Personal reactions to projects:	Few reflections include personal reactions. Reactions are vague or repetitive.	Some reflections include personal reactions. Reactions may be vague or repetitive.	Reflections include personal reaction that clearly reflect the student's feelings.	All reflections include personal reactions that are descriptive and insightful.

Source: www.essdack.org/port/rubric.html

SAMPLE LESSON: eLEARNING

The principal asked Jim to submit a sample lesson plan with his proposal for distance AP science courses. The lesson is to be an example of what might be posted to the electronic forum used for the distance courses. Because the students will see the lessons and use them to direct their learning, Jim needs to ensure the lesson is student-friendly. Jim understands that other teachers have created wonderful lessons for online learning and, after searching the Web, he selects a ninth/tenth-grade lesson in the form of a WebQuest created by K. Nuthall, a science teacher in Poway, California (www. powayschools.com/projects/elnino/ default.htm). The stated standards addressed by this lesson include math standards such as problem solving, reasoning, connections, and skills (statistics); content reading standards such as variety of sources, information access, and evaluation; and writing content standards such as modes.

Following is the lesson Jim chose.

EL NIÑO OR EL NO-NO

Have you ever watched the evening news with your folks and wondered how the weather person could have been so wrong? You wore shorts to school that day only to find yourself freezing during lunch. Predicting the weather is a very difficult task. The many factors which impact your daily local weather can be thousands of miles away, so Meteorologists use a variety of different remote tools including satellites and buoys to help them make predictions. These experts make their predictions by building models using historical and current data.

El Niño and La Niña cycles are examples of these complex patterns. In this investigation, you will learn more about El Niño and La Niña cycles, and how they impact the weather in your area. To accomplish this task, you will be logging into one of same ocean buoys that scientists use to develop their models.

Your Task

You will be part of an expert team. Your team will be responsible for collecting data, organizing it in an appropriate graphic form, and analyzing it for the purpose of making weather predictions in your community. After making your prediction, you will write a speculation paper that details how you reached your conclusion. Your last task will be to share your findings with the scientific community.

As winter approaches, you will be on the hot seat, and you'll get a taste of what it's like to be a weather person. To be successful, you need to ask great questions, seek out the answers, develop new relationships, and take a stand.

The Process

Your team will be taking a seven-step approach to accomplishing the project. You will begin by learning more about El Niño and La Niña. After gaining a solid understand of these cycles, you will log into an ocean buoy and begin gathering your data and building a model. Your final task will be to craft an effective speculation paper about the coming winter, and share your findings with the scientific world.

Step 1: In the news

El Niño and La Niña cycles have a tremendous impact on the world's weather. It is hard to believe that ocean water temperatures in the Pacific Ocean can impact mid-America states, but the national news organizations have reported on the extensive impact of the cycle. Read the two articles below, and write a short summary of each one.

- La Niña leaves states high and dry - CNN News
- Flotilla of sensors to monitor world's oceans - CNN News

Step 2: Background information

Split up and assign each member of your group one of the Web pages listed below. After exploring the Web pages individually, get back together in your group and answer the following questions.

1. What is the difference between El Niño and La Niña?
2. Why is predicting these cycles important?
3. What are the possible impacts on weather due to a La Niña cycle?

4. What are the possible impacts on weather due to an El Niño cycle?
5. Is the earth always in either an El Niño or El Niña cycle?
6. Write and answer four additional questions that you believe would help people understand the El Niño and La Niña Cycles.

Resources

- <u>About La Niña and El Niño</u> - Climate Prediction Center
- <u>Global La Niña Impacts</u> - Climate Prediction Center
- <u>El Niño Impacts</u> - Climate Prediction Center
- <u>El Niño Basics</u> - Climate Prediction Center

Step 3: Real-time data

It's time to start gathering sea surface temperatures (SST), so your team can begin to build a useful model. You will be using a buoy located at <u>110 degrees West and 0 degrees North</u>. You will begin by gathering today's real-time data, and then adding that value to the temperatures for the last 14-days.

Current Real-Time Data
<u>Java Applet #1</u>
<u>Java Applet #2</u>
<u>Last 14-days</u>
(Make sure you use the data from the buoy at 110 W)

1. Use the link above to collect the today's daily (SST) for the <u>110 W 0 N buoy.</u>
   (Note: When you place the mouse on the correct buoy, the window below will show the real-time information.)
2. Access and print the data for the last 14-days.
3. Calculate <u>anomaly</u> for each day. (<u>Mean SST Values</u>)
4. Place the data and calculations in a well-constructed table. Be sure to include a table title, column headings, and units.
5. Create a line graph for both the SST data and your calculated anomalies. (<u>Example anomaly graph</u> | <u>Example SST graph</u>)

Step 4: Historical model

Scientists have been tracking SST for many years, and it has allowed them to create a historical model that helps them predict El Niño and La Niña cycles. Use the link below to answer the following questions:

- Which two years show the greatest "positive" anomalies?
- Which two years show the greatest "negative" anomalies?
- Compare the anomaly graph you created in step 5 with the historical anomaly graph. Does it look like the current year is either an El Niño or La Niña cycle?
- How could you make your model a better predictor of the cycle?

<u>Historical Anomaly Graph</u> - TOA/TRITON

Step 5: Temperatures and participation

The buoy we have been tracking is several thousand miles away, so it is hard to believe that sea surface temperatures can have an impact on your local weather. Use the links below to investigate how the El Niño and La Niña cycles impact your local weather. You may want to split up the links between each of your team members, and allow each individual to become a site expert. Be prepared to use this information when you write your final speculation paper.

- <u>La Niña Seasonal U.S. Temperature & Precipitation</u> - Climate Prediction Center
- <u>Seasonal Mean Temperatures and Precipitation for the United States during Strong El Niños</u> - Climate Prediction Center

(continued)

- Words of CAUTION - by William S. Kessler NOAA / Pacific Marine Environmental Laboratory
- Cold and Warm Episodes by Season - Climate Prediction Center

Step 6: Speculation

It's time for you to take a stand. The model you developed in step 5 was only for a 15-day period, so you may also want to extend your graph to include a longer period of time. You can access additional SST by visiting the TOA / TRITON Data Delivery System. (Note: Make sure you are gathering data from the correct buoy.)

Is the world currently in an El Niño or La Niña cycle? What are your predictions for temperature and precipitation in your local area? You will be required to provide solid support when making your case. Your group needs to work together to reach consensus. After your group has reached consensus, your task is to construct a solid speculation essay, so you may want to read a few Tips on Writing Speculation Papers. You may also want to view a possible grading rubric before beginning.

Step 7: Share your prediction

Your last step is to share your speculation with the world. Access the Climate Prediction Center Feedback Form, and cut and paste your paper into the form. Maybe you'll hear back.

Conclusion

Good Luck! Remember, luck only occurs where opportunity and preparation meet. Read, write, gather data and create your model with care. This winter you may actually live out your speculation.

Source: Project Design Team: Keith Nuthall, Cindy DeClercq, and John Windbury. Poway Unified School District, Poway, California.

Jim read the lesson carefully to analyze its appropriateness for the ninth/tenth-grade AP course he is envisioning and to adapt it to his teaching context. He completed a Lesson Analysis and Adaptation Worksheet (found in chapter 1 on page 33 and on the Lesson Planning module of the Companion Website, http://www.prenhall.com/egbert) and concluded these things about the lesson:

- The standards, objectives, and task are aligned.
- The standards and objectives are appropriate for ninth/tenth graders. The NETS*S could be mentioned, but technology is also mentioned in the content standards.
- In each of the steps students are asked to search for and analyze data. The overall project goal is to create an informed speculation, an important skill.
- Graphs and data charts address visual literacy; students use technology in new ways; students use a variety of media—a real strength of this lesson.
- This lesson addresses all the learning goals through its emphasis on working in teams, coming to consensus, developing summaries and tables, searching for data to answer the question, and delivering a product to an authentic audience.
- The Web materials/resources in the lesson are not marked for reading level or content. There is limited variety in materials since almost all of them are other Web sites. This needs to be expanded so that all students can access them at an appropriate level.
- Roles are not outlined specifically—the students need more guidance here. A good connection is made to real life in both the introduction and the conclusion. "How does weather work?" is an essential question.
- The raw data sources are completely authentic, as are the news articles. The communication supported by the technology makes the task easier for most students, but ELLs may need other types of input. It is unknown whether the students will learn faster, but they will probably be very engaged, so they may. The goal of understanding is foremost.

SAMPLE LESSON

- The vocabulary and instructions are repeated, which helps with comprehensibility. However, some instructions need more explanation. There need to be more offline resources and models of finished products. Choices of resources would help students work in different ways, but more choice in other areas would also help.

- The rubric is too simple and does not explain clearly what is required. It seems to focus as much on writing as content—maybe these should be separate rubrics so that the focus is on the thought process first. It would be useful for students to help with the rubric creation, but that might be difficult from a distance. Maybe they can write a reflection based on what they see as the main points of their work.

This lesson has many outstanding aspects. However, based on his analysis and his knowledge of his students, Jim decides to make some small but important changes to the lesson. He especially wants to make sure that his adaptations meet the needs of the ELLs and other students with challenges who will take the course. He decides to make these changes based on his analysis:

- Link content words that some students might need to have explained (such as "remote," "cycle," and "historical") to an online dictionary.
- Boldface important words such as "buoy" so that students will notice them.
- Bullet the content of the Task section to separate the goals and make it easier to read.
- Create a link to simple instructions for summary writing.
- Add models of the assignments.
- Annotate the Web links for reading level and content.
- Add additional resources such as books, magazine articles, and links to scientists.
- Include more graphics that help explain the goals and content of the lesson.
- Provide detailed suggestions for assigning roles within teams.
- Create a new rubric that includes more specific guidelines for each part of the task, and include guiding questions for students to reflect on their learning. Also include a rubric for discussions, such as:
  Quality (Do you show reflection in your posting? Do you integrate readings, resources, and activities? Do you refer to your experiences and others' ideas? Do your comments add something to the discussion?)
  Support (Do you provide evidence for your assertions?)
  Professionalism (Do you get to the point? Do you use strategies to enhance others' understanding [e.g., give examples]? Are you a positive and supportive participant? Do you welcome different opinions and perspectives? Do you show respect to others in the discussion?)

Jim also decides to note places where the teacher will provide direct facilitation; how chat, video, and other tools of the learning environment will be integrated into the assignment; and how course management issues will be addressed. With these changes, Jim feels that this lesson will work well not only for his students but for students from other classrooms participating in the online ninth/tenth-grade AP course.

What other changes, if any, should Jim make to this lesson? Why?

_____

_____

_____

Conclusion

Bailey (2001) sums up the focus and importance of eLearning:

1. We need to move beyond the notion that education is about school buildings, school days, and classrooms. For us to move forward with not just eLearning, but learning in general, we

must accept the reality that education can now be delivered to students wherever they are located.

2. Schools need to become education centers. With distance education, schools become access points to a whole range of educational opportunities. Until schools recognize that their mission is fundamentally changing as a result of eLearning, we're only going to make incremental progress toward this important objective.

3. Every educational program is a technology opportunity and every technology program is an educational opportunity. While our investment in technology does help schools purchase computers and networks, it is also fundamentally about purchasing math courses and additional online resources and distance education classes for their students. It isn't about the boxes and the wires. It is about teaching and learning. It is the instructional content and its applications that should drive technology, not the other way around.

4. Online assessment, particularly online assessment with eLearning technologies, is one of the next generation "killer applications" that is waiting for us out there. When online assessment results are tied into eLearning systems, the potential benefits become very significant. The result should be more effective use of class time and a system of education that isn't based on mass production, but is instead based on mass customization.

5. Finally, together as industry and as government, we need to be relentless in measuring and assessing the impact that technology has on education and on academic achievement. We need evidence that teaching and learning are improved as the result of technology. Using technology to teach using traditional methods will only lead to traditional results.

As better, faster, cheaper, and more accessible technologies are developed and classrooms move more toward online learning, these issues will be crucial to understand and implement. However, we must also remember the face-to-face interactions that students need and value.

Which information in this chapter is most valuable to you? Why? How will you use it in your teaching?

_____

_____

_____

CHAPTER REVIEW

Key Points

- **Explain eLearning and how it can help meet learning goals.**

  eLearning consists of three basic components: (1) instructional and learning strategies, (2) pedagogical models or constructs, and (3) learning technologies. eLearning contexts range from hybrid classes to those completely online and at a distance from the teacher. eLearning can help schools meet the needs of a variety of students.

- **Discuss guidelines for creating eLearning opportunities.**

  Although guidelines and tips for eLearning can also apply to f2f classrooms, they are especially crucial to follow in eLearning contexts. Teachers must work toward building a community of learners and consider what the hidden curriculum means for the students in the class. To facilitate online learning, teachers can organize ahead of time and work toward giving clear instructions.

- **Describe eLearning tools.**

  Almost any electronic tool, and many other types of tools, can be and are used as part of eLearning. The tools must, however, support and enhance student learning and not impede it.

- **Develop and evaluate effective technology-enhanced eLearning activities.**

    Features of effective eLearning activities are much the same as for those in f2f contexts, but with the added elements of technology and differences in how time is used. Activities that follow guidelines for good teaching will be effective both online and off, as long as the medium in which they are employed is considered.

- **Create appropriate assessments for technology-enhanced eLearning activities.**

    Although this book outlines many kinds of assessment that are available for eLearning, ePortfolios have many benefits for teachers, students, and other educational stakeholders.

CASE QUESTIONS REVIEW

Reread the case at the beginning of the chapter and review your answers. In light of what you learned during this chapter, how do your answers change? Note any changes here.

1. *What other information does Jim need before he writes his proposal?*

    _____

    _____

    _____

2. *What are some potential benefits of eLearning?*

    _____

    _____

    _____

3. *What are some potential disadvantages of eLearning?*

    _____

    _____

    _____

4. *How could Jim most easily teach and assess students who are at a distance from him?*

    _____

    _____

    _____

5. *If you were Jim's principal, how would you react to this proposal? Why?*

    _____

    _____

    _____

CHAPTER EXTENSIONS • • • • • • • • • • • •

Find additional exercises, questions, and resources on the Companion Website (http://www.prenhall.com/egbert).

Adapt • • • •

Choose a lesson for your potential subject area and grade level from the Lesson Plan Library at Discovery Schools (http://school.discovery.com/lessonplans/). Use the Lesson Analysis and Adaptation Worksheet from chapter 1 on page 33 (also available on the Companion Website), to consider the lesson in the context of *blended* or *completely online eLearning*. Use your responses to the worksheet to suggest general changes to the lesson based on your future students and context.

Practice • • • •

1. *Give online instructions.* Using a classroom document in which you have outlined instructions for students or a lesson that you have created, write specific instructions that students could follow in a setting *without* immediate access to a teacher. Use the examples in the Guidelines section of this chapter. Check to see if a classmate can follow the instructions exactly as you intended without your help, and if not, revise them.

2. *Review an eLearning tool.* Choose an eLearning tool mentioned in this chapter. Go to the ISTE Web site and follow the instructions to choose an appropriate evaluation form for the tool you choose (http://cnets.iste.org/teachers/web/t_form_software-eval.html). Use the form to review the features and uses of the tool. Write a short reflection about your findings.

3. *Interview a teacher.* After reading this chapter, what questions do you have? List them. Now, interview a teacher who you think has the experience or understanding to answer your questions. Report your answers to the class.

4. *Develop an ePortfolio rubric.* First, list a goal for the portfolio and create a brief table of contents. Then use one of the tools mentioned in this text to develop a rubric to assess the expected contents.

Explore • • • •

1. *Avoid plagiarism.* Brainstorm with your classmates how teachers might ensure that the assignments turned in have actually been completed by the student rather than someone else. Check online for solutions that other teachers have found and share them with your class.

2. *Reconstruct an activity.* Choose a lesson you have developed or one that you find for your content and grade level on the Web (see the Lesson Planning module of the Companion Website, http://www.prenhall.com/egbert, for lesson plan sites). Using information from this chapter, examine the activity. Are there parts of it that are too high in content and not high enough in process? If so, revise the activity. If not, explain why the level of process in the activity would be appropriate for eLearning.

3. *Explore resources.* Find a technology not listed in this book that could be used for eLearning. How can this tool support eLearning? Your answer should contain an explanation of the instructional and learning strategies, pedagogical models or constructs, and other learning technologies that could support eLearning with this tool.

4. *Create an ePortfolio assignment.* Revisit the standards for your grade level and content area(s). Outline requirements for an ePortfolio that would help your future students show how they have met the standards.

REFERENCES

Abate, L. (2004, September 1). Blended model in the elementary classroom. *tech*learning*. Available: http://www.techlearning.com/story/showArticle.php?articleID=45200032.

Bailey, J. (2001, October). Keynote address presented at the Center for Internet Technology in Education (CiTE) Virtual High School Symposium, Chicago, IL.

Barrett, H. (2000a). *Electronic portfolios = Multimedia development + Portfolio development: The electronic portfolio development process*. Available: http://electronicportfolios.com/portfolios/EPDevProcess.html.

Barrett, H. (2000b). *How to create your own electronic portfolio*. Available: http://electronicportfolios.com/portfolios/howto/index.html.

Barrett, H. (2005). *Alternative assessment and electronic portfolios*. Available: http://electronicportfolios.com/portfolios/bookmarks.html.

Blomeyer, R. (2002). E-learning policy implications for K–12 educators and decision makers. NCREL/Learning Point Associates. Available: http://www.ncrel.org/policy/pubs/html/pivol11/apr2002d.htm.

Bowman, M. (1999). What is distributed learning? Tech Sheet 2.1. Available: http://techcollab.csumb.edu/techsheet2.1/distributed.html.

Cavanaugh, C., Gillan, K., Kromrey, J., Hess, M., & Blomeyer, R. (2004). *The effects of distance education on K–12 student outcomes: A meta-analysis*. Naperville, IL: Learning Point Associates.

Chamberlain, C. (2001). *Creating online portfolios*. Available: http://www.electricteacher.com/onlineportfolio/presteps.htm.

Clyde, L. (2004). M-learning. *Teacher Librarian, 32*(1), 45–46.

Conceicao, S., & Drummond, S. (2005, Fall). Online learning in secondary education: A new frontier. *Educational Considerations, 33*(1), 31–37.

Dabbagh, N., & Bannan-Ritland, B. (2005). *Online learning: Concepts, strategies, and application*. Upper Saddle River, NJ: Prentice Hall.

Davis, N., & Robyler, M. (2005). Preparing teachers for the "schools that technology built": Evaluation of a program to train teachers for virtual schooling. *Journal of Research on Technology in Education, 37*(4), 399–409.

Jackson, R. (2004). Web learning resources, page 1 of 3. Available: http://www.knowledgeability.biz/weblearning/#CoursewareandContentPublishers.

Lucas, C. (2005, July). Pod people. *Edutopia, 1*(5), 12.

Moore, M., & Koble, M. (1997). *K–12 distance education: Learning, instruction, and teacher training*. American Center for the Study of Distance Education: The Pennsylvania State University.

NEA. (2006). Guide to online high school courses. http://www.nea.org/technology/onlinecourseguide.html.

Niguidula, D. (2002). *Getting started with digital portfolios*. Available: http://www.essentialschools.org/lpt/ces_docs/224.

Office of Education Technology. (2004). *National education technology plan Web site*. Available: http://nationaledtechplan.org/.

Setzer. J., & Greene, B. (2005, March). *Distance education courses for public elementary and secondary school students: 2002–2003 (NCES 2005-010)*. Washington, DC: National Center for Education Statistics, U.S. Department of Education.

Tallent-Runnels, J., Thomas, J., Lan, W., Cooper, S., Ahern, T., Shaw, S., et al. (2006, Spring). Teaching courses online: A review of the research. *Review of Educational Research, 76*(1), 93–135.

Tumulty, K., and Locke, L. (2005, August 8). Al Gore, businessman. *TIME*, pp. 32–34.

Zucker, A., & Kozma, R. (2003). *The virtual high school: Teaching generation V*. New York: Teachers College Press.

9

Supporting Teacher Development

My oldest cousin is Ryan, who is in college. He has a little sister Emily who is my third oldest cousin. These are the names of my cousins on my mom's side in order of how old they are: Ryan, Jarrod, Emily, Anthony, Marissa, Camille, Liam and Donald, Brier and Ellie. I like it when me and my family go to New Jersey because it is hot and is very fun too. I think the most fun part is the beach and miniature golf because those are the tings we do together most of the time. Even though my uncle owns a big golf course in Florida, where he lives, this is the first time we have all gone to the miniature golf course together with all of my relatives.

Me and my family and relatives have lots of fun in New Jersey!

Case: Lifelong Learning

As you read the following scenario, think about how you will continue to develop professionally in technology-supported learning.

• •

The teachers at Pierce Junior High School had just participated in an in-service provided by the state education department. The focus of the meeting was the new state technology standards for students. The teachers learned that, in addition to content area standards and grade level indicators, the state was requiring all teachers to address the technology standards throughout the curriculum. During the workshop the presenter provided a resource list that included many print and electronic resources that teachers could use to help them learn about the technology standards and integrate them into instruction.

Patricia Morello, an eighth-grade English teacher, used technology regularly in her classes, particularly word processing. Her students typed their essays, looked for resources on the Web, and sometimes made graphic organizers to lay out the structure of a text. Patricia felt that she could probably meet the majority of the standards with little change. Just to make sure that she was working in the right direction, she decided to complete the Learning with Technology Profile Tool at www.ncrtec.org/capacity/profile/profwww.htm, which the workshop presenter had highly recommended. When she received her responses in graphical form, she discovered to her dismay that there was a lot more that she could do to use technology to engage learners. She also found that the technology she was using in her classes was neither very challenging nor very functional for students. Patricia understood why the standards should be addressed well and decided that she needed to learn more about the use of technology to meet standards, but she was unsure where to begin and how she could fit professional development in technology into her already-busy schedule.

• •

Answer these questions about the case. There are no right or wrong answers to this chapter preview—the goal is for you to respond before you read the chapter. Then, as you interact with the chapter contents, think about how your answers might change.

1. *Where should Patricia start her professional development? Why?*

    _____

    _____

    _____

2. *How can new teachers fit professional development about technology into their busy professional lives?*

    _____

    _____

    _____

3. *Should all teachers know about technology and its uses? Why or why not?*

    _____

    _____

    _____

4. *How can teachers learn about technology use? List 3–5 ways.*

    _____

    _____

    _____

Patricia understands the importance of helping students to meet standards, but she also is realistic about what she can do with the amount of time and current knowledge that she has. She, like many other teachers, is willing to learn more but has a number of barriers to overcome to be able to do so. The goal of this chapter is to help you to understand the role of professional development in learning to teach with technology and how some of these barriers might be bridged. Although you may not be thinking about professional development yet, you should be aware of the opportunities that exist so that you can plan appropriately when the time comes. After reading this chapter, you will be able to:

- Understand the role of professional development in technology-supported learning in student achievement and school change.
- Discuss guidelines for professional development in technology-supported learning.
- Evaluate tools for teacher development in technology-supported learning.
- Discover and participate in effective activities to support technical and pedagogical development.
- Assess your own development in technology-supported learning and teaching.

*When you have completed this chapter, which NETS*T will you have addressed?*

    _____

    _____

    _____

The sample activities and tools will help you understand the many opportunities available for professional development in technology. To begin, review the standards that guide teacher professional development in technology-supported learning in this chapter's Meeting the Standards.

• • • • **Meeting the Standards:** Supporting Teacher Development • • • •

The International Society for Technology in Education (ISTE), in addition to developing the widely used national education technology standards for students (NETS*S), has developed a set of standards that you have been applying throughout this text that outline "the fundamental concepts, knowledge, skills, and attitudes for applying technology in educational settings" (ISTE NETS Project, 2005, n.p.). These teacher standards, called NETS*T, focus on pre-service teacher education, and they also provide guidelines for teachers who are still learning about technology. As you have seen, the NETS*T recommend that:

I. Teachers demonstrate a sound understanding of technology operations and concepts.

II. Teachers plan and design effective learning environments and experiences supported by technology.

III. Teachers implement curriculum plans that include methods and strategies for applying technology to maximize student learning.

IV. Teachers apply technology to facilitate a variety of effective assessment and evaluation strategies.

V. Teachers use technology to enhance their productivity and professional practice.

VI. Teachers understand the social, ethical, legal, and human issues surrounding the use of technology in PK-12 schools and apply those principles in practice.

ISTE also provides guidelines for the essential conditions for general teacher preparation, professional preparation, student teaching/internship, and first-year teachers (see www.iste.org/inhouse/nets/cnets/teachers/t_esscond.html).

Part of what these standards require is that teachers understand and can use technology to work toward student creativity, production, critical thinking, and other learning goals outlined in the NETS*S, state and national content standards, and this book. In other words, teachers are charged with not only learning the technical aspects of technology, but also practicing how to meet learning goals and discovering the technology that allows and enhances such opportunities. Rubrics, lessons, and other resources that can help teachers to measure and use the standards can be found at http://cnets.iste.org/teachers/t_resources.html. Cases and other explanations are located on the Web at http://cnets.iste.org/teachers/ t_stands.html.

It should be noted that, although many states and districts use the ISTE standards, they are themselves not law. However, there is a federal requirement, presented in the reauthorized Elementary and Secondary Education Act, for states to meet these goals:

• Improving student academic achievement through the use of technology

• Assisting students in becoming technologically literate by the time they finish eighth grade

• Ensuring that teachers can integrate technology into the curriculum (Loschert, 2003, p. 2)

In whatever way states choose to make sure these goals are met, whether by adopting the NETS*T or developing their own standards, teachers no longer have a choice about using technology in their instruction. How well they do so may depend in large part on the effectiveness of their professional development experiences in technology-supported learning.

How can these standards help Patricia and other teachers focus on what they need to do? Which of these standards do you think you have mastered? What evidence do you have?

_____

_____

_____

 For your state technology standards, see the Standards section in the Resources module of the Companion Website (http://www.prenhall.com/egbert).

• • • •

OVERVIEW OF PROFESSIONAL DEVELOPMENT IN TECHNOLOGY-SUPPORTED LEARNING

What Is Professional Development?

Professional development (PD) is an opportunity that leads to an increase or change in skills, knowledge, abilities, and understandings. These changes can occur through any number of means. PD experiences include individual study, action research, in-service workshops, online graduate courses, internships, temporary residencies in organizations, curriculum writing, peer collaboration, school or district study groups, peer coaching or mentoring, or work with a mentor or master. Most states or districts require teachers to participate in specific amounts of some kind of PD to keep their teaching certification current or to meet the requirements of their Professional Improvement Plans, and it's a good idea for pre-service teachers to keep this in mind as they plan their first years of teaching. However, the outcomes of PD typically are not measured in any substantive way, the thought being that any PD is effective in helping teachers to teach well. The photo shows teachers in Pullman, Washington, collaborating on strategies to teach ELLs.

Russell Robinson

Unfortunately, not all PD opportunities are the same, and certainly not all are useful. While investing in staff development and supporting good teaching are the best ways for schools to make sure that technology use leads to student achievement, PD experiences cannot simply consist of learning new techniques to apply "tomorrow." Rather, PD must help teachers to "transform their role" by understanding current educational issues, implementing innovations, and improving their overall practice (Cook, Fine, Sparks, & Hirsch, 1996). In other words, the purpose of PD is not for teachers to teach better in traditional ways, but to learn better and different ways to teach. Both incremental and fundamental changes are important to the change process. However, teacher changes and related changes to the education system are complex and dynamic and cannot happen through short-term, one-shot opportunities for professional development.

Teacher Uses of Technology

Key to understanding the issues of professional development in technology-supported learning is understanding teachers' uses of and attitudes toward technology. In general, there are three categories into which teacher technology use falls: personal, administrative/productivity, and academic. Figure 9.1 outlines these three uses.

All of these technology uses are important in the development of competent technology-using teachers. Most important for professional development is that teachers see that PD is linked to their immediate needs and interests (Kanaya, Light, & McMillan-Culp, 2005).

FIGURE 9.1 **Teacher Uses of Technology**		
Use	**Purpose**	**Examples**
Personal	Highly relevant uses that help them in their daily lives	Use email to keep in contact with family members; write letters and other documents.
Administrative	Make their school lives more efficient	Send and receive emails about meetings and announcements; create worksheets and other handouts; post word processed documents; record attendance and assessments; grading and seating charts.
Academic	Directly support classroom learning goals	Help students find resources and perform procedures such as typing essays; encourage students to produce, solve problems, communicate, think critically and creatively, explore and learn content more deeply.

The Need for Professional Development Opportunities in Technology

After a single pre-service teacher education technology course, many practicing teachers discover that they are unprepared for the realities of teaching and using technology to transform their classrooms and schools (Cattani, 2002). In addition, few teachers emerge from their teacher education programs equally competent in each of the three categories of technology use mentioned previously. Although teachers often seek out and take advantage of chances to learn about technology for personal and administrative uses, typically fewer informal opportunities to learn about academic uses are available.

According to Cook et al. (1996), new learning standards in all areas and the need to develop better ways to assess students are pushing teachers to change their roles in classrooms and schools. Many teachers feel the stress of trying to keep up with academic uses of technology, of meeting new and changing standards for both students and teachers, and of working to help all their students succeed. Separately these are daunting tasks; together they may constitute an overwhelming burden, especially when teachers see that these goals may change in unpredictable ways at any time. However, effective professional development opportunities can support teachers in reaching these goals and lead to change in the system itself.

What should the general goals for Patricia's PD be? Why?

_____

_____

_____

Characteristics of Effective Professional Development in Technology-Supported Learning

The traditional model for professional development is a deficit model of learning in which teacher-students are expected to learn from listening to experts. In the same way that education is trying to move away from this model for students, we must employ a more teacher-centered growth model for PD. Effective PD tasks:

- Consider the needs and learning styles of teachers.
- Present information in authentic contexts with direct links to classrooms and provide feedback while teachers try new strategies in their classrooms.
- Allow time for reflection and experience.
- Are social in nature, allowing teachers to interact with colleagues and mentors.
- Present ways to get from A to B, not just new ideas that require an instant and complete transformation.
- Focus on tools that teachers use for their own productivity.
- Present information in a variety of formats.
- Are made at the teacher's level. Teachers are more likely to use information that is for their grade and content than that which they have to adapt or revise to use.
- Continue over time. (Feiman-Nemser & Remillard, 1995; Lowenberg Ball & Cohen, 2000; NCTRL, 1993; Wells, 2007)

The most important aspect of PD tasks is that they result in improved student learning and performance over time.

What can Patricia Morello do to make sure that her PD choices will be effective?

_____

_____

_____

Benefits of Professional Development in Technology-Supported Learning

PD that follows the guidelines for effectiveness noted above can lead to a number of important teacher, classroom, and school changes. As Cook et al. (1996) note, professional development of teachers is central to school change. In fact, research shows that teacher quality is the most important variable in student learning (Rodriguez & Knuth, 2000). Teacher improvement can lead to higher student achievement and to systemic changes in schools. In addition, teachers can be refreshed and reenergized by working with peers, solving classroom problems, and learning more effective ways to support the learning of all students.

What other benefits can you think of that teachers may derive from participating in PD? Who else benefits, and in what ways?

_____

_____

_____

THE TECHNOLOGY PROFESSIONAL DEVELOPMENT PROCESS

PD is essentially an individual enterprise because growth first takes place in individual teachers. Coughlin and Lemke (1999) and others propose an iterative, or repetitive, growth process that teachers generally go through during effective technology PD:

Entry: Teachers do not yet have the skills and knowledge to change their practice. During this stage they
- Build knowledge.
- Understand possible changes.

Adaptation: Teachers use technology to support existing practice rather than to change the classroom. At this stage they
- Apply (try new ideas and understandings, assess their effectiveness, adapt and change as needed, try again).
- Revise their practice.
- Repeat.

Transformation: Teachers use technology to help them change their practice in important ways. During transformation they
- Share with colleagues.
- Document successes and failures.
- Evaluate the changes in both the environment and learner achievement.

Any stage can be revisited an unlimited number of times, or even skipped, as teachers work through their individual learning processes. Of course, learning and change are more complex than this simple process implies, but teachers can use this description to generally understand the process and their place in it.

Also important to succeeding in the PD process are these suggestions from enGauge (2004):

- Stay focused on the goal of helping students.
- Take on goals that are challenging but doable.
- Convince others that technology and thinking skills can lead to higher student achievement.
- Build on the good work that is already underway.
- Collaborate to support a systemwide culture of innovation.

The PD process is similar to the independent learning processes that teachers must encourage their students to work toward. By experiencing it for themselves, teachers may be better able to support this process for their students.

At what stage in her development in technology-supported learning is Patricia? What stage are you in? Describe why you think so.

_____

_____

_____

Challenges for Teachers in Technology Professional Development

There can be many challenges for teachers who want to participate in PD and for those who want to work toward change based on their PD experiences. However, for each barrier there are a variety of possible solutions.

Time

Sometimes teachers are unaware of technologies that can make their classrooms contexts more effective and efficient learning environments; sometimes, when they do know, the belief that learning to use these technologies will take longer than it is worth stops them from trying. According to Cook and Fine (1997b), time is the most crucial barrier to teacher development. This may be in part because teachers and others in the educational community see PD as something that individual teachers have to set aside large chunks of time for. But Cook and Fine state that for PD to be effective it must become "part of the daily work life of educators." In other words, time must be made by schools and districts and a community culture developed that not only allows ongoing learning but supports it as much as possible. Piexotto and Pager (1998) suggest some useful and effective ways to provide the time necessary for sustained PD experiences:

- Restructure the school calendar.
- Use permanent substitutes.
- Schedule common planning time.

In the end, it may come down to a trade-off—spend time learning to then teach more efficiently and effectively.

Access

Teachers cannot use technology that they cannot get to at all, and some teachers cannot get to it as often or as well as they would like. Without access to technology teachers also cannot practice new skills. Examples throughout this book and the cases in Rodriguez and Knuth (2000) provide examples of how administrators, teachers, and other stakeholders can work together to make sure that teachers have the access they need. Many teachers who have not been able to secure access to school and district resources have obtained their own technology funding through grants available from a wide array of organizations. More on funding is presented in the Guidelines section of this chapter.

Knowledge

As previously noted, there are many sources of information for teacher PD in technology-supported learning. However, sometimes local resources are the most useful. For example,

- *Students.* Often students have technical know-how that teachers do not and can provide instruction for their whole class. Coughlin and Lemke (1999) propose that schools develop student support specialists who receive training before and after school for a specific amount of time and then obtain a special status and limited access to the school network. Their identifying badges let peers know whom they can call on for help and let the teacher know whom she can count on for on-the-spot instruction. Generation Yes (www.genyes.org) offers several great programs to teach students to use technology.
- *Colleagues and other staff members.* In-school staff may have a just-in-time answer that can save a frustrating wait for technical support people.
- *Teachers' guides.* Guides that accompany and support software packages often focus on process and provide many additional relevant activities; this is especially true of the outstanding manuals that accompany software from Tom Snyder Productions and Teacher Created Materials kits.

FROM THE CLASSROOM

Connections

When I attended [a conference] this year, the state PTA president gave a workshop around parent involvement. One example they gave was the use of classroom-produced videos. Some students have parents unable to read, unable to attend open house, etc., but most families now have a television and VCR. Videos were created by teacher and students (could get volunteers to do the recording) showing parents: students at work, classroom goals, suggestions for helping with homework. In other words, an overall picture of the child's classroom. The response has been tremendous, and the payoff is that more parents want to come to the school. Another suggestion, which has been tried at our school, is the use of technology during staff meetings. PowerPoint presentations are made (the principal has tapped into the staff members with technology knowledge and skill), staff use the AlphaSmarts during staff meetings to look up info or type notes, videos are shown showing teachers (from our school) using examples of good teaching practices. (Jean, middle school teacher)

FROM THE CLASSROOM

Barriers

Our school applied for a grant and received five computers for every sixth-grade classroom. We have had mostly problems. As teachers, we attended staff development, continued to learn on our own, have the students use the computers for drill-n-practice, to gather information. Unfortunately, as the computers crashed, the district did not provide technical support. We have had to pay for any maintenance and for additional wiring. In several of the sixth-grade classrooms, nonfunctioning computers sit on the floor because no one seems to want to fix them or take them away. Other schools have received fewer computers, but they were bought by the district and technical support is provided. This is a good example of where more information and asking questions should have happened before accepting the "free" computers. (Jean, middle school teacher)

The person in charge of choosing the software in our building is very well trained and knowledgeable about the software we purchase. The problem? Well, our tech coordinator is also our librarian. She is always swamped with questions and troubleshooting. . . . The problem has become so huge, we now have a little basket where we fill out our questions/headaches, etc., and a district technician comes by about once a week to go over the "yellow slips." (Andrea, elementary bilingual teacher)

- *Local conferences, workshops, and in-services.* Many school districts, professional organizations, and state education agencies offer workshops, seminars, and conferences that either focus on technology or have a technology strand. Typically cheaper and more personal than the large national conferences such as the National Educational Computing Conference (NECC, sponsored by ISTE), these opportunities can offer a wealth of resources, data, and relationships with interested peers.

Parents, community volunteers, school library media specialists, and school technology coordinators can also be excellent sources of knowledge and support.

Working with parents

Communicating with parents, particularly helping them to understand technology use in schools, takes time and thought. Getting parents on board with technology PD can sometimes be a struggle. To make communication with parents easier, teachers can build on other teachers' experience and download forms and letters from great sites like TeacherTools (www.teachertools.org/) or timesaversforteachers.com. Teachers might also kill two birds with one stone by employing Web- and telephone-based software such as CONNECT-ED (Notification Technologies) or ParentOrganizer, which helps teachers to notify parents about what is happening in classrooms.

Read as one teacher describes connecting with parents and other PD practices in From the Classroom: Connections.

Working with ELL and special-needs children

In the past PD for content-area teachers did not often address the needs of all the student populations in a class; rather, issues of special needs and ELL children were addressed separately. However, with the current understandings of the effectiveness of differentiated instruction and the focus on inclusion, many more PD experiences deal with the success of all students.

Read what two teachers have to say about barriers to learning about and using technology in From the Classroom: Barriers.

Clearly, teachers cannot make all of these changes themselves. Schools and communities need to support teacher PD and provide ways to meet these challenges.

How can Patricia gain the support she needs from her colleagues, school, and district?

_____

_____

_____

GUIDELINES FOR WORKING TOWARD EFFECTIVE TECHNOLOGY PROFESSIONAL DEVELOPMENT

Like student learning, effective teacher growth can only happen when the support and encouragement that teachers need is available. The guidelines in this section provide ideas about some ways for teachers to gain both support and encouragement and to have rewarding and effective PD experiences.

Guideline #1: Be a part of the decisions. Being on the school or district technology committee does take a commitment of time and effort. However, teachers who understand what it takes to effectively integrate technology into learning can help to make sure that technology funds pay for both the hardware *and* the training that is necessary. Simpler, temporary solutions also exist—for one, see the Tool CloseUp: netTrekker.

Guideline #2: Explore alternative funding sources. Although experts recommend that 25–30% of technology budgets be devoted to professional development, it rarely is (Fletcher, 2005). In addition, millions of technology dollars each year are left sitting in organizational coffers, unclaimed by the teachers that they are meant to help. There are a variety of reasons for this, some dealing with teachers' lack of time for grant writing and knowledge of resources, others with the misunderstanding that technology grants are hopelessly complicated to complete and win. Large grants, especially those from the federal government, typically require a lot of work and are not always successful, but can offer years of support and extensive funding. Pairing with faculty at universities or local civic organizations who can help with grant preparation and administration can be effective for all participants.

In addition, there are a large number of foundations and other organizations working to fund teachers needing specific hardware such as handhelds (e.g., Handspring.com) or software in areas such as reading improvement. Even a small grant can provide impetus for PD and access to the technology that can make it happen.

Many commercial software and hardware publishers offer their own grants of money and/or materials, and some, such as Riverdeep (www.riverdeep.net/) and Tom Snyder Productions (www.tomsnyder.com) offer links and other information to help teachers. In many cases securing funding requires only a one-page description of the need; in others it is more involved, but resources exist across the Web to assist teachers in preparing grant documents. See the Grants and Funding section of the Resources module on the Companion Website for some of these resources (http://www.prenhall.com/egbert).

Guideline #3: Take it slowly. Time is a crucial component in teacher professional development (Kanaya et al., 2005). Learning to use technology well does not happen quickly, but rather is a process of learning, testing, revising, and evaluating. Just as students should not be expected to become critical or creative thinkers overnight, teachers should not be expected, or expect themselves, to become instant technology integration experts. It may be frustrating to take only small steps, but learning and change are slow processes, and in the end the small steps can add up to large gains. Read as one teacher provides advice for a colleague in From the Classroom: Sharing.

Guideline #4: Do not do it alone. As other parts of this book have stressed, there are many education stakeholders, both direct and indirect, who can be called on to work with teachers and students. Stevenson's (2004/2005) research shows that these kinds of informal collaborations can lead to effective technology integration in the classroom, and other studies have shown the importance of school and other technology partners to successful PD (cf. Ludwig & Taymans, 2005). To support teacher PD, parents can be asked to help in all kinds of ways. For example, they can participate in funding drives, be part of dissemination or reading groups with teachers, work with the results of PD by sharing and commenting

FROM THE CLASSROOM

Sharing

Accountability to the state is important, but what about to the students? If they are only being trained how to take a test that is not a fair representation of their knowledge, how are they learning the valuable skills of working collaboratively to solve complex and real-life problems? Perhaps you could start slowly, by adding a few authentic learning activities where students will be learning the discrete knowledge they need for the test, but can also have an opportunity to apply it in some manner—perhaps with technology. Your situation with computers that do not have Internet access or word processing programs is quite eye-opening! It sounds as if you are in need of at least one decent computer with a basic software program to start with. If that isn't available, there are other forms of technology that some parents in the community might be willing to loan the classroom for a day or two: video cameras, laptops, digital cameras, tape recorders, typewriters, etc. And once you can get a few of these technologies, you can begin to help your students meet the NETS standards for students. Now, it sounds as if you aren't very comfortable with teaching students how to use these technologies. No fear! I've known many teachers who use various strategies to get around this barrier. First, begin with what you do know and teach a few select students. Those students can then become experts and share their "knowledge" with others in the class. Perhaps there are older students in the school or high school who would be willing to volunteer an hour or two every week and do the same. I think you'll be surprised with the wealth of knowledge available to you in the form of your students in your own district. To help your students become independent users of the technology to save you time for teaching and instruction, you can make a list of various skills and knowledge and have student experts sign their names under each that they qualify for, so that the class will know where to go when they encounter a question or problem. Also, as you have various groups of students coming and going throughout the day, it might be helpful to open up your classroom during recess once a month or so and train a few of your experts. While these are only suggestions, I want to encourage you not to give up on technology but to continue making baby steps with what you can do and do have available to you by using a few creative strategies to overcome the barriers you encounter. (Jennie, elementary teacher)

T O O L S

Tool CloseUp: netTrekker

Sometimes the easiest way to address PD is to buy technology that requires little teacher training and that includes everything teachers need. This sounds like an impossible dream, but netTrekker (school.nettrekker. com) almost makes it come true.

netTrekker is basically a Web search engine for classrooms, but it is constructed to make Web resources easy to find, relevant, appropriate, and available. Rather than searching the entire Web, netTrekker searches a massive database of Web pages that have been preselected by educators (who identify themselves and provide annotations of the sites). The sites are grouped into three categories—elementary, middle school, and high school—with a separate "channel" for English language learners in the d.i. (differentiated instruction) version. In the ELL channel, shown in the top screenshot, two additional areas are added: skills development and the multicultural pavilion.

ELL

Searches can be refined easily to focus on grade-level lesson plans, images, maps/charts, or games. Choices can also be made of audio, video, primary source, and bibliographic results. In addition, the d.i. version of the software contains a readability meter for each Web site so that searchers can find topical readings at one level or differentiate for a variety of students. Some of these features are in the bottom screenshot.

Inclusion

State standards are included in netTrekker for every state. There are two ways for teachers to use them. First, after a search the teacher can click on the state standard and see which links from the results match the standard. Or, the teacher can pick a standard first and conduct a keyword search to find sites that meet that standard. Other available search types include themes (producing results in a variety of content areas), famous people (using a built-in criteria search), and news.

The netTrekker Web site describes additional features that help teachers organize, plan, and instruct efficiently and effectively, including a dynamic timeline, "save your search," and current events from over 3,600 sources.

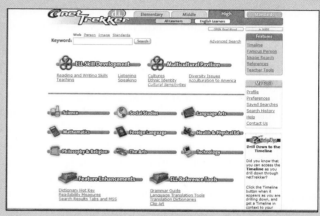

(continued)

Tool CloseUp: Continued

Equally as important as these other features, the complete and well-designed help area includes parent letters (to send home the student's username and password, for example) and a teacher's guide, among other documents and links shown to the right.

Among other benefits, using netTrekker can save teachers time that they might otherwise spend lost on the Web, help focus their teaching toward state standards, provide resources for differentiation for special-needs and ELL students, and give them peace of mind that their students will not be exposed to inappropriate materials. More important, the learning curve for netTrekker is small, so teachers do not need extensive PD to understand and integrate it into classroom instruction.

What goals would using technologies like netTrekker help Patricia achieve?

Source: © 1999–2007 by Thinkronize, Inc. All rights reserved.

_____

_____

_____

_____

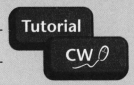

Find netTrekker tutorials in the Tutorials module of the Companion Website (http://www.prenhall.com/egbert).

on their children's electronic portfolios, or make contact with teachers through telephony software such as Connect-ED (Notification Technologies). Peers at the same school and colleagues throughout a district or across districts who have the same needs for PD can form working groups, and administrators can be invited to join to see the effect of the efforts. Even students can support teacher PD by being willing to try new ideas and tasks and to participate honestly and openly in their evaluation. Because learning is social and teachers are already isolated enough in their classrooms, PD should happen with the support and participation of others. Read as one teacher describes her successful experience in From the Classroom: Professional Development. Figure 9.2 summarizes the guidelines for this chapter.

FIGURE 9.2 Guidelines for Effective Professional Development

Guideline #1: Be a part of the decisions.	Become a member of the technology committee or other organization that decides on how to allocate funding.
Guideline #2: Look for alternative funding sources.	Apply for small grants and/or enlist help from the community.
Guideline #3: Take it slowly.	Outline small steps that can lead toward large gains.
Guideline #4: Do not do it alone.	Work with peers, administrators, parents, and the community.

FROM THE CLASSROOM

Professional Development

When I came to be a part of the first group of teachers in my school to learn about technology use and curriculum software from the technology team leader, one of our assignments was to share activities or tips during our staff meetings. It was great! We all share and learn a lot from each other. Things that I will never think to concentrate on but at the same time considered to be important were demonstrated by another teacher. We also share tips on how to deal with computer problems. It took less time for me to learn different things than if I had to do it all by myself. I think collaboration can melt some of those barriers that we find when using technology. (Maria, elementary teacher)

TEACHER TOOLS FOR TECHNOLOGY-SUPPORTED LEARNING

This chapter started by describing three categories of teacher technology use. This section addresses administrative tools for teachers for several reasons. First, personal uses of technology are just that—personal—and so cannot be prescribed. Most teachers will find and use the tools that they need for personal productivity. Second, academic uses of technology have been described already in every other chapter of this text. Finally, the effective use of administrative tools can free time for teachers to participate in PD experiences. Administrative tools include any that help teachers prepare for, carry out, and monitor instruction (versus academic tools, which are integrated into learning tasks). Many administrative tools have been mentioned in other chapters. These include Web site generators, rubric creators, and puzzle and other activity makers. Others are described here.

Administrative Tools for Teachers

- *Translators/parent letters.* In addition to professional development opportunities, 4Teachers has links to administrative tools. Try Casa Notes to send home notes in Spanish. www.4teachers.org/
- *Clip art.* For great free school clip art, see discoveryschool .com's Clip Art Gallery.
- *Forms and handout templates.* An amazing number of ready-made templates can be found at Education World's Tools and Templates page (www.education-world.com/). Essential Word Worksheets and Essential Math Worksheets (Essential Tools for Teachers, Tom Snyder Productions, Version 1.2) allow teachers to build their own worksheets using a variety of scaffolds or to use/adapt premade worksheets.
- *Screen timer.* This handy gadget from www.ncrtec.org/ timer.com allows everyone in the classroom to see how much time is left, which is useful for students who need to pace themselves during tasks. It has a variety of settings for different contexts.
- *Classroom management tools.* Administrative tools from Scholastic.com include a calendar and classroom layout tool. See Figure 9.3 for some of the other Scholastic tools. Other available tools include attendance, grade management, and test generation software and Web sites.
- *Lesson planner.* The NCRTEC Lesson Planner (http://www.ncrtec.org/tl/lp/) provides guidance for teachers to write complete, standards-based, content-focused lessons.

There are other tools that can function both as administrative and academic support for teachers and help teachers work toward PD. These include resources such as:

- *Apple's Learning Interchange 2006* (http://edcommunity.apple.com/ali/). This site provides media libraries, teacher support, and connections with peers.
- *Atomic Learning* (www.atomiclearning.com/). Teachers can subscribe to participate in multimedia tutorials of their choice or incorporate student tutorials into instruction.
- *Social bookmarking managers* that allow teachers to share resources with others. These include furl (www.furl.net/), del.icio.us (http://del.icio.us/), and scuttle (http://scuttle.org/).
- *MarcoPolo* (www.mped.org/teacher/teacher_about.aspx). Sponsored by Verizon, MarcoPolo offers free teacher resources and professional development.

For another example of a resource for both administrative and academic use, see the Tool CloseUp: teAchnology.

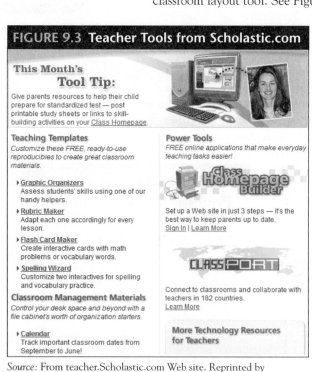

FIGURE 9.3 Teacher Tools from Scholastic.com

This Month's Tool Tip:

Give parents resources to help their child prepare for standardized test — post printable study sheets or links to skill-building activities on your Class Homepage.

Teaching Templates
Customize these FREE, ready-to-use reproducibles to create great classroom materials.

▸ Graphic Organizers
Assess students' skills using one of our handy helpers.

▸ Rubric Maker
Adapt each one accordingly for every lesson.

▸ Flash Card Maker
Create interactive cards with math problems or vocabulary words.

▸ Spelling Wizard
Customize two interactives for spelling and vocabulary practice.

Classroom Management Materials
Control your desk space and beyond with a file cabinet's worth of organization starters.

▸ Calendar
Track important classroom dates from September to June!

Power Tools
FREE online applications that make everyday teaching tasks easier!

Class Homepage Builder

Set up a Web site in just 3 steps — it's the best way to keep parents up to date.
Sign In | Learn More

CLASSPORT

Connect to classrooms and collaborate with teachers in 182 countries.
Learn More

More Technology Resources for Teachers

Source: From teacher.Scholastic.com Web site. Reprinted by permission of Scholastic Inc.

Which of these tools might be most appropriate for Patricia to learn? Why do you think so?

_____

_____

_____

Tool CloseUp: teAchnology

Teachers learn and apply their knowledge and experience in different ways; some teachers prefer to develop their own original ideas, others adapt premade resources, and others are adept at using ready-made materials without change. Whichever they choose, all teachers are interested in saving time and involving students in effective learning experiences. Although there are thousands of useful teacher resources on the Web, teAchnology (www.teachnology.com/) has more free resources than most teachers will be able to use. It can also save teachers time—unlike some Web sites, this site is highly organized and very easy to follow. A series of indexes helps teachers find just what they need quickly and easily. The site focus is on lesson plans, worksheets, teaching tips, and rubrics, many of which focus on the use of technology in classrooms.

The 26,000 free teacher-created lesson plans are arranged into content areas and topics for easy searching. The 6,000 worksheets are also arranged in logical order. Teaching tips from teachers around the world address "Technology in your class," content areas, computing, questioning techniques, and a variety of issues mentioned throughout this text. Links to additional resources are also provided.

Teachers who use sites like teAchnology need to be sure to employ the materials provided to meet their classroom and curricular goals. The old adage "you get what you pay for" applies here—just because it is available does not necessarily mean that it is useful, and teachers must be discriminating in the resources that they choose.

Although the teAchnology site does have some commercial pop-ups, they do not take away from the effectiveness of the content. To access even more content and tools, teachers can join teAchnology for a nominal fee.

Source: Used with permission of Teachnology, Inc.

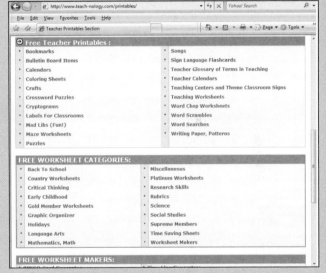

Source: Used with permission of Teachnology, Inc.

Would this tool be useful for Patricia in meeting her goals? Why or why not?

_____

_____

_____

_____

LEARNING ACTIVITIES: PROFESSIONAL DEVELOPMENT

Whether teachers want to take it fast or slow, make incremental or fundamental changes, there are all kinds of activities to get them started. Right now, while waiting for funding, the district technology plan, more resources, or other support, teachers can take a step toward their larger goals and participate in any of these activities to make immediate changes in their instruction:

- View sample activities from the *Handbook of Engaged Learning Projects* (HELP) (www-ed .fnal.gov/help/index.html). See Figure 9.4 for a partial listing of projects.

- Explore two teachers' technology uses; listen to audio and/or watch video about these experiences at the NCRTEC Web site: http://www .ncrtec.org/pd/cw/midschl .htm.

- Ask questions at teacher electronic discussion groups or join communities such as Learning-Times.org. For ideas and information, see *A Busy Educator's Guide to Listserv Discussions* at www .middleweb.com/.

- Get inspired by cruising some of the coolest sites for kids on the Web. *Definitely* start at http:// yucky.com. Then visit www.iknowthat.com (see Figure 9.5).

- Set up a cooperative group with your colleagues at Yahoo.com. Use the system from home to share useful Web sites and other resources.

- Get free PD materials from NETC to share with colleagues. Try the classrooms@work: tools@ hand CD.

- Create a literature circle for teachers and administrators within the district and work through Peterson's (1999) text, *Teachers and Technology*.

- Make a Web page using the Filamentality Tool (www.kn.pacbell.com/ wired/fil/index.html). It is simple to do and requires no understanding of any technical aspects. See Figure 9.6 on page 253 for an introduction to Filamentality.

- Take an inspirational virtual journey. Take a private museum tour through one of the 33,000 museums connected to http://museumnetwork.com. Be sure to check the MuseumEducator.org link to access teacher resources from museums across the United States.

- Download resources from NCREL to help you look at your own teaching (www.ncrtec.org/pd/ lwtres/resource.htm), such as the Engaged Learning Tool that helps teachers support engaged learning with technology.

- Subscribe to an online educational technology journal, magazine, or newsletter. Try *From Now On* (http://fno.org) for an easy and useful read or any of the newsletters from Education World.

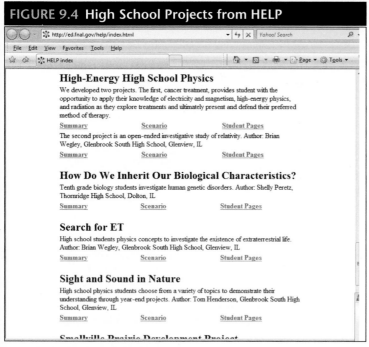

FIGURE 9.4 High School Projects from HELP

Source: Fermilab Education Office.

FIGURE 9.5 Science Topics from iknowthat.com

Source: Used with permission of iknowthat.com.

- Choose a relevant tutorial from i4c (www.internet4 classrooms.com/on-line2.htm; see Figure 9.7), Technology Tutorials for Teachers (eduscapes.com/tap/ topic76.htm), 2learn.ca (www.2learn.ca/teachertools/ teachertools.html), or PBS Technology Tutorials (www .pbs.org/teachersource/teachtech/tutorials.shtm). Be sure to share when done.

- Visit the Motivating Moments Web site at www .motivateus.com/teachers.htm for inspiration.

- Read a book to obtain a different view of educational technology. Classics include:
  ✓ Johnstone, B. (2003). *Never mind the laptops: Kids, computers, and the transformation of learning.* New York: iUniverse.
  ✓ Cuban, L. (2002). *Oversold and underused: Computers in the classroom.* Cambridge, MA: Harvard University Press.
  ✓ Bowers, C. (2000). *Let them eat data. How computers affect education, cultural diversity, and the prospects of ecological sustainability.* Athens, GA: University of Georgia Press.
  ✓ Ferneding, K. (2003). *Questioning technology: Electronic technologies and educational reform.* New York: Peter Lang.
  ✓ Khine, M., & Fisher, D. (2003). *Technology-rich learning environments: A future perspective.* New Jersey: World Scientific Publishing.

  There are many ways that teachers can jumpstart their PD—the activities listed above constitute only a small portion of them.

Which of these activities might be good for Patricia to start with? Why? Which is most interesting/useful for you? Why?

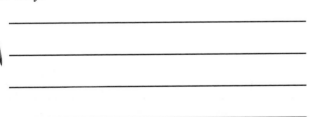

_____

_____

_____

_____

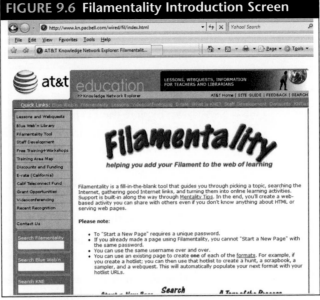

FIGURE 9.6 Filamentality Introduction Screen

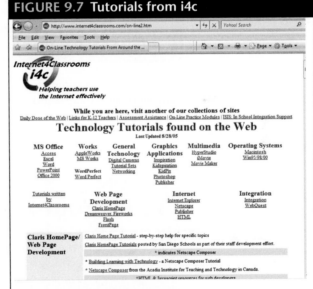

FIGURE 9.7 Tutorials from i4c

Source: Used by permission of Internet4classrooms.com.

ASSESSING PROFESSIONAL DEVELOPMENT

The ultimate goal of evaluating teacher technology PD is to determine whether professional development promotes using technology to improve student achievement. Assessment of PD can take many forms and involve many people, such as:

- *An evaluation team.* Cook and Fine (1997a) recommend that a team be created to ensure the quality of the professional development experience(s) and help perform both formative and summative analyses of the process. This team can consist of an administrator, a technology staff member, a content-area peer, and the teacher, or any combination of participants who are able to evaluate the experience.

- *Teacher self-assessments.* Teachers can reflect both on the experience and on the long-term effects.

- *Student data.* Achievement data in the form of test scores, grades, and student self-reflections can be collected over time to evaluate the impact of the changes.

Like planning classroom experiences, evaluation of PD experiences should be part of the process from the beginning. NCREL (2004) recommends the following evaluation process:

1. Clarify goals and assess their value.
2. Analyze the context.
3. Explore the PD program's research base and evidence of effectiveness.
4. Determine multiple indicators for assessing goals and define who will gather what evidence when.
5. Collect and analyze evidence on participants' reactions, learning, and use of new knowledge and skills. Also look at evidence of organizational support and change and student outcomes.
6. Present the results to all stakeholders and suggest possible changes.

The results of these assessments can help teachers and others to choose effective PD experiences and to work toward technology integration in a purposeful way.

How do you evaluate your own learning? What criteria do you use? Are there others that you should consider? Why?

_____

_____

_____

PROFESSIONAL DEVELOPMENT PLAN EXAMPLE

Patricia decides to complete a formal learning plan, not only to guide her own learning but to share with her principal and others from whom she will ask support. Her plan, using the district form, is presented here.

TECHNOLOGY LEARNING PLAN

1. Write information about your strengths/weaknesses, knowledge and skills, and/or practical technology use. Include the source of the information.

   From the Learning with Technology Profile Tool at www.ncrtec.org/capacity/ profile/profwww.htm, I learned that I need to give students more choices, use more and different kinds of group work, and apply classroom activities more to authentic contexts for students. I need to make sure that all students get to use the technology and that the appropriate technology is available for what I ask them to do. They do too many papers and not enough projects and explorations, but the book is not a good enough resource. The technology access is okay but not great, and it's as equitable as it can be given the context. I have to remember that students can help me learn technology as I help them understand curricular goals and issues.

2. Reflect on what your answer to Question 1 means for potential areas of improvement, questions to be answered, skills to be learned, and/or problems to be addressed.

(continued)

I need to learn more about software and Web sites that can be used to support the English curriculum. I know my students well, so I can figure out flexible groupings that will work without having to study about it. I have to remind myself to make connections to students' lives more often. Maybe I could find a checklist or lessons that other teachers have done to help with this? I need to find more ways to access the Web for students—maybe handhelds? I need to find more resources that support what's in the book but allow students to investigate and inquire. Maybe WebQuests already exist that can do that. I'd like to talk to other teachers in the district about what they do with technology, especially in English. If I had time I would learn different software packages and search the Web for greater familiarity.

3. Create several goal statements based on your answer to Question 2. Include your specific, obtainable learning goal, a measurable outcome, and how you expect to achieve it (an online course? a conference? a learning circle?). Prioritize the goals, and note when you expect to have achieved each one.

   Goal 1: *Become more informed.* I'll talk to colleagues, make time to search the Web, and join a teacher technology listserv discussion to find out what other teachers do in eighth-grade English with technology. I'll keep notes to guide my other goals. This will take all fall semester.

   Goal 2: *Collect resources.* I'll make lists of 10 Web sites and software packages for each major theme in the eighth-grade English curriculum. I'll have students help so it won't take so long and I'll find sites that work and that they're interested in. They can test any software we find. We'll start working on this halfway through fall and continue until we're satisfied that we have a core list of excellent resources.

   Goal 3: *Learn one new technology.* I'll ask the district to buy me a handheld computer with my resource funds that I can use while I work on Goals 1 and 2. I'll analyze this technology in light of what the goals for my classroom are. I should know this technology well by the end of the school year.

4. How will you measure progress toward your goals?

   I will keep a journal of my activities and of how I implement them in class. I'll also collect copies of the artifacts we produce, including Web site lists and activity ideas. I will present my new understandings at the last staff meeting of the year.

Patricia could have easily used the NETS*T standards, her state technology standards, and/or her school curriculum to guide her in developing her learning plan. Notice that in her plan Patricia is following many of the guidelines from this chapter—she is giving herself enough time to accomplish her goals within her busy schedule, is counting on her students and colleagues for help and collaboration, and has chosen goals that relate directly to the needs of her classroom and in which she is invested.

How likely is Patricia to stick to her plan? Why do you think so? How should her principal evaluate her plan? Why?

_____

_____

_____

There is plenty more that can be said about professional development. There are more resources, more ideas for assessment of PD plans and experiences, more explanations for why PD is necessary and how it can best be done. However, the essential ideas have been included in this chapter. PD becomes even more important as both technologies and the focus of education change. These changes are the focus of chapter 10.

CHAPTER REVIEW

Key Points

- **Understand the role of professional development in technology-supported learning in student achievement and school change.**

  Teacher quality is the most important variable in student learning. Although many factors determine how teachers think and act, it is clear that they hold the key to student achievement.

- **Discuss guidelines for professional development in technology-supported learning.**

  A thoughtful, reflective approach to PD will help teachers get the most out of each experience. Working with peers and other stakeholders and being part of the decisions, whether on funding, class size, or technology purchases, can also make a difference.

- **Evaluate tools for teacher development in technology-supported learning.**

  An amazing array of tools exists for teachers' personal, administrative, and academic uses.

- **Discover and participate in effective activities to support technical and pedagogical development.**

  Teachers must develop their understandings about learning and about technology. Even activities as simple as reading an article or playing with a new tool can play a role in teacher learning.

- **Assess your own development in technology-supported learning and teaching.**

  Although multipoint, multi-evaluator assessment provides a clearer overall picture of PD experiences, teachers can use many of the self-assessment tools found in books and on the Web to reflect on their own changes and on changes to their classrooms and schools.

Which information in this chapter is most valuable to you? Why? How will you use it in your teaching?

_____

_____

_____

CASE QUESTIONS REVIEW

Reread the case at the beginning of the chapter and review your answers. In light of what you learned during this chapter, how do your answers change? Note any changes below.

1. *Where should Patricia start her professional development? Why?*

   _____

   _____

   _____

2. *How can new teachers fit professional development about technology into their busy professional lives?*

   _____

   _____

   _____

3. Should all teachers know about technology and its uses? Why or why not?

_____

_____

_____

4. How can teachers learn about technology use? List 3–5 ways.

_____

_____

_____

CHAPTER EXTENSIONS • • • • • • • • • • •

To answer any of the following questions online, go to the chapter 9 Extensions module of this text's Companion Website. Also find additional exercises, questions, and resources on the Companion Website (http://www.prenhall.com/egbert).

Adapt • • • •

Develop a personal technology learning plan. Use the Technology Learning Plan form shown here, also available in the Lesson Planning section of the Companion Website (http://www.prenhall.com/egbert). As you answer the questions, think about your own individual interests in technology. List ways that work with your learning style that can help you to learn more about those things you are interested in. Decide how you can best assess your learning.

Technology Learning Plan

1. Write information about your strengths/weaknesses, knowledge and skills, and/or practical technology use. Include the source of the information.
2. Reflect on what your answer to Question 1 means for potential areas of improvement, questions to be answered, skills to be learned, and/or problems to be addressed.
3. Create several goal statements based on your answer to Question 2. Include your specific, obtainable learning goal, a measurable outcome, and how you expect to achieve it (an online course? a conference? a learning circle?). Prioritize the goals, and note when you expect to have achieved each one.
4. How will you measure progress toward your goals?

Practice • • • • • • •

1. *Start a technology resource list.* Develop a system to keep your important links and technology resources in some efficient manner. Start this resource list by going back through this book and picking out important resources and also by copying anything that you want to keep for the future from the Companion Website (http://www .prenhall.com/egbert). Use one of the social bookmarking managers mentioned in this chapter if you want.
2. *Test PD tools.* See if any of the PD tools mentioned in this chapter are interesting to you and/or work with your time and teaching style. Note which and why.

3. *Describe a tool that you use regularly.* Brainstorm how you might move it from personal use into more administrative or academic purposes.

4. *Apply the NETS*T.* Map the standards onto knowledge that you have gained while using this text, giving specific examples of how you have met these standards for teachers. Note gaps that you hope to fill.

Explore • • • •

1. *Make a dissemination plan.* Many of your colleagues will not have the same information, learning, and technology that you have. How will you share what you know with your colleagues? Outline a plan.

2. *Find new resources.* Look at technology magazines online or in the library and note which you would like to consult on a regular basis and why. Which do not seem as useful?

3. *Interview a teacher.* Choose a local teacher to interview. What does her school or district provide in the way of PD in technology-supported learning? What does she wish it would provide? What steps is she taking to make it happen? Summarize your findings.

REFERENCES

Cattani, D. (2002). *A classroom of her own: How new teachers develop instructional, professional, and cultural competence.* Thousand Oaks, CA: Sage.

Cook, C., & Fine, C. (1997a). *Critical issue: Evaluating professional growth and development.* Oak Brook, IL: North Central Regional Education Laboratory. Available: http://www.ncrel.org/sdrs/areas/issues/educatrs/profdevl/pd500.htm.

Cook, C., & Fine, C. (1997b). *Critical issue: Finding time for professional development.* Oak Brook, IL: North Central Regional Education Laboratory. Available: http://www.ncrel.org/sdrs/areas/issues/educatrs/profdevl/pd300.htm.

Cook, C., Fine, C., Sparks, D., & Hirsch, S. (1996). *Critical issue: Realizing new learning for all students through professional development.* Oak Brook, IL: North Central Regional Education Laboratory. Available: http://www.ncrel.org/sdrs/areas/issues/educatrs/profdevl/pd200.htm.

Coughlin, E., & Lemke, C. (1999). *Professional competency continuum: Professional skills for the digital age classroom.* Santa Monica, CA: Milken Family Foundation. Available www.mff.org/publications/publications.taf?page-159.

enGauge. (2004). *21st century skills: Getting there from here.* Available: http://www.ncrel.org/engauge/skills/there.htm.

Feiman-Nemser, S., & Remillard, J. (1995). *Perspectives on learning to teach* (Issue Paper 95-3). East Lansing: Michigan State University.

Fletcher, G. (2005, June). Why aren't dollars following need? *T.H.E. Journal, 32*(11), 4.

ISTE NETS Project (2005). *National Educational Technology Standards.* Available: cnets.ste.org.

Kanaya, T., Light, D., & McMillan-Culp, K. (2005, Spring). Factors influencing outcomes from a technology-focused professional development program. *Journal of Research on Technology in Education, 37*(3), 313–329.

Loschert, K. (2003, April). Are you ready? *NEA Today.* Available: http://www.nea.org/neatoday/0304/cover.html.

Lowenberg Ball, D., & Cohen, D. (2000). Developing practice, developing practitioners: Toward a practice-based theory of professional education (chap 1). In L. Darling-Hammond and G. Sykes (Eds.), *Teaching as a learning profession: Handbook of policy and practice.* San Francisco: Jossey-Bass.

Ludwig, M., & Taymans, J. (2005). Teaming: Constructing high-quality faculty development in a PT3 project. *Journal of Technology and Teacher Education, 13*(3), 357–372.

NCREL (2004). Guidelines for evaluating professional development. *Pathways Home.* North Central Regional Educational Laboratory. Available: http://www.ncrel.org/sdrs/areas/issues/methods/technlgy/te91k17.htm.

NCTRL (1993). *Findings on learning to teach*. East Lansing, MI: Michigan State University.

Peterson, S. (1999). *Teachers and technology: Understanding the teacher's perspective of technology*. San Francisco: International Scholars Publications.

Piexotto, K., & Pager, J. (1998, June). High quality professional development: Finding time for professional development. *By request*. Available: http://www.nwrel.org/request/june98/article8.html.

Rodriguez, G., & Knuth, R. (2000). *Critical issue: Providing professional development for effective technology use*. Oak Brook, IL: North Center Regional Educational Laboratory. Available: http://www.ncrel.org/sdrs/areas/issues/methods/technlgy/te1000.htm.

Stevenson, H. (2004/2005, Winter). Teachers' informal collaboration regarding technology. *Journal of Research on Technology in Education, 37*(2), 129–144.

Wells, J. (2007, January). Key design factors in durable instructional technology professional development. *Journal of Technology and Teacher Education, 15*(1), 101–122.

10

Supporting Your Students' Futures

About the Author

Daisy Solomon-Ward lives in Pullman Washington and is in second grade and every summer goes to New Jersey with her family and relatives.

Case: The Future Is Now

As you read the case, notice how learning for a student of the future might be supported by technology.

● ●

Jan McCubbin, a senior high student, logs into her virtual school's Web site and uses voice commands to download information about her remaining assignments. She then uses her wireless hand-held phone/computer to check the class audioblog for messages from the facilitator about her previous project. She is delighted to learn that she has passed the critical thinking, creativity, and production requirements for her senior year. Deciding that her communication assignment is the most interesting of those remaining, she downloads the content. Because she has strengths as both an aural and a visual learner, she chooses to complete the assignment by watching a communication-based lecture on a topic that she likes and exploring the accompanying visuals on her computing eyewear as she travels to a museum across town. At the museum she will meet a docent for the last of her 10 required face-to-face meetings with an expert. She will then prepare a multimedia report on her new understandings that will be peer-reviewed by classmates from around the world and discussed at the next class video conference. Jan is satisfied with the way that her senior year is going and expects to complete the requirements on time.

● ●

Answer these questions about the case. There are no right or wrong answers to this chapter preview—the goal is for you to respond before you read the chapter. Then, as you interact with the chapter contents, think about how your answers might change.

1. *How likely do you think this scenario is? Why?*

_____

_____

_____

2. What are the advantages of the type of education that Jan is participating in? What are some disadvantages?

_____

_____

_____

This is not a real case, although it could happen in the near future. All of the technologies are currently available, but they are not yet widely used in these ways in education. This case shows one vision for the future of education supported by technology. There are many other ways that the future of education could take shape, each with its own advantages and disadvantages as described in this chapter.

This chapter is a bit different from the others. First, it is shorter than the others because only so much speculation is useful. Second, the focus is to prepare you for the relatively unknown. Although guidelines are possible, concrete applications for the future are probably not as useful as they are for the present. This is particularly true not only because technology will change, but because standards, goals, and curricula will also change. Even the definitions of "schooling" and "education" may change while you are in the classroom. Therefore, the goal of this chapter is to help you to understand current trends in learning to teach with technology to help you prepare as much as possible for the future. Although it may be hard to look ahead when you're just getting started, you should be aware of changes that might affect your classroom so that you can work with the changes instead of being surprised by them.

After reading this chapter, you will be able to:

- Understand trends that indicate where learning and educational technology might be headed.
- Describe guidelines to help you support students in the technology-enhanced future.
- Reflect on current trends in technologies.
- Help students think about the future through technology-supported activities.
- Assess how well your students are prepared for their technology-enhanced futures.

When you have completed this chapter, which NETS*T will you have addressed?

_____

_____

_____

The discussion, sample activities, and tool descriptions throughout this chapter will help you understand the many opportunities that the future may present. As you read this chapter, consider how you might work to make the best of these opportunities. To begin, read the discussion of future standards in this chapter's Meeting the Standards.

• • • • Meeting the Standards: Supporting Students • • • •

It's hard to say what learning goals will be in the future—the pendulum between learning to think and learning test-focused basic skills swings back and forth with regularity. It seems logical to be able to have students do both. Other chapters in this text show that basic skills are crucial to more open-ended learning, and students can mix skill learning with other more open instructional goals and succeed in both. For now, it appears that this dual focus will serve students well in the future.

In addition, organizations that have developed national standards suggest that these standards will carry us far into the future. They note that the emphasis on thinking skills, building communities of learners, and both process and outcomes not only will take some time to implement fully, but will also prepare students for future challenges.

• • • • **Meeting the Standards:** *continued* • • • •

Do you agree that current standards in your content area are also effective standards for the future? Why or why not? What would you add or delete from the standards to make sure that your students are prepared for the future?

_____

_____

_____

CW For the current state standards for your content area, see the Standards section in the Resource module of the Companion Website (http://www.prenhall.com/egbert).

OVERVIEW OF FUTURE TRENDS AND EDUCATIONAL TECHNOLOGY

Rapid technology changes occur constantly in health, medicine, science, and other fields. Many of these advances will eventually arrive in educational settings, but which and how useful they will be is a question. Many people are making predictions, suggestions, and statements about the future of education and educational technology. Some predict that schools built of brick and mortar will no longer exist and that the boundaries of education will be as broad as cyberspace. Others suggest that technology will increase the distance between the educational haves and the have-nots.

No one knows what the future will bring. However, it is possible to look at the past and present and develop some general predictions. Why should teachers look 5 years, 10 years, and even longer into the future? Teachers should have an idea what their students will have to be able to do in 2015 or 2020 in order to understand how to prepare them.

LEARNING TRENDS

Looking at current trends is a fruitful way to predict what the future might bring. Information on the trends discussed in this chapter has been gleaned from the popular press, the Internet, and other media outlets. There are as many alternative views as there are trends described here, and they make for interesting reading and discussion for teachers and students alike. The trends highlighted here are likely to affect education in important areas such as funding, demographics, and sources of information.

Trend 1: Universal Access and Use

At the turn of the recent century, according to the Forum on the Future of Technology in Education (U.S. Department of Education, 2000; http://www.air.org/forum/issues.htm), the following priorities were emerging for technology in education:

1. All students and teachers will have universal access to effective information technology in their classrooms, schools, communities, and homes.
2. All teachers will effectively use technology.
3. All students will be technologically literate and responsible cybercitizens.
4. Research, development and evaluation will shape the next generation of technology applications for teaching and learning.
5. Education will drive the eLearning economy.

Almost a decade later, these priorities for universal access and use of educational technology are still trends. In other words, they have not been realized. This may be in part because many of the same barriers noted in the U.S. Department of Commerce report *Falling Through the Net: Toward Digital Inclusion* (2000) still exist. The report showed that students with disabilities or those living in impoverished conditions had less access to technology than others. First language, level of education, and age also continue to affect how technology is accessed and used. In addition, although the U.S. gender gap that previously existed in *who* used technology has closed, reports show that there are differences in *why* and *how* males and females use technology such as the Internet (Pew Internet and American Life Project, 2007).

If, in fact, the priorities of universal access and use are to be met, attention must be paid to students' circumstances both within and outside of school. Administrators and teachers need to think about new ways to allocate the computers in their buildings, as noted in chapter 2. They also need to notice which students are using computers more frequently and support those with less confidence or less assertiveness. In addition, schools need to help students be flexible and effective in why and how they use technology.

Communities are working toward addressing these issues in a number of ways, including starting financially supported student laptop programs (e.g., see a story about East Rock School District at www.education-world.com/a_issues/schools/schools020.shtml), creating community computing centers such as the Community Technology Empowerment Project (www .newcurriculum.com/2002/ed5-20.htm), and funding more technology for public libraries (e.g., see the Public Library Association site at www.pla.org/). The results of these programs are not yet in, and some have generated controversy (for example, see reports supporting laptop programs in *eSchool News online* at www.eschoolnews.com/news/showStory.cfm?ArticleID=4910 and in *The New Curriculum* at www.newcurriculum.com/2002/ed5-20.htm, and an argument against it in McKenzie, 2002). However, if these solutions prove workable they should have an impact on this trend.

Trend 2: Digital Natives and Digital Immigrants

Marc Prensky (2001a, 2001b), in his now-famous articles on the state of education and technology, suggests that a real divide exists between children who have been brought up with technology (the digital natives) and those teachers who have only recently come to it (digital immigrants). Based on studies from neurobiology, psychology, and game use, Prensky argues that digital native students' brain structures are actually different and require a different kind of instruction. These differences mean that traditional ways of teaching, such as lecture and drill, do not suit the attention spans, interests, or needs of such students. Prensky (2001a, b) claims that digital native students expect constant and ongoing interactivity, pay attention strategically, and use information selectively. Digital natives can be bored with traditional instruction. This is particularly true because on average, during traditional instruction students get to ask a question only every 10 hours (Prensky, 2001b).

Additionally, Levin, Arafeh, Lenhart, and Rainie (2002) note that schools are not responding to the many ways that students are using technology outside the school for educational purposes. Student expectations and skills are changing with Internet use, and they perceive a disconnect with what is allowed and accessible at school.

Prensky's solution is for teachers to learn to use new approaches that include parallel processing, graphics awareness, and random access—skills that digital natives are increasingly better at. Such approaches employ the use of well-designed, content-based computer games integrated into effective instruction. Research seems to back up his assertions, particularly that digital natives learn better through alternative instruction with alternative tools.

If Prensky's assumptions are correct, it means that teachers have a choice—to change their way of teaching or to fail to meet the needs of these students. As more of our students become digital natives, solutions to this trend will become more pressing, until, of course, digital natives become teachers themselves. VanSlyke (2003), while acknowledging that there are differences between natives and immigrants, disagrees with Prensky's assumptions. He claims that the gap is not so wide, and that students and teachers must meet in the middle rather than teachers changing how they teach. He adds,

> *Education does need to adapt and evolve with the times, and educators need to understand the learning styles of their students, but we do not have to assume that our students are incapable of learning from or communicating with the Digital Immigrants even if we suspect that their*

thought patterns are different from our own . . . a range of teaching methods does not necessarily suggest an unwillingness to adapt to new circumstances, but rather an understanding that the incorporation of technology in the learning process is always context-specific, always determined by the particular circumstances of a given course. (n.p.)

Time will tell which, if either, of these views is correct. In the meantime, teachers should continue to address the needs of the students in their classrooms in a variety of ways.

Trend 3: Web 2.0

An important trend in technology in general is that more people can contribute to and participate in media. With the advent of social computing, called "Web 2.0," students are building social networks and connecting to other users through blogging, creating wikis, programming virtual worlds, developing lists of social bookmarks, and supplying video, audio, graphics, and text to be shared with millions of unknown users around the world.

According to Lenhart and Madden (2007, p. 2):

55% of online teens have created a personal profile online, and 55% have used social networking sites like MySpace or Facebook.

66% of teens who have created a profile say that their profile is not visible to all Internet users. They limit access to their profiles.

48% of teens visit social networking websites daily or more often; 26% visit once a day, 22% visit several times a day.

Older girls ages 15–17 are more likely to have used social networking sites and created online profiles; 70% of older girls have used an online social network compared with 54% of older boys, and 70% of older girls have created an online profile, while only 57% of older boys have done so.

Most of this happens outside of classrooms, but teachers can learn to take advantage of this trend and use some of these tools in effective instruction. These tools can be used to help learners see different perspectives, learn to write for an audience, create information that should be shared, and meet other learning goals.

A possible disadvantage of the proliferation of social Web sites and other tools is the tendency of students to believe what they read. Exercises and tools that facilitate student critical thinking (such as those in chapter 4) will be more crucial than ever if this trend continues. In addition, risks inherent in Internet use by minors increase with more time and information online, and all stakeholders must ensure that safety policies (chapter 3) are effective.

Figure 10.1 summarizes these trends and provides suggestions for what teachers can do to address them. These trends may or may not continue and may or may not have the suggested impacts on education that their supporters believe. However, teachers must be aware and prepared to respond to these changes.

As a whole, what implications do these trends have for future teachers?

_____

_____

_____

FIGURE 10.1 Summary of Trends in Learning and Technology

Trend	Possible Teacher Actions
Priorities	Help develop solutions to the gaps in computer availability and access in the classroom, school, and community.
Digital natives and digital immigrants	Consider how students learn best and integrate this knowledge into instruction.
Changes in sources	Help students understand clearly how the source affects the information. Take advantage of the benefits of social computing tools in the classroom.

Future Roles of Teachers

The traditional role of teachers as information-givers is changing, as noted throughout this text. Teachers need to and are becoming facilitators, co-learners, and mentors. Change is slow in education. Although new technologies are often seen as the agents of change, only *teachers* can make changes in pedagogy (such as creating new kinds of tasks, integrating technology in effective ways, and providing support and feedback that meets the needs of individual students).

As the availability and importance of technologies change, teachers must be able to address the academic, linguistic, and social needs of students so that all students have opportunities to learn. Trends that are beginning to help teachers become change agents in their students' lives include emphasis on social justice, equity, cultural responsiveness, differentiation, and access to information. The guidelines throughout this text that focus on these issues may play an even more important role in the future.

What are some of the guidelines that you remember reading about in this text that you can use to support the learning of all students? List some here.

GUIDELINES FOR SUPPORTING STUDENTS IN THE TECHNOLOGY-ENHANCED FUTURE

All of the learning goals outlined in this text aim at supporting students' learning, and in doing so also address students' futures. Teachers can implement the following guidelines now to help students meet the goals and be ready for the future.

Guideline #1: Help students handle information. Students are often bombarded with information from multiple sources when they are using computers, cell phones, and other technologies in class. Teachers must be aware of "continuous partial attention" (Roush, 2005) that results from the overwhelming amount of information. Teachers need to help students sort out what is important in the information stream and how to organize and use it. Some students will feel at home with the flow of data, and others might get lost. Strategies for teachers include:

- For students who are comfortable with it, "continuous connectivity" allows them to tap into what is called the "back channel," gathering information to support the task or event they are working on through numerous resources. Teachers can allow these students to access a variety of resources at the same time and teach them how to give credit to the authors of the sites they access.

- Other students may need more structured, selective use of technology. Teachers should carefully preselect Web sites or software modules and provide step-by-step instructions on how to proceed.

A flood of information can support learning for those who can multitask, but it can also create barriers to true, face-to-face social interaction from too much attention to technology. By observing and working with students, teachers can work toward an appropriate balance of technology use and social interaction for each student.

Guideline #2: Keep an eye on trends. Knowing where education and educational technology are going (and should go) means being aware. Teachers should consult useful resources such as ISTE's *Leading and Learning with Technology* magazine, news media Web sites such as CNN and MSNBC, and electronic discussion lists and blogs that directly address the future of technology. Teachers can also enlist students in finding and presenting information about trends, documenting where the trends seem to be going, and mapping the trend as it progresses.

One interesting site to review is *Imagining the Internet: A History and Forecast*, provided by Elon University and the Pew Internet Project (www.elon.edu/e-web/predictions/publications .xhtml). The 2006 survey, *The Future of the Internet II*, asked hundreds of technology experts to look at trends and predictions for the year 2020. The site creators provide teacher tips and tools for teaching about the future and working with predictions, including "Back 150 Years," "Forward 150 Years," and a KidZone.

Figure 10.2 on page 266 summarizes the guidelines for supporting students' futures with technology.

In what other ways could you learn about trends and prepare yourself for educational technology changes?

_____

_____

_____

FIGURE 10.2 Guidelines for Supporting Students' Futures with Technology	
Guideline	**Example**
Guideline #1: Help students handle information.	Evaluate the appropriate balance between technology and social interaction for your students by observing how much information they can handle at once. Provide scaffolds such as preselected Web sites and simple tasks for students who are not as adept at multitasking or handling information overload.
Guideline #2: Keep an eye on trends.	Consult resources that address trends and ask students to participate in tracking them. Check outstanding resources such as the Pew Internet and American Life Project at www.pewinternet.org/ and Imagining the Internet at www.elon.edu.

TRENDS IN TOOLS AND TOOL USE

There are so many emerging technologies and changing uses of tools that it is often difficult to keep track. By the time this book is published, blogs, wikis, podcasts, and other "new" technologies may be commonly used in schools, increasing online interactions and collaboration and providing a variety of students with access to content and skills. For example, Lindsay (2006) notes that she uses Bloglines (www.bloglines.com) to get one-page access to the blogs she's interested in, and Writely (accessible through www.google.com) allows her to write proposals with colleagues and help students collaborate.

This section lists tool trends that could affect education in the near and far futures. They are not listed in any particular order, because all could equally signal important changes to educators.

1. *A move away from commercial operating systems from Microsoft and Apple to Linux and other open-source, free programs.* This is currently a slow-moving trend that is gaining momentum. Since many of the programs that schools currently use may not work on these new operating systems, it may impact school economics.

2. *A move away from desktop machines to integrated mobile units.* Technologies are combining, and some of them are wearable. For example, GPS, cell phones, and watches; blogs with video (e.g., www.vidblogs.com); courseware that will include telephony software such as Skype. The trend toward mobile computing means that students can access information almost anywhere. This implies that the classroom of the future might be wherever the student is. See the Sample Lesson on page 33 in this chapter that addresses this trend.

3. *Really Simple Syndication.* RSS allows teachers and students to "subscribe" to their favorite blogs and podcasts and receive new entries in one place instead of logging in to each site. This is an advance in efficiency that will become more common as the number of blogs and other types of posts increases exponentially, and it can save time and effort in keeping up with the trends in learning and educational technology.

4. *New Web search varieties.* In addition to the typical Web search, Google search already provides 3-D satellite photos of everywhere, specialized searches of images, scholarly articles, catalogs, and many other choices for searchers, as seen in Figure 10.3. Other search companies are gearing up to compete, which means that more types of search engines are on the

horizon. This trend could make searches not only easier but more specific to the user, which could help teachers and students save time and make more accurate searches.

5. *Social networking.* An already exploding trend, social networking (also known as Web 2.0) includes sites such as myspace .com, YouTube.com, Friendster.com, Facebook.com, and meetup.com. These sites have more than 90 million participants (Barrett, 2006). Table 10.1 presents additional examples of Web 2.0 sites.

Teachers can use these sites to find experts and help students answer questions. For example, Wondir (www.wondir .com/) allows a user to enter any question and be connected to an expert who knows the answer. The use of these sites has implications for student safety because predators and other dangers do exist. Teachers and parents can help ensure children's safety with information from WiredSafety (www.wiredsafety.com). The site includes many excellent resources, including the "Guide to Keeping Your Kids Safe Online" by Parry Aftab, shown in Figure 10.4 on page 268.

FIGURE 10.3 Google Searches

Source: Google screenshot © Google Inc. Used with permission.

6. *Internet telephony* (Voice over Internet/VoIP). Programs such as Skype are taking the financial burden out of instant voice connections. These free programs are changing the economics of electronic voice connection and the possibilities for schools to use it. VoIP can give students the ability to communicate synchronously with peers and experts all over the world. However, VoIP requires a fast connection, so it will not be available in some schools for quite a while.

7. *Ease of use.* Technologies are getting easier to use as interfaces become more supportive, more visual, and more user-friendly. For example, to find specific items in a Web or site search, users had to type special symbols and order terms in a certain way. Now most

TABLE 10.1 Social Networking (Web 2.0) Sites

Type of Site	Description	Examples
Podcasting	Allows users to upload or download audio and/or video in MP3 format. Available in all content areas.	www.eslpod.com, www.podcast.net, www.npr.org, podcasts.yahoo.com, and thousands of others
Editing	Users can edit documents, videos, photos, and other projects online without additional software or cost.	Snipshot.com; jumpcut.com; slide.com, docs.google.com
Blogs	Users can create blogs, add entries, read or view others' blogs.	wordpress.org; www.vidblogs.com; dandelife.com; www.blogger.com; DeKita.org
Virtual Environments	Users can create their own spaces and interact with a variety of other users. In some environments they are immersed in content-area information.	Secondlife.com; Rainbow MOO (http://it.uwp.edu/rainbow/); schmooze University (http://schmooze.hunter.cuny.edu/)
Wikis	Information resources constructed by users.	www.mediawiki.org; www.wikipedia.org; wikia.com; quizlet.com

Tutorial

CW

browsers do not even require the "http://" in front of the URL, and symbols are rarely needed. Additionally, animation software like Animation Master (hash.com) makes it easy for people to do simple animations. Students can create animations of stories, concepts, and ideas to help their audience understand their presentations. Also, Web sites are using new coding and software to make them more interactive and responsive to users' needs. Many sites include visuals created in Flash, site searches provided by Google, and instant technical support through telephony software. All of this makes these tools and information more accessible to a wider range of users.

FIGURE 10.4 Guide to Keeping Your Kids Safe Online

Parry Aftab's Guide to Keeping Your Kids Safe Online

MySpace, Facebook and Xanga, Oh! My!
Keeping yourself and your kids safe on social networks

The quick tips for teens:

- Put everything behind password protected walls, where only friends can see
- Protect your password and make sure you really know who someone is before you allow them onto your friends list
- Blur or morph your photos a bit so they won't be abused by cyberbullies or predators
- Don't post anything your parents, principal or a predator couldn't see
- What you post online stays online - forever!!!! So thinkb4uClick!
- Don't do or say anything online you wouldn't say offline
- Protect your privacy and your friends' privacy too . . . get their okay before posting something about them or their pic online
- Check what your friends are posting/saying about you. Even if you are careful, they may not be and may be putting you at risk.
- That cute 14-year old boy may not be cute, may not be 14 and may not be a boy! You never know!
- And, unless you're prepared to attach your MySpace to your college/job/internship/scholarship or sports team application . . . don't post it publicly!

And for parents:

- Talk to your kids – ask questions (and then confirm to make sure they are telling you the truth!)
- Ask to see their profile page (for the first time) . . . tomorrow! (It gives them a chance to remove everything that isn't appropriate or safe . . . and it becomes a way to teach them what not to post instead of being a gotcha moment! Think of it as the loud announcement before walking downstairs to a teen party you're hosting.)
- Don't panic . . . there are ways of keeping your kids safe online. It's easier than you think!
- Be involved and work with others in your community. (Think about joining WiredSafety.org and help create a local cyber-neighborhood watch program in your community.)
- Remember what you did that your parents would have killed you had they known, when you were fifteen.
- This too will pass! Most kids really do use social networks just to communicate with their friends. Take a breath, gather your thoughts and get help when you need it. (You can reach out to WiredSafety.org.)
- It's not an invasion of their privacy if strangers can see it. There is a difference between reading their paper diary that is tucked away in their sock drawer . . . and reading their MySpace. One is between them and the paper it's written on; the other between them and 700 million people online!
- Don't believe everything you read online – especially if your teen posts it on her MySpace!
- And, finally. . . . repeat after me – "I'm still the parent!" If they don't listen or follow your rules, unplug the computer . . . the walk to the library will do them good.

For more information, visit WiredSafety.org.

Figure 10.5 presents a summary of these tool trends. In the *far* future, advances in virtual reality, wearable computing, and other technologies may allow even greater access to information and communication. However, teachers must make sure that these and other technologies are used effectively, responsibly, and in pursuit of learning goals, as outlined throughout this text. For an extensive list of resources that look at educational technology trends, see d'Eca's site at http://64.71.48.37/teresadeca/webheads/online-learning-environments.htm.

Which of these tool trends do you think has the most potential to support students' futures in your classroom? Why do you think so?

_____

_____

_____

FIGURE 10.5 Summary of Tool Trends

Trend	Implications
1. A move away from commercial operating systems to Linux and other open-source, free programs	Schools may end up with a lot of legacy, or unusable, software. Teachers and school technology leaders need to keep an eye on this trend to be prepared.
2. A move away from desktop machines to integrated mobile units	The end of static labs and the beginning of learning that happens anywhere, anytime.
3. RSS	Teachers and students can keep up on trends more efficiently.
4. New varieties of Web search	Advanced search engines may make it possible to find anything with one click. This gives students faster access to information, but it may not mean better information.
5. Social networking	Students and teachers will have access to peers and experts across the globe. Safety issues will be paramount.
6. Internet telephony	Classrooms will not have to deal with scheduling the video equipment, sending voice mails, or working with distorted audio.
7. Ease of use	More technologies will be accessible to a great number of people. However, just because it's there doesn't mean students and teachers need to use it.

ACTIVITIES TO PREPARE STUDENTS FOR THE FUTURE

One way to prepare students for the future is to facilitate their progress toward the learning goals that frame this text. Another way is to have them start thinking about the future using both real and fantastic approaches. The activities in this section incorporate both of these ways. Each activity is listed with a short description and possible resources. All of the examples address a set of the learning goals. Each activity can be adapted to suit student needs, interests, and context.

FIGURE 10.6 Resource for Time Travel from PBS

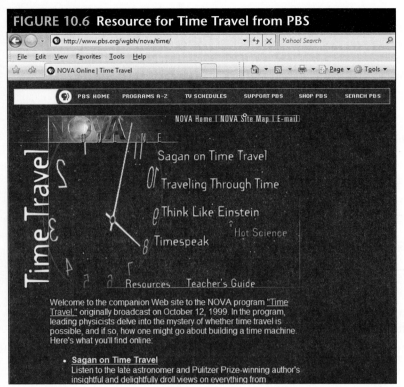

Source: Courtesy of Nova/WGBH Educational Foundation. Copyright © 1999. WGBH/Boston.

FIGURE 10.7 Bureau of Labor Statistics Resources

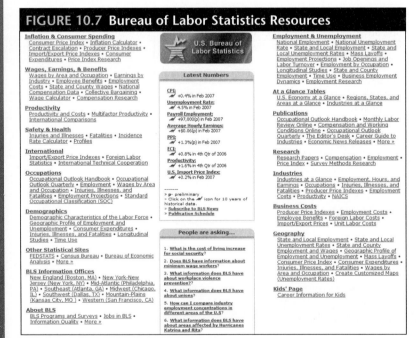

Source: U.S. Bureau of Labor.

Example 1. Tools of the future

Students:

• Think about what technology might be able to do in the future.

• List current problems that technology use could solve.

• Predict what problems the technology could cause.

• Create a "documentary" or opinion piece to present their ideas.

Use Time Travel resources from Nova (Figure 10.6) to engage students in the unit and get them thinking and other Web sites for support and development (e.g., Creating a Documentary from Apple at www.apple.com/education/documentary/).

Example 2. Future occupations

Students:

• Access lists of current occupations.

• Chart the current and future need for the occupation based on data.

• Note how technology might change the occupation.

• Create an advisory bulletin (news report, pamphlet, FAQ file) for students making career decisions.

Use occupational trend data found in the *Occupational Outlook Handbook* from the Bureau of Labor Statistics (BLS), (www.bls.gov/emp/) to get started. Resources from the BLS are shown in Figure 10.7.

Example 3. Fortune-telling

Students:

• Examine the basis for and veracity of fortune-telling.

• Choose a type of fortune-telling—e.g., palm reading, tarot cards, the stars, a crystal ball—that is of interest to them (and that does not go against any of their beliefs or expected behaviors).

• Explore the background of their chosen method, including its cultural significance.

• Create a presentation or product to show others what they found and what they believe about it based on evidence they collected.

Resources include library- and Internet-based texts, Web sites, experts, readings, and practitioners. Students can start with definitions in encyclopedias such as Encarta and wikipedia, then check fun sites such as iVillage's Crystal Ball (http://predictions.astrology .com/cb/), Fortune Cookie (http://predictions.astrology.com/fc/), and GenieSays.com's Genie (www. geniesays.com/). Other background information can be found in Leland's historical account of fortune-telling (www.sacred-texts.com/pag/gsft/index.htm), and Haider's brief article at www.dawn.com/weekly/yworld/ archive/051112/yworld2.htm.

Example 4. The most important question

Students:

- Determine the most essential questions to answer about the future.
- Brainstorm, consult peers, family, and experts, and use feedback from a data-collection site on the Web to compile a list of questions.
- Develop criteria for narrowing their list (perhaps "affects the most people," or "easiest to answer").
- Debate, survey, or use other methods to determine which questions best fit their criteria.
- Figure out ways to try to answer the questions.
- Share their answers in an appropriate format with those who provided input.

Resources can include blogs or Web forms, email, articles and readings, and production technologies. Students can get ideas and opinions from The Specialist blog (Seven Questions about the Future; www.speculist.com/archives/000019.html) or ABC News experts (http://abcnews.go.com/Technology/FutureTech/story?id=2629071&page=1).

These brief examples show how teachers can integrate knowledge and ideas about the future, crucial learning goals, and educational technologies to support student learning.

What other topics can you think of that can be used to help students think about the future? List some of them here.

ASSESSING STUDENT PREPAREDNESS FOR THE FUTURE

Students will need to be more independent, resourceful, and technologically literate in the future. Many of the assessments described throughout this text can help you to understand where your learners are proficient and where they need more support. The three assessments shown on pages 272–273 from Intel Education (Figures 10.8, 10.9, and 10.10) help teachers and students to understand what skills and inclinations students currently possess. This evaluation will assist teachers and students in understanding where to put more effort so that students meet the goals they need to be successful. Teachers and students can adapt these checklists and rubrics to their contexts and beliefs about the future. For example, the language may need to be simplified or examples provided for some learners, while additional criteria addressing what students need in the future could be added.

Students can use these checklists to evaluate their skills as independent, resourceful, prepared learners. Students can complete the appropriate rubric one or more times and reflect with their teacher on where they need to improve. Then teachers and students can make a plan for how to achieve the goals on the checklist. For example, to use time more wisely, students may make a list of ways that they typically do not do so and then have a peer or the teacher remind them to check it. Likewise, students can keep running records of their progress on a criterion such as participating in the group, noting when they participate most effectively and working to enhance those group features that help them to participate. The checklist criteria could also be posted around the room to remind students to reflect upon them every day. These evaluation checklists could be usefully integrated into a portfolio or a progress report.

Through assessments like these, teachers can help students to invest their time and effort in tasks and skill-building that will serve them well in their futures.

Based on your current beliefs about the future, how would you change these rubrics for your students? Why?

FIGURE 10.8 Elementary Self-Direction Checklist from Intel Education's Assessment Library

Elementary Self-Direction Checklist

☐	I use my time wisely
☐	I make an action plan and can revise my plan
☐	I set goals
☐	I anticipate resources I might need to reach my goals
☐	I keep track of my progress in my learning log
☐	I persevere when I meet obstacles or problems
☐	I ask for help when needed
☐	I complete my tasks
☐	I set high standards for my work
☐	I review my work when completed
☐	I am willing to improve on my work when needed
☐	I explain how I can learn from my successes and failures

Source: Used with permission of Intel Corporation.

FIGURE 10.9 Middle School Accountability Rubric from Intel Education's Assessment Library

Middle School Accountability Rubric

4	3	2	1
I always take a thoughtful, active role in my own learning, challenging myself on a daily basis so that I can contribute wholeheartedly to the group.	I consistently take an active role in my own learning so that I can contribute my best to the group.	I sometimes take an active role in my own learning, sharing relevant ideas and asking appropriate questions.	I rarely take an active role in my own learning. I often do not participate and rarely share ideas or ask questions.
I consistently demonstrate a genuine desire to learn and share my ideas with my classmates.	I participate regularly in discussions and frequently volunteer my ideas, ask thoughtful questions, and defend my opinions.	Although reluctant to take risks, I contribute to discussions.	I have poor listening skills, and may be intolerant of the opinions of others.
I initiate discussions, ask significant questions, and act as a leader within the group. I am willing to take risks, to assert an opinion and support it, and to listen actively to others.	I listen respectfully to my classmates and am willing to share ideas.	I listen to my classmates and respect their opinions most of the time.	I participate only when prompted.
I am always well prepared to contribute to the group as a result of having thoughtfully completed my tasks, and the thoroughness of my work demonstrates the high regard I have for learning.	I complete my tasks and am prepared to contribute to the group.	I may need occasional reminders to stay on task, to make the most of my group time, and to increase my contributions to the group.	I do not complete my tasks so am not prepared to contribute thoughtfully with detail or substance. I need regular reminders to stay on task.

Source: Used with permission of Intel Corporation.

FIGURE 10.10 High School Self-Direction Checklist from Intel Education's Assessment Library

High School Self-Direction Checklist

Creating a Personal Vision:

☐	I self assess using input/feedback from others, criteria and my own observations to make decisions and complete goals
☐	I explain ways my behavior and choices help and hinder my achievement and progress toward my goals
☐	I use techniques to remind myself of my strengths and preferred learning modes and styles and can adapt and adjust to different learning modes and styles
☐	I seek out opportunities to challenge myself
☐	I evaluate successes and failures and what I learned about myself
☐	I assess how fear of failure limits my possibilities and options

Setting Goals, Priorities, Plans:

☐	I recognize and assume responsibility for planning and performance of projects and future plans
☐	I prioritize and organize my work using an action plan model which incorporates goals and steps to reach them and which accommodates numerous or conflicting goals and priorities
☐	I determine and use an effective system for managing time and materials
☐	I structure a plan which clearly outlines strategies, time factors, resource needs and overall constraints

Managing Self:

☐	I use time management techniques and tools, e.g., day planners, assignment calendars
☐	I make informed choices based on information or data and an understanding of responsibility, e.g., cause/effect, consequences
☐	I make plans and contingency plans which address stresses and avoid procrastination
☐	I identify personal motivational patterns, distribute work according to perceived strengths and use techniques for areas needing improvement
☐	I explain that mistakes are opportunities for learning and demonstrate learning from my mistakes
☐	I develop and use self sufficiency and self management skills, e.g., look for own solutions to problems before seeking help, yet know when and how to access appropriate, timely help
☐	I demonstrate and evaluate my work habits and attitudes and describe areas of strength and those needing improvement (e.g., collaboration, positive attitude, desire to exceed standard, task completion)

Source: Used with permission of Intel Corporation.

SAMPLE LESSON: THE FUTURE

This lesson, adapted from NASA Explores (http://media.nasaexplores.com/lessons/01-029/5-8_2.pdf), helps students think about technologies they might expect to see in the future and those that they might even help invent.

SEEING WHAT CAN'T BE SEEN: FUTURE TECHNOLOGIES

Grade Level: 5–8

Subjects: Science, Technology

National Education Standards				
Science	Mathematics	Technology		Geography
		ISTA	ITEA	
6a, 8c			1c, 3a	

Objective: Students will be able to produce and explain a combination of technologies that lead to a new and/or improved technological application.

Step 1: Read Background

Teacher has students read and discuss this background statement to establish prior knowledge:

> The challenge of advanced technology is to design and assemble machines that are increasingly integrated and miniaturized while providing higher performance. We are surrounded by products that integrate technologies once thought of as separate. The telephone was a breakthrough because it was the first device to integrate telegraph and analog microphone technologies. Now, we have devices that fuse telephone, fax, printer, answering machine, and other functions. We have cordless phones, cellular phones, pagers, and pocket-sized remote answering machines. We can communicate face-to-face in real time via the Internet using a computer and phone lines. As we become accustomed to these new devices, we grow to think of them as a single technology.

Teacher uses photos and other supplements (e.g., video, other text, a real-time Skype session) to illustrate the concepts in the reading. Provide other scaffolds for students who need them, such as reading aloud, using bilingual dictionaries, and providing a chart for students to list separate technologies and their combined result. Students can take notes, draw pictures, and discuss their understandings with guided questions from the teacher.

Step 2: Brainstorm and Discuss

Ask the students in small groups to list additional products that integrate technologies, identifying the different technologies that are combined. Examples are hearing aids combined with eyeglasses; telephones that are also answering machines, faxes, and printers; and monitors that can be used to watch TV, play video games, and cruise the Internet. Bring students back together as a class and review their additions.

Students can add their additions to their notes from Step 1. Assess students' understanding in light of their responses to questions such as: What are some differences between the separate and combined technologies? What emerges as a working definition for *technology?* For *integration?*

Step 3: Predict

Have students suggest future products that integrate different technologies. Consider different ways of thinking about integrated technologies. Also, consider such issues as materials (availability, usefulness for multiple purposes), energy (various sources of power), functions (multiple purposes, combined efforts), and applications (specialized uses, general applications).

Provide a worksheet or chart for students that provides space for these and other examples to be written or drawn. Be sure to write student responses where everyone can see in order to provide multimodal access to the information.

Step 4: Produce

Have student teams create and provide support for a "future technology." Students can choose how to present their technology (a graphic, a poster, a 3D mockup) but they must accompany it with a written explanation to convince an audience that not only is their product plausible, but it's useful and beneficial too. Student roles can include illustrator, labeler, writer, computer operator, and researcher, among others. Students can use the library, classroom computers, and other school resources to support their work.

Step 5: Assess

Help students find the appropriate audience (as nearly as possible) for their product and present it to that audience. This may necessitate scanning or photographing their product and emailing the files to the audience or having a member of the appropriate audience visit the class. The audience member(s) should provide feedback on the product's plausibility and usefulness.

Students should use this feedback to reflect on their product. They should also complete a team reflection on the group process. The teacher can use a product rubric (such as those presented in chapter 7) to evaluate the products on the ideas and skills she sees as central and also make observations on student group work, process, and understanding based on their notes and charts.

This lesson plan meets the criteria on the Lesson Analysis and Adaptation Worksheet (available in chapter 1 on page 33 and on the Companion Website) in these ways:

- It provides standards for students and a measurable objective for students to meet.
- It addresses technological, communicative, and other nontraditional literacies.
- It integrates critical thinking, communication, creativity, content knowledge, problem solving, research, and production.
- It presents information in a variety of modes and scaffolds instruction for a variety of learners. Students have choices of media to use and levels of texts to refer to.
- Students have roles and connections to their future lives. Students search for answers about the future.
- It uses technology as a tool that helps students accomplish the task more easily and with more information.
- It considers the needs of diverse students by providing choices and scaffolds.
- It includes appropriate and thorough assessments of process and product. It involves all the participants in the assessment process.

In addition, this lesson helps students think about the future of technology and what it may mean for them.

Based on your understanding of this chapter, your beliefs about the future, and your philosophy of teaching, what would you add to or delete from this lesson? Why?

_____

_____

_____

It is not certain that the changes suggested in this chapter will or even should happen. In fact, with every gain, some kind of loss is experienced. This idea is underscored by some of the trends presented in this chapter. For example, when networking becomes more social, the amount of face-to-face interaction might decrease. Or, when computing becomes more mobile, student expectations of schooling might change in ways that schools are not ready for.

According to Bruce Sterling (2005), author of *Shaping Things*, there are two future scenarios that technology might help bring about—greater community around the world that leads to peace, prosperity, and a cleaner, fairer world, or a government-ruled, 1984-type future where the flow of information is controlled by the elite. Either is just as likely as a lot of other visions, but teachers must prepare to have an important role to play in the outcome.

CHAPTER REVIEW

Key Points

- **Understand trends that indicate where learning and educational technology might be headed.**

  Experts and others continue to make a variety of predictions about the future, some of which appear more likely than others to happen. What seems clear is that technology and education will change.

- **Describe guidelines to help you support students in the technology-enhanced future.**

  Teachers must help students find a comfortable place in the flow of information and keep up on trends that might affect their teaching contexts.

SAMPLE LESSON

- **Reflect on current trends in technologies.**
  Many technologies are changing so rapidly that it seems impossible to keep up with them. It is important to be aware of those that can help students meet their learning goals and to focus on effective use of whatever technology is employed.

- **Help students think about the future through technology-supported activities.**
  Well-crafted activities can help students meet learning goals as they think about and imagine what the future may bring.

- **Assess how well your students are prepared for their technology-enhanced futures.**
  Part of this assessment is helping students be aware of their current knowledge and skills and to understand where they need to be better prepared for their futures.

Which information in this chapter is most valuable to you? Why? How will you use it in your teaching?

_____

_____

_____

CASE QUESTIONS REVIEW

Reread the case at the beginning of the chapter and review your answers. In light of what you learned during this chapter, how do your answers change? Note any changes here.

1. *How likely do you think this scenario is?*

_____

_____

_____

2. *What are the advantages of the type of education that Jan is participating in? What are some disadvantages?*

_____

_____

_____

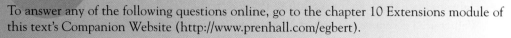

CHAPTER EXTENSIONS

To answer any of the following questions online, go to the chapter 10 Extensions module of this text's Companion Website (http://www.prenhall.com/egbert).

Adapt

Choose a lesson for your potential subject area and grade level from one of the lesson plan archives online (see the Companion Website if you need help finding resources). Use the Lesson Analysis and Adaptation Worksheet from chapter 1 on page 33 (also available in the Lesson Planning module of the Companion Website) to consider the lesson in the context of *your students' futures*. Use your responses to the worksheet to suggest general changes to the lesson based on your current or future students and context.

Practice

1. *Research a technology trend.* Find more information about one of the trends in the learning and technology trends section of this chapter. What additional information did you find? What is the significance of this information to future teaching?

2. *Explore a technology tool.* Find and review one of the tools mentioned in the tool trends section of this chapter. What are some ways that you think this tool could eventually be used in classrooms? What benefits would its use bring? What disadvantages might also come with this tool's use?

3. *Make an assessment.* Use the assessment frameworks in the assessment part of the chapter to create an assessment for one of the activities presented. What questions will you ask students to reflect on? Why?

Explore

1. *Create a technology-supported future activity.* Use the format of the activities in the text to list the steps and resources students will use to learn future-themed content and address learning goals. Note how technology will be integrated and why.

2. *Read about teachers' roles.* Find articles that address the goals of technology-supported social justice, equity, and access to opportunities. See some of the Beyond the Classroom essays on the Companion Website. Summarize what you find and describe how your role as a teacher can help support these goals.

REFERENCES

Barrett, J. (2006, September). My space or yours? *Leading and Learning with Technology, 34*(1), 15–19.

Lenhart, A., & Madden, M. (2007). Social networking websites and teens: An overview. *Pew Internet and American Life Project.* Available: www.pewinternet.org/pdfs/PIP_SNS_Data_Memo_ Jan_ 2007.pdf.

Levin, D., Arafeh, S., Lenhart, A., & Rainie, L. (2002). *The digital disconnect: The widening gap between Internet-savvy students and their schools.* The Pew Internet and American Life Project Report. Available: www.pewinternet.org/report_display.asp?r=67.

Lindsay, J. (2006, September). Online tools for sharing and collaboration. *Leading and Learning with Technology, 34*(1), 34–35.

McKenzie, J. (2002). After laptop. *From Now On, 7*(11). Available: www.fno.org/apr02/afterlaptop.html.

Pew Internet and American Life Project. (2007). *Demographics of Internet users.* Available: www.pewinternet.org/trends/User_Demo_1.11.07.htm.

Prensky, M. (2001a). Digital natives, digital immigrants. *On the Horizon, 9*(5). Available: www.marcprensky.com/writing/default.asp.

Prensky, M. (2001b). Do they really *think* differently? *On the Horizon, 9*(6). Available: www .marcprensky.com/writing/default.asp.

Roush, W. (2005, August). Social machines. *Technology Review, 108*(8), 45–53.

Sterling, B. (2005). *Shaping things.* Cambridge, MA: MIT Press.

U.S. Department of Commerce (2000). *Falling through the Net: Toward digital inclusion.* Available: www.ntia.doc.gov/ntiahome/fttn00/contents00.html.

U.S. Department of Education (2000). Emerging priorities. Forum on the Future of Technology in Education: Envisioning the Future. Available: www.air.org/forum/issues.htm.

VanSlyke, T. (2003, May/June). Digital natives, digital immigrants: Some thoughts from the generation gap. *The Technology Source.* Available: http://ts.mivu.org/default.asp?show=article&id=1011.

Glossary

A

active learning: learning activities in which students do something actively and think about what they do.

assistive devices: special hardware and software technologies designed for specific needs. They can help teachers to provide larger text for sight-impaired students, voice recognition for students with physical disabilities, and extra wait time, feedback, or practice for those who need it.

asynchronous (interaction): communicators interact one after the other at different times.

authentic audience: people that share and work toward similar goals for their communication.

authorable: able to be changed by users.

B

behaviorism: learning theory/philosophy that emphasizes the importance of practice and rote learning.

bells and whistles: parts of a software program that are extra and are included just for fun.

blended (also hybrid, or mixed-mode): A combination of face-to-face and electronic learning.

browser (Web): software that can translate HTML into a readable display.

C

close-ended problems: problems with known solutions.

collaboration: social interaction in which participants must plan and accomplish something specific together.

communication: a general term that implies the conveyance of information either one-way or through an exchange with two or more partners.

communication devices: hardware and software that connect computers to each other.

connection components: allow computers to communicate.

constructivism philosophy of learning that emphasizes that knowledge is socially constructed.

content-high tasks: one-way resource dumps from instructor to student with little interaction.

controlling feedback: evaluates only how well students did compared to other students or to their previous work.

convergent thinking: emphasizes working quickly to get to *the* right answer and is typically used for information learning.

cooperation: implies that students each have separate roles in a structured task and pool their data to a specific end.

creativity: the creation of original ideas, processes, experiences, or objects.

critical literacy: reading beyond the text.

critical thinking skills: abilities to analyze, evaluate, infer, interpret, explain, and self-regulate.

culturally relevant: celebrates the lives and heritages of all students and reflects the contributions of all groups.

D

declarative knowledge: discrete pieces of information that help us identify things and events.

differentiated instruction: way to provide enrichment for students' abilities, interests, and learning needs. In differentiated instruction, the goals and concepts are the same for all students, but the challenge varies.

divergent thinking: out of the norm and goes in many different ways.

domain: part of a URL that shows where the document can be found.

E

educational technology: electronic technologies, with an emphasis on computing, that are used for learning and teaching.

elearning: instruction that uses technology to enhance learning, often when the teacher and students are not in the same location.

eportfolio: a digital version of a portfolio.

external document: a handout or worksheet that enhances the use of technology.

F

flotilla: a set of computers that rotate among classrooms.

formative assessment: feedback and support that help students during the task process.

freeware: software that is distributed freely (without charge).

G

group dynamics: how people interact in a group.

H

hardware: One component of technology. The three main types are input, processing, and output.

hidden curriculum: elements that are not explicitly taught.

higher order thinking skills: a group of cognitive abilities and personal characteristics including analysis, synthesis, and evaluation.

homegrown: locally produced.

hypertext markup language (HTML): formatting language used for Web pages.

I

information literacy: the ability to recognize when information is needed and have the ability to locate, evaluate, and use effectively the needed information.

informational feedback: helps students to understand how their audience understands their work and what the strengths and weaknesses of their work are.

input devices: used to enter information into the computer.

inquiry: sometimes called *research, investigation,* or *guided discovery*. During inquiry, students ask questions and then search for answers to those questions.

Internet: a massive global network of linked computers.

J

jigsaw learning: a group structure in which students become experts on a topic in their "home" groups and then share their knowledge in new groups with members of other home group.

just-in-time (JIT) learning: learning that occurs just when it is needed.

L

learning goals: expected outcomes of teaching and learning.

literacies: ways of being knowledgeable.

M

media literacy: critically thinking about the influences of media.

mediated: bridged by technology.

metacognition: thinking about the process of one's decision making.

N

negotiation of meaning: working toward common understanding during social interaction.

O

open-ended (or loosely structured) problems: those with many or unknown solutions rather than one correct answer.

operating system (OS): manages the rest of the software on the computer.

output devices: display or deliver the information in a format that users can understand.

overlay keyboards (concept keyboards): flat input devices connected to a computer.

P

platform: a framework that allows software to run, e.g., Windows, Mac, or Unix operating systems.

plug-ins: special components used on Web pages to display a variety of content.

podcasts: digital media files shared over the Web.

portfolio: a collection of student work, typically accompanied by one or more reflections.

problem-based learning (PBL): a teaching approach that combines critical thinking, problem-solving skills, and inquiry as students explore real-world problems.

problem solving: a process that centers on a *problem*. The end result of problem solving is typically some kind of decision, in other words, choosing a solution and then evaluating it.

procedural knowledge: the knowledge of action, or the knowledge of how to do something.

process-high tasks: acknowledge the importance of interaction and communication among students and instructors before, during, and after the task.

processing devices: change electronic input into output.

product: a concrete artifac.

production: a form of learning whereby students create a concrete artifact.

productivity tools: those that maximize or extend students' ability to create products and to solve problems.

professional development (PD): an opportunity that leads to an increase or change in skills, knowledge, abilities, and understandings.

R

rubric: a detailed scoring outline.

S

scaffolds: structures and reinforcements that help guide learners toward independent critical thinking.

scoring guides: like rubrics, but used to evaluate learning in a broader sense.

shareware: software that users can test; if they decide to keep it, they pay a small fee to the developer.

social interaction: communication with an authentic audience that shares some of the goals of the communication.

software: instructions written in a computer language that tell the computer how and when to perform certain tasks.

spam: unsolicited, unwanted, or inappropriate email messages.

spreadsheet: a table arranged in columns and rows that is used to calculate numerical data.

structural knowledge: an understanding of how pieces of declarative knowledge fit together.

summative assessment: overall evaluation of the student's performance on a task.

synchronous: communication in real time.

T

teachable moment: a spontaneous opportunity to introduce a new concept or idea.

technological literacy: understanding the many ways in which technology affects lives for both good and bad.

technology: hardware, software, and related tools.

twenty-first century skills: critical thinking, communication, problem-solving, production, creativity.

U

uniform resource locator (URL): a Web address.

usability test: an observation of the actual use of the product by a target user.

W

Web (World Wide Web): a way of accessing information over the medium of the Internet. It is an information-sharing model that is built on top of the Internet.

Web browser: displays Web files in an easily readable format, e.g., Mosaic, Netscape, Explorer, Lynx, and many others.

Web 2.0: social networking.

Name Index

Subject Index